MULTISTATE EXAMINATION WORKBOOK

Volume I

By
Jeff A. Fleming
Attorney at Law

Edited by
Susan P. Sneidmiller
Attorney at Law

Published by: FLEMING'S FUNDAMENTALS OF LAW
26170 Enterprise Way, Suite 500, Lake Forest, CA 92630
(949) 770-7030 • (800) LAW EXAM
FAX (949) 454-8556
WEB www.lawprepare.com • EMAIL info@ffol.com

Distributed by: LEGAL BOOKS DISTRIBUTING
4247 Whiteside Street
Los Angeles, CA 90063
(800) 200-7112

All Rights Reserved (© 2015)

SUPERVISING WRITER AND EDITOR

Jeff A. Fleming
Attorney at Law

MANAGING WRITER AND EDITORS

Susan P. Sneidmiller
Attorney at Law

LAYOUT:

Donald F. Bayley II
    IMAGEN Company   Irvine, CA.

CONTRIBUTING WRITERS:

Professor Leah Christensen
    University of Iowa College of Law, J.D.

Professor Sam Frizell
    University Of California, Hastings College Of The Law, J.D.

Jared Gross
    University Of Santa Clara School Of Law, J.D.

Professor Philip Merkel
    University Of Illinois, J.D.

Professor Jeremy Miller
    Tulane School Of Law, J.D.

CONTRIBUTING EDITORS:

Anita Stuppler
    University of Baltimore School of Law, J.D.

Josh Effron
    Loyola Law School of Los Angeles, J.D.

Copyright 2004, 2006, 2011, 2015 by Fleming's Fundamentals Of Law. Seventh Edition. All rights reserved. No part of this book may be reproduced in any form or by any electronic or mechanical means, including photocopy, recording, or any information storage and retrieval system, without permission from the publisher in writing. Printed in the U.S.A.

CONTENTS – Volume I

THE RULES OF THE ROAD – An Introduction to the Multistate Method 3

CONTRACTS – Question Breakdown 47
CONTRACTS Questions 53
CONTRACTS Answers 111
CRIMINAL LAW – Question Breakdown 167
CRIMINAL LAW Questions 171
CRIMINAL LAW Answers 197

TORTS – Question Breakdown 231
TORTS Questions 235
TORTS Answers 277

SIMULATED BAR Questions 319
SIMULATED BAR Answers 361

PROFESSIONAL RESPONSIBILITY – Question Breakdown 393
PROFESSIONAL RESPONSIBILITY Questions 395
PROFESSIONAL RESPONSIBILITY Answers 417

INTRODUCTION

THE RULES OF THE ROAD – AN INTRODUCTION TO THE MULTISTATE METHOD

As we traveled down the road of higher education, each milestone had a cryptic name – the PSAT, the SAT, and the LSAT, among others. Although each successive exam seemed to intimidate more than the last, with some determination, we arrive at the ultimate milestone – the Multistate Bar Examination, or MBE.

Created in 1972 by the National Conference of Bar Examiners (or NCBE), in cooperation with the Educational Testing Service, the MBE is a full-day, 200-question, mind numbing, multiple choice exam. One hundred questions are administered, randomly as to subject area, in two three-hour testing sessions. The exam seeks to cover a breadth of subjects that would be impossible to cover in a few selected essays.

The MBE has become the standard for most multiple choice exams that seek to test on legal reasoning skills, as well as familiarity with generally accepted legal principles. Presently, it covers the eight core areas of Torts, Criminal Law and Procedure, Contracts, Real Property, Constitutional Law, Evidence and, the most recently added subject, Civil Procedure. As constituted, the MBE is a major portion of the bar exam in virtually every jurisdiction, with Louisiana and Puerto Rico being among the few exceptions.

The MBE has also been the model for countless objective law school exams, as well as the California First Year Law Student Exam administered by the State Bar (also referred to as the Baby Bar). However, the MBE is perhaps the most subjective objective test ever created. It attempts to test those analytical skills that we have honed and perfected, or have attempted to perfect, in the law school classroom through case study.

This introduction will review preparation methods and offer test-taking techniques that will also be of value to the law student facing objective testing in virtually any area of the law and California students preparing for the Bar and/or Baby Bar Exam. The methodology discussed herein can be applied to any multiple choice testing format that uses, or has used, the MBE as a model. It must be noted, however, that the NCBE has endeavored to make the testing items on the MBE more "straight forward," more "concise" and more "focused." As a result, some of the techniques addressed herein will be of great value to the law student (or California Baby Bar Examinee), but of lesser importance to the candidate sitting for the MBE as a part of that state's bar examination.

As part of a continuing evolution, the National Conference of Bar Examiners (or "NCBE") has instituted important changes (2008/2009) in their multiple-choice testing programs. One of the changes is the inclusion of "pre-test" questions, which are not calculated as part of the applicant's score. Of greater significance to those taking the exam are the changes in style and format.

Based on psychometric research, changes were made in the drafting process, involving a more focused approach. The result has been more concise and more consistent examination questions. The style revision has yielded a less unwieldy testing format. The drafters are encouraged to write questions covering a range of skills and tasks— e.g., the ability to gather information, the ability to spot dispositive issues and the ability to synthesize the law with the facts.

It is through the evaluation of these questions that they can be used as "equators," allowing for the exam to be scaled, or weighted, to reflect the level of difficulty. By comparing performance on the equator questions, the NCBE can create a scaling factor so that each exam is no more difficult than the previous exam.

RULE #1 – FAMILIARIZE YOURSELF WITH THE MBE TERRAIN.

Material released by the NCBE indicates, in an almost lawyer-like disclaimer fashion, that the MBE is fraught with a long-held mythos, stating as follows:

"Bar Examiners across the country often encounter questions and myths relating to the Multistate Bar Examination (MBE), one of the important parts of their test of minimum competence for licensure to practice law. Over the years, significant research has been conducted that dispels these myths.

Myth 1: **Examinees can pass the MBE by guessing. The MBE is a test of memory and test-taking ability, not of legal knowledge or analytical skill.**

Fact: Research indicates that the MBE is not a "multiple-guess test" or an examination that rewards test-taking ability. In research conducted in July 1986, in-coming law students took the morning session of the MBE, and their scores were compared to graduates of the same law schools who had taken the same examination. The novices and graduates had virtually identical mean LSAT scores, so if the ability to take multiple-choice tests were the major factor influencing MBE scores, both groups should have had very similar MBE scores. In fact, the highest MBE score earned by the novices was lower than the lowest score earned by any of the graduates.

Second, research on the MBE indicates that MBE scores are highly correlated with other measures of legal skills and knowledge, such as scores on state essay examinations and law school grades. These correlations provide empirical evidence that the MBE is testing legal ability rather than general test-taking ability. Similarly, a panel of experts convened in 1992 as part of a content validity study concluded that MBE items were material to the practice of law and that their emphasis was balanced between legal reasoning skills and memorization of legal principles.

Myth 2: **MBE questions are needlessly difficult, arcane, and tricky.**

Fact: MBE questions are designed to be a fair index of whether an applicant has the ability to practice law. MBE questions are written by Drafting Committees composed of men and women who are law teachers and practitioners. Before it is administered, every MBE question is reviewed at several levels: at least twice as it is edited by the Drafting Committee; by psychometric experts to insure that it is fair and unbiased, by the practitioner members of the MBE Policy Committee and their academic consultants; and by the members of Boards of Bar Examiners across the country. After a form of the MBE is administered, any question that performs in an unanticipated manner—is very difficult or is missed by applicants who did well on the rest of the test—is flagged by psychometric experts and reviewed again by content experts on the Drafting Committees to insure that no ambiguity exists in the question and that the key is unequivocally correct. Should an error be detected even after this thorough scrutiny, two or more answers may be deemed correct in order to insure that no applicant is disadvantaged by having a particular question appear on the form of the MBE he or she took.

In a 1992 study, expert panelists reported that they believed MBE items were generally easy; correctly estimating that about 66 percent of candidates would select the right answer to a typical item.

Myth 3: **Not enough time is allotted to answer MBE questions.**

Fact: Research shows that the time allotted to take the MBE is sufficient for 99 percent of applicants. The MBE is designed to be answered by a reasonably competent applicant in the amount of time available. The rate of correct responses at the end of three-hour sessions is not significantly different than the rate of right answers at other, earlier points in the test.

A research project in which applicants were given virtually unlimited time to answer the MBE resulted in an average increase in score of about 6 raw (unscaled) points. Since all groups benefit from an increase in time to the same degree, and since the test is scaled to account for differences in difficulty, an increase in average score would be offset in the scaling process and additional time would not increase applicants' scaled scores.

Myth 4: **Essay examinations and performance tests are a better way to measure minimum competency to practice law.**

Fact: While essay examinations and performance tests provide important information about candidates, there are several significant advantages to including multiple-choice tests on a bar examination. First, multiple choice testing offers the opportunity for a breadth of coverage of subject areas which cannot be duplicated using only essay questions or performance tests. This breadth of coverage improves the reliability of the examination. Second, multiple-choice questions can be scored objectively, and scores can be scaled to adjust for changes in difficulty from one test to the next. There are two sources of variation in difficulty in essay examinations and performance tests: variations in the difficulty of the test items themselves, and variations in how strict or lenient graders are. In contrast, scores on the MBE are equated through a process that insures that a new form of the MBE is no more nor less difficult than a previous form by comparing the performance of applicants on a common set of items, raw scores on the test can be converted to adjusted, "scaled" scores that are directly comparable to one another. Because scores are equated, the MBE provides an anchor for other, more subjective test scores; the National Conference recommends that scores on essay examinations and performance tests be scaled to the MBE. And finally, this scaling of MBE scores allows direct comparisons of performance to be made among tests. An applicant taking a current examination is on a level playing field with other applicants taking tests at other times.

Myth 5: **The MBE discriminates against minority applicants.**

Fact: The MBE neither widens nor narrows the gap in performance level between minority and majority applicants. Research indicates that differences in mean scores among racial and ethnic groups correspond closely to differences in those groups' mean LSAT scores, law school grade point averages, and scores on other measures of ability to practice law, such as bar examination essay scores or performance test scores. Individual items on the MBE that are relatively difficult for one group are relatively difficult for all groups; the relative difficulty of the items within a subtest (e.g., the Constitutional Law items versus the Torts items) does not differ from group to group. Finally, total MBE scores are not higher or lower from group to group than they are on other test formats.

All items on the MBE are reviewed for potential bias. Men and women serve on each Drafting Committee, and members of ethnic minority groups assist in the preparation and review of items at both the Drafting Committee level and at the level of MBE Committee and State Board review. The National Conference of Bar Examiners is committed to diverse representation on all its Drafting and Policy Committees.

Myth 6: **The MBE is getting easier; scores keep increasing while applicants are getting *less* able.**

Fact: The MBE is a reliable measure of applicant ability. The average scaled score on the MBE has varied by less than 2 1/2 points from year to year, indicating that the ability level of the candidate pool has been fairly stable. Changes in MBE scores follow closely the variations in average scores on other measures of candidate ability, such as the LSAT. This correlation between changes in MBE and LSAT scores indicates that increases in the average score mirror increases in the general ability level of the group being tested rather than a decline in the difficulty of the test."

So, the examiners are saying, in essence, that the MBE is:

1. Not a multiple-guess test, or a test of test-taking skills, but of legal skills and knowledge, with a high correlation to performance on the essays;

2. Not a needlessly difficult, arcane or tricky test, but is designed to be a fair and unbiased index of whether the applicant has the ability to practice law, regardless or race or ethnicity;

3. Not a test in which time is a statistically significant factor, as the time allotted is sufficient for 99 percent of the test takers;

4. Not inferior to essay and performance exams as a measure of minimum competency to practice law, because the MBE can cover a greater breadth of subjects, can be scored

objectively and scaled to account for variations in difficulty from test to test; and

5. Not getting easier from year to year.

Perhaps this last representation can go without dispute, but even the less gifted advocates among us may, after a trip down the MBE road, be able to raise an issue or two.

The landscape on the MBE road looks something like this:

Effective with the February, 2015 administration of the Multistate Bar Examination (MBE), a eighth content area – Civil Procedure – will be covered for the first time. The timing of the exam has not changed.

The MBE consists of 200 multiple-choice questions, of which 190 are scored items and 10 are unscored pretest items. They are divided as follows:

1. Torts: 27 questions;

2. Contracts: 28 questions;

3. Real Property: 27 questions;

4. Criminal Law and Procedure: 27 questions;

5. Evidence: 27 questions;

6. Constitutional Law: 27 questions; and

7. Civil Procedure: 27 questions.

So a scored section may look about like this:

A. **TORTS** (27 questions)

   50% - Negligence, Proximate Cause, Damages (Apportionment), Defenses, Vicarious Liability

   50% - Divided among remaining Tort areas

Questions here are based on the common law, the majority rule, and, increasingly, on the Restatement of the Law of Torts. The importance of Torts, and specifically of negligence, cannot be overstated. The remaining emphasis is primarily on the intentional torts and strict liability, with nuisance, defamation, privacy and misrepresentation also being represented. You can count on at least one question from each of these seven topics.

The specifications (i.e., subject matter outline) for the Torts MBE questions feature five main headings. Nuisance, defamation, privacy and misrepresentation fall under a single heading of Other Torts. Products liability is segregated from strict liability, and the Other Torts heading also includes intentional interference with business relations. The significance of the headings is that the examiners will always post at least one entry from each category. Of the 27 Torts questions, 50% will test on negligence.

PERCENTAGE BREAKDOWN OF MBE SUBJECTS

A. **Constitutional Law** (27 questions)

1. 50% - State action, due process, equal protection, privileges and immunities clauses, bill of attainder, ex-post facto laws, takings, contract clause, First Amendment (speech, association, press, and religion)

2. 50% - Procedure, separation of powers, intergovernmental immunities, Tenth Amendment and federal/state conflicts – Federalism-based limits on state authority

The principles tested in Constitutional Law are derived from the U.S. Constitution, the decisions of the U.S. Supreme Court, and, apparently, from obscure footnotes in Nowak's or other hornbooks on Constitutional Law. The good news is that the questions in this area tend to be the most straightforward on the MBE, accounting for the highest percentage scores.

B. **Contracts/U.C.C.** (28 questions)

1. 50% - Formation, performance, discharge of contractual duties and breach

2. 50% - Defenses, parol evidence and interpretation, third party rights and remedies

   *Note: 25% of the Contracts questions for each MBE will be based on the U.C.C.

INTRODUCTION: THE RULES OF THE ROAD

The source of law in this area is the common law, the majority rule, the Restatement 2d, Contracts, and the Uniform Commercial Code (U.C.C.) Articles 1 and 2. The bad news is that the questions in this area feature some of the longest, most complex fact patterns on the MBE; the good news is that the concepts tested generally tend toward the basic.

C. Criminal Law/Procedure (27 questions)

1. 50% - Homicide, theft crimes, assault and battery, rape, kidnapping, arson, pre-commission crimes, accomplice liability, mens rea and actus reus and defenses

2. 50% - Criminal Procedure - Fourth, Fifth, Sixth and Eighth Amendment, burdens of proof and persuasion and appeal and error

The common law, the modern law, the majority rule, the Model Penal Code, and, sometimes, a statute contained within the problem form the basis for the Criminal Law questions. The decisions of the U.S. Supreme Court form the basis for the Criminal Procedure questions.

D. Evidence (27 questions)

1. 33% - Presentation of evidence

2. 33% - Hearsay

3. 33% - Relevancy, authentication, character, habit, expert testimony, real and demonstrative and scientific evidence, authentication, privileges, public policy exclusions and the best evidence rule

The questions are based on the Federal Rules of Evidence. For purposes of the MBE, throw out those old outlines based on the common law, with one possible exception – from time to time, you may see a federal court sitting in diversity jurisdiction. In those situations, apply state rules of procedure that may be outcome determinative, including state rules of Evidence, as spelled out in the problem. Your state essays may require you to have knowledge of both state and federal rules.

E Property (27 questions)

1. 20% - Interests in land, co-tenancies and landlord & tenant

2. 20% - Covenants, servitudes, easements, profits, licenses, fixtures (Article 9, U.C.C.), and zoning

3. 20% - Land sales contract, risk of loss and marketable title

4. 20% - Mortgages and security devices

5. 20% - Adverse possession, deeds, transfers by operation of law and by will, the recording act and title insurance

The common law, the modern law, the majority rule, and the U.C.C. (Article 9 – Fixtures) are tested in Real Property. The problems are, along with Contracts, the longest and most complex on the MBE; unfortunately, most students would agree that the concepts tested are anything but basic. Traditionally, the lowest percentages come out of Real Property. On recent MBEs, there has been a significant rise in testing on mortgages.

F. **Torts** (27 questions)

1. 50% - Negligence, proximate cause, damages (apportionment), defenses and vicarious liability

2. 50% - Intentional torts and defenses, strict liability, products liability and other remaining torts and defenses

(Question sources for Torts discussed above).

G. **Civil Procedure** (27 questions)

1. 75% - Jurisdiction, venue, pretrial procedures, and motions

2. 25% - Law applied by federal courts, jury trials, verdicts and judgments, and appealability and review

The source for the Civil Procedure items on the MBE will be, by and large, the Federal Rules of Civil Procedure ("FRCP"), along with the development of case law in the areas indicated above, and an occasional statutory provision.

The subjects of Civil Procedure, Criminal Law, Evidence and Torts tend to emphasize, and will likely continue to emphasize, the elements of the rule invoked by the facts; in Constitutional Law, Contracts, Criminal Procedure and Real Property factual analysis and reading comprehension is emphasized.

Unlike the essays, cross-over testing is the exception rather that the rule. This is due, at least in part, to the fact that the questions are drafted by individual committees, each responsible for one of the MBE areas.

INTRODUCTION: THE RULES OF THE ROAD

Prior MBE questions have tested the Erie doctrine in Constitutional Law, have used a will or trust to get to an issue in Real Property, have used a federal court sitting in diversity jurisdiction to get to an Evidence issue, or have used a contract to get into a Real Property issue. Expect to see as many as three or four questions that could cross-over between Evidence and Criminal Procedure. Remedies, including damages and equitable relief, will arise in the context of in Contracts, Real Property (e.g., specific performance), Torts, and, possibly, Constitutional Law (e.g., injunctive relief).

It is highly unlikely that anything resembling a cross-over pattern will be seen on the Baby Bar, as the examiner is unable to assume that you have any knowledge beyond the Contracts, Crimes or Torts material covered in your first year of law school.

RULE #2 – PREPARE FOR THE LONG HAUL (or, You Have to Get out of the Driveway before You Can Ride the MBE Fast Lane.)

The foregoing subject breakdowns are to be used as study guides, along with comprehensive outlines, such as the Gilbert series recommended by Fleming's Fundamentals of Law in the MBE areas. It is recommended that one outline be reviewed every one and one-half weeks for long term and review two outlines per week for short term. Greater emphasis should be placed on weak or highly testable areas, combined with practice problems as discussed below.

The essentials of preparation for the MBE can be addressed in three words – **practice, practice, and practice.**

In gearing up for the practice runs, the student must sort through a potentially overwhelming assortment of materials. At the outset, a schedule should be prepared that considers the outlines to be covered, as well as the practice problems to be done. A series of goals, both long term (overall) and short term (daily), will be helpful, but only if these goals are realistic and within reach.

A successful performance on the MBE requires more than the ability to regurgitate rules of law and a rote memorization of the outlines. An examinee must be able to master the rules, the exceptions, the exceptions to the exceptions, the footnotes in the hornbooks, the Restatement comments and illustrations, the ability to function in a stress-filled environment, the ability to think on one's feet, and the ability to apply all of this in 1.8 minutes per question.

Unquestionably, success on the MBE is grounded on a solid foundation of the black letter law. By itself, however, this is not enough. Each rule, as it is studied, must be put into a factual context so that the application of the rule is understood and the associative process is enhanced.

Generally, the commercial outlines, such as the Gilbert series, or the bar review outlines, will be a sufficient source of the law needed. Despite all of our experience with last-minute cramming, merely reading the outlines will not be enough to vanquish the MBE. The study of the law must be incorporated into an approach that contemplates problem-solving as the goal, rather than rote memorization.

The recommended **first step** is to break down each subject area into its component parts and to master each of these areas before moving on to the next. For example, one cannot learn Crimes without first mastering the general requirements of **actus reus** (the criminal act) and **mens rea** (the mental state) **before** moving on to homicide and theft crimes.

While studying the outline materials, take the time to discern the necessary elements of each rule reviewed. List these elements in your mind, on a piece of paper or on a flash card and then **contextualize**. This means putting the outline aside for a moment to consider or imagine a set of facts that will call up the rule, element or exception to be applied. For example, while reviewing contract offers, consider a number of situations in which an offer may or may not exist, such as Do you want to go to the movies? (merely an inquiry); If you pay for the movies, I'll pay for the food (possibly an offer, despite its indefiniteness, if another would be justified in believing that a power of acceptance has been created); or I'll pay you $5.00 an hour to come over at 7:00 P.M. this Saturday and watch my kids while I go to the movies (clearly an offer). If at first this seems difficult, there are a number of flash card sets on the market that list examples or hypotheticals that may prove helpful in helping initiate the process.

The **next step** is to turn to a source of practice questions, such as the Finz Multistate Method book utilized by Fleming's Fundamentals of Law, starting with the table of contents. You will see, for example, in the Criminal Law section, that following the heading **General Principles** is a listing of 13 questions that test in that specific area. Working questions in the subtopic immediately following its review will not only help you place the rules in context, i.e., to apply the rules, it will also help you to determine whether or not there is sufficient comprehension of the rules so as to allow you to move on to the next area of testing. Again, it is vital to achieve some sense of mastery in each area before moving to the next.

When taking the practice test questions, always time yourself, allowing no more than 1.8 minutes per question. If you are aware of the time pressure from the very beginning, then you will start to develop a rhythm or an almost instinctive awareness of the passage of time as you work the problems.

RULE #3 – KEEP YOUR EYES ON THE ROAD (or, the Zen of testing.)

One of the attributes of the successful examinee is the ability to focus, to the exclusion of all else, while in testing mode. This can be thought of as finding a quiet place, both externally and internally, in which to perform. The distractions may be external, such as the continued groans of a neighboring test taker; or the distractions may be internal, such as wondering what impulse possessed you to sit for the exam.

The key is to block out everything but the test question, and to be able to do that for an extended period of time. By doing test questions in blocks of no less than 17 at a time, one half hour per set, you can consciously put yourself in the exam for that period of time to the exclusion of all else. Consider continuing to practice the half hour sets until you have mastered the ability to go for thirty minutes without thinking about anything but the test questions. Once you have mastered this ability, then expand to one hour of testing, or 33 questions, and so on, until you can sit for three hours without a significant break in concentration.

This does mean, however, that no matter how great the temptation, you cannot look at the answer key until you have completed the set. When you do review the answers, look at the explanations for both the correct and incorrect responses to ensure a well-reasoned basis for your selections and to reinforce your grasp of the rule being tested.

Some students will find it helpful to write out the rule on a flash card for those problems they got wrong. This, again, helps to reinforce your grasp of the rule, will help you keep track of areas of difficulty, and will create a valuable study tool.

It is also important to sit for at least one simulated exam so as to test your ability to focus over the long haul. Use the simulation as an opportunity to diagnose areas of weakness, not only substantively, but technically or procedurally as well, i.e., Does the brain completely fade somewhere around question 75? Does it take 10 to 15 questions to establish a rhythm? Does the brain think of nothing but lunch as the clock nears the noon hour?

As the exam draws nearer, the emphasis should shift from outline review to problem solving, with outlines being used primarily to refresh or supplement the problems. Again, the exam is testing on problem solving skills, not the ability to regurgitate the black letter law. The final month should be devoted to doing practice MBE's.

RULE #4 – MAXIMIZE YOUR FUEL EFFICIENCY.

As mentioned above, study time should be allotted to reflect the relative importance of each subject area. Factor in the testing on the essays, where typically half of the test on the same rules as the MBE, and the result is that at least 75% of the black letter law needed to pass any given bar exam. This same basic principle, that studying for the MBE will help on the essays, also applies to the Baby Bar essay questions, but is limited to the topics of Contracts, Crimes and Torts.

Emphasis in study time for the bar should be placed on the MBE areas. Generally, each MBE area could be studied three times as much as any individual essay-only subject, such as Wills or Community Property, given the likely importance of the MBE subjects on the essays.

As we saw in the subject breakdowns, above, within each MBE subject can be found certain key areas, for example:

CONSTITUTIONAL LAW:..... Individual Rights And The First Amendment.................

CONTRACTS: .... Formation (Including U.C.C.), Defenses ....

EVIDENCE: .... Hearsay, Character Evidence And Impeachment............

TORTS: .... Negligence ....

PROPERTY:............................. Establishing And Conveying Title ....

Obviously, the key areas require a greater expenditure of time. Again, the subject breakdowns will be an important tool in emphasizing specific areas, and getting the most efficient use of your study time.

RULE #5 – KNOW WHERE YOU ARE HEADED *(Before You Leave the House.)*

In order to maximize your reading comprehension and initiate your analysis of an MBE test question, it will help to know the area of testing, and, if possible, to determine the rule of application, before you start to read the facts. The area being tested will not be specifically identified for you.

The typical MBE question (item) is composed of three parts – the **stem** (fact pattern); the **lead-in** (call of the question); and the **options** (answer choices), as in the following example:

> *Question 1 is based on the following facts:*
>
> A student was a candidate for Student Body President at an exclusive college preparatory school. This student was scheduled to debate the other presidential candidates before the assembled student body in the school's auditorium. After the students had taken their seats, the faculty advisor called the first student to the podium. Just as this student was crossing the stage to get to the podium, an opponent stuck out a foot, causing the first student to fall off of the stage. As a result, the student was deeply humiliated, but suffered no physical harm.
>
> 1. If the first student asserts a claim against the opposing student that stuck out a foot due to the humiliation that was suffered, will the first student prevail?
>
>   A. Yes, if the opposing student knew that the first student had to walk across the stage in front of the opposing candidate at the precise moment the opposing student stuck out a foot.
>
>   B. Yes, if the opposing candidate carelessly failed to notice that first student had to walk across the stage in front of opposing candidate.

INTRODUCTION: THE RULES OF THE ROAD

> C. No, because first student suffered no physical harm.
>
> D. No, only if in sticking out his leg the opposing candidate did not intend to cause physical harm to first student.

The answer to this example can be found in the Rule #7 Section that follows.

Prior to reading the facts, read the lead-in. In the above example, the first student asserts a claim language identified the area of testing – Torts. Now the stem (fact pattern) can be read with a eye toward the appropriate cause of action. This is essentially the same as issue spotting an essay. The facts are designed to trigger the application of a rule. The examinee's job is to recognize those trigger facts and apply the appropriate rule.

Getting a sense of the ultimate destination helps to initiate the reasoning process that goes into analyzing the facts. Again, this is the same process that goes into issue spotting an essay, i.e., Do the facts support a particular outcome or result? Have all elements been satisfied? Are there additional facts that must be evaluated? Are there missing facts that must be considered before the outcome can be determined? Is there an exception that will apply?

In the above example, once the area of law was established, the various rules, which might apply, e.g., negligence, intentional tort or strict liability, can now be considered. Which facts become significant? The facts state that as the first student was crossing the stage, the opposing candidate stuck out a foot. There is no mention of whether or not it was intentional or accidental. It does not appear that any of the categories of strict liability (products liability, wild animals, abnormally dangerous activities) can be supported by the facts, so this area can be eliminated. Negligence is possible, but given the lack of physical harm, we will need to continue the search for a more appropriate rule. The claim asserted will likely arise out of the intentional torts, perhaps battery or intentional infliction of emotional distress. The facts must be scrutinized to see if they will support the claim, or if something more will be needed.

On occasion, the lead-in may go farther in establishing the rule of application, e.g., if Defendant is charged with murder..., or if Plaintiff asserts a claim in strict liability due to the injuries caused by the defective product.... This may allow you to get further along in the distillation process, but it does not mean that your analytical skills will not be called into play.

In those rare problems where the stem is followed by more than one lead-in, i.e., multiple questions follow a single fact pattern, try to read each stem so as to get a general sense of the issues or areas being tested. Later, when working through the responses, you can deal with each stem independently. You will find this is one of the question types that is being used with less and less frequency on the MBE.

If the lead-in does not provide you with sufficient information to determine the area of testing, then glance at the options. This means allowing your eyes to drop down an imaginary centerline through the potential responses, so that you recognize key words. This should be enough to enable you to determine, at a minimum, the area of testing. In the above example, you may have noted the words know and carelessly in the first two options, suggesting that the key, or correct answer, will be coming out of intentional torts or negligence, and may possibly require a distinction to be made as to those two areas.

Consider the following example:

> 2. In a common-law jurisdiction, Defendant should be found guilty of:
>
> A. Burglary only.
>
> B. Arson only.
>
> C. Burglary and arson.
>
> D. Neither burglary nor arson.

As you have likely observed, the lead-in did identify the rule of application, the common-law rules. It did not identify the rule of law; however, a quick glance at the options clarified the area (Criminal Law) and the crimes of burglary and arson. Once you have identified the rule or rules of application, your job may merely be the accounting of all essential elements.

In some examples, the lead-in essentially replaces or supplements the existing facts by asking you to assume additional facts. In this situation, reading the entire lead-in first may not be as desirable. It may be helpful to first read the last sentence or phrase of the longer lead-in, so as to learn the objective of the problem, and then read the additional facts contained in the lead-in. Consider the following example:

> **Assume for the purposes of this question only** that instead of doing the job herself, the builder delegated the remodeling work to an experienced cabinetmaker. Although the cabinetmaker had never worked on a job of this exact type, size and complexity, she eagerly accepted the delegation because she owed a sizable gambling debt to the builder. The builder did not inform the owner of the delegation. The builder then assigned the contract proceeds to a third party to pay off a car loan owed to that third party.
>
> 3. Will the owner be required to accept the builder's delegation of duties to the cabinetmaker?

In this example, glancing at the lead-in reveals testing on a delegation of contract duties. By having this knowledge, the important facts are easily distinguished from those immaterial to the inquiry (e.g., that the cabinetmaker was inexperienced with the type of job versus the cabinetmaker's experience as a cabinetmaker or the assignment to the assignment to the third party). Note also that where the lead-in instructs you to "Assume for the purposes of this question only," **do not** carry those additional facts on to other questions and **do not** allow the new facts to influence your reading of the basic fact pattern. Although this has been a popular testing format in general, the NCBE has sought to move away from pattern of this type.

RULE #6 – USE ROAD MAPS.

Reading the lead-in, or glancing at the answers, to establish the objective or direction the problem is taking will help boost your reading comprehension. This can be compared to using a road map to establish which direction to take in order to reach your ultimate destination, i.e., the objective of the problem.

Reading comprehension is enhanced if you have a sense of direction, that is, an idea of which facts are likely to be important and which facts are set forth as mere distracters. Whole paragraphs may be skimmed if you know in advance that such paragraphs will not have a bearing on the result. Parties are more easily identified; issues are more easily narrowed.

Once the objective has been established, it becomes easier to recognize the details that may be important in resolving the issues presented. For example, the fact that the plaintiff was an anticipated or known trespasser, and thus a duty was owed, may be determinative in Torts; or that the seller was an unemployed ballerina, and thus not a merchant, may help resolve the issue as to whether or not a written option contract not supported by consideration is enforceable; or that the seller was planning to sell, rather than presently intending to sell, may indicate that there is no offer on which to base a contract.

As indicated above, a fact critical to the outcome may be buried within the details of the fact pattern, which, in essence, is identical to the essays. These details may be seen in adjectives, verbs, adverbs, times, dates, places, quotations, personal characteristics, names, or intentions. The question to ask is: What is the **legal significance** of each fact or detail as it relates to our inquiry or call of the question?

In some problems, but not all, a simple, quickly executed diagram may be helpful to set out, for example, the chronology or the relationships that are central to the question. This can be done right in the test booklet, or on the scratch paper provided by the proctors. Consider the following example:

> *Question 4 is based on the following facts:*
>
> A man is the owner in fee simple absolute of a 13,000-acre ranch. On May 2, the owner conveyed the ranch to his employee for the

price of $150,000.00 by means of a quitclaim deed. The employee did not immediately record this conveyance. On June 16, the owner conveyed the ranch by warranty deed to an investor in consideration of a $250,000.00 debt owed by the owner to the investor, which the investor forgave. The investor recorded this conveyance immediately. On July 1, the employee recorded his quitclaim deed.

On July 10, the employee conveyed the ranch to his friend as a gift.

The friend recorded the conveyance immediately. On July 15, the investor conveyed the ranch to a speculator by quitclaim deed for the price of $300,000.00. The speculator recorded immediately.

4. Assume for the purposes of this question only that the jurisdiction has a recording statute that reads as follows:

> *No conveyance is good as against a subsequent purchaser for valuable consideration and without notice, unless such conveyance be recorded prior to subsequent purchase.*

If all necessary parties are joined in a quiet title action, title will be found in which of the following parties?

This problem can be diagrammed to strip the facts down to the essentials. The key is to identify the bona fide purchasers, and when each recorded relative to the other, so as to establish the absence or presence of notice in this race notice jurisdiction. A diagram may look something like the following:

O to E/BFP, O to I, I rec., E rec., E to F/gift, F rec., I to S/BFP, P rec.
–|–––––––|––––|–––––|–––|–––––––––|––––––|–––|--------|------

Of course, the diagram can be distilled further by using arrows instead of "to" or abbreviating "recorded" to the letter R, so long as there is no confusion as to meaning or a party.

The areas that are most likely to call on diagramming skills would be Contracts and

22 INTRODUCTION: THE RULES OF THE ROAD

Real Property. It is recommended that you practice diagramming, if that technique is to be employed, wherever appropriate in the practice questions. The objective is to distill the information into a useful format as quickly as possible, keeping in mind that if you spend more than 1.8 minutes with each item, that time must be made up elsewhere.

Some students may wish to highlight or underline the facts. This can either be helpful, or a waste of time. In order to highlight effectively, there must still be some awareness of the relative importance of the material highlighted. You may recall how much material you highlighted in your casebooks during the first weeks of law school. Soon, as you grew more sensitive to the relevant facts and law, less and less was being highlighted. This was a product of learning how to read a case. In much the same way, you will learn how to recognize the vital facts, and disregard the immaterial.

In reading the root of the student-opposing candidate example, above, it may not be as important to note that first student was running for office as it was to note that the accident occurred in front of the assembled student body, thus increasing the probability that student would be humiliated. This is not to completely discount the student's purpose for being in the auditorium, or that the opposing candidate was an opponent. The fact that the student was there to participate in a debate makes it clear that the audience would likely watch the first student's every move. The facts are not clear on the opposing candidate's intent in sticking out his leg; while it might appear that he intended to trip the first student, we have to be careful in making an unwarranted assumption. In this example, we appear to be missing a critical fact, and cannot make up for it with imagination. The resolution of this issue is likely the key to the problem, and will be dealt with in the answer choices.

It is important that you follow the facts and do not fight or respond emotionally to the facts that are given. This means taking the facts at face value, without reading too much into the facts. In this regard, you may need to stifle some of the natural inclinations of an advocate, as arguing or assuming facts may do little except waste time or lead to an incorrect response. Where the facts state that the arresting officer had a valid warrant, do not attempt to challenge the warrant. Where the facts state that the police made a random stop, do not go on to consider the possible exceptions to the warrant requirement. Where the facts state that a deed is valid and has been properly executed, there is no need to ask if the description is sufficient.

Some rules may seem unfair, perhaps even illogical, in applying the facts. For example, why shouldn't a physician be required to act to render assistance to another who may be seriously injured as a result of the physician's inaction, where there is no risk to the physician, and despite the fact that the victim was placed in peril by another? Why shouldn't a party be allowed to prove up a subsequent remedial measure to prove negligence or culpability, when such remedy is logically connected to the dangerous condition causing injury? The MBE is not the place to argue policy, and attempting to do so will exact a very high toll. Again, do not respond with emotion, but rather, respond with a reasoned approach to applying the law to the facts.

If a straightforward interpretation is available, do not over-analyze or seek out an unnecessarily convoluted interpretation. A reasonable, logical inference may, however, be required. Ensure that the inferred fact logically and necessarily follows from the information given. Making assumptions, creating new facts, or working with conclusions that are not warranted by the existing facts will, in most instances, generate an incorrect response.

Constitutional Law, Contracts and Real Property are where the subjects that are more demanding on reading comprehension, given the nature of the subject matter and the tendency that the examiners have to use longer, more complex fact patterns with multiple parties to test in these areas. Fact patterns in these areas will often require greater scrutiny, and therefore require more time.

Testing in Crimes, Evidence and Torts tends to emphasize elements and command of the black letter law. As a result, the fact patterns tend to be shorter, and may require less in the way of reading comprehension, and more in the way of substantive knowledge of the rules of law.

When reading the facts, regardless of the subject, keep in mind that the examiner is testing on lawyering skills. Cases very often turn on details, so an effective reading of the facts will often depend on the examinee's ability to discern the operative from the inoperative, the relevant from the immaterial, and the substantial from the inconsequential. Also, you must be as flexible and as adaptable as conditions may demand. This is known as thinking on one's feet. These are qualities that lead to a successful performance.

As with all the methods and techniques discussed in this introduction, including the following materials on selecting a response, success is dependent on practicing until the approach is virtually unconscious. Techniques must be adjusted to fit each individual's approach, and that only comes through practice. You must sort through each suggestion, and incorporate only that which has produced the greatest result with the practice questions.

Arguably, if the work done in reading the facts and the call of the question has been successful, then there should be little effort expended in reaching your destination, i.e., selecting a correct answer. In the most basic terms, we are usually seeking the best legal basis on which to support a particular or given outcome.

RULE #7 – DON'T GET SIDETRACKED.

On occasion, the correct answer may appear obvious. Certainly, if the answer is obvious, do not fight it. In other instances, however, it will seem as though the examiner has taken great pains to hide the ball. The incorrect answers, referred to as distracters by the examiners, are aptly named.

Consider Question 1, above. It would appear that the opposing candidate acted intentionally to trip the first student; however, the facts say nothing about the opposing candidate's state of mind, and we cannot afford to guess at what the opposing candidate was thinking. The facts state that the first student was not injured, so the (B) response, based on negligence, is improbable. The (C) response can be ruled out, because an action for battery or intentional infliction of emotional distress can be maintained even in the absence of actual physical harm. The (D) response can also be eliminated, as it limits liability to intent to cause physical harm; however, a cause of action can be based on the offense to the student's dignity or the intent to cause emotional distress. The (A) response, therefore, is the **key**, or correct response. By using the word "knew," it addresses the missing element of intent.

Typically, the person drafting the question is or has been a law professor. As a result, he or she has ample experience with the phrasings that are likely to lure an examinee into an incorrect response. There must be something attractive in a distracter. It may be an inaccurate or incomplete statement of the law. It may trigger some faint memory of an arcane rule. It may be a concept that has been drilled into you. Or, more likely, the distracter may reflect an incomplete understanding of a rule that has traditionally led to confusion.

In the student-opposing candidate example, the examiner may have been counting on the difficulty some students may have in distinguishing negligence and the intentional torts, or the requirement of physical harm that accompanies a negligence action.

One concept that routinely turns up in distracters is promissory estoppel. The same people who taught you to love and cherish the concept, law professors, now turn it against you. In the absence of a promise and a reasonable expectation on the part of the promisor that the promise will induce some action or inaction, the doctrine does not apply. Yet students have routinely attempted to use promissory estoppel as an all-purpose substitute for consideration, despite the absence of a promise, or the presence of a more appropriate response that has very real consideration.

In other situations, the distracter may prey on an examinee's confusion as to the identity of the holder of a right, or when the right arises. In a problem where the government is maintaining an action in inverse condemnation, an examinee must realize the action is one properly maintained against the government. In a problem where a defendant seeks to assert the last clear chance doctrine, an examinee must realize that only a plaintiff can assert the doctrine. Where there is a claim of privilege against self-incrimination, be sure that there is a statement in issue and that the statement is testimonial in nature.

Other distracters may seek to create whole new, incorrect concepts. Only a student with sufficient familiarity with the hearsay exceptions under the Federal Rules will know that there is no exception for a recent sense impression. Bargained-for reliance, a concept that withers in daylight, might get a second glance from an examinee unsure of his or her knowledge of Contracts. Keep in mind that after reading outlines in each of the subject areas, and doing thousands of practice questions, if there such a thing as bargained-for reliance existed, the concept would be recognized.

This is not intended to mean that you will necessarily be familiar with all potential phrasings. In an area such as negligence, we cannot expect to see 14 problems that may be answered Liable, if negligent. Some synonyms are in order, such as recklessly, carelessly, unreasonably, without due care, and so on. This does not mean, on the other hand, that new, special duties can be created, e.g., in a negligence, the defendant owes the "highest" or an "utmost duty of care."

Ultimately, the best cure is a thorough substantive review, followed by judicious amounts of practice questions. Adequate preparation will thwart the intentions of the examiner seeking to trap the unwary examinee.

RULE #8 – REMEMBER TO READ THE TRAFFIC SIGNS.

A clear understanding of the language in the lead-in and the options will be critical to achieving a sense of direction, or, in other words, the objective of the problem and arriving at the correct response.

The language in the lead-in may cast the examinee in a specific role, which in turn will have a bearing on which response is the most appropriate. For example, a lead-in that asks for the best basis on which to support a judge's decision is asking you, in essence, to act as that judge's law clerk. A question asking for the strongest or weakest argument is calling for an advocate. On the other hand, a lead-in seeking the most probable outcome may require a neutral approach in analyzing the most appropriate response.

Consider the following example to determine how much information is contained in the lead-in:

Question 5 is based on the following facts:

Two men operate a private courier service. They contracted with a law firm for the delivery of the firm's promotional calendars to clients throughout the city. Prior to commencing the deliveries, one man suggested that the two of them throw away the calendars, pocket the money paid for the deliveries, and spend the rest of day at the local race track. The other man said nothing. The first man then proceeded to dispose of the calendars.

5. If both men are charged with conspiracy to commit larceny in a common law jurisdiction, which of the following constitutes the second man's **weakest** defense?

    A. He did not have the required intent.

    B. He did not form an agreement with the first man, either explicitly or implicitly, as to a criminal objective.

> C. He did not act to take the calendars out of the law firm's possession.
>
> D. He was feigning agreement.

In the above example, the question lead-in is identifying the following: (1) the area of law, (2) the specific rule being tested, (3) the law of the jurisdiction, (4) the defendant to focus on in applying the rule, and (5) the role to assume in responding to the question. Actually, very little is needed from the root in this example. The criminal charge has been set out, so in order to respond, apply the rule of conspiracy.

The fact that the question seeks the weakest defense should not dramatically affect your analysis. This question may be more easily solved by working it in reverse; in other words, re-phrase the call to read "Which of the following constitutes the *strongest* defenses to conspiracy?" In this example, the (A), (B) and (D) responses are all negating an element of conspiracy, i.e., the specific intent to commit larceny or the agreement between two or more actors, and as such, are very strong defenses. Option (C) appears to be dealing with the crime of larceny, and not the inchoate crime of conspiracy, and would not be an adequate defense, is therefore the key in this example. Note that in the areas of Crimes and Torts the strongest, best defenses are those that negate an element of the charge or claim.

The same care must be used in analyzing the options. Consider the following example:

> ### *Question 6 is based on the following facts:*
>
> A skier was skiing in an area, which he was not familiar with, and inadvertently skied out of bounds. As he attempted to get back on the ski trail, a blizzard started, making it impossible for him to find his way back. As darkness descended, the skier started to fear that he would suffer from hypothermia unless he found shelter. As he was making his way through the waist-high snow, the skier spotted a ski cabin. Despite seeing a sign which read Private Property – Keep

Out!, the skier immediately made his way to the cabin and was able to gain entry by forcing the door open. The cabin was unoccupied.

Once inside the cabin, the skier started a fire in the fireplace. Without realizing there was a defect in the fireplace screen that allowed sparks to escape, the skier went to sleep. A fire broke out, which destroyed the cabin and caused serious injury to the skier.

6. If the skier asserts a claim against the owner for his injuries, will he be successful?

   A. Yes, **if** the owner was aware of the defective fireplace screen.

   B. Yes, **only if** the owner could have discovered the defective fire screen by a reasonable inspection.

   C. No, **unless** the owner had reason to anticipate a skier might break into the cabin.

   D. No, **because** the skier assumed the risk that a fire might break out when he went to sleep.

Notice that each option has a result, followed by a suggested basis on which to support that result. This is the most common formulation of answers on the MBE. Look closer, and you will notice that each outcome is joined to the basis by a conjunction, which can be referred to as the modifier, or operative term. Each different modifier has its own connotation or usage.

The modifier in option (A), **if**, suggests that the outcome **must** follow as a result of the statement of law of fact given, and no other outcome is possible. The determination that must be made is whether the logical connection is sufficient to justify the result. In a problem where there is one missing element in order for the plaintiff to prevail, and that missing element is preceded by an "if" modifier, then no other result is possible. This would be a very strong choice. The if modifier may be followed by a new fact, in which case the inquiry is whether no other result logically follows the new information. In the above example, we do not need to question whether or not the owner actually knew of the defect. The inquiry is whether or not the owner would necessarily be liable, given this awareness. Your knowledge of Torts will tell you that absent some duty owed, this result does not necessarily follow, and this answer may be rejected.

The **only if** modifier in option (B) suggests that the basis that follows the outcome is the exclusive means of arriving at the outcome, and that there is no other way to logically arrive at the outcome. The word only is a word of restriction or limitation. If there is another way to arrive at the outcome, then this modifier would indicate an incorrect response. In this example, the duty to inspect (owed to invitees) would not be the exclusive basis on which to predicate the owner's liability to the skier, and therefore must be rejected.

Option (C) features the **unless** modifier, which requires a reversal of the analysis of the only if modifier in options (A). In other words, the outcome stated could only be avoided by the statement that follows. The "unless" modifier should be treated as the logical opposite of "only if." Your knowledge of Torts will tell you that the owner will prevail if the skier is unable to satisfy all of the elements of negligence. All of the elements needed to find for the skier have been supplied except one – duty. Another way to view this option is to rephrase it to the skier will recover **only if** the owner had reason to anticipate the skier's presence in the cabin. This logically follows, because, based on the facts, duty to the trespassing skier will only arise where the owner has reason to know or anticipate his presence in the cabin; therefore, this is the key response.

The modifier in option (D), **because**, can be used interchangeably with the conjunctions since and as. Here the inquiry is two-fold. First examine the basis as a correct statement of law or fact. If it is correct, then ask if the outcome stated logically and necessarily follows from the basis. In this example, there is nothing in the facts that indicates the skier voluntarily and unreasonably encountered the known risk of a defective fireplace screen. As a result of this, this option must be rejected.

The analysis of the language above may seem awkward, even somewhat convoluted at first. After working through a substantial number of practice questions, you will find that familiarity and comfort with the language increases at a rapid pace. Fortunately for the MBE-examinee, the questions have increasingly relied on the "because" conjunction, as the other options start a ride into the testing sunset.

RULE #9 – BE ALERT FOR CHANGING ROAD CONDITIONS.

The three complete examples above followed a fairly standard format. The root was followed by the lead-in, which in turn was followed by options that each listed an outcome, followed by a proposed basis on which to support the outcome. The method used to arrive at the correct response in the explanations above was the process of elimination. Once we eliminated the false statements, whatever remained became our selection.

Another way to view the exam is as a multiple true-false test, rather than multiple choice. That means looking at each option, independently, as a true-false question. It will be helpful to mark a T or an F next to each option as you read through them. Alternately, you might use a system of pluses or minuses, or crossing out the false statements. Selecting the correct option then becomes a function of looking for a T, a plus, or an option that has not been crossed out.

But what about the options with a question mark next to them? What if you can only narrow it down to two choices?

If you are able to narrow it down to two choices, one of which is correct, you are definitely on the right track. You will have increased the odds of getting the problem correct by 100%. This is one reason why you may wish to indicate your second choice as you work through the practice questions. As you read through the explanatory answers, you will seek to develop a sense of why the examiner prefers one choice over another.

Remember that the examiner, at least in the problem types we have reviewed so far, is putting you on the hunt for the **best legal basis** on which to support a given outcome. Consequently, the answer that can be seen as narrower or more specific to the result is usually preferred; the same is true when comparing a legal basis with a factual basis. The legal basis is generally preferred. For example, Not guilty, because the facts do not state that Defendant had an improper motive does not present as good a legal basis as Not guilty, because Defendant lacked the intent to steal in exculpating the defendant in an example testing on larceny.

Be on the alert for those answer choices that are "underinclusive" or "overinclusive" in stating the basis for the outcome. For example, the option stating "Constitutional because the 1st Amendment only protects" is likely to be wrong in a Constitutional Law problem, because certain acts of expressive conduct may be within the scope of

1st Amendment protection. If you find the rationale in an option eliminates a right that should be included, or encompasses a right or result that does not follow from your understanding of the law, then such option is to be avoided.

The examiners use a number of variations on the problem-types illustrated above, such as where the result is the only thing contained in the option. Consider the following example:

> ### Question 7 is based on the following facts:
>
> During the night, a drug addict broke into the apartment of a reputed drug dealer, with the intention of stealing the dealer's supply of rock cocaine. Although the addict did not find any cocaine, he did find some methedrine, an illegal stimulant. The drug addict took the methedrine with him when he left the apartment.
>
> 7. In a common law jurisdiction, the drug addict is guilty of:
>
>   A. Burglary only.
>
>   B. Larceny only.
>
>   C. Burglary and larceny.
>
>   D. No crime.

Although the options are not the compound type that we have looked at, the approach is similar, in that we must still go through each possible response and deem it either true or false. We do this by reviewing the elements of each charge, and determining whether or not the facts will support the charge. Where there are multiple charges (or outcomes), deal with the elements of each individual charge.

In this example, we are in a common-law jurisdiction, and the facts state that the addict broke into the purported drug dealer's apartment at nighttime with the intent to steal drugs. We do not have to struggle with the elements of breaking and entering because they are there in the facts. The examiner is hoping for an emotional response, that somehow stealing illegal drugs is not morally wrong. But the facts make it clear that the addict had the intent to commit a larceny at the time of breaking and entering, therefore the addict has committed burglary. He has also taken the drugs, which are the personal property of another, with the intent to steal; therefore the addict has also committed larceny, and choice (C) is correct. Keep in mind that each crime requires satisfaction of an element the other does not, so there is no double jeopardy prohibition.

Another problem type, now used only rarely on the MBE but continually used in law school exams and other testing formats incorporates the facts into the options themselves, which may be referred to as a **squib-option** format, as in the following example:

> 8. In which of the following fact situations will the contract most likely be enforceable despite the absence of a written agreement?
>
> A. A homeowner and a cable company have a dispute over the placement of the company's use of the utility poles on the homeowner's land. In an effort to settle the matter, the company offers to purchase an easement from the homeowner, and the homeowner accepts.
>
> B. A vendor operates vending machines throughout the city. A supplier offers to sell $5,000.00 worth of snack foods to the vendor for only $3,000.00. The vendor accepts.
>
> C. An agent hears a singer perform in a nightclub and on the spot offers her a two-year recording contract. In reliance on the offer, the singer quits her job at the nightclub, and accepts the offer.
>
> D. An owner asks a builder to submit a bid for the construction of addition to the owner's house. The builder offers to build the addition for $10,000.00. The owner accepts.

Problems of this type can generally be attacked with a two-step approach. Ask yourself the following: What is the rule being tested (as identified by the stem)? And, How is it to be applied, i.e., what is the task to perform? In this example, the stem indicates that the rule being tested is the Statute of Frauds (requiring a writing in order to enforce certain types of agreements), and the task is to classify each contract to see whether it falls within the Statute. Options (A), (B), and (C) each reflect an agreement that requires a writing under the Statute of Frauds – a contract for the sale of an interest in land, a contract for the sale of goods for the price of $500 or more, and a contract that is not to be performed within one year from the making thereof, respectively. Only (D), involving a construction contract, clearly falls outside of the Statute, and is the key response.

Answer choice (C) may present a problem for some students, as they might want to argue the element of reliance. The examiners are counting on this, expecting some students will waste time wanting to argue. If you have an arguable response, versus a clear-,cut response, do not waste time. Answer the question, and then completely erase it from your mind. One of the pitfalls of the exam is that certain problems are so challenging that a student will continue to work it in the back of the head, long after a response has been marked. Resist this temptation, as it will only slow you down, frustrate you and destroy your effectiveness.

Another problem type the examiners have used in the past is the **tiered** question, as in the following example:

> ### Question 9 is based on the following facts:
>
> A company operates a factory that manufactures air conditioners. One of the ingredients used in the manufacturing process is freon gas, which when exposed to the welding torches necessary to the manufacturing process creates the highly toxic phosgene gas. The phosgene gas is pulled out of the inside of the factory by means of large exhaust fans, which are vented directly to the atmosphere. No other means are available to the company for the removal of the phosgene gas. A little girl who lives next to the factory, inhaled the fumes and was severely injured.
>
> 9. If the girl asserts a claim against the company for her injuries, which of the following must be established if she is to be successful?
>
>   I.   The company operated the factory in a negligent manner.

> II. The factory constituted a public nuisance.
>
> III. The toxic gas released by the factory caused her injuries.
>
> A. III only.
>
> B. I and III only.
>
> C. II, and III only.
>
> D. I, II, and III.

The most efficient, effective way to work this problem is to treat it in the same way that we have already seen, that is, to treat it as a compound true-false question. The stem is asking which of the following is an absolute requirement, regardless of the cause of action. We can cross out or write an F next to statement I and statement II, because the company is involved in an abnormally dangerous activity giving rise to strict liability, i.e., disbursing highly toxic gases into the atmosphere in a populated area. The girl can therefore prevail even in the absence of proof of negligence or nuisance. Option (A) is therefore correct. This question-type has fallen into disfavor with the NCBE.

Yet another problem type is the **complex case precedent**. In this problem type, a series of case precedents are set out, with the stems being fact patterns, and the options designating which of the precedents will be controlling, as in the following example:

> *Questions 10 - 12 are based on the following facts:*
>
> Read the summaries in the four cases (A – D) below. Then, decide which is the most applicable as a precedent to each of the cases in the questions that follow, and indicate each choice by marking the corresponding space on your answer sheet.

36 INTRODUCTION: THE RULES OF THE ROAD

(A) Defendant, while in the process of robbing a liquor store, dropped his revolver. The gun discharged, and the bullet struck and killed a customer in the store. Defendant fled, but is later apprehended and charged with murder. At trial, Defendant testifies that the killing was accidental, and requests that an instruction for manslaughter be given. **Held**: Guilty of murder.

(B) Defendant, angered over not being invited to her next-door neighbor's housewarming party, discharged her gun into their common wall while the party was ongoing. The bullet struck a lighting fixture, and the shards of glass in turn struck and killed a partygoer. Defendant was apprehended and charged with murder. At trial, Defendant testifies that she never intended to harm anyone and requests that an instruction for manslaughter be given. **Held**: Guilty of murder.

(C) Defendant, while in the desert, decided to practice target shooting with her new rifle. Taking aim at a cactus, she discharged a round. The bullet struck a rock, ricocheted off of another rock, and struck and killed a person standing 10 yards behind Defendant. Defendant is apprehended and charged with murder. At trial, Defendant testifies that she did not know that the victim was present, and requests that an instruction for manslaughter be given. **Held**: Guilty of manslaughter.

(D) Defendant was away on a two-week lecture tour. On her return home, she discovered her husband having sex with her sister. Defendant then removed a revolver from her briefcase and fired it in the general direction of her husband and sister. The sister is struck by the bullet and dies. Defendant is apprehended and charged with murder. At trial, Defendant testifies that she only intended to shoot her husband, that the shooting of her sister was accidental, and she only discharged the gun because she had lost control and was unable to regain her composure. Defendant also requested an instruction for manslaughter. **Held**: Guilty of manslaughter.

10. Defendant, intending to collect on an insurance claim, sets fire to his warehouse. The fire spreads to an adjoining building, which apparently had been abandoned several years earlier. A vagrant who was living in this adjoining building was sleeping at the time and was overcome by the smoke. As a result, the vagrant was unable to escape in time, and was killed in the ensuing blaze.

A statute in the jurisdiction defines arson as the malicious burning of any structure.

11. Defendant, while driving his car at the posted speed limit on the freeway, began to be perturbed at the close proximity of the car immediately behind him. In an effort to send a message to the tailgating driver, the defendant abruptly slammed on his brakes. The other driver attempted to avoid the impact by swerving his car, but instead struck the concrete center median barrier and the other driver was killed.

12. Two men were fellow employees of IDF, a communications software developer. One night the two of them began to argue over a technical matter. One man then reached into his desk drawer, and started to pull out something that appeared metallic. Defendant believed that the man was pulling out a gun and was about to shoot him, so Defendant pulled out a gun and shot the first man. The first man, who was merely taking out a letter opener, died.

The temptation will be to match the facts in the stems with the facts in the precedents, which will usually result in confusion and one or more incorrect answers. In the above example, the facts in the question cases did not closely resemble the precedents. The key is to distinguish each precedent as to the legal basis as it relates to the result, use your knowledge of the law to determine the result in each stem, and then match result for result. In the above example, this means identifying the following:

A. Murder/Felony murder rule – robbery.

B. Murder/Depraved heart murder.

C. Manslaughter/involuntary – act of criminal recklessness.

D. Manslaughter/voluntary – adequate provocation.

Now, it becomes a task of matching result and basis with each of the ensuing fact patterns. This means that the correct answer to Question 10 is (A), because the accidental killing arose as a foreseeable consequence of the commission of an inherently dangerous felony, arson. Question 11 was an example of involuntary manslaughter involving criminal recklessness, and not depraved heart murder, because the necessary showing of the Defendant's awareness of the high probability of death was not present; thus, option (C) is correct. Finally, Question 12, is an example of voluntary manslaughter because of mistaken justification – Defendant had a mistaken belief in an imminent threat of death or serious bodily injury. The result must be matched with the result in one of the precedents; consequently, option (D) is correct. Thankfully for many students, this question type does not appear with frequency; when it does, usually in Criminal Law/Procedure, you may recognize that with a workable approach, these questions will not seem overly difficult. This extremely complex question-type has fallen into general disfavor, but could appear on a law school or state exam.

In the **supposition stem** problem type, the lead-in will ask which of the facts contained in the options, if true, will best support a particular result. The goal here is to treat each of the options as true, combine it with the existing facts, and determine if it logically and necessarily leads to the desired outcome, as in the following example:

> ### *Question 13 is based on the following fact situation:*
>
> On May 28, a woman and a man who was a dealer of vintage cars, entered into a written, signed agreement whereby the dealer offered to give the woman 30 days in which to decide whether or not to purchase the dealer's extremely rare automobile for $1,000,000.00. Only 50 of these automobiles were imported to the United States, and only five are currently known to exist. On June 1, the woman tendered a cashier's check for $1,000,000.00. The dealer refused to convey title to the automobile. The woman brings an action for specific performance.
>
> 13. Which of the following facts, if true, would provide the dealer with his **strongest** defense?
>
>   A. The woman did not give any form of consideration for the option to purchase the automobile.

> B. The woman had entered into an agreement with another dealer for the purchase of a different automobile after May 28, and had communicated that fact to the dealer.
>
> C. At the time of commencing the action, the woman knew that another one of the same automobiles was available for $1,500,000.00.
>
> D. Both parties thought the agreement was for the purchase of another one of the dealer's extremely rare automobiles.

Again, as each option is examined, it is assumed that it is true. Option (A) does not have legal significance, as the facts state that the dealer was a dealer in this type of automobile. Under the U.C.C., a merchant who gives assurance in a signed writing that an offer will not be revoked cannot later claim lack of consideration as a defense to an option contract. Option (B) appears to state that the woman revoked his offer; however, this does not follow from the facts, as the woman is an offeree who has not yet rejected the dealer's offer. Option (C) cuts against the remedy of specific performance, yet it is incomplete in that it does not state that the two automobiles were alike in all practical respects. Option (D), although it flies in the face of the facts, is the "key" response, because if mutual mistake is present, the contract is necessarily voidable at the election of either party. Remember, in this problem type each additional fact must be treated as true.

In the **three-one split** problem type, there will be one option that stands alone as to result. Do not attach any special significance to this, as it probably has a one in four chance of being correct. Work it through as you would any other example, but pay special attention to the modifiers, particularly one that would affect the result such as unless. If one option does not include a basis or rationale, select it only if the facts provide sufficient support for the outcome. Consider the following example:

Question 14 is based on the following fact situation.

A professional ice skater stopped in a bar for a drink after performing one evening. After having several drinks, the ice skater began to speak with a woman who was seated next to him at the bar. The discussion turned into a disagreement and the disagreement was so fierce that the skater took a swing at the woman. The contact was slight, but it was enough to knock the woman off of her bar stool. Unbeknownst to the skater, the woman was a federal undercover agent, and was at the bar in order to make a drug buy.

Subsequently, the skater was arrested and charged with assaulting a federal officer. At trial, the skater testified that he was unaware that the woman was a federal officer and that, if he had known, he would have never struck her.

14. If the jury believes the skater, it should find him:

   A. Guilty.

   B. Not guilty, because he lacked the specific intent to assault a federal officer.

   C. Not guilty, unless assault of this type is considered a general intent crime.

   D. Not guilty, because the skater was mistaken as to the woman's identity.

In the above example, the only requirement as to mens rea is that the skater intended the assault. The skater's awareness of the woman as a federal officer is immaterial. No mental awareness of the jurisdictional element of this type of offense is necessary to convict. Note that option (B) can be eliminated on this basis. Option (C), which has the modifier unless, can be eliminated on the basis that the facts indicate that the skater intended the assault, and so the classification does not have a bearing on guilt. Option (D) is incorrect, because mistake is no defense on these facts. Again, only after eliminating all other choices can we properly arrive at the correct answer, option (A).

Other problem types may appear from time to time. It is the ability to think on your feet and apply the law to the facts in a lawyer-like fashion that will allow you to vanquish each problem, and, ultimately, the MBE.

RULE #10 – ENSURE THAT SPEED IS ADEQUATE TO PASS.

Be aware that a number of problems do not appear to test your minimum competency to practice, but rather, are designed to play with your mind. As the exam is a test against time, you cannot afford to get bogged down on any one problem. If the answer proves elusive, mark down a response, and move on. If the facts are lengthy, and there is only one problem, consider skipping it to conserve time, especially if it is testing on arcane or obscure material. For example, if the problem has two full columns of facts, and a single question testing on planned unit developments and the mutuality of equitable servitudes in Real Property, Burby, a well-known Property scholar himself, might have skipped it. Before moving on, though, glance at the options to see if any can be eliminated as clear false statements of law, so as to improve the odds of a guess.

Always be sure to mark down an answer so as to avoid skewing the "Scantron." If you have skewed the answer grid, say around problem 15, you cannot afford to discover this as the proctor is calling time. You must always be aware of time and speed, so that you do not run into the situation where no time remains, and yet you are still trying to fill in the bubbles.

Avoid changing answers unless you specifically see where you have misread a problem, or later remember the formulation of a rule that applies in a earlier problem; however, if you are still thinking about an earlier problem, the concentration is not there, and speed is likely lagging. If you spend enough time practicing, your first guess will probably be correct anyway.

Remember, no one gets them all, not even the law professors who take the exam. In fact, the examiners will typically throw out two to three questions on each exam due to ambiguity or inconsistency. Of the 190 scored questions on the MBE, most examinees will get at least 100 correct. The key to success is getting the next 35 to 60 problems correct.

Always, always remain positive. Indicate to yourself that you are ready to pass by doing the things that you, and only you, know you need to do. Treat the exam like a game, and do it for the sake of the game. Don't think about the result or the stakes - just enjoy the ride!

THE RULES OF THE MBE ROAD, IN REVIEW:

1. Familiarize Yourself With The MBE Terrain;

2. Prepare For The Long Haul;

3. Keep Your Eyes On The Road;

4. Maximize Your Fuel Efficiency;

5. Know Where You Are Headed;

6. Use Road Maps;

7. Don't Get Sidetracked;

8. Remember To Read The Traffic Signs;

9. Be Alert For Changing Road Conditions; and

10. Ensure That Speed Is Adequate To Pass.

Good luck on the MBE!

CONTRACTS – QUESTION BREAKDOWN

1. Statute of Frauds - Written Confirmation Between Merchants
2. Offer - Meeting of the Minds
3. Consideration - Bargained for Exchange
4. Consideration - Donative Promise
5. Consideration - Reasonable Reliance
6. U.C.C. - Predominant Purpose Test
7. U.C.C. - Firm Offer
8. Consideration - Pre-existing Duty
9. Formation - Additional Different Terms
10. Formation - Additional Terms
11. U.C.C. - Place of Delivery
12. Unilateral Contract
13. Offer - Communication to Offeree
14. Anticipatory Repudiation
15. Express Condition
16. U.C.C. - Risk of Loss
17. Defenses - Mistake
18. U.C.C. - Nonconforming Goods
19. Incidental Damages
20. Express Warranty - Sample or Model
21. Third Party Beneficiary - Vesting
22. Contract Liability
23. Third Party Beneficiary - Incidental
24. Excuse - Part Performance/Substantial Performance
25. Third Party Beneficiary - Vesting
26. Conditions - Implied in Fact
27. Third Party Beneficiary - Detrimental Reliance
28. Third Party Beneficiary
29. Assignments - Non-Assignment Clause
30. Third Party Beneficiary
31. Defenses - Failure to Perform
32. Assignments
33. Assignments – Delegation of Duty
34. Assignment/Third Party Beneficiary
35. Assignment – Delegation of Duty

36. Warranty of Title – Disclaimer
37. Express Warranty
38. U.C.C. – Method of Acceptance
39. U.C.C. – Shipment of Goods
40. U.C.C. – Firm Offer
41. Acceptance – Additional Terms
42. U.C.C. – Perfect Tender Rule
43. U.C.C. – Acceptance
44. Statute of Frauds - Merchants
45. Express Warranty – Affirmation of Fact
46. Formation
47. Acceptance – Unilateral
48. Revocation
49. Statute of Frauds
50. Divisibility of Contract
51. Parol Evidence Rule
52. U.C.C. – Perfect Tender Rule
53. Liquidated Damages
54. Shipment Contract
55. Risk of Loss

56. Remedies – Rescission
57. Third Party Beneficiary
58. U.C.C. – Perfect Tender Rule
59. U.C.C. – Right to Cure
60. Contract Damages
61. Consideration – Promissory Estoppel
62. Mutual Assent
63. U.C.C. – Firm Offer
64. U.C.C. – Additional Terms
65. U.C.C. – Tender of Goods – Notice of Non-Conformity
66. Repudiation
67. Damages – Loss of Bargain
68. Parol Evidence Rule
69. Leases
70. Breach – Material
71. Statute of Frauds
72. Parol Evidence Rule – Mistake in Integration
73. Consideration
74. Consideration

75. Unjust Enrichment
76. Statute of Frauds
77. Statute of Frauds – Exception
78. Defenses – Mutual Mistake
79. Contracts with Minors
80. Contracts with Minors
81. Misrepresentation
82. Defenses – Unilateral Mistake
83. U.C.C. – Right to Inspect
84. Non-Conforming Goods – Damages
85. Non-Conforming Goods – Disposal
86. Unilateral Contract
87. Firm Offer
88. Option Contract
89. Option Contract/Counteroffer
90. U.C.C. – Acceptance/Additional Terms
91. Bilateral Contracts
92. Statute of Frauds – Sufficient Memo
93. Defenses – Mistake
94. Pre-existing Duty Rule

95. Conditions
96. Acceptance/Rejection
97. Discharge of Duties
98. Mistake
99. Pre-existing Duty Rule
100. Modification
101. U.C.C. – Predominant Purpose
102. Consideration
103. Detrimental Reliance
104. Consideration
105. Consideration
106. Assignment – Defenses
107. Third Party Beneficiary - Vesting
108. Third Party Beneficiary – Donee
109. Assignments
110. Assignments – Defenses
111. Defenses – Ratification
112. Statute of Frauds
113. Accord and Satisfaction
114. Novation

115. Remedies – Cover/Specific Performance

116. Consideration – Moral Obligation

117. Offer

118. Measure of Damages

119. U.C.C. – Resale of Non-conforming Goods

120. Waiver

121. Assignments – Delegation of Duty

122. Assignments – Delegation of Duty – Liability

123. Offer – Advertisement

124. Assignment

125. Risk of Loss

126. Unilateral Mistake

127. Formation

128. Statute of Frauds

129. Consideration

130. Consideration

131. Offer

132. Revocation – Detrimental Reliance

133. Unilateral Contract

134. Conditions

135. Revocation

136. Repudiation

137. Breach – Material

138. Damages

139. Statute of Frauds

140. Rescission

141. Quasi-Contract

142. Quasi-Contract

143. Warranty Disclaimer

144. U.C.C. - Acceptance

145. U.C.C. – Method of Acceptance

146. U.C.C. – Sec. 9-313 Security Interest

147. U.C.C. – FOB – Risk of Loss

148. U.C.C. – Security Interest

149. U.C.C. – §9-313(4)(B) – Perfect Security Interest

150. U.C.C. – §9-313(4)(A) – Defeat of Pre-Existing Realty Interest

151. U.C.C. – §9-401(2) – Good Faith Filing

152. Article 9 – Removal of Secured

Property

153. Article 9 – Removal of Secured Property

154. Implied Warranty of Merchantability – Disclaimer

155. U.C.C. – §2-312 – Warranty of Title

CONTRACTS QUESTIONS

1. A distributor of stereo equipment phones a merchant-customer and agrees that it will sell 1,200 stereo systems to that merchant-customer for $500 each - if delivery can be made before August 1. The merchant-customer states that he will think about it. The merchant-customer then sends a confirmation form to the distributor, signed by the merchant-customer, stating the price of the goods and the quantity of the stereo systems. The distributor receives this form on July 1. On July 16, the distributor informs the merchant-customer that it will not perform, due to an increase in production costs. The merchant-customer sues the distributor for breach of contract. Which of the following statements are most correct?

    A. Given the above facts, the Parol Evidence Rule is applicable, and the merchant-customer would win.

    B. If the distributor asserts the Statute of Frauds as a defense, the distributor would win.

    C. The Statute of Frauds requires that the merchant-customer should have signed a written contract with the distributor.

    D. If the distributor asserts the Statute of Frauds, it will probably be unsuccessful.

2. A woman had been working for a company for a long time. When she was ready to retire, her boss promised to pay her $500 a month for the rest of her life, in appreciation for her years of service. The woman exclaimed, "Thank you, this is the biggest surprise I've ever gotten!" The woman knew that the company did not have a retirement plan for any of its employees.

    What was the legal effect, if any, of the woman's statement after hearing the promise of lifetime income?

    A. There was a valid and binding acceptance by the woman.

    B. At the moment of the statement, there was an objective meeting of the minds.

    C. It created acceptance, only if the woman expressly promised not to be self-indulgent with the funds.

    D. It has no binding legal effect.

3. A charitable boy picked up trash at the beach one weekend. His neighbor found out what the boy had done and promised to give the boy $100 on his birthday for his charitable work picking up the trash. The boy's birthday arrived, but the neighbor did not pay him. The boy sued the neighbor.

    What will be the most likely outcome?

CONTRACTS

A. The boy will recover because the neighbor made a legally enforceable gratuitous promise.

B. The boy will recover because the neighbor had a moral obligation to pay him.

C. The boy will recover under a promissory estoppel theory.

D. The boy will not recover.

4. A woman just found out that she had passed the Bar Examination. She was so overjoyed that she called her former Bar Examination tutor and promised to give the tutor a new Ferrari automobile as a token of her appreciation for the tutoring that helped her pass the Bar Examination. The tutor immediately gave away her car and then went to a Ferrari dealership and picked out a red Ferrari that she loved. The tutor then called the woman to make arrangements for the woman to come to the dealership and pay for the car. The woman laughed and said, "Surely you didn't believe me, did you?" The tutor said, "Yes I did, and I'll see you in court. I'm going to sue you."

In evaluating the woman's statement about paying for the Ferrari, which of the following rules will the court most likely find to be the correct and applicable law to the case:

A. A gratuitous promise is not enforceable against the promisor in the absence of special circumstances.

B. A gratuitous promise is a substitute for consideration and has the same legal effect as consideration.

C. A gratuitous promise, coupled with detrimental reliance, is binding upon the promisor because there was a bargained-for exchange.

D. A promisor cannot unilaterally change the terms of a gratuitous promise.

5. A woman promises her boyfriend that she will pay his rent for an entire school year. At the time, the boyfriend was living in low-cost student housing. After the woman made her promise, the boyfriend immediately moved into a high-rent penthouse apartment with a view of the ocean. When the woman found out that the boyfriend's rent in the new apartment was quadruple the amount of his prior rent, she refused to pay the boyfriend's rent for the rest of the school year. The boyfriend contends that he will be successful in enforcing the woman's promise, under the theory of promissory estoppel. However, the woman will most likely prevail under which of the following arguments?

A. The boyfriend's conduct in reliance on the woman's promise was unforeseeable.

B. The woman did not intend for the boyfriend to rely upon her promise.

C. The boyfriend's conduct was not sufficient legal detriment to support the enforceability of the woman's promise.

D. Since the woman was only joking, she had no intent to be bound.

6. A boater purchased a ski boat at a police auction. After one outing, the boater realized the boat had a slow leak and needed to be repaired. The boater took the boat to a boat repair shop. After the shop had repaired the boat, the boater discovered it still leaked. The repair bill showed that the boater was charged $350 for parts and $400 for labor. A dispute arose over this transaction. Does Article 2 of the U.C.C. apply to this transaction?

A. Article 2 may apply depending on a determination of whether the predominant factor in the transaction was for services.

B. Article 2 may apply depending on a determination of whether the predominant factor in the transaction was the sale of goods.

C. Article 2 does not apply.

D. Article 2 applies only to the labor.

7. A man works as a merchant dealing strictly in turbo engines. He sends another merchant, a woman, a signed offer that he will sell her 2 (two) top-notch supreme turbo engines for $6,000.00 each at any time during the next five months. She receives the signed offer the following day. Which of the following is most correct?

A. The offer is not valid because it was not supported by consideration.

B. Under Article 2 of the U.C.C., the offer will remain irrevocable for five months.

C. Under Article 2 of the U.C.C., she must accept the offer within three months, or the offer will have expired.

D. She must accept the offer by return mail.

8. On August 1, a woman borrowed $600.00 from her brother to enroll in beauty school. The woman had promised to pay her brother on October 1. On October 2, the brother phones the woman and says, "I really need the money you owe me to pay for my bar application, which is now due. If you give me $400.00 by Sunday, I will relieve you from payment of the additional $200.00." The woman, noting a bargain, pays her brother the $400.00. The brother does not give the woman a discharge of the debt. The brother

then sues the woman for the additional $200.00. The outcome will be for:

A. The woman, since any pre-existing duty was extinguished.

B. The brother, since the woman was under a pre-existing duty to pay the original amount of the debt.

C. The woman because the $400 payment was sufficient consideration.

D. None of the above.

9. A merchant mailed an order form to another merchant. The form stated that the first merchant would sell 12 tons of sunflower seeds to the second merchant for total sum of $600.00. Delivery was to be made at the second merchant's store on December 1. Payment was due upon delivery.

The second merchant returned the order form to the first merchant. However, the second merchant added some terms stating that the first merchant would be liable if delivery were delayed and that payment was due within 30 days of delivery.

Which of the following statements are most correct?

A. A contract was created when the second merchant returned the order form.

B. No contract was created until the first merchant received the order form back from the second merchant.

C. No contract was created because the forms varied.

D. No contract was created because the second merchant made a counteroffer.

10. A man sold his neighbor a bicycle at a garage sale. The man and the neighbor agreed in writing that the neighbor would pay the sum of $100 for the bicycle the following day. The next day, the neighbor brought back the signed agreement, but added that before turning over the bicycle, the man would paint it. The man refused to sell the neighbor the bicycle. The neighbor sued the man. Will the neighbor prevail?

A. Yes because a contract was formed and the contract terms would include those proposed by the man (the seller).

B. No because a contract was not formed in that the additional terms materially altered the contract.

C. No because a contract was formed on the terms upon which the parties agreed, and the added terms by the neighbor would be construed as mere proposals to the contract.

D. No because requiring the man to paint the bicycle is unconscionable.

11. A seller agrees to sell ten tons of peanuts to a buyer. The agreement does not mention the place of delivery. The place of delivery is:

    A. A carrier's terminal in the buyer's city.

    B. The buyer's place of business.

    C. The buyer's loading facility.

    D. The seller's place of business, if that is where the peanuts were located.

12. A store wanted to increase business, so it published an ad in a local newspaper stating that it would give a small computer worth $1,800 to the first 100 people who arrived at the store on Wednesday. The offer in the newspaper constituted:

    A. A bilateral contract.

    B. An offer to negotiate.

    C. A unilateral contract.

    D. A unilateral contract that became a bilateral contract to the first 100 people who arrived at the store.

13. A woman lost her dog and posted an ad in the local newspaper offering a $5,000 reward for the dog's safe return. Her neighbor, unaware of the reward, found and recognized the dog and returned the dog to the woman. The neighbor then learned about the reward and demanded it. If the neighbor sues to recover the $5,000 reward, he will:

    A. Succeed.

    B. Succeed, since a contract implied by law was formed.

    C. Not succeed because there was no bargained for exchange.

    D. Not succeed.

14. On September 1, a man offered to sell his motorcycle to his girlfriend for $2,500. The man was to deliver the motorcycle on September 9, and his girlfriend was to pay the $2,500 on September 15. The man delivered the motorcycle on September 9. However, on September 10, his girlfriend refused to pay. When will the man have a cause of action against his girlfriend?

    A. September 9.

    B. September 10.

    C. On September 1 only.

    D. September 15, or after.

15. A seller offered to sell his house to a buyer on January 30 if that buyer could obtain a mortgage by January 15. The

requirement for the buyer to obtain a mortgage by January 15 is:

   A. An express condition.

   B. An implied condition.

   C. A constructive condition precedent.

   D. A concurrent condition.

16. A woman who deals in special industrial engines agrees to construct and sell a special industrial engine grinder for a merchant. The cost to construct this special grinder is $50,000. Upon completion of the grinder, it was agreed that the woman was to ship the machine to the merchant. However, before the engine was completely finished, the warehouse containing the engine burned to the ground, completely destroying the engine. The fire was not the fault of anyone. Which is the correct statement?

   A. The woman's performance is excused.

   B. The woman must pay damages.

   C. The merchant may collect from the woman the loss not covered by the insurance.

   D. The merchant may sue for breach of contract.

17. A major contractor agreed to build a large enclosed shopping mall for a corporation. After long hours of deliberation, the parties agreed on the price of 30 million dollars. The contract was signed on January 1. The completion of the new mall was set for May 1. As the contractor started digging, it struck solid rock. Removing this rock would increase the cost by one-half million dollars. Other builders who made bids had been aware of the rock and had submitted much higher bids. The most probable outcome is:

   A. The contractor will be excused from performance.

   B. The contractor and his corporation will split the increased costs.

   C. The contract is void due to impracticability.

   D. The contractor will be bound to finish the work originally contracted for and will suffer the increased costs.

18. A seller contracted with a buyer to sell 12 dozen roller blades for $1,200 to the buyer. Payment was due 20 days after delivery. When the roller blades arrived, they were found to be non-conforming. The buyer rejected the shipment of roller blades. The buyer is now required to:

   A. Send the roller blades back to the seller.

   B. Sell the roller blades at a discount

and give the proceeds to the seller.

C. Accept the roller blades and sue for breach of contract.

D. Hold the roller blades with reasonable care for disposition as the seller instructs.

19. A company owner was about to go to a seminar, where he planned to hand out pens containing his business logo. He, thus, called a supplier and ordered 1,000 ballpoint pens to be inscribed with his business logo. The pens were supposed to be black ink pens, and the logo was to be inscribed in black. When the pens arrived, they were red ink pens with a competitor's logo. The company owner then contacted another supplier to make the pens in time for the seminar. That supplier charged a sales commission in addition to the regular fee because of the rush order. The company owner then sued the original supplier for damages. In a general claim for damages, which would not be incidental damages?

A. An expected profit by the company owner of which the original supplier was aware at the time the contract was made.

B. Expenses incurred in inspecting the non-conforming pens.

C. The cost of storing the non-conforming pens.

D. A sales commission paid to accomplish cover.

20. A model sees a demonstration of a new curling iron that curls hair in 30 seconds. She is interested because she always has to do her hair in a hurry. The curling iron that the model purchases takes 2 minutes to curl her hair. Is the curling iron's performance sufficient to create a cause of action for the model?

A. No because she has no privity of contract with the seller of the curling iron.

B. Yes because there was a warranty of fitness for a particular purpose.

C. Yes because there was an express warranty.

D. None of the above.

21. A city awards a contract to a general contractor to build a sports complex. The general contractor then engages the services of a sub-contractor to do the electrical work and informs the city representatives that he has engaged the services of the sub-contractor. The city's representatives then approve of the sub-contractor's engagement in this project. Subsequently, the sub-contractor fails to perform. Can the city sue the sub-contractor?

A. No because the city had no donative intent towards the sub-contractor.

B. No because the city is not a creditor beneficiary.

C. Yes because the city is a creditor beneficiary.

D. Yes because the city is a creditor beneficiary whose rights against the sub-contractor have vested.

22. A general contractor is awarded a contract by a county. The general contractor engages a sub-contractor to do the plumbing work by signing a valid contract. The sub-contractor fails to install all the right plumbing equipment. If the county sues the general contractor, may the general contractor sue the sub-contractor?

    A. No because the general contractor has no rights against the sub-contractor.

    B. Yes because the sub-contractor is the obligor.

    C. No because a general contractor can never sue a sub-contractor as a matter of law.

    D. Yes, if the general contractor and the sub-contractor had a valid enforceable contract.

23. A restaurant owner attends a city council meeting and voices his support for the construction of a new sports arena that is going to be built a block away from his restaurant because he expects to have an increase in his business from the arena. The city council subsequently adopts a resolution for the sports arena to be built. Before the arena is completed, a fire breaks out at the sports arena construction site because of the negligence of the general contractor, and the sports arena construction project is never completed. Can the restaurant owner, as a third party beneficiary, sue the general contractor?

    A. Yes, if the negligence of the general contractor is proven in court.

    B. No because the restaurant owner is an officious intermeddler.

    C. No, the restaurant owner did not have the right to receive any duty.

    D. No because the restaurant owner's rights have not vested.

24. A boutique enters into a contract with a dress supplier. The dress supplier gets its dresses from a wholesaler. When the wholesaler delivers the dresses to the dress supplier, some of the dresses are damaged, but the dress supplier nonetheless sends the dresses on to the boutique. The boutique refuses to pay the dress supplier. The dress supplier then fails to pay the wholesaler. The wholesaler sues the boutique. What is the most likely outcome?

    A. The boutique's damages will be offset by any breach of the dress supplier.

B. The boutique's damages will be offset by any breach of the wholesaler.

C. The wholesaler has suffered a "legal" detriment.

D. The wholesaler is an incidental beneficiary of the contract between the boutique and the dress supplier.

25. A woman owes her mother some money. The woman enters into a contract with a man for the woman to perform services. She tells the man that her fee should be paid to her mother. The woman fails to tell her mother about the agreement that she has entered into with the man. When the mother asks the woman for the money that is owed to her, the woman says, "Didn't the man pay you?" Since the man has not paid the mother, can the mother sue the man?

A. Yes because the mother has suffered a bargained-for legal detriment.

B. Yes because the mother has reasonably relied.

C. No because the mother was not a party to the contract between the woman and the man.

D. No because since the mother was not aware of the contract between the woman and the man, her rights had not vested.

26. A motorcyclist is hit by a hit and run driver and is lying on the side of the road. A doctor drives by and sees the motorcyclist lying on the side of the road. The doctor gets out of his car and offers medical assistance until the ambulance arrives. The motorcyclist's father calls the doctor and promises to pay him. The doctor sends a bill to the motorcyclist, and the motorcyclist refuses to pay. What is the doctor's best theory of recovery against the motorcyclist?

A. The doctor provided necessary health services.

B. The doctor has a valid claim based upon an implied-in-fact contract.

C. The doctor is a creditor beneficiary.

D. The doctor is a donee beneficiary.

27. A litigant hires an attorney. Part of the retainer agreement states that the attorney will pay the creditor of the litigant $1,500 from any settlement that is recovered. The creditor is unaware of the agreement between the litigant and the attorney. Ultimately, over $1,500 is recovered in the litigant's lawsuit, but the creditor is not paid. The creditor contacts the litigant for payment, but the litigant refers the creditor to the attorney, citing the retainer agreement clause that states that the attorney will

pay $1,500 to the creditor. If the creditor brings an action against the attorney based on the retainer agreement with the litigant, the attorney's best defense argument would be:

A. The creditor did not change his position in reliance.

B. The creditor's rights have not vested.

C. The litigant owes the money, not the attorney.

D. The creditor is an incidental beneficiary.

28. An indigent taxpayer hires an accountant to do his taxes. The accountant promises to pay the taxpayer's Internal Revenue Service (IRS) tax bill. However, before the tax bill comes due, the accountant retires and refers the taxpayer to a second accountant. If the IRS brings an action against the second accountant, the second accountant will most likely argue:

A. There is no evidence supporting that the IRS changed its position in reliance.

B. There is no evidence supporting a finding that the IRS was either a creditor or donee beneficiary of the second accountant's promise to the original accountant.

C. The second accountant only made a gratuitous promise.

D. The IRS is an unidentified beneficiary.

29. A business that manufactures yo-yos enters into a written agreement to purchase all of its requirements of hard plastic for two years from a plastic manufacturer. The contracting parties agree on a unit price, delivery, and payment terms. The agreement also states that the parties promise not to assign the contract and that the first four months of payments due to the plastic manufacturer by the yo-yo manufacturer would be made to a creditor of the plastic manufacturer. The plastic manufacturer then makes an assignment of the contract to a third party for security on a loan. In regards to the non-assignment clause, which statement is correct?

A. The assignment is completely ineffective.

B. The non-assignment clause has no legal effect.

C. The plastic manufacturer's assignment is a breach of contract with the yo-yo manufacturer, but there is still an effective transfer to the third party.

D. The assignment is void as against public policy.

30. A businesswoman owes money to a creditor. She enters into a contract with a designer and tells the designer to pay the creditor instead of her. What is the

creditor's status regarding the contract between the businesswoman and the designer?

A. An incidental beneficiary.

B. A creditor beneficiary.

C. A donee beneficiary.

D. An intended beneficiary.

31. A man is contracted to do some gardening work for a woman. As part of the contract, the woman is to pay the man's niece instead of the man. The niece is aware of this contract at the time it is entered into. The man fails to do the work. The niece sues the woman. Will she recover?

A. No because the woman must pay man, not the niece.

B. No because the woman will successfully assert the defense that the man failed to perform the gardening work.

C. Yes because the niece's rights were vested.

D. Yes because no defenses are applicable in this fact situation.

32. One evening at a concert, a songwriter meets and falls in love with an opera singer. She moves in with him and does all the housework. After, he writes a beautiful song promising to give her 20% of any future royalties he receives from the song. Soon afterward, the songwriter is killed in a car accident. One week later, his estate enters into a contract with a record company, and his song becomes a hit. The opera singer brings a cause of action against the songwriter's estate to recover her 20% of the royalties. What result will most likely happen?

A. She will win because the assignment is enforceable.

B. She will win because her housework constitutes valuable consideration.

C. She will lose because future contract claims are not assignable.

D. She will lose because royalty contracts are not assignable.

33. A museum wishes to acquire a rare spoon. It enters into a $50,000 contract with a well-known spoon dealer, to acquire the spoon. The owner of the spoon offers to sell it to the dealer for $60,000. The dealer rejects the offer, explaining that it would lose $10,000 in the deal. The dealer offers to assign its contract with the museum to the owner of the spoon for $5,000. The owner of the spoon agrees. The dealer then sends a telegram to the museum explaining the assignment. The owner of the spoon tenders the spoon to the museum. The owner of the spoon then requests payment of $50,000. The museum refuses,

stating that there is no obligation. The owner of the spoon brings a breach of contract action. What will the most likely result be?

A. The owner of the spoon will lose because the performance is too personal.

B. The owner of the spoon will lose because there is no existing privity.

C. The owner of the spoon will win because she paid valuable consideration for the assignment.

D. The owner of the spoon will win because the duty was delegable.

34. A debutant owns an exclusive dress. An exclusive pre-owned dress shop makes a contract with the debutant to purchase the exclusive dress for $50,000. For $5,000, the pre-owned dress shop assigns its contract with the debutant to a customer with which it has a long-standing relationship. The customer agrees. The pre-owned dress shop then sends a telegram to the debutant explaining the assignment. The debutant refuses to sell the dress to the customer, and the customer sues the debutant for breach of contract. Who will prevail?

A. The customer will win because the assignment of rights resulted in a third-party beneficiary contract, giving the customer a cause of action.

B. The customer will win because it has a long-standing relationship with the pre-owned dress shop.

C. The debutant will lose because there is no privity of contract.

D. The debutant will lose because contracts for exclusive items cannot be assigned.

35. A landlord enters into a contract with a tenant to rent an apartment for $1,500. The tenant then assigns to his sister his right to reside in the apartment and his duty to pay the rent. The sister refuses to pay the rent, so the landlord sues the original tenant for breach of contract. Who will prevail?

A. The tenant because he delegated the contract to his sister.

B. The tenant because of the doctrine of impossibility.

C. The landlord because the tenant remains the guarantor for the performance of his sister.

D. The landlord because the tenant's duty was too personal to delegate.

36. A woman sold gym equipment to a fitness instructor. The bill of sale provided that:

"Seller does hereby sell, convey and transfer to Buyer any right, title and interest seller may have in the gym equipment. It is expressly understood and agreed that Seller shall not be obligated, liable or accountable for any warranties on the gym equipment sold to Buyer."

Unknown to the fitness instructor, the woman had obtained the gym equipment from a third party. After the fitness instructor purchased the equipment, the third party sued the woman for title and possession of the equipment. The third party prevailed and repossessed the equipment from the fitness instructor. The fitness instructor now sues the woman for the loss. Who prevails?

A. The fitness instructor because the warranty of title cannot be disclaimed.

B. The fitness instructor because the woman did not specifically disclaim the warranty of title.

C. The woman because the language in the bill of sale effectively disclaimed the implied warranty of title.

D. The woman, provided the disclaimer of warranty was conspicuous.

37. A man contacts a boating store to buy a motorboat. The man indicates that he needs to use the boat at a water ski show and that the boat would be pulling 10 skiers at a time, at 35 miles per hour. The motorboat salesman directs the man to a used boat and states, "This baby has a lot of power and you'll be able to pull 20 skiers at 35 miles per hour if you decide to increase the size of your show."

When the man tries to pull 5 skiers, the boat is unable to muster more than 15 miles per hour. The man contacts the motorboat salesman about the problems. The motorboat salesman refuses to refund the man. The man then sues the boating store for breach of contract. What result?

A. The man wins because the motorboat salesman made an express warranty to the man.

B. The man wins because of the motorboat salesman's implied warranty of merchantability, which accompanied the sale to the man.

C. The man will lose because he should have tried out the boat before his purchase.

D. The man will lose because the U.C.C. does not apply to used goods.

38. A boat supply store sent a purchase order to a wholesaler on July 7. The purchase order stated, "Please send immediately two Number 100 outboard motors at your current list price."

The wholesaler received the order on July 9. Since it only had one Number 100 outboard motor in stock, it shipped one Number 100 motor and one Number 200 motor to the boat supply store. The Number 200 motor had comparable features to the Number 100 motor but sold for $100 less than the Number 100 motor. Was an enforceable contract formed upon wholesaler's shipment of the motors?

A. Yes because the wholesaler's shipment constituted an acceptance.

B. Yes because the wholesaler acted in good faith in shipping the Number 200 motor.

C. No, since the wholesaler could only accept the boat supply store's offer by a return promise.

D. No because the wholesaler's shipment of non-conforming goods was not an acceptance, but a counteroffer.

39. A woman orders from a shirt supplier 500 gray t-shirts with her company's logo, to be printed on the back of the t-shirts in black ink. The woman states that she needs the t-shirts by April 15. On April 14, the shirt supplier sends 400 gray t-shirts with the woman's logo printed in black and states that it will send another 100 t-shirts in a month. What are the woman's rights upon receiving the 400 t-shirts?

A. The woman may accept all or part of the shipment without giving notice to the shirt supplier.

B. The woman may either accept or reject all or part of the shipment, upon reasonable notice to the shirt supplier.

C. The woman must either accept all or none of the shipment.

D. The woman must accept all of the order shipped and sue the shirt supplier for breach.

40. On February 1, a blouse manufacturer sends a written offer to a retail store to supply the store with 1,000 blouses for the spring season and states that the offer will be held open until March 31. May the blouse manufacturer revoke the offer prior to March 31?

A. No because the blouse manufacturer had given the retail store assurance that the offer would remain open.

B. No because both parties are merchants.

C. Yes because there was no consideration for keeping the offer open.

D. Yes, since the retail store relied to its detriment.

41. On August 21, a vegetable canning company, sent the following letter to a grocer:

"Have 50 cases of canned corn available at $10.50 per case. Please reply if interested."

On September 1, the grocer sent a fax to the vegetable canning company that stated:

"Please be advised that I accept your offer dated August 21. However, I would appreciate delivery of 25 cases in October and 25 cases in November, if possible." The grocer's fax on September 1 had the following effect:

A. It had no legal effect because the mode of acceptance was not the same as the offer from the vegetable canning company.

B. It operates as a rejection of the offer and creates a counteroffer, since the grocer changed the terms.

C. A contract for 50 cases of corn was formed.

D. A contract for 50 cases of corn was formed for delivery in October and November.

42. A shoe store ordered 1,000 pairs of children's shoes in specified sizes and styles from a shoe distributor. Delivery was requested on May 1, with payment to be due 30 days from delivery. The shoe distributor found it could only fill the order to the extent of 900 pairs. Without communicating with the shoe store, the shoe distributor shipped the 900 pairs of shoes. On receipt of the shoes on April 30, the shoe store rejected the shipment. The shoe distributor sued the shoe store for breach of contract. Which of the following is the most likely outcome?

A. Judgment will be for the shoe distributor because it substantially performed.

B. Judgment will be for the shoe distributor, but the shoe store will be entitled to offset any damages attributable to the non-delivery of the 100 pairs of shoes.

C. Judgment will be for the shoe store because the shoe distributor had not filled the order according to its specified terms.

D. Judgment will be for the shoe store, but only because a 10% deficiency in the amount delivered would be considered a substantial failure of performance.

43. A law school orders 1,000 brochures from a printer. The brochures are to be delivered by April 1. On April 1, the printer delivers 900 brochures. The law school nonetheless accepts the 900 brochures and gives the printer notice that the shipment was incomplete. Upon receiving no reply from the printer, the law school brings suit against the printer for damages caused by the printer's failure to deliver the remaining 100

brochures. Which of the following is the most likely outcome of the suit?

A. The law school will recover damages against the printer.

B. The law school will recover, but only if the printer's failure to deliver the remaining 100 brochures could be considered a material breach.

C. The law school will not recover because it waived the printer's breach by accepting the 900 brochures.

D. The law school will not recover because the printer shipped the brochures that it had.

44. A silk manufacturer and a silk retailer had a phone conversation, during which an agreement was reached that the retailer would buy 500 yards of silk at $10 per yard from the manufacturer. The manufacturer then sent a signed letter to the retailer to confirm the transaction. The letter omitted the price term. A month later, the manufacturer called to confirm the date of delivery but was told by the retailer that she did not need the order. Assuming that the manufacturer sues retailer for a breach of contract, what is the most likely outcome?

A. There will be judgment for the retailer because the written confirmation was not signed by the party to be charged.

B. There will be judgment for the retailer because the confirmation was insufficient since the price was omitted.

C. There will be judgment for the retailer because the manufacturer did not verify the order with the retailer within 10 days of sending the confirmation.

D. There will be judgment for the manufacturer because both parties are merchants.

45. A woman is considering buying a 4-wheel drive truck but is concerned about rollover safety. She asks a car salesman about the rollover safety of a new 4-wheel truck. The salesman assures the woman that all 4-wheel trucks that he sells have always come with an integral rollbar built into the cab structure, as shown in the truck's brochure. The brochure explains the cab provides complete rollover protection.

The woman's friend rolled an identical truck the prior week when she was off-roading and was seriously injured when the cab was completely crushed. The woman knew of her friend's accident but purchased the truck because she thought the salesman was convincing. The woman rolls her truck and is also injured. She sues the truck company for her injuries. Who prevails?

A. The woman, since the truck company made an express warranty on which she relied.

B. The woman, since her truck was totaled.

C. The truck company, since the woman should not have relied on the affirmations in entering the contract.

D. The truck company, since the salesman actually made the representations to the woman.

46. A man accidentally left a brief case containing valuable items at the airport. The next morning, he posted flyers all around the airport. The flyers stated:

"Lost - one black brief case, contains the name 'Smith.' Will pay $500.00 to anyone for its return. Call (213) 555-2645 to arrange a meeting place for the return of the briefcase."

Later that evening, a woman at the airport read one of the flyers while waiting for her baggage and noticed the black brief case described on the flyer on the luggage carousel. She picked up the brief case, tore a flyer off the wall and left the airport.

A few days later, the man realized that he had put the valuable items in his suitcase, which he had with him, thus making the brief case worth less than $500.00. He, therefore, decided that he did not need the brief case returned. However, before he could take down the fliers at the airport, the woman called and said that she had found the black brief case at the airport. The man replied that he no longer needed the brief case and was cancelling the reward offer. If the woman claims the $500.00 reward from the man, she will:

A. Recover because a contract was formed when she called the man to return his brief case.

B. Recover because the man created a unilateral contract upon the posting of the flyers, and once the woman performed, it became irrevocable.

C. Not recover because no contract was formed.

D. Not recover, unless she returns the brief case.

47. On May 15, a woman sends a letter to a man stating, "If you walk across the Brooklyn Bridge on or before May 30 and come to my office afterward, I will pay you $100." The man receives the letter and on May 17 sends a letter back to the woman in which he promises to walk across the Brooklyn Bridge on or before May 30 and come to the woman's office afterward. The woman never receives the man's letter. On May 20, the woman sends the man a letter stating, "I have changed my mind and am revoking my May 15 offer." What legal effect does the man's May 17 letter have?

A. The May 17 letter bound both parties to a bilateral contract because the man could accept by an act or a promise.

B. The May 17 letter bound both parties to a unilateral contract as soon as the man mailed the letter.

C. The May 17 letter had no legal effect, thus, allowing the woman to revoke her offer.

D. The May 17 letter would only be an acceptance if the woman had received the man's letter.

48. On January 2, a homeowner offers to sell his home to a buyer. The offer stated that it would be held open until January 30. The homeowner sells his home to another buyer on January 15 and sends the original potential buyer a letter revoking his offer. On Jan 16, the potential buyer receives the homeowner's revocation letter. Nonetheless, on January 17, the potential buyer sends his purchase payment to the homeowner. The homeowner returns the money to the potential buyer, stating that his home has already been sold. The potential buyer sues the homeowner for specific performance, citing the homeowner's promise to hold the offer open until January 30. Who will prevail?

A. The potential buyer will prevail because the homeowner's sale of the home to another party prior to January 30 constituted a breach.

B. The potential buyer will prevail because even though he knew that a new buyer had purchased, he still paid his purchase money to the owner prior to January 30.

C. The homeowner because he revoked his offer by selling his home to another party before the potential buyer could accept the offer.

D. The homeowner because he effectively revoked his offer by sending the potential buyer a letter of revocation before the potential buyer accepted.

49. A woman orally contracted with a man on March 10 for the woman to build a swimming pool. The pool was to be completed by June 15. The total price of the job is $28,000. The man completes the swimming pool, but the woman, dissatisfied with the quality of the finished pool, refuses to pay the man. If the man sues the woman for breach of contract, which defense can the woman successfully use?

A. The agreement was not in writing.

B. Under the U.C.C., if a person is dissatisfied with the quality of the finished product, that person does not have to pay.

C. The woman sold her home and no longer needed the pool.

D. No defense is available to the woman.

50. A supplier of widgets enters into an agreement with a retail store. The supplier agrees to supply the store with 15,000 widgets, to be delivered in three installments of 5,000 each. The store agrees to pay $10,000 for each of the three deliveries. After the supplier delivers the first installment, and the store pays for that installment, when the supplier is ready to send the second installment, the store owner repudiates the contract and says, "Do not send it. We are not going to pay." Which of the following is correct?

    A. The supplier has a cause of action against the store for $10,000 in damages.

    B. The supplier can refuse to send the second and third installments and will not be liable for breach of contract.

    C. Both A and B.

    D. Neither A nor B.

51. A bar candidate orally agreed to sell his bar materials to a law student for $1,500 on the condition that the bar candidate pass the Bar Examination. Two weeks later, the bar candidate and the law student reduced their agreement into a writing, but no mention was made in the writing that the sale would be contingent upon the bar candidate passing the Bar Examination.

The bar candidate failed the Bar Examination and refused to sell his materials to the law student. The law student sues the bar candidate for breach of contract. The bar candidate asserts in his defense that the contract was contingent upon him passing the Bar Examination.

How should the court rule on the bar candidate's offer of proof that he did not pass the Bar Examination?

    A. The evidence is admissible because the bar candidate's purpose of the contract was frustrated.

    B. The evidence is admissible because the final writing was not a full integration of the parties' oral agreement.

    C. The evidence is barred because of the Statute of Frauds.

    D. The evidence is barred because the oral agreement contradicts the written agreement.

52. A seller contracted in writing to deliver 10,000 cartons of milk to a buyer on May 1 at $1.00 a carton. Because the farmers who supplied the seller with his milk did not deliver enough milk, the seller only had 9,000 cartons of milk to fulfill his contract with the buyer. If the seller tenders only 9,000 cartons of milk to the buyer on May 1, and the buyer refuses to accept or pay for them, which is the best statement regarding their contractual relationship?

A. The doctrine of impossibility of performance excuses the seller from performing the contact.

B. The seller can sue the buyer, since the seller substantially performed the contract.

C. The buyer is obligated to give the seller time to cure.

D. The buyer has a cause of action against the seller for the seller's failure to deliver 10,000 cartons of milk.

53. A car wash owner leased his equipment from a lessor under a five-year lease that was renewable for 3 one-year periods. At the end of eight years, the lessor would "abandon" the equipment to the car wash (since he would have paid for it in full). After four years, the car wash owner defaulted. The lessor repossessed and resold the equipment. The lessor claims that the lessor is owed $2,000 by the car wash owner under a lease provision, which provides that the lessor could collect 10% of the equipment's total cost in the event of any default. The car wash owner claims the liquidated damages clause is invalid. Is the liquidated damages clause valid?

A. Yes because there was a meeting of the minds.

B. Yes because it must be determined whether or not the car wash owner would default at the inception of the lease.

C. No because a 10% liquidated damages clause in any contract is unconscionable as a matter of law.

D. No because the damages to the lessor would not be difficult to ascertain.

54. In a written contract, a manufacturer agreed to deliver to a store owner 200 described chairs at $100 each F.O.B., at the manufacturer's place of business. The contract provided that "neither party will assign the contract without written consent of the other." The manufacturer placed the chairs on the carrier on August 31. On September 1, the manufacturer, in a signed writing, assigned to a third party all his rights under the contract between the manufacturer and the store owner. On September 3, the chairs were destroyed by fire while in transit. The store owner refused to pay for the chairs. In an action by the third party against the store owner for breach of contract, the third party will recover:

A. $20,000, the contract price.

B. The difference between the contract price and the market value of the chairs.

C. Nothing because the chairs had not been delivered.

D. Nothing because the contract between the manufacturer and the store owner forbids an assignment.

55. A car dealership orders 10,000 automobiles from the automobile manufacturer. The contract has a clause, indicating that the merchandise (the automobiles) is "F.O.B., at the manufacturer's place of business." The manufacturer delivers the automobiles to its carrier. On the way to the dealership, the motor in the carrier explodes, and all the automobiles are destroyed. The dealership refuses to pay. The manufacturer sues for breach of contract. The dealership will probably:

   A. Succeed, since the risk of loss was on the manufacturer.

   B. Succeed because the explosion was an Act of God.

   C. Not succeed, since the risk of loss was on the dealership.

   D. Not succeed, since the automobiles were destroyed, making it impossible for the manufacturer to perform.

56. A woman contracted to purchase a certain piece of land from a man for the purpose of building a tourist attraction. The man assured her that the land was properly zoned for this purpose. After she purchased the property, she discovered that zoning laws did not in fact permit her to build the tourist attraction. She sued the man. Can the woman recover damages, rescind the contract, or both?

   A. She can only recover damages.

   B. She can only rescind the contract.

   C. She can either recover damages or rescind the contract.

   D. She cannot recover damages or rescind the contract.

57. A bank loaned money to a corporation. As a condition of the loan, a majority shareholder in the corporation agreed in writing to personally guarantee the loan. Thereafter, the corporation defaulted on the loan and entered into a repayment agreement with the bank. This agreement provided that the bank would use maximum efforts in selling the corporation's assets at the highest possible price to discharge the corporation's indebtedness. The bank proceeded to sell the corporation's assets, discharging the indebtedness of the corporation.

Later, it was ascertained that the bank did not realize the highest possible price in administering the sale of the corporation's assets.

The aforementioned majority shareholder brought an appropriate action against the bank to recover her investment in the corporation's stock. She will most likely:

A. Not prevail because she was an incidental beneficiary of the bank's sale of the corporation's assets.

B. Not prevail because the bank's sale of the corporation's assets discharged whatever contractual relationship existed between her and the bank.

C. Prevail because the bank did not realize the highest possible price from the sale of the corporation's assets.

D. Prevail because the bank breached its fiduciary duty to the shareholder under the terms of the agreement between the bank and the corporation.

58. On January 5, a manufacturer of steel security blinds for homes, received the following order from a builder: "Please ship 500 4' x 6' security shutters. Delivery by March 10." On February 10, the manufacturer shipped 500 4' x 8' security shutters, which were received by the builder on February 12. The following day the builder sent the following fax to the manufacturer: "Be advised that your shipment is rejected. Order stipulated 4' x 6' security shutters." The fax was received by the manufacturer on February 15. Did the builder properly reject the shipment?

A. No because the shipment was an almost perfect tender.

B. No because the manufacturer could accept the builder's offer by prompt shipment of either conforming or nonconforming goods.

C. Yes because the security shutters were nonconforming.

D. Yes because the manufacturer did not notify the builder that the 4' x 8' security shutters were for accommodation only.

59. On March 1, a retailer ordered from its supplier 5,000 teddy bears dressed in Christmas outfits, to be delivered by December 1. On November 15, the supplier sent 4,000 teddy bears dressed in Halloween costumes without an explanation. The retailer promptly rejected the shipment as nonconforming and returned the teddy bears to the supplier. The supplier immediately notified the retailer that it would be shipping 5,000 teddy bears dressed in Christmas outfits on or before the original December 1 deadline. On November 28, the supplier sent 5,000 teddy bears in Christmas outfits to the retailer, which the retailer also rejected. Did the retailer properly reject the teddy bears on November 28?

A. No because, under the U.C.C., a contract for the sale of goods can be modified without consideration.

B. No because the supplier cured the November 15 defective shipment by tender of conforming goods on November 28.

C. Yes because the supplier's shipping of the teddy bears in Halloween costumes on November 15 constituted anticipatory breach.

D. Yes because the supplier's shipping of the teddy bears in Halloween costumes on November 15 constituted a present breach.

60. A grocery store enters into a contract with its supplier to supply 10,000 oranges for $5,000. The supplier always gets its oranges from a grower in Florida. However, due to an unusually cold winter, the entire Florida orange crop is wiped out, and the supplier has to get its oranges from a more expensive supplier in another location. The supplier contacts the grocery store and says that it will not be able to supply the oranges for less than $6,000. The grocery store replies that it will hold the supplier to the $5,000 price stated in the contract. The supplier goes ahead and delivers the oranges to the grocery store. The supplier immediately demands payment of $6,000. The grocery store refuses to pay. In an action by the supplier against the grocery store, the supplier will be able to recover:

A. $5,000 because that was the contract price.

B. $6,000 because of an unanticipated change of circumstances.

C. Only in quantum merit because the supplier did not intend to operate at a loss.

D. Only in quantum meruit because by demanding $6,000 the supplier repudiated its contract with the grocery store.

61. A man contacted several companies to install a burglar alarm at his home. On October 1, a security company sent the man a bid for $5,000 for the security system and its installation. The security company based its bid on its wholesaler's quoted price of $1,000 for burglar alarm components. On October 9, the wholesaler notified the security company that the wholesaler would be unable to supply any burglar alarm components to the security company. On October 11, the man accepted the security company's $5,000 bid.

The security company had to pay another wholesaler $1,000 above the quoted price by the first wholesaler for the burglar alarm components. What argument best supports the claim for the additional $1,000 by the security company against the first wholesaler?

A. The first wholesaler had made an offer to the security company that was accepted when the security company submitted its bid to the man.

B. The first wholesaler had made an offer that the security company

accepted by using the wholesaler's bid in computing the bid it submitted to the man.

C. The first wholesaler's bid was an offer that it was obligated to hold open because of the fact that the first wholesaler and the security company were both merchants.

D. An option contract was created when the security company used the first wholesaler's bid.

62. A law student who was on the school's moot court team needed sponsorship for the team. A bar owner at the local watering hole offered to sponsor the school's moot court team. The student and the bar owner then entered into a written agreement that provided that the bar owner would pay for all the "usual sponsoring fees."

The bar owner had understood the agreement to mean merely that he would supply the keg of beer following each moot court competition. Conversely, the student thought that the bar owner would be reimbursing the team for 1) transportation costs, 2) research and material costs, 3) the keg of beer, and 4) plaques to the competition finalists. Did a contract exist between the student and the bar owner?

A. No contract exists.

B. Yes, a contract exists on the terms understood by the law student.

C. Yes, a contract exists on the terms understood by the bar owner.

D. Yes, a contract exists, but only on the consistent terms between the parties.

63. On May 1, a fan wholesaler sends a hardware store a signed letter stating, "We have 400 industrial fans available at $500 each for delivery on July 1. This offer will remain open for acceptance until June 1. Please reply if interested." According to the given facts, is it possible that the fan wholesaler could have revoked the offer before June 1?

A. No because it had given the hardware store assurance that the offer would be held open until June 1.

B. No because the fan wholesaler and the hardware store are both merchants.

C. Yes because there is no consideration to support an option contract.

D. Yes, unless the hardware store detrimentally relied on the offer.

64. On September 1, an olive wholesaler sent to the owner of an Italian restaurant the following signed letter:

"Have 300 pounds of large fresh olives available at $3.00 per pound for October delivery. Please reply if interested."

76 CONTRACTS

On September 30, the restaurant owner wired the following telegram to the olive wholesaler, which it received the following day:

"Please be advised that I hereby accept your offer dated September 1. However, I would appreciate your delivering 150 pounds in October and 150 pounds in November if you possibly can." The restaurant owner's telegram of September 30 has which of the following effects?

A. It has no legal effect because the mode of acceptance was not by the same means as the offer.

B. It operates as a rejection of the olive wholesaler's offer and a proposal of a counteroffer.

C. It creates a contract for 150 pounds of olives for October delivery and 150 pounds of olives for November delivery.

D. It creates a contract for 300 pounds of olives for October delivery.

65. A mattress store orders from a wholesaler 500 waterbed mattresses for delivery on February 23. On February 23, the wholesaler shipped and the mattress store received 500 spring mattresses. If the mattress store accepts the spring mattresses, even though they are nonconforming tender, he probably has:

A. A remedy against the wholesaler whether or not it gives the wholesaler notice of the breach.

B. A remedy against the wholesaler, provided that the mattress store gives the wholesaler notice of the breach.

C. No remedy against the wholesaler because the mattress store waives whatever claim it may have by accepting the nonconforming mattresses.

D. No remedy against the mattress wholesaler because the risk of loss was not spelled out in the contract.

66. On March 1, a hotel owner entered into a written contract with a contractor in which the contractor agreed to remodel the hotel for $2 million. According to the terms of the agreement, the hotel owner promised to pay the contractor $1 million when work was to commence on May 1, with the balance payable upon completion of the job on September 1.

On April 1, the contractor sent the hotel owner a letter stating that the cost of building materials had increased from his original estimate. Consequently, the contractor indicated that he did not think he could perform the remodeling work, unless the hotel owner agreed to increase the price to $2.5 million. Without notifying the contractor, the hotel

owner went ahead and hired another contractor to perform the remodeling.

On May 1, the contractor showed up at the hotel. The contractor told the hotel owner that he reconsidered and was ready to begin remodeling the hotel at the original contract price. The hotel owner then informed him that he had hired someone else and dismissed the contractor from the job. The contractor brings suit against the hotel owner for breach of contract. Who will prevail?

A. The contractor because the hotel owner did not inform him before May 1 that he was hiring someone else to perform the remodeling work.

B. The contractor because he attempted to perform the remodeling work as contractually agreed.

C. The hotel owner because he hired another contractor.

D. The hotel owner because the contractor's April 1 letter manifested his prospective inability to perform, thereby justifying the hotel owner treating such as an anticipatory breach.

67. On May 20, a bar candidate hires a tutor for tutorial services to begin on June 1. The bar candidate is to pay the tutor her fee of $5,000 on June 1. On May 31, the tutor informs the candidate that she will be in the hospital and will not be able to tutor him. The bar candidate hires another tutor for $7,500. He fails the bar exam and blames the second tutor, with whose services he is dissatisfied. Nevertheless, he sues the original tutor for breach of contract. The bar candidate should recover:

A. $2,500 or the difference between the original tutor's contract price and the new tutor's contract price.

B. $7,500 because he is dissatisfied with the second tutor's services.

C. $12,500 or the amount he was to pay the first tutor plus the amount he paid the second tutor.

D. Nothing because he failed the bar exam.

68. On December 1, the owner of a ranch and a buyer orally agreed that the buyer would pay the owner the sum of $1,000 and upon receipt, the owner would hold open for thirty days the owner's offer to sell the ranch to the buyer for $150,000. On December 5, the owner sent the following written document to the buyer. The document stated: "The owner hereby offers to sell the ranch to the buyer for $150,000. All terms are incorporated." Both parties then signed the document.

The buyer then paid the owner $1,000. Notwithstanding, on December 20, the owner sent the buyer a signed letter stating:

"Have offer for the purchase of the ranch from another person for $160,000. I hereby withdraw my offer to you for the sale of the ranch for $150,000 and refund your $1,000 already paid."

The next day, the buyer tendered $150,000 cash to the owner for the purchase of the ranch and demanded the deed to the ranch. The owner refused. The buyer brought an action against the owner for specific performance.

The buyer seeks to introduce the fact that he and the owner orally agreed that upon the owner's receipt of the buyer's payment of $1,000, the offer to sell the ranch to the buyer for $150,000 would remain open for thirty days. Upon the owner's objection, will the trial court permit the testimony?

A. Yes because the Parol Evidence Rule allows the introduction of prior or contemporaneous oral terms contradicting the terms of the parties' written agreement.

B. Yes because the Parol Evidence Rule does not operate to exclude evidence of contemporaneous or subsequent oral modifications of the written term.

C. No because the written instrument is a complete integration of the parties' agreement.

D. No because the doctrine of promissory estoppel will only apply if the buyer relied on the December 1 agreement to his detriment.

69. In 1982, a building owner leased a shop to a tenant under a written ten-year lease. Both the owner and the tenant knew that a highway ran directly to the shop. During the sixth year of the lease, the city reconstructed the highway leading to the shop. Because of the reconstruction, the highway no longer led up to the shop. This caused a substantial decline in the tenant's business.

Neither the building owner nor the tenant had knowledge of the city's intent to change that highway at the time they entered into the lease agreement. The tenant contacted building owner and told him of the circumstances. The tenant asked the building owner to renegotiate the lease agreement, but the building owner refused. The tenant decided to abandon the shop and refused to pay the building owner any rent. The building owner brought an action against the tenant to recover the unpaid rent. Who will prevail?

A. The tenant because of the doctrine of impossibility of performance.

B. The tenant because both parties were wrong in their assumption that the highway would continue to lead to the shop.

C. The building owner because the tenant assumed the risk of any

change in circumstances when he entered into the lease.

D. The building owner because he was entitled to rent whether or not there was a change in the highway.

70. A producer engaged an actress to do a role in a new play for a period of six months. The actress turned down a role in another play in order to accept this engagement. On the third day of the run, the actress was hospitalized, and another actress was hired to do the part. A week later, the first actress recovered, but the producer refused to accept her services for the remainder of the run. The first actress brought a breach of contract action against the producer. Which of the following is first actress' best legal theory?

A. Her acting contract with the producer was legally severable into weekly units.

B. Her performance of the literal terms of the contract was physically impossible.

C. She had relied on the engagement with the producer by declining another acting role.

D. Her failure to perform for one week was not a material failure.

71. On March 5, a seller orally agreed to sell his land to a buyer for $135,000, to be paid on March 31. On March 31, the buyer refused to pay the seller and informed the seller that he would not be going through with the deal. The seller sued the buyer. Who will prevail?

A. The buyer because he could successfully raise the Statute of Frauds as a defense, since the agreement between the buyer and the seller was for the sale of an interest in land.

B. The buyer because the price of the land was unconscionable.

C. The seller because he was prepared to sell on March 31 and the buyer was in breach.

D. The seller because he detrimentally relied on the buyer's promise to purchase the land.

72. A water supplier and a grocery store owner orally negotiate a contract for the supplier to provide 5,000 cases of water to the grocery store for $10,000. However, when the contract is typed up, the typist mistakenly types the purchase price as $1,000. Neither the supplier nor the grocery store owner notices the mistake. The contract also contains a provision stating that it is fully integrated. The supplier and the grocery store owner both sign the contract. The grocery store owner later reads the written contract and sees the $1,000 purchase price that was typed. He promptly pays the water supplier

$1,000 for the water. The water supplier sues the grocery store owner for $9,000. It would be to the water supplier's advantage to try to prove that:

A. The writing was intended only as a sham.

B. The writing was only a partial integration.

C. There was a mistake in integration.

D. There was a misunderstanding between the supplier and the grocery store owner concerning the purchase price.

73. A man crashed a motorcycle into a woman's car. The woman, who was inside the car at the time, was injured and was rushed to the hospital. The man orally told the woman that he would reimburse her for any expenses and losses as a result of the accident. In an action by the woman against the man for lost wages while she was incapacitated as a result of the accident, which of the following would be the man's best defense?

A. The Statute of Frauds.

B. There was a lack of consideration.

C. Promissory estoppel.

D. The statement was a mere promise.

74. A law student contacted a tutor for the Bar Examination. The next day, the law student's father called the tutor and promised to pay for the law student's tutoring. The tutor began tutoring the law student. The father, however, refused to pay the tutor because he did not approve of the tutoring services. The tutor brought suit against the father for breach. Who will prevail?

A. The father because there was no consideration for his promise.

B. The father because he did not approve of the tutoring services.

C. The tutor because she commenced her tutoring services after the father made the promise to pay her.

D. The tutor because, otherwise, the law student would be unjustly enriched.

75. A man mows his neighbor's lawn, expecting to be paid his normal fee of $25, which the neighbor has always paid the man after the lawn has been mowed. This time, however, the neighbor refuses to pay the man. The man brings suit against the neighbor. Who will prevail?

A. The man because the neighbor would be unjustly enriched.

B. The man because of the previous course of dealing between the man and the neighbor.

C. The neighbor because the contract was not in writing.

D. The neighbor because the contract was not supported by consideration.

76. A man and a woman enter into an oral agreement for the woman to purchase the man's car for $600. The woman is to present a check to the man for $600 the following day and receive the car. The following day, the woman arrives at the man's home with her $600 check, but the man refuses to sell the car. The woman sues for breach of contract. Who will prevail?

   A. The man because the sale of the car under the terms of this particular agreement needed to be in writing.

   B. The man because he is a non-merchant.

   C. The woman because she is a non-merchant.

   D. The woman because this contract could be performed in less than a year.

77. A property owner enters into an oral agreement with a buyer to rent a piece of land for $5,000 per month for four years. According to the terms of the contract, if the buyer makes $4,000 in improvements to the land over the course of the four years, the property owner will deed the land to the buyer for $50,000. Over the next four years, the buyer pays his rent on time and makes $4,000 in improvements to the land. At the end of the four years, the buyer gives $50,000 to the property owner and demands the deed to the land. The property owner refuses to tender the deed to the land. The buyer sues for specific performance. The property owner claims the Statute of Frauds as a defense. Who will prevail?

   A. The buyer because the improvements show the buyer detrimentally relied on the oral agreement.

   B. The buyer because the improvements constitute partial performance.

   C. The property owner because contracts for the sale of land must be in writing to be enforced.

   D. The property owner because the contract was not supported by consideration.

78. A retail coin dealer purchased a rare coin for $500. He examined the coin before the purchase. The coin dealer resold the rare coin to a collector for $750. The collector later found out that the coin was a counterfeit. The collector sued to rescind his purchase of the coin from the coin dealer. The court will:

   A. Allow rescission of the contract because of a misrepresentation.

B. Allow rescission of the contract because there was mutual mistake.

C. Not allow the contract to be rescinded because there was no warranty made.

D. Not allow rescission of the contract because buyer assumed the risk upon purchase.

79. On August 15, 1992, a teenager entered into a contract with an electronics store to purchase a flat screen television for $5,000 to be paid in ten equal monthly payments of $500. The teenager was 17 years old at the time and would be turning 18 on December 18 of the same year. For the next nine months, the teenager made his monthly payments on time. Before he made his tenth payment, he voluntarily returned the television to the electronics store. The electronics store refused to accept the television and sued the teenager for the balance owed. Judgment will be for:

A. The electronics store because the teenager affirmed the contract.

B. The electronics store because a minor cannot disaffirm a contract after reaching the age of majority.

C. The teenager because contracts entered into by minors are void.

D. The teenager because, by returning the television to the electronics store, the teenager properly disaffirmed the contract.

80. A sixteen-year-old boy purchased a $3,000 diamond ring from a department store. He intended to give the ring to his girlfriend. The store contract provided that the boy was to make monthly payments in the amount of $300 per month for the next ten months. The boy failed to make any payments and disaffirmed the contract. The store brought suit against the boy for $3,000. Who will prevail?

A. The store because the boy did not return the ring.

B. The store because the boy did not make any payments.

C. The boy because under the U.C.C., it is illegal for merchants to sell goods in excess of $1,000 to minors.

D. The boy because he disaffirmed the contract.

81. A woman consulted a local real estate agency to purchase a new home. The agent showed her several homes. One home obtained its water supply from a well located on the property. The current owner received information indicating that the well was contaminated after the woman had looked at the house. The woman had the agent write up an offer for the property. The current owner accepted the offer but did

not disclose the information about the contaminated well. After escrow closed, the woman moved into the property and discovered that the well was contaminated. The woman now brings suit to rescind the contract. The court will find for:

A. The prior owner because there was no duty to disclose newly-discovered information.

B. The prior owner because escrow closed, releasing him from any further obligations.

C. The woman because the prior owner failed to disclose the contaminated well.

D. The woman, but she can only recover money damages.

82. A contractor submitted a bid to a city to do piping work for a sewer project. The city required that ten percent of the bid price be posted as a bond, in favor of the city, guaranteeing that the bidder would do the job for the bid price if awarded the contract. The contractor gave a bid. Three competing bids were higher. A few hours later, after the bids were opened, the contractor discovered that there was a significant error in his computations on which he relied upon in making the bid. The contractor explained the error to the city and withdrew his bid, but the city accepted the bid anyway.

The contractor refuses to enter into a contract with the city at the mistaken bid price. The contractor sues to rescind the bid. The contractor will:

A. Prevail because he made a material mistake.

B. Prevail because the city would be unjustly enriched if the contractor has to perform.

C. Not prevail because the city relied on the contractor's bid.

D. Not prevail because once a bid is submitted, it cannot be withdrawn.

83. A company purchased pinball machines from a supplier. Their contract required the company to pay for the pinball machines upon delivery, prior to inspection. Which of the following statements regarding the contract provision for pre-inspection payment is correct?

A. It constitutes an acceptance of the goods.

B. It constitutes a waiver of the buyer's remedy of private sale in the case of nonconforming goods.

C. It does not impair a buyer's right of inspection or his remedies.

D. It is invalid.

84. A fabric company contracted with a supplier for the fabric company to purchase 100 bolts of lightweight wool fabric of No. 1 quality. The 100 bolts were shipped to the fabric company. Upon the fabric company's inspection, the company discovered that the wool was No. 2 quality. The company returned the wool to the supplier and demanded return of its payment. The supplier refused on the ground that there is no difference between No. 1 quality wool and No. 2 quality wool. What is the company's remedy because the wool was nonconforming?

    A. Specific performance.

    B. Damages measured by the difference between the value of the goods delivered and the value of conforming goods.

    C. Damages measured by the price paid, plus the difference between the contract price and the cost of buying substitute goods.

    D. No remedy because the goods shipped were of an equal quality.

85. An electronics store contracted with a wholesaler for delivery of 10,000 laser jet printers. The wholesaler, however, delivered 10,000 ink jet printers. The electronics store sued the wholesaler for breach because of the nonconforming printers. Can the electronics store resell the nonconforming printers?

    A. Yes, in a private sale.

    B. Yes, in a private sale - but only after giving the wholesaler reasonable notice of its intention to resell.

    C. Yes, but only at a public sale.

    D. No because such an act is inconsistent with the claim such goods were nonconforming.

86. On Wednesday, a woman wrote a letter to a man stating, "If you will pick up the computer at my office this coming Friday at five o'clock in the afternoon, I will sell it to you for $1,000." On Thursday, the man sent a letter to the woman saying, "I accept your offer and will pick up the computer on Friday at five o'clock in the afternoon." What is the legal effect of the man's Thursday letter to the woman?

    A. It is an ineffective attempt by the man to accept the woman's offer.

    B. A unilateral contract was created when the man mailed the letter.

    C. It constituted notice to the woman that the man would buy the computer.

    D. A bilateral contract was created when the woman received the letter.

87. A woman has a garage sale. A man admires her antique typewriter and asks

the price. The woman replies, "$500." The man says that he will come back later that day with the money. The woman promises the man that she will not sell the typewriter to anyone and that she will hold open the $500 offer to the man if the man returns with the $500 by five o'clock in the afternoon that day. What is the effect of woman's promise not to revoke the offer?

A. It prevents the woman from revoking the offer.

B. It has no effect because the woman did not state a date for termination.

C. It has no effect.

D. It prevents any implied revocation.

88. On April 1, a woman offered to sell her prize mare to a man for $10,000. The man handed the woman a $100 bill. In return, the woman handed the man a written statement that included the offer and also stated that the woman promised not to revoke the offer for a 60-day period. The woman signed the offer.

On April 4, the woman sold the mare to someone else. The man was unaware of the sale. On April 5, the man wrote to the woman, "I accept your offer to purchase the mare for $10,000." The woman writes back, "I cannot sell you the mare because I sold her to someone else yesterday." If the man sues the woman for damages, the most likely outcome will be:

A. The man will prevail because the woman was precluded from selling the mare to another party.

B. The man will prevail because acceptance any time during the 60 days was effective.

C. The woman will prevail because $100 is not sufficient consideration to hold an offer open.

D. The woman will prevail because she effectively revoked her original offer when she sold the mare to another party.

89. On March 1, a woman offered to sell a piano to her neighbor for $500. The woman stated that if the neighbor would pay her $10, she would hold open the offer to sell the piano for 60 days. The neighbor paid her the $10. On March 11, the neighbor wrote a letter to the woman stating he could only afford to pay $400 and that if the woman would not lower the price, he could not buy the piano. Thus, on March 15, the woman sold the piano to her piano teacher. On March 16, the neighbor learned that the woman had sold the piano. The neighbor's power to accept the woman's offer would be:

A. Good for 60 days because the neighbor paid $10 for a 60-day option.

B. Terminated on March 11.

C. Terminated when the woman received the neighbor's March 11 letter.

D. Terminated when the woman sold the piano.

90. On April 1, a convenience store owner offered to sell his leftover stock of ice chests to a grocery store owner for $5,000 by April 15. On April 2, the grocery store owner sent a $5,000 check, along with a reply letter that stated, "I accept and will pick up the ice chests in 30 days. I will pay for any storage fees." The grocery store owner's April 2 letter is:

   A. A counteroffer because it changes the terms of the original offer.

   B. A counteroffer because it was not definite.

   C. An acceptance, and the convenience store owner must store the ice chests.

   D. An acceptance, and the convenience store owner may refuse to store the ice chests.

91. A man began to work for a company at a rate below union scale, in exchange for a promise that the company would employ him "for life." Twenty years later, another corporation bought the company. The new corporate managers assured all employees that existing employment contracts would be honored. The man went to his new supervisor and explained the terms of his employment agreement. The supervisor stated that he would look into the matter, but never got back to the man. The man was then fired by the new owners of the business. The man brought suit for breach of a contract. The man will most likely:

   A. Win because new owners are not obligated to honor previous owners' existing contracts.

   B. Win because he agreed to work below scale in exchange for lifetime employment.

   C. Lose because traditional law did not uphold unilateral contracts.

   D. Lose because one cannot promise to employ someone for life.

92. A window manufacturer and a glass company have been doing business with each other for many years. As was their custom, the window manufacturer phoned the glass company and placed an order for 1,200 glass window panes to be delivered in sets of 100, one set each month. The panes were $500 each. After the glass company delivered the first set, the window manufacturer sent the glass company a check for $5,000 and a signed letter stating, "$500 a pane is too high; cancel the remainder of my order." The glass company sues the window manufacturer for breach

of contract. The window manufacturer pleads the Statute of Frauds as a defense, claiming that the oral agreement did not constitute a valid contract and that the remainder of the order could, thus, be cancelled. The most likely outcome will be that:

A. The glass company prevails because 100 panes have been received by the window manufacturer.

B. The glass company prevails because the signed letter constituted a writing sufficient to satisfy the Statute of Frauds.

C. The window manufacturer prevails because he repudiated the remaining contract.

D. The window manufacturer prevails because the signed letter does not satisfy the Statute of Frauds.

93. A general contractor was commissioned to build a new motel. He took bids from several sub-contractors for the plumbing. One sub-contractor submitted a bid for $80,000. The next lowest bid was $85,000. The remaining bids ranged between $86,000 to $87,500. The general contractor gave the contract to the sub-contractor on March 1. Work was to begin on April 1. One week before the sub-contractor was to begin working, he discovered that he had made an error in his calculations. The sub-contractor immediately called the general contractor and told him that he had made a mistake and the bid should have been $84,000, instead of $80,000. The sub-contractor refuses to work, unless the general contractor agrees to pay $84,000. The general contractor refuses to pay the additional amount to the sub-contractor and brings suit for breach of contract. The court will most likely rule for:

A. The general contractor because the sub-contractor is bound by a valid contract.

B. The general contractor, but only if he neither knew nor could have known of the sub-contractor's mistake in calculations of the bid.

C. The sub-contractor because the general contractor should not have accepted such a low bid.

D. The sub-contractor because time of performance was not due.

94. A piano teacher makes a contract with the parent of a student to give the student five piano lessons for $500 to be paid after the five lessons. After entering into the contract, but before performance has begun, the piano teacher realizes that she cannot pay her bills with what she charges her students. The piano teacher informs the parent of the student that she will not be able to give the lessons for less than $600. The parent agrees to pay the $600 at the

conclusion of the five lessons. After the piano teacher completes five lessons, the parent pays only $500. The piano teacher sues the parent for the additional $100. Who will prevail?

A. The parent because of the piano teacher's obligation to perform the work for $500.

B. The parent because $600 for five piano lessons is unconscionable.

C. The piano teacher because she intended to work only for the amount of $600.

D. The piano teacher because the parties mutually agreed to the new price of $600 for five piano lessons.

95. A rare coin dealer took out an insurance policy covering the coins that he had in stock in his coin shop. There was a written provision in the policy that stated all records describing the coins were to be kept off the store premises in a place where they would not be stolen.

The coin dealer was updating his records, since he had received new inventory. He decided to finish the records the next day. He went home and left the records in the coin shop. The shop was robbed that night. All the coins and the records of the coins were stolen. The insurance company refuses to pay on the policy. The coin dealer brings suit to recover on the policy. He will most likely:

A. Not prevail because the coin dealer breached the contract by leaving the records in the coin shop.

B. Not prevail because the policy specifically stated the records must be stored in a safe place.

C. Prevail because the provision in the policy regarding the records has been reasonably satisfied.

D. Prevail because of the unfairness of the provision.

96. On April 1, a woman drafted a contract for the sale of her car to a man. She mailed the contract to the man the same day. The man received the contract on April 3. He signed it and mailed it back the same day. Later that day, he changed his mind. The man immediately called the woman and told her to ignore the signed contract when she received it because the man was no longer in the financial position to purchase the car. The woman received the signed contract in the mail on April 5. Can the woman enforce the contract for the sale of her car to the man?

A. No because the man communicated his retraction before the woman received the signed contract in the mail.

B. No because the mail is not a reliable source of communication.

C. Yes because the man made his retraction by phone instead of by mail.

D. Yes because the man act of mailing the signed contract was an effective acceptance.

97. On March 1, a woman contracts with a man to tutor her for the LSAT with tutoring services to begin on March 15. On March 5, the woman realizes that she does not want to go to law school and, therefore, does not have to take the LSAT. The woman calls the man that day and informs him that she does not need the tutoring. The man responds that it is just as well because he is now too busy to do the tutoring. The woman changes her mind and calls the man on March 6 wanting tutoring as originally agreed. Does the woman have an enforceable contract for the tutoring services?

A. No because woman stated her intent to rescind the original contract, and the man accepted the offer to rescind.

B. No because there was no manifestation of contractual intent to make a contract in the first place.

C. Yes because a contract cannot be rescinded.

D. Yes because there was no valid consideration for rescission.

98. A homeowner received bids for painting the exterior of his house, ranging from $6,000 to $7,500. He then received a call from a painter, who submitted a bid to do the work for $5,500. The homeowner entered into a contract with the painter to have the exterior of his home painted for $5,500. The work was to begin on January 2. On December 30, the painter called the homeowner and stated, "My foreman made a mistake in adding the figures. I can't possibly do the work for less than $6,100, or I will lose money." If the homeowner sues the painter for breach of contract, who prevails?

A. The painter because he had not started painting.

B. The painter because of the defense of mistake.

C. The homeowner, unless he can still accept the bid of the next lowest bidder.

D. The homeowner, only if he had no reason to know of the painter's error.

99. An exterminator entered into a contract with a homeowner to spray the homeowner's home for $2,000. Before the exterminator was to commence the spraying, he contacted the homeowner and stated that, "I cannot do the spraying for less than $2,500 because of an increase in the cost of my materials." The homeowner responded to the exter-

minator's statement by stating, "I'll pay the extra money, but I really think it's unfair." After the exterminator finished spraying the homeowner's home, the homeowner tendered a check for $2,000 to the exterminator. If the exterminator brings suit for the additional $500, the court will most likely rule for:

A. The homeowner because he did not put his promise to pay the extra $500 in a valid writing.

B. The homeowner because the exterminator was under a pre-existing duty to spray the house for $2,000.

C. The exterminator because he detrimentally relied on the homeowner's promise to pay the additional $500.

D. The exterminator because public policy would mandate enforcing the homeowner's promise to pay.

100. A shipper contracts with a truck driver to haul a load of goods from California to New York for $2,000. Just before the truck driver reaches New York, the shipper calls the truck driver on his cell phone and says, "I will pay you an additional $500 if you pick up some more goods in New York and drive them to Pennsylvania." The truck driver agrees and after unloading the original goods in New York, loads the new goods and drives them to Pennsylvania. After the truck driver unloads the goods in Pennsylvania, the shipper tenders a check for $2,000, refusing to pay the additional $500. If the truck driver brings suit for the additional $500, who will prevail?

A. The shipper because the truck driver was under a pre-existing duty to haul the goods for $2,000.

B. The shipper because the promise to pay the additional $500 was not in writing.

C. The truck driver because there was a valid modification of the contract.

D. The truck driver because he detrimentally relied on the shipper's promise.

101. A subcontractor agrees to install the plumbing in a motel being contracted by a contractor. Before the subcontractor is to begin work, the contractor learns that the sub-contractor's employees went on strike. The contractor demands that the subcontractor explain how the subcontractor will perform the plumbing work. When the subcontractor does not explain, the contractor withholds an advance payment due to the subcontractor under the terms of the contract, and hires a different subcontractor to perform the plumbing work. The first subcontractor sues the contractor for breach of contract. The first subcontractor will most likely:

A. Prevail because the U.C.C. does not apply to service contracts.

B. Prevail because the subcontractor intended to do the work himself.

C. Lose because another subcontractor finished the work.

D. Lose because the contractor could demand "assurance of performance."

102. A man promises to buy a woman a diamond ring for her birthday because he loves her. The woman's birthday comes and goes, but the man does not buy the diamond ring. The woman sues the man for breach. Which is the man's best defense?

A. Illusory promise.

B. Lack of consideration.

C. Statute of Frauds.

D. No mutual assent between the parties.

103. On June 1, a man promises to pay a nursing home $500 per month for the care of his elderly mother. Before the mother can move into the nursing home, she becomes ill and has to be hospitalized. On June 30, the man informs the nursing home that he will not be able to pay for his mother's care there because he intends to have her live with him when she comes home from the hospital. The nursing home tells the man that they denied the application of another applicant because they were expecting man's mother to come to the nursing home. The nursing home brings suit against the man for the amount of money that they lost by denying the application of the other applicant. Who will prevail?

A. The man because the agreement was not in writing.

B. The man because his mother became ill.

C. The nursing home because it turned down other applicants in anticipation of the man's mother coming to live there.

D. The nursing home because it should not have relied on the man's promise, since elderly people get sick all the time.

104. A man has an automobile accident and dies on the spot. A week later, one of the man's creditors calls the man's father and says that he was going to file a claim against the man's estate. The father tells the creditor that if he does not file a claim, the father will pay the creditor $500 on May 15. On May 15, the creditor contacts the father for payment. The father refuses to pay, so the creditor sues him. Will the creditor be successful?

A. No because one cannot sue a deceased person.

B. No because there was a lack of consideration.

C. Yes because there was detrimental reliance by the credit card companies.

D. Yes because there was consideration.

105. A man and a woman are neighbors. The woman helps the man landscape his backyard. The man is so excited about his backyard, he decides to throw a barbecue and invite his whole block. At the barbecue, the man tells his neighbors how the woman helped. He then says to the woman, "Because you helped me landscape my backyard and it looks so great, I am going to install your new water heater for you." Subsequently, the man refuses to install the woman's water heater. Can the woman bring a successful suit against the man for breach?

A. Yes because there was consideration.

B. Yes because the man owed a duty to perform.

C. No because of involuntary servitude.

D. No because the consideration was not sufficient to render the party's promise enforceable.

106. A roofer agrees to put a new roof on a building. Payment is due upon completion of the work. The roofer begins work on schedule. Two days later, the roofer sends a letter to the owner of the building, telling them to make the payment to one of the roofer's creditors. A copy of the letter is sent to the creditor who is to receive the payment. The roofer completes the roof. The building owner now refuses to pay. What is the building owner's best defense if the creditor brings suit?

A. The creditor was incapable of putting on the roof himself.

B. The roofer failed to perform his work in a professional manner.

C. The roofer had promised not to assign the contract.

D. The creditor is not an intended beneficiary.

107. In 1980, a man took out a life insurance policy for $100,000. The policy stated that the insured had power to change the beneficiary and to assign the policy. In 1990, the man named his wife as the beneficiary. The wife did not know of the insurance policy. In 1991, he changed the beneficiary from his wife to his only daughter. The man wrote the daughter and informed her of the policy. He died two years later. The wife learned of the insurance policy and sued insurance company to collect the proceeds. The wife will:

A. Not prevail because she was no longer the intended beneficiary.

B. Not prevail because she was merely an incidental beneficiary.

C. Prevail because public policy would warrant a wife being provided for.

D. Prevail because the wife is a donee beneficiary.

108. A woman has a contract with a house painter for the painter to paint her house for $5,000. The painter tells the woman that when he finishes painting, she should pay his girlfriend instead of him. The painter tells his girlfriend about the contract with the woman and that the girlfriend will be getting a $5,000 payment. Before the man finishes painting, he breaks up with the girlfriend and tells the woman to pay him the $5,000 directly. The man then finishes painting the house, and the woman pays him directly. The girlfriend then sues the woman to collect her $5,000. Who will prevail?

A. The woman because the girlfriend was no longer entitled to the $5,000.

B. The woman because paying a girlfriend is against public policy.

C. The girlfriend because she detrimentally relied on the painter's promise.

D. The girlfriend because she was a donee beneficiary of the original contract between the painter and the woman.

109. An actor enters into a contract with a film producer. The first draft of the contract states that the actor is to be paid $1 million. The final contract states that the actor's girlfriend is to be paid the $1 million when the film is produced and that the contract is freely assignable. The actor immediately informs his girlfriend that she is to be paid $1 million upon completion of the film. The film producer assigns the contract to a studio. The film is produced, but the studio refuses to pay the actor's girlfriend. The girlfriend sues the studio for $1 million. The court will most likely hold for:

A. The studio because assignees prevail over donee beneficiaries.

B. The studio because the Screen Actor's Guild will not allow payment to a non-actor.

C. The girlfriend because her third party beneficiary rights had vested.

D. The girlfriend because she is a creditor beneficiary.

110. A wedding planner agreed with a bride to plan the bride's wedding, with payment to be made upon completion of the performance. While the perfor-

mance was still incomplete, the wedding planner told a florist that if the florist would give the wedding planner the flowers she needed, the wedding planner would have the bride pay directly for the floral arrangements. The florist agreed, and the wedding planner sent a letter to the bride stating the agreement between the wedding planner and the florist. After the wedding, the bride refused to pay the florist any money. The florist brought suit against the bride. What is the bride's best defense?

A. The florist was not an intended beneficiary of the contract between the wedding planner and the bride.

B. The florist did not detrimentally rely on the promise.

C. The wedding planner assigned her rights before completion, and an assignment, before personal services are performed, is invalid.

D. The wedding was not performed in a proper manner, if the wedding planner's performance is below accepted standards.

111. A seller fraudulently induced a buyer to purchase the seller's cabin, by falsely representing that the cabin was in immaculate condition. In reality, the cabin was about to slide down the hill into a lake. When the buyer saw the cabin, he was outraged. However, the buyer's wife fell in love with the cabin and wanted to purchase it. The buyer then wrote a note stating, "Dear seller, you lied about the cabin; however, my wife loves it, so I have decided to purchase it. Enclosed is a check for the amount we discussed." The next day, the buyer decided that he really was being cheated and put a stop payment on the check. Can the seller enforce the promise made in the note?

A. No because the original promise was based on fraud.

B. No because the seller lied to the buyer.

C. Yes because the promise was written.

D. Yes because the promise was a ratification.

112. In January, a car manufacturer orally agreed to supply automobiles to a car dealership at 15% below the usual $90,000 price of the cars. In March, the car manufacturer delivered all of the cars required under the contract. In April, the car manufacturer sent the car dealership an invoice showing a balance owing of $90,000. The car dealership sent the car manufacturer a check for $76,500. The car dealership also enclosed a letter stating that the car manufacturer had not deducted the 15% discount. The car manufacturer sent a letter demanding the additional

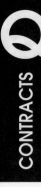

$13,500, asserting that there was no written contract for the discounted amount and that the price was based on their usual course of dealing ($90,000). The car manufacturer brings suit against the car dealership for $13,500. The car manufacturer will most likely:

A. Prevail because of the normal course of dealing between merchants.

B. Prevail because the sale of goods in excess of $500 must be evidenced by a sufficient writing.

C. Not prevail because the additional amount is unconscionable as against public policy.

D. Not prevail because the car dealership's protest letter is a sufficient writing.

113. A bookstore orders 1,000 binders from its regular supplier for a total price of $4,000, which represents the normal 20% discount that the supplier offers to the bookstore. The supplier sends the 1,000 binders to the bookstore, along with an invoice in the amount of $5,000, stating that the state of the economy is forcing it to charge more. The bookstore sends a check for $4,000 marked "paid in full." The supplier deposits the check and then brings suit against the bookstore for the additional $1,000. The bookstore's best argument would be:

A. Accord and Satisfaction.

B. Promissory Estoppel.

C. Novation.

D. Implied Novation.

114. A husband and wife own an antique store. They have an existing written contract with an estate seller to supply it with antique desks for $1,000 each. The husband and wife owe the estate seller $5,000. The husband and wife separate, and the husband decides to terminate the business relationship with his wife. He executes a document assigning all of his rights and delegating all of his obligations in the antique store to his wife. The wife, in return, agrees to be solely liable for all of the antique store's business obligations. The estate seller knows of the assignment and delegation. The wife pays $4,000 to satisfy the $5,000 debt, along with a note stating that because she is having financial problems, she cannot pay any more money to the estate seller. The estate seller sues the husband for the remaining $1,000. The husband's best argument is:

A. There is a valid accord and satisfaction.

B. The Statute of Frauds has been violated.

C. There is an implied novation.

D. None of the above.

115. A museum orders ten Ming Vases from a supplier in China. The supplier sends five instead of ten. The museum immediately contacts the supplier, demanding the additional five vases, but the supplier refuses to supply them. The museum brings suit against the supplier for breach of contract. What is or are the museum's remedies:

   A. Damages only.

   B. Damages or specific performance.

   C. Specific performance only.

   D. Damages, specific performance, or reformation of the contract.

116. A doctor is attending a play one evening. A woman falls out of her balcony seat into the crowd. The doctor hears the woman screaming in pain, "If there's a doctor in the house, please help me. I'll pay you later." The doctor administers first aid, and then the woman is taken to the hospital. Later, the woman receives a bill from the doctor for the emergency services rendered at the play. The woman refuses to pay. The doctor sues. The court will most likely rule for:

   A. The doctor, under the Good Samaritan Rule.

   B. The doctor because the woman contracted for his services.

   C. The woman because the doctor was under a moral duty to treat her.

   D. The woman because there was insufficient consideration.

117. A woman and a man were drinking alcohol at the man's house. The woman admired the man's rug. The man said that he would sell it to her for a specified amount of money. The woman agreed. The man then wrote on a piece of tissue the terms of their agreement, namely the price and the item in question (the rug). Both signed the tissue. The next day, the woman wrote a check to the man for the specified amount and demanded the rug. The man claimed that that they were both too drunk to know what they were doing and that there is no contract. The woman sued the man for breach of contract. What result is most likely?

   A. The court will find a contract, and the woman can seek specific performance if the man understood the effect of his actions.

   B. The court will find a contract, but will not enforce it under the temporary incapacity rule.

   C. The court will not find a contract because both parties lacked the requisite capacity due to intoxication.

   D. The court will not find a contract because the man made the offer in jest.

118. A designer contracted with a supplier to purchase 200 bolts of number one quality fine linen. Upon inspection, the designer discovered that the linen was not number one quality. For this reason, the designer returned the linen back to the supplier. The designer then purchased number one quality linen from another supplier. However, the new supplier charged a higher price than the first supplier charged. The designer sued the original supplier. If the designer prevails, what will be his remedy or remedies?

    A. Damages, measured by the difference between the price of the replacement conforming goods and the contract price.

    B. Damages, measured by the difference in value of conforming goods versus the value of the goods delivered.

    C. Specific performance.

    D. There are no remedies.

119. A coffee restaurant orders 100 bags of Turkish coffee from its supplier, to be delivered COD on November 20. On November 20, the supplier sends, and the coffee restaurant receives, 100 bags of Colombian coffee. The coffee restaurant immediately pays the supplier for the coffee. After paying, it inspects the coffee and discovers that it is not Turkish coffee as it had ordered. The coffee restaurant demands a refund from the supplier. The supplier refuses. May the coffee restaurant resell the Colombian coffee?

    A. No, unless at a public sale.

    B. Yes, but only at a private sale.

    C. Yes, in a private sale, after the coffee restaurant gives reasonable notice of its intent to resell.

    D. No because the Colombian coffee is nonconforming.

120. In a contract for the sale of goods, which is a correct statement with regard to a contract provision for payment in advance of inspection?

    A. It is invalid.

    B. It waives the buyer's remedies.

    C. It constitutes immediate acceptance of the goods.

    D. It does not impair the buyer's right to inspect or its remedies.

121. A well-known landscaper has been landscaping private residences for over 17 years. The landscaper has a contract with a homeowner to landscape the backyard of her condominium. The condo has a standard backyard. The contract contains no provisions regarding assignment. The landscaper assigns the contract to his son, who has worked with him for 10 years. The son

has a comparable reputation. Which one of the following statements are correct?

A. A novation has occurred.

B. The homeowner must accept performance by the landscaper's son.

C. The homeowner may refuse to accept performance by the landscaper's son.

D. There is a breach of contract.

122. A proofreader has a contract with an author to proofread the author's manuscript. The contract is silent as to whether or not it can be assigned. Because proofreading services are not unique, the proofreader assigns her rights and delegates her duties under the contract to a co-worker. The co-worker makes many mistakes. Does the author have a cause of action?

A. Yes, only against the first proofreader for damages.

B. Yes, only against the co-worker.

C. Yes, against the first proofreader, but only after all exhaustion of remedies against the co-worker.

D. No because when the author allowed the co-worker to perform, she waived any cause of action she had against the original proofreader.

123. A ski shop owner places an advertisement in the paper: "One set of premium skis-- last one only $250, first come first serve." A skier, seeing the ad in the paper, is the first one at the store in the morning. She asks to purchase the skis, and the owner refuses to sell them to her at $250. The owner claims the advertisement was merely an invitation for an offer. The woman sues the owner for specific performance. Most likely the court will find that the advertisement is:

A. Only a mere invitation to deal.

B. A valid offer.

C. An allowable advertisement gimmick to lure customers.

D. None of the above.

124. A telephone company enters into a contract with a woman for cell phone service. The contract states that neither party will assign without the consent of the other. Nonetheless, the telephone company assigns to another company without informing the woman. The woman fails to pay her telephone bills. The new company brings suit against the woman. The new company will most likely recover:

A. Nothing because the woman was unaware of the assignment.

B. Nothing because the assignment was invalid.

C. The outstanding balance, minus a punitive offset for the assignment.

D. The outstanding balance on her bills.

125. A buyer and a seller enter into a contract for the seller to deliver 50 boats at $500 each F.O.B., at the seller's place of business. The seller ships the boats on June 1. On June 3, the boats are destroyed in transit. If the buyer brings a suit against the seller for breach of contract, the buyer will most likely:

A. Not succeed because the risk of loss has shifted.

B. Not succeed because of the doctrine of impossibility.

C. Succeed because the seller has the risk of loss.

D. Succeed because of public policy.

126. A violinist decides to sell his expensive Stradivarius violin. He puts out a written advertisement stating: "I am selling my Stradivarius for $10,000. I will sell to the first person who offers me the price in cash." A music lover sees the notice. The violinist had actually intended to ask $100,000, a cheap price for a Stradivarious. The music lover gives the violinist $10,000, in cash and demands the violin. The violinist refuses. If the music lover brings suit for specific performance, he will most likely:

A. Lose because specific performance is not equitable.

B. Lose because there was a unilateral mistake.

C. Win because there is a valid offer.

D. Win because the violinist should have known about the typographical error.

127. On May 25, a builder wrote to a subcontractor, "I will pay you $2,000, if you electrically wire a building for me according to the enclosed specifications. I must have your reply by June 1." On May 27, the subcontractor wrote the builder stating, "Can't do the work for less than $2,500." On May 28, the subcontractor wrote again to the builder stating, "Okay," I'll do the work for $2,000." Without hearing from the builder, and without the builder's knowledge, the subcontractor began work on June 1. What is the legal relationship of the builder and the subcontractor on June 1?

A. There is no contract between the parties.

B. A contract was formed when the subcontractor began work on June 1.

C. A contract was formed after the builder's receipt of the subcontractor's May 28 letter.

D. A contract was formed when the subcontractor mailed his letter of May 28.

128. A man stated to his cousin, "If you attend law school for the next three years, I will pay for your tuition, room and board. In addition, I will give you $2,000 for each 4.0 you earn." The cousin immediately enrolls in law school. At the end of the first semester, the cousin earns three 4.0s. The man refuses to pay any tuition, room or board and refuses to give the cousin $6,000 for her three 4.0s. She sues the man to enforce his promise. What is the man's best defense?

A. There was no legal detriment to the cousin.

B. The man was not serious about paying.

C. The cousin and the man did not manifestly intend a contract.

D. The agreement was not in writing.

129. A father tells his son, "If you join the army for the next five years, I will pay you $5,000 per year." The son joins the army. After his first year, he asks his father for the first $5,000. The father refuses to pay. If the son brings suit against the father for payment of the $5,000, he will most likely:

A. Not succeed because there was no consideration.

B. Not succeed because the father's promise was a gratuitous promise and thus not enforceable.

C. Succeed, under promissory estoppel.

D. Succeed because there was a bargained-for exchange.

130. A woman promises to pay a man $800 if he promises to paint her house. The man promises to paint the house and immediately begins work. After the man is over one-third of the way finished painting, the woman learns that another painter will paint her house for $500. She fires the man. The man brings suit for breach of contract. The man will most likely:

A. Succeed because he has already begun performance.

B. Succeed because he agreed to perform.

C. Not succeed because his price was too high.

D. Not succeed because there had not been substantial performance.

131. A law school, posted the following notice on its bulletin board: "Any student who wins the current moot court competition will be given the additional prize of $1,000. All moot court briefs must be submitted to academics by April 20." The notice constitutes:

   A. An offer, creating the power of acceptance.

   B. An invitation to deal.

   C. Merely a preliminary invitation because no offeree is named.

   D. A conditional promise.

132. On February 20, a private health foundation posts an ad at local health clubs, offering to give the winner of an April 4 marathon $5,000 on top of the marathon's own prize money. Participants interested in accepting the $5,000 are required to contact the health foundation by March 15. A runner reads the ad and contacts the health foundation on February 28. She then intensifies her training for the marathon as a result. On March 30, the health foundation writes, "Revoked" on all the ads at the health clubs. As to the runner, was the offer validly revoked?

   A. Yes because of the posting of the March 30 "Revoked" notice on the ads.

   B. Yes because it is a private health foundation.

   C. No because the runner detrimentally relied on the ad, prior to March 30.

   D. No because the runner might not have read the March 30 "Revoked" notice.

133. A store offers to pay $100 to the first customer who comes to the store on Monday morning. The offer constitutes a:

   A. Bilateral offer only.

   B. Bilateral and/or a unilateral offer.

   C. Unilateral offer only.

   D. Unilateral offer, which became a bilateral offer.

134. A girl scout troop offers to pay $500 to any girl who wins a school's spelling bee. How will a girl's winning the spelling bee affect the enforceability of the girl scout troop's promise?

   A. It will act as a condition precedent to the girl scout troop's performance and, thus, make the girl scout troop's promise enforceable.

   B. It will be unenforceable as a promise to make a gift.

   C. The girl scout troop's promise will be enforceable under the pre-existing duty rule.

D. None of the above.

135. A merchant offers to pay a diamond cutter $10,000 thirty days after the diamond cutter cuts a diamond. The diamond cutter cuts the diamond. The following day, diamond cutter dies. What is the effect of the diamond cutter's death on the merchant's duty to pay?

   A. It is not enforceable because death of any party voids the duties of the surviving parties as a matter of law.

   B. It is not enforceable.

   C. It is enforceable because of the diamond cutter's detrimental reliance.

   D. It is enforceable, by the executor of the diamond cutter's estate.

136. On December 26, a singer entered into a contract with a nightclub owner to sing at the nightclub on January 1. On December 29, the singer calls the nightclub owner and states that he may not be ready to start until January 10. Will the court allow the nightclub owner to bring an immediate suit against the singer?

   A. No because a repudiation must be in writing.

   B. No because there was no repudiation.

   C. Yes because there was a repudiation.

   D. Yes because the nightclub owner will lose money and is entitled to damages.

137. A contractor enters into a contract with a homeowner to renovate the homeowner's home. Work is to begin on May 1 and is to be completed by December 31. On May 1, the homeowner receives an e-mail from the contractor, stating that the contractor will not start work until May 10. May the homeowner cancel the existing contract?

   A. No because the contractor notified the homeowner.

   B. No because there was no material breach.

   C. Yes because the homeowner will be inconvenienced.

   D. Yes because there was a material breach.

138. A travel agency hires a tour guide to conduct tours each month for a salary $5,000 per month for twelve months. The tour guide is to assume his duties effective June 1. The tour guide fails to appear for the month of June, so the travel agency hires another tour guide for $6,000 per month for twelve months. The travel agency files suit against the original tour guide. What is the most likely amount it will recover?

A. $1,000 damages.

B. $1,000 damages for the month of June, and present value of the $1,000 per month salary difference for the remaining 11 months.

C. Nothing.

D. The full contract price of the contract between the travel agency and the original tour guide.

139. A builder entered into a contract with a homeowner to build a pool in the homeowner's backyard for $10,000. The price is to include all building materials. The week before performance was to begin, the homeowner called the builder and said, "I've changed my mind, the deal is off." The builder brought a lawsuit against the homeowner for breach of contract. The homeowner raised the Statute of Frauds as a defense. What will the court most likely rule?

A. If the building materials were to exceed $500, the contract would have to be in writing.

B. The building of a pool is a service. Thus, no writing is required.

C. Since this contract involves both goods and services, it does not need to be in writing.

D. Since this contract involves goods (over $500) and services, it has to be in writing.

140. On November 1, a woman and a man agreed in writing that the woman would purchase the man's car for $25,000. The sale was to take place November 15. On November 10, the woman told the man, "I really can't afford the car, the deal is off." The man said, "Okay, I'll let you out of the deal." The next day, the man told the woman he decided not to let her out of the deal because he needed the money. If the man sues the woman for breach of contract, will he recover?

A. Yes because contracts cannot be rescinded orally.

B. Yes because on November 1 there was a contract.

C. No because the woman does not have the money.

D. No because the contract was rescinded.

141. A contractor agrees to build a barn and stable for a farmer, for $200,000. After finishing 50% of the work, the contractor goes broke and is unable to finish the job. The farmer has to hire another contractor to finish the job. The original contractor has spent $100,000 in expenses and wants to recover his expenditures. What is his best theory of recovery?

A. Quasi-contract.

B. Impossibility of performance.

C. Material breach.

D. None of the above.

142. An auto repair company contracted with an automobile owner to restore the owner's antique car. The owner agreed to pay $300,000 for the work. When the auto repair company had done 50% of the work, it notified the owner that it would not complete the work. The owner takes his car to another repair company to complete the remaining work. If the auto repair company sues the owner, what may it recover?

    A. No amount because it is in material breach.

    B. No amount because it did not complete performance as promised.

    C. The $150,000 benefit it had conferred on the owner, less any expenses the owner incurred in having someone else complete the work due to the original the auto repair company's breach.

    D. Nothing because the breach was willful.

143. A man buys a new car and is injured when the brakes fail twenty days later. He sues both the car dealer where he purchased the car and the car manufacturer on an implied warranty theory. The defendants claim that the warranty is disclaimed in fine print on the back of the contract. How will the court rule?

    A. For the man because he has been injured.

    B. For the man because the vehicle is not merchantable.

    C. For the defendants because they have a valid disclaimer.

    D. For the defendants because there was equality of bargaining position.

144. A buyer sends an order for 10,000 tennis balls to a manufacturer, with instructions to ship immediately. The manufacturer ships immediately, via common carrier. Later that day, the buyer wires a revocation of his order. Is there an enforceable contract?

    A. Yes because the manufacturer has shipped the tennis balls.

    B. Yes, under the "mirror image" rule.

    C. No because the buyer made a timely revocation.

    D. No because the manufacturer can sell the balls to someone else.

145. A shoe retail store orders 1,000 pairs of green sandals from a shoe manufacturer. The manufacturer ships $1,000 pairs of blue sandals because it is out of green sandals. Is there a contract?

    A. No because the goods were nonconforming.

    B. No because the blue sandals constitute a breach.

    C. Yes because it is only an accommodation.

    D. Yes because shipment is an acceptance.

146. A man purchases a restaurant, secured by purchase money financing. The man buys an air conditioning system from a store on credit. The store takes a security interest in the equipment sold to the man and timely files a security interest under Article 9 of the Uniform Commercial Code.

    The man fails to pay for the equipment and goes bankrupt. The store claims a priority interest in the system over the man's other creditors. The bankruptcy trustee claims an interest in the system for the benefit of all creditors. Whose interest in the system has priority?

    A. All the general creditors because they are owed money from the man for supplies sold to the man on credit for the restaurant.

    B. The store because any supplier of fixtures sold on credit has a secured interest in the fixture until paid for.

    C. The store because of the store's perfected security interest in the equipment.

    D. Neither the store nor the creditors because once the equipment was installed, it became part of the real property.

147. A sugar exporter offers to sell to a food company five thousand 100-pound bags of sugar. The food company places the order on its own order form by filling in the description and quantity of the goods. In the space for price, the food company writes: "FOB FOOD COMPANY'S PLANT PER 100 POUND BAG $15.25."

    The exporter agreed to load up the food company's shipping container with the sugar. The loaded container was stolen from the exporter's plant before the food company's carrier was able to pick it up. The exporter sues the food company for the contract price when the food company refuses to pay. Who will prevail?

    A. The exporter, since it had already loaded up the shipping container.

    B. The exporter because the parties had "agreed otherwise" to pass the risk of loss at the time and the shipping container was loaded.

C. The food company because the risk of loss cannot pass when identified goods have been stolen – although neither party is at fault.

D. The food company because the term "FOB EXPORTER'S PLANT" requires delivery to the carrier before the risk of loss passes.

148. In 2002, a man purchased a home and assumed the existing mortgage with the bank. He then purchased lumber on credit from a hardware store to build a larger garage. The hardware store's credit application stated that it has a secured interest in the lumber until the goods are paid for.

After completing his new garage, the man defaulted on his debts to the hardware store and the bank. Which party's claimed interest in the lumber prevails?

A. The bank, if its secured interest in the realty is first in time.

B. The bank, since the lumber was ordinary building materials.

C. The hardware store, if it filed its security interest in the lumber prior to construction of the garage.

D. The hardware store because the lumber became a fixture upon incorporation into the construction of the garage.

149. A motel purchases a new furnace on credit from a store, which the store installs the same day. The store files its security interest in the furnace three weeks after the sale to the motel. The motel then takes out a second mortgage from a bank, which the bank promptly records. The motel defaults on all of its debts before they are repaid. Whose interest in the furnace has priority between the store and the bank?

A. The store because the store's security interest was filed before the bank recorded its mortgage.

B. The store because its security interest was filed within the 21-day grace period after installation of the fixture.

C. The bank, since the store did not file its security interest within the grace period, in order to have priority over a subsequent interest.

D. The bank because the furnace became realty, which is subject to a mortgagee's claim.

150. A homeowner has a recorded preexisting mortgage from a bank on his home. He purchases a hot water heater on credit from a store. The store files its security interest in the hot water heater four months later. The homeowner defaults on all his debts before they

CONTRACTS 107

are repaid. Whose security interest prevails between the store and the bank?

A. The store because it filed its security interest within the 21-day grace period.

B. The store because a fixture financier is entitled to a security interest when it extends credit.

C. The bank, due to its pre-existing security interest in the home.

D. The bank, since the store failed to file its security interest within the Article 9 grace period.

151. The owner of a tanning salon sold his tanning equipment on credit to customers and installed the equipment at his customers' businesses. The equipment was affixed to the realty of his customers' businesses.

The tanning salon owner attempted to file a secured interest in some tanning equipment sold and installed for one customer. Because the tanning salon owner was unfamiliar with the filing process, he misidentified some of the equipment in the financing statement. He filed the financing statement without discovering his error. Is the filing effective?

A. No, an erroneous filing is never effective.

B. No because unfamiliarity is no excuse for the tanning salon owner's mistake.

C. No, except as to the extent the descriptions were proper.

D. Yes because the tanning salon owner's attempt to file the security interest was in good faith, even though he did not pay the filing fee.

152. A restaurant purchased booths on credit from a booth supplier. The booths were then affixed to the restaurant building. The booth supplier properly filed its security interest in the booths.

The restaurant defaulted on its debt to the booth supplier. The booth supplier immediately took back the booths by smashing a large window to extract the booths. Were the booth supplier's actions proper in repossessing the booths?

A. Yes because it had timely obtained a secured interest in the fixtures prior to repossession.

B. Yes because the booth supplier had the right to repossession without resort to the judicial process.

C. No because the booth supplier breached the peace in order to repossess the booths.

D. No because it was impracticable to remove the booths and the booth supplier should have made them unusable, instead.

153. A hunting lodge purchased toilets on credit from a plumber. The plumber promptly recorded its security interest in the toilets. The hunting lodge defaulted, and the plumber removed the toilets in a legally proper manner that nonetheless caused some damage to the hunting lodge's property. Must the plumber reimburse the hunting lodge for the damage to the lodge's property?

   A. Yes, for the diminution in value to the hunting lodge.

   B. Yes, for the repair cost for the hunting lodge.

   C. Yes, for either the diminution in value or repair cost, whichever is less.

   D. No because the hunting lodge is the debtor.

154. A woman purchased a bird from a pet shop. The pet shop's bill of sale conspicuously stated the following:

   "HEALTH GUARANTEE FOR 72 HOURS FROM TIME OF PURCHASE. EXCHANGES WILL BE PERMITTED ONLY UPON PRESENTATION OF VETERINARIAN'S REPORT WITHIN THE 72-HOUR PERIOD. NOT RESPONSIBLE FOR INJURY, ACCIDENT OR LOSS AFTER 72 HOURS."

   The woman had the bird examined the next day by a veterinarian, but no disease or defect was discovered. However, 3 weeks later, the bird died for no apparent reason. An autopsy of the bird could not identify the cause of death. The woman asked the pet shop to replace the bird, but the pet shop refused. The woman sued the pet shop to recover her purchase price. What is the most likely result?

   A. The woman prevails because the pet shop failed to disclaim the implied warranty of merchantability.

   B. The woman prevails because 72 hours is not sufficient time to discover defects or disease in a bird.

   C. The woman loses because she could not prove the bird's cause of death.

   D. The woman loses because the implied warranties of merchantability and fitness for intended use were expressly disclaimed.

155. A thief steals a CD player and later sells the equipment to a woman. The woman, unaware of the thief's wrongdoings, sells the equipment to a man. The original owner of the CD player locates it and repossesses it from the man. The man sues the woman for breach of warranty of title. What is the most likely outcome?

A. The woman will lose because she was not a merchant.

B. The woman will lose because the CD player had been stolen.

C. The woman will lose because she could not pass good title.

D. The woman will win because, although the woman was unaware of the thief's theft of the CD player, she was a bona fide purchaser of the CD player from the thief and, thus, rightfully conveyed title to the man.

END OF QUESTIONS

CONTRACTS ANSWERS

1. D is the correct answer. A written letter of confirmation, sent by a merchant within a reasonable time after the oral contract is made, will satisfy the Statue of Frauds, if the receiving party is a merchant and does not object to the contents thereof within 10 days after receipt. Here, the merchant-customer is a merchant, and he signed the confirmation letter. Furthermore, the distributor received the signed confirmation on July 1, and the closest it came to objecting was when it informed the merchant-customer that it would not perform, but this did not occur until July 16, which is more than ten days later.

    A is an incorrect statement because the Parol Evidence Rule is only applicable to alleged conditions of a contract not included in the written contract, itself. Such is not the situation here because the facts here only deal with the written contents of the contract; no one here is alleging any oral conversations were added to the contract. B is incorrect because the merchant-customer sent a signed confirmation letter, complying with the merchant's confirmation letter exception to the Statute of Frauds. C is an incorrect statement because the merchant's exception does not require the merchant-customer's signature on a written contract; all it requires is a signed confirmation, which we have here.

2. D is the correct answer. There was no legal effect as to the woman's exclamation because there was no binding contract here. A binding contract requires there to have been an offer, acceptance, and consideration. Here, the boss' statement that he would pay the woman $500 a month for the rest of her life could be considered a valid offer because it indicated an intent to be bound, had definite and certain terms, and was communicated to the woman. However, the woman's response ("Thank you, this is the biggest surprise I have ever gotten!") is not a mirror-image acceptance of the offer, as required by common law. In addition, there was no consideration because the woman did not take on a legal detriment in exchange for the lifetime income. Her past services to the company do not constitute consideration because past services are not valid consideration. A is incorrect for the reasons stated in answer D. B is incorrect because it is irrelevant, since there was no binding contract, as discussed in answer D. C is incorrect because no expressed qualifications were imposed upon the woman for her to receive the gift. There are no facts that show that the woman was aware that this was her boss' preference.

3. D is the correct answer. The boy will not recover because he encountered no legal detriment. His charitable work at the beach was done before the neighbor made the promise and could, thus, not be considered a legal detriment in reliance on the neighbor's promise. A is incorrect. Modern law holds that if a

donative promise induces reliance by the promisee in a manner that the promisor should reasonably have expected, the promise will be legally enforceable. However, here the promissor (the neighbor) could not have expected his promise to induce reliance by the promissee (the boy), since the boy had already finished the work at the beach at the time the neighbor's promise was made. B is incorrect because the traditional rule holds that a promise based on moral obligation is unenforceable. C is incorrect because promissory estoppel requires reliance and, as discussed, there was no reliance here because the boy's work at the beach occurred before the promise was made.

4. A is the correct answer. The general rule is that a donative promise is unenforceable because there is a lack of consideration. Here, the woman promised to give the Ferrari to the tutor as a gift for the tutor's tutoring. The tutoring occurred before the woman's promise was made. Thus, the woman's promise was a donative promise. B is incorrect because a gratuitous promise is not a substitute for consideration, as discussed in Answer A. C is an incorrect statement because by its very nature, a gratuitous promise does not involve a bargained-for exchange; where there is a bargained-for exchange, the promise may be binding, rather than gratuitous. D is an incorrect statement. A promisor can always change the terms of a gratuitous promise because the promisor is not legally bound to carry out the promise, in any case.

5. A is the correct answer. Restatement First §90 of Contracts provides that a promise that the promisor should reasonably expect to induce action or forbearance and that does induce such is binding if injustice can be avoided only by enforcement of the promise. Here, it can be said that the woman would have no reason to foresee that the boyfriend would move into an apartment with significantly higher rent. Thus, her promise to pay his rent would not be binding. B is incorrect because, whether or not the woman intended reliance is irrelevant to the applicable rule of law. C is incorrect because it incorrectly states the law. While the boyfriend's conduct in renting a new apartment with a significantly higher rent may have been a legally sufficient detriment, promissory estoppel requires foreseeable reliance on the promise, which was not the case here for the reasons stated in Answer A. D is incorrect because even if she made the offer in jest, if the boyfriend's reliance was reasonably foreseeable under the circumstances, the boyfriend would prevail. As discussed, however, the actions that the boyfriend took (namely, renting an apartment with a significantly higher rent) was not reasonably foreseeable. Therefore, the boyfriend will not prevail here and Answer A is the correct choice.

6. B is the correct answer. When a contract calls for goods and services, the court applies the Predominant Purpose Test. Under this test, if it is decided that the predominant purpose of the contract was for goods, then the Uniform Commer-

cial Code (U.C.C.) will apply. Here, the contract was broken down into $350 for parts (goods) and $400 for labor (services). Thus, it is a close call here. It must, therefore, be determined which was the predominant purpose of the contract – the goods (the parts) or the services (the labor). A is incorrect because it states precisely the opposite of what the law is. As discussed, the U.C.C. applies if the predominant purpose of the contract was for goods, not services. C is incorrect, as the courts may, under the Predominant Purpose Test, decide that the U.C.C. applies. D is an incorrect statement as the U.C.C. applies to goods, not services, and under the Predominant Purpose Test may apply to goods and services if the predominant purpose of the contract was goods, but the U.C.C. never applies to contracts that are strictly for services.

7. C is the correct answer. A merchant's firm offer is irrevocable without consideration for a reasonable time, or for the time specified in the contract; but in no event for a period of time longer than three months. The offer must be made by a merchant and involve the sale of goods. Here, the offer to sell goods (the engines) was made by a merchant and the rule applies. A is incorrect, since no consideration is needed for a merchant's firm offer. B is incorrect because the U.C.C. holds firm offers open for three months, no longer. Therefore, even though five months were specified here, this would violate the firm offer rule's three-month provision. D is an incorrect statement of law. A signed acceptance by mail is not required by the U.C.C.

8. B is the correct answer. Payment of a smaller amount than was due on a claim is valid consideration if it is made in good faith and there is a bona fide dispute as to the claim. This is called an accord. The satisfaction is the performance of that accord. It has the effect of completely extinguishing the previous debt. The problem here is that, although the woman's payment of the lesser sum ($400) was in good faith because her brother needed the money sooner, there was no bona fide dispute as to the amount owed ($600). Therefore, the payment by the woman is not valid consideration. Consequently, the brother's previous promise to accept the lesser sum as a complete satisfaction of the debt is not enforceable and the brother will recover the additional $200. A is an incorrect statement of law. As explained in B, the entire debt was not extinguished by the $400 payment. C is incorrect because payment of a lesser sum than is due (here, $400, versus $600) when a debt is not disputed is not sufficient consideration for an accord and satisfaction. D is an incorrect answer for the same reasons that A and C are incorrect.

9. A is the correct answer. Under U.C.C. §2-207, when there are dealings between merchants, additional or different terms become part of the contract automatically after a reasonable period of time, unless: 1) the offer expressly limits acceptance to the terms of the offer, 2) the additional or different terms are a material alteration of the offer, or 3) the original offeror notifies the offeree that he objects to the

additional or different terms within a commercially reasonable period of time. Here, the facts expressly state that both parties are merchants. The initial offer did not expressly limit acceptance to its terms and, even though the new terms may have materially altered the offer, the facts do not indicate that the offeror (the first merchant) objected to the new terms. Thus, a contract was created when the second merchant mailed the order form to the first merchant. B is incorrect because conduct by both parties that recognizes the existence of a contract is sufficient to establish a contract. Here, both merchants understood the terms of the proposed contract, and it was unnecessary to wait until the first merchant received the second merchant's order form back, in order to create a contract. C is incorrect because contracts for the sale of goods between merchants allow for additional terms under U.C.C. §2-207, as discussed in Answer A. Thus, a contract was created, even though the forms varied. D is incorrect. It is true that under common law, an offeree must accept a mirror-image of the offer, and any additional terms will be construed to be a counteroffer. However, here, the facts are dealing with the sale of goods and, thus, the U.C.C. controls. U.C.C. §2-207 provides for additional terms, as discussed in Answer A. Thus, the second merchant's order form was not a counteroffer.

10. C is the correct answer. When a non-merchant offeree proposes additional or different terms in his acceptance, a contract exists consisting of the terms agreed upon, while the additional terms are deemed a proposal for additional or different terms. Here, the neighbor is a non-merchant, and he is proposing the additional term that the man paint the bicycle before turning it over to the neighbor. However, this additional term is a mere proposal, and a contract was formed on the terms originally agreed upon. A is incorrect for the same reasons that C is correct. B is incorrect because the additional terms would merely be considered proposals, as discussed in A. As such, they do not materially alter the contract. D is incorrect because, although unconscionability is a defense to contract formation, the neighbor's request that the man paint the bicycle is merely a proposal and, thus, unconscionability is not an issue here.

11. This contract is for the sale of peanuts, which are goods rather than services. Thus, the U.C.C. applies here. Under the U.C.C., D is the correct answer. Where no place is specified for delivery of the goods, the place of delivery is the seller's place of business, or, if there is none, the seller's residence. Here, no place of delivery was given. Therefore, the seller's place of business is the place of delivery, as stated in Answer D. Answers A, B, and C are all incorrect for the reason stated in the correct answer D.

12. C is the correct answer. A unilateral contract is one in which an offer requires performance of an act as bargained-for consideration. The unilateral contract is

formed by doing the required act. Here, the store offered to give a small computer to the first 100 people who arrived at the store on Wednesday. Arriving at the store on Wednesday (and being among the first 100 people to do so) is the required act. Thus, the store made a promise that required performance in exchange for that promise, making this a unilateral contract. A is incorrect because the newspaper ad constituted an offer, not an offer to negotiate. The newspaper ad contained all the required terms: subject matter (computer), quantity (1 computer per customer), time (Wednesday, first 100 to arrive), parties (the store and the first 100 customers to arrive on Wednesday), and the price ($1,800). B is incorrect because the reward was not intended as negotiation. It was intended to induce action (in this case, getting customers to come to the store). D is an incorrect statement because a bilateral contract requires a promise in exchange for a promise. Here, the first 100 people were not required to promise to come to the store. They were required to actually take the action of coming to the store.

13. D is the correct answer. A reward offer must be accepted by an offeree who knows of the offer. Here, the neighbor did not learn of the reward until after the dog's return. A and B are incorrect for the reasons discussed in correct Answer D. Here, since the neighbor did not know of the reward offer before he returned the dog, he will not succeed in an action whether or not a contract implied in law could be formed. A contract implied in law occurs when a person takes an action expecting to be compensated. Here, the neighbor gratuitously found and returned the dog. There is nothing indicating that the neighbor expected to be compensated at the time that he returned the dog. C is not correct because the issue is not consideration, but whether or not the offeree knew of the offer.

14. D is the correct answer. Anticipatory repudiation does not apply in a contract fully performed on the side of the non-repudiating party. Here, the non-repudiating party (the man) has fully performed by delivering the motorcycle on time (on September 9). Thus, since anticipatory repudiation does not apply under these facts, the man must wait at least until the promised payment date of September 15 before he has a cause of action against his girlfriend. A is incorrect because on September 9, although the man had fully performed by delivering the motorcycle, his girlfriend had not yet breached because her payment was not due until September 15. B is incorrect because, although the girlfriend repudiated on September 10 by stating that she did not intend to pay, this was not an anticipatory repudiation because anticipatory repudiation does not apply under these facts, as discussed above. C is incorrect because on the date the contract was made, there was no repudiation by either party.

15. A is the correct answer. The agreement expressly stated that the buyer was to obtain a mortgage by January 15 as a

condition for the seller to sell the house to the buyer on January 30. B is incorrect because the condition is expressed in the contract. There is no implied situation here. C is incorrect because, although the buyer's requirement to obtain a mortgage by January 15 is a condition precedent of the seller's duty to sell on January 30, this condition was expressed in the contract. It was not an implied or constructive condition. D is incorrect because the buyer had to obtain a mortgage on January 15, which was before the seller's duty to sell on January 30. Concurrent conditions must occur at the same time.

16. A is the correct answer. The contract here is for the sale and construction of a special engine. While construction is a service, a court would likely conclude that the primary purpose of the contract was the ultimate sale of the engine, which is a good. Thus, the U.C.C. applies here. U.C.C. §2-613 states that if the contract involves goods that were identified when the contract was made and the goods are destroyed without fault of either party before the risk of loss passed, the contract is voided. Here, the engine is a special engine, which makes it different from most engines. Thus, there is no doubt about which engine the contract is dealing. Hence, the goods in question are clearly identified (the special engine), and the facts state that the fire was not the fault of anyone. Therefore, the woman's performance is excused, and the contract is voided, making B, C and D incorrect.

17. D is the correct answer. A party bears the risk of a mistake when he is aware at the time that the contract is made, that he has only limited knowledge with respect to the facts to which the mistake relates, but treats his limited knowledge as sufficient. In this case, the contractor is obligated to build the mall and pay the increased costs. The contractor assumed the risks when it started the job. A is incorrect because the contractor's mistake will not excuse its performance. B is incorrect, as the corporation is not obligated to share in the increased costs. C is an incorrect statement. Impracticability requires extreme and unreasonable difficulty or expense that was not anticipated. Here, the facts indicate that the existence of the rock was known to other builders who had made bids and who had submitted higher bids based on this. Through simple due diligence, the contractor could have likewise become aware of this fact and cannot take advantage of its failure to do so by discharging the contract through impracticability. Thus, although removing the rock will cut into the contractor's profits, the contract is not impracticable to perform.

18. D is the correct answer. The buyer must notify the seller of the rejection within a reasonable time and must hold the goods with reasonable care for a reasonable time sufficient for the seller to remove the goods. A is incorrect, as the buyer is under no obligation to send the roller blades back. Answers B and C are incorrect because the buyer only

needs to hold the rejected items (here, the roller blades). The buyer is not required to sell them at a discount and give the proceeds to the seller or to accept the roller blades and sue for breach of contract, as discussed in Answer D.

19. A is the correct answer. Incidental damages allow the buyer to recover any cost or expense reasonably incurred that are incidental to the seller's delay or delivery of defective goods. Loss of expected profit is not considered to be an incidental damage and is, therefore, not recoverable. Here, the seller (the original supplier) delivered non-conforming pens. Although the buyer (the business owner) may have been able to recover lost profits, the question specifically asked about incidental damages, not consequential damages. Answers B, C and D are all incorrect because they all constitute incidental damages and could be recovered. (U.C.C. §2-815(1)). Here, the expenses incurred in inspecting and storing the non-conforming pens, as well as the extra sales commission that the company owner had to pay the new supplier for the rush order of replacement pens, are all examples of incidental damages.

20. C is the correct answer. An express warranty can be created by any sample or model that is made part of the basis of the bargain. Here, the demonstration would create an express warranty that the curling iron shall conform to the model used. In the demonstration, it took thirty seconds to curl hair. Thus, the fact that it, instead, took the model 2 minutes to curl her hair using the curling iron would be a breach of the express warranty. A is an incorrect statement of law. Here, the contract is for a curling iron, which is a good. Thus, the U.C.C. applies here. Under U.C.C. §2-318, direct privity between the manufacturer and the ultimate buyer is not required for there to be a cause of action. B is incorrect because this warranty requires that the seller have reason to know of the particular use of goods contemplated by the buyer, and the seller must also be aware that the buyer is relying on the seller's judgment. The facts here do not indicate that the seller had any reason to know the purpose for which the model purchased the curling iron and that the model was relying on the seller's judgment. D is incorrect for the same reasons that C is correct.

21. D is the correct answer because the city is a third party creditor beneficiary of the contract between the general contractor and the sub-contractor, and the city's rights have vested. When a third party creditor beneficiary's rights have vested, that third party creditor beneficiary has the right to sue if a breach occurs. Vesting occurs when a third party assents to a contract between two other parties after being made aware of this contract. Here, the city awarded the contract to the general contractor. The general contractor then made a separate contract with the sub-contractor. This made the city a third party beneficiary of the contract between the general contractor and the sub-contractor. The

city then assented to the contract between the general contractor and the sub-contractor. In this way, the city's rights in the contract between the general contractor and the sub-contractor vested. Hence, the city has the right to sue the sub-contractor here. A is incorrect because the city is a third party creditor beneficiary, as discussed above. It is not a donee beneficiary. B is incorrect because, as discussed above, the city is a creditor beneficiary. C is incorrect because, although the city is a third party creditor beneficiary, its rights must vest in order for the city to be able to sue. Thus, D is the correct answer, rather than C.

22. D is the correct answer. In this case, the general contractor will be looking for indemnification from the sub-contractor because of the sub-contractor's breach that resulted in the county suing the general contractor. Indemnification is the part of a contract that provides for one party (here, the sub-contractor) to bear the monetary costs, either directly or by reimbursement, for losses incurred by a second party (here, the general contractor). For the general contractor to be able to indemnify himself, there must obviously be a valid contract between himself and the subcontractor. Here, the facts indicate that there was such a valid contract. A is incorrect because the general contractor has the right to be indemnified by the sub-contractor, as discussed above. B is incorrect because, even though the sub-contractor has to perform the duties called for under the contract between it and the general contractor, this does not prevent a third party from suing the general contractor. C is an incorrect statement of law. As discussed in Answer D, a general contractor may sue a sub-contractor for indemnification.

23. C is the correct answer. The restaurant owner is an incidental beneficiary. An incidental beneficiary is someone who benefits as a result of a contract, but is not a direct intended beneficiary. Here, the restaurant owner expected to increase business when the sports arena was built, but he was not an intended beneficiary of any contract to build the sports arena. Incidental beneficiaries do not have the right to sue for breach. A is incorrect because it is irrelevant if the general contractor's negligence is proven in court, since incidental third party beneficiaries cannot sue, as discussed. B is incorrect. An officious intermeddler is a volunteer who assists and/or benefits another without contractual responsibility or legal duty to do so, but nevertheless wants compensation for his/her actions. Here, the restaurant owner has not volunteered to do anything and is, thus, not an officious intermeddler. D is incorrect because an incidental beneficiary's rights never vest because incidental beneficiaries have no contractual rights, as discussed above.

24. B is the correct answer. If the wholesaler has made partial performance or a substandard performance, the bou-

tique had the right to offset against any incompleteness to the performance of the contract. Also, the boutique could actually be owed damages, if it has been placed in a position that is worse than before the wholesaler performed the duty under the contract. A is incorrect. The dress supplier's actions are not related to the suit between wholesaler and the boutique. C is incorrect as "legal detriment" refers to action of the promisee taken in reliance upon the actions of the promisor. Here, the wholesaler did not fully perform because some of the dresses it delivered were damaged. For the wholesaler to remedy this situation would not be a "legal detriment," but simply the fulfillment of its contractual obligations. D is incorrect because the wholesaler is an intended, not an incidental, beneficiary of the contract between the dress supplier and the boutique.

25. D is the correct answer. When a third party creditor beneficiary's rights have vested, that third party creditor beneficiary has the right to sue if a breach occurs. Vesting occurs when a third party assents to a contract between two other parties after being made aware of this contract. Because the mother was owed money from the woman, the mother would have been a third party creditor beneficiary of the contract between the woman and the man, and the mother could have then sued the man when her rights vested. However, the mother did not become aware of the contract between the woman and the man at the time it was entered into and did not assent to it. Thus, the mother's rights have not vested and she cannot sue the man. A and B are incorrect because the mother has neither suffered a bargained-for legal detriment nor relied on the contract between the woman and the man because the mother was unaware of this contract, as discussed above. C is incorrect because a third party beneficiary, while not a party to the contract, may still sue if that third party beneficiary's rights have vested. However, as discussed, the mother's rights have not vested and she, thus, cannot sue the man.

26. B is the correct answer. The motorcyclist received medical treatment from the doctor, which implies a promise by the motorcyclist to pay for the services received. Answers C and D are incorrect because the status of the doctor as a beneficiary would give him the right to sue the motorcyclist's father, not the motorcyclist. Instead, the fact that the doctor has rendered services to the motorcyclist is what gives the doctor the right to sue the motorcyclist. A is incorrect because an implied-in-fact contract is an actual contract. Quasi-contractual relief is granted if there is no contract and party would be unjustly enriched if it were not required to pay the other party the quantum meruit of their services. Here, the doctor rendered medical services under an implied-in-fact contract because when the doctor rendered treatment, it was understood that the doctor would be paid for his services.

27. A is the correct answer because the creditor could only proceed against the attorney as a third party beneficiary of the retainer agreement between the litigant and the attorney. In order for a third party beneficiary to have rights to sue, he must be aware of the contract between the two originally contracting parties and change his position in reliance on the contract. Here, the creditor did not become aware of the contract between the attorney and the litigant and, thus, did nothing in reliance on that contract until after the attorney had paid the money to the litigant. B is incorrect because once the creditor's rights have vested, the creditor must also change his position in reliance on the vested rights in order to sue. C is incorrect because, even though the litigant owes his creditor the money, if the creditor had been aware of the contract between the litigant and the attorney and the creditor had changed his position in reliance on that contract, he could have sued the attorney for the money owed to him by the litigant. D is incorrect because the creditor is an intended beneficiary as per the language of the retainer agreement.

28. B is the correct answer. The second accountant only promised to work for the taxpayer. He did not promise to pay the IRS. Thus, the IRS is neither a creditor nor a donee beneficiary of the second accountant's promise to the taxpayer. A is incorrect because there is no evidence that the IRS changed its position in reliance on the first accountant's promise to pay the IRS, since the IRS was unaware of this promise. C is an incorrect statement of fact. The second accountant made no promise to pay the IRS, gratuitous or otherwise. The second accountant only promised to prepare the taxpayer's taxes. D is incorrect because the IRS is not a beneficiary of the second accountant's promise to work for the taxpayer.

29. C is the correct answer. When a contract contains a non-assignment clause, and a party makes an assignment in violation of this clause, the non-assigning party has a right to sue for breach of the non-assignment clause. However, the non-assigning party must accept the new party (assignee) to whom the assignment has been made. For the reasoning discussed in correct answer C, A and B are both incorrect. D is incorrect, since it is an incorrect statement of law.

30. D is the correct answer (for Bar Exam purposes). The Restatement II of Contracts is followed where the terms "creditor" and "donee" beneficiary (see Restatement I) have been replaced with the term "intended" beneficiary. (Note that a majority of states still follow the Restatement I, which results in a different answer.) Here, the businesswoman's creditor is an intended beneficiary of the contract between the businesswoman and the designer. A, B, and C are incorrect for the reasons D is correct.

31. B is the correct answer. The niece is an intended beneficiary of the contract between the woman and the man and is, thus, subject to any defenses that may

arise. Here, the woman can successfully assert the defense of nonperformance by the man. Thus, the niece will not recover. A is incorrect because the contract provides that the woman is to pay the niece, not the man. C is incorrect because, although the niece's rights were vested, she is still subject to the defenses that can be asserted here, as discussed in Answer B. D is an incorrect statement. As discussed above, there are defenses that can be asserted here.

32. C is the correct answer. In order to assign rights in a contract, there must be a contract in existence at the time of the assignment. Here, the songwriter promised to give 20% of the royalties from the song to the opera singer, but he did not have a contract with any companies to sell the song at the time. Even though after his death his estate entered into a contract to sell the song, this would not give assignment rights to the opera singer for the reasons stated above. A is incorrect because at the time of the songwriter's promise, there was no contract to be assigned. D is incorrect because royalty contracts are assignable, but in the facts here, there was no contract in existence at the time of the alleged assignment. B is incorrect because her housekeeping services were not given as consideration, since the promise to assign the royalties came after the opera singer rendered the housekeeping services.

33. D is the correct answer. Contracts are freely assignable, so long as they are not personal service contracts. Du-

ties can also be delegated, so long as they do not increase the risk. Here, the dealer had a contract with the museum in which the dealer was to supply the museum with a spoon, in exchange for a payment of $50,000. Subsequently, the dealer assigned to the owner of the spoon its rights to collect the $50,000. The contract between the dealer and the museum was not a personal service contract, and, thus, the dealer's duty to deliver the spoon was delegable to the owner of the spoon. Here, the dealer's assignment to the owner of the spoon was a delegation of its duty. Thus, when the owner of the spoon performed, the museum's duty to pay became absolute. A is incorrect because, as discussed in Answer D, the contract between the museum and the dealer was not a personal service contract. B is incorrect because the assignment and delegation act as a substitute for privity. C is incorrect because that fact alone is not enough to subject the museum to liability.

34. A is the correct answer. Every assignment gives rise to a third-party beneficiary contract. Here, when the pre-owned dress shop assigned its rights to the customer to purchase the dress from the debutant, a third party beneficiary contract was created. Thus, the customer (assignee) was the third party beneficiary and had the right to sue the debutant when the debutant refused to sell the dress. B is incorrect because it is irrelevant how long the customer has had a relationship with the pre-owned dress shop. C is incorrect because the debutant had privity

of contract with the pre-owned dress shop. Thus, when the pre-owned dress shop assigned its rights to the customer, that privity of contract passed on to the customer. D is incorrect because there is no such law regarding exclusive items.

35. C is the correct answer. When a party to a contract delegates its duty, it remains liable as a guarantor for the performance of the delegatee. Here, the tenant (the original contracting party) delegated to his sister his duty to pay rent. Nonetheless, the tenant as guarantor for the performance of the delegatee (his sister) remains liable if she does not pay. Therefore, the landlord will prevail in a lawsuit against the tenant. A is incorrect for the reasons discussed in Answer C; the delegator (the tenant) remains liable. B is incorrect because there is no impossibility here. It is not impossible for the tenant to pay the rent. D is incorrect because the delegation of the duty to pay rent is not too personal.

36. B is the correct answer. Under U.C.C. §2-312, a warranty of title must be disclaimed by specific language. The provision for sale of "any right, title and interest" is not an exclusion or disclaimer of the warranty of title. Further, the provision disclaiming warranties is ineffective as to title for its failure to disclaim the warranty of title specifically. A, C and D are incorrect for the reasons stated in correct answer B.

37. A is the correct answer. The motorboat salesman made an express warranty to the man, regarding specific attributes of the boat that were not true. Specifically, the motorboat salesman said, "This baby has a lot of power and you'll be able to pull 20 skiers at 35 miles per hour if you decide to increase the size of your show." As the facts show, however, the boat was unable to exceed 15 miles per hour with just 5 skiers. B is incorrect because, although all sales provide for the implied warranty of merchantability, which basically states that the item will conform to normal use for the item in question, here the motorboat operated as a motorboat and, as such, was merchantable. If anything, the implied warranty of fitness for a particular purpose may have also been breached by the motorboat salesman, but since the salesman expressly stated the amount of people that the motorboat could pull at 35 miles per hour, A is the better answer. C and D are incorrect for the reasons stated in the explanation to answer A. Furthermore, C is incorrect because a buyer is not required to try out the goods before purchasing, and if a buyer fails to test the goods prior to purchase, this does not eliminate his right to sue for breach of contract. D is an incorrect statement of law; the U.C.C. applies to the sale of all goods, whether new or used.

38. A is the correct answer. This contract involves the sale of motors, which are goods. Thus, the U.C.C. is the governing law here. Under U.C.C. §2-206, an offer may be accepted by any reasonable medium. An offer may be

accepted by either a return promise or by specific acts. Here the wholesaler's act of shipping the motors constituted acceptance of the boat supply store's offer, even though the wholesaler shipped nonconforming goods. There is still a valid contract here, although the boat supplier can pursue remedies for the nonconforming goods. B is incorrect because the U.C.C. requires acceptance by any reasonable medium, as discussed above. The good faith of the wholesaler is not at issue. C is incorrect because, as discussed in Answer A, the wholesaler could accept the boat supply store's offer either by a return promise or by shipment. Here, the wholesaler shipped, thereby accepting the offer. D is incorrect because under the U.C.C., the shipment of nonconforming goods still constitutes an acceptance and, thus, the formation of a contract, as discussed in Answer A.

39. B is correct. U.C.C. §2-608 provides that when a buyer receives nonconforming goods, the buyer may upon reasonable notice to the sender revoke or reject the whole shipment, or accept any commercial unit, and reject the rest. Here, the woman (the buyer) was to receive 500 gray t-shirts with her logo. She instead received 400 gray t-shirts with her logo. Thus, the shipment was nonconforming, and the woman can pursue her remedies under U.C.C. §2-608. A is incorrect because a buyer must give notice within a reasonable time of rejection. C and D are incorrect statements of law, for the reasons discussed in Answer B.

40. A is the correct answer. Under U.C.C. §2-205, an offer by a merchant, in a signed writing, which by its terms gives assurances to keep the offer open, is not revocable for a period not to exceed three months. Here, the blouse manufacturer is a merchant, and its offer to the retail store included assurances that the offer would remain open until March 31, which is within the three-month time frame. Therefore, the blouse manufacturer may not revoke until March 31. B is incorrect because having merchants as parties is not sufficient for the merchant's firm offer rule. As discussed in Answer A, the offeror must give assurances that the offer will remain open for a period not to exceed three months. C is incorrect because under the U.C.C., consideration is not required for the merchant's firm offer rule. D is incorrect both because there are no facts to indicate that the retail store relied on the promise to keep the offer open and because reliance is not necessary under the merchant's firm offer rule.

41. D is the correct answer. Under U.C.C. §2-207(2), where parties to a contract for the sale of goods are both merchants, the proposed additional terms become part of the contract, unless: (1) the offer expressly limits acceptance to the terms of the offer; (2) the additional terms would materially alter the contract; or (3) the offeror notifies the offeree within a reasonable period of time that he ob-

jects to the additional terms. Because the grocer's response was an inquiry to the vegetable canning company's offer, the terms will be construed as a proposal and will become part of the contract. In addition, the grocer's request that 25 cases be delivered in October and 25 in November, rather than a single delivery of 50 cases, does not materially alter the terms of the contract. A is incorrect because under the U.C.C., acceptance does not need to be done using the same mode as the offer; acceptance may occur through any reasonable means. B is an incorrect statement of law. Under the common law, this would have been a counteroffer. However, as discussed in Answer D, the U.C.C. provides for additional terms without making this a counteroffer. C is incorrect because it does not include the additional terms for delivery, which under the U.C.C. become part of the contract.

42. C is the correct answer. This contract deals with shoes, which are goods. Therefore, the U.C.C. governs this contract. U.C.C. §2-601 provides where goods or tender of delivery fails in any respect to conform to the contract, the buyer may reject tender (perfect tender rule). Here, the shoe distributor failed to provide a perfect tender by only shipping 900 pairs of shoes instead of the required 1,000 pairs. Because this did not perfectly conform to the terms of the contract, the shoe store may reject them. A is incorrect because the perfect tender rule requires that the shipment conform perfectly to the requirements of the contract; substantial performance is not enough. B is incorrect because the shoe store is not required to accept an offset for damages. Due to the perfect tender rule, it is entitled to the entire 1,000 pairs of shoes. If the shoe store does not receive 1,000 pairs of shoes, it may reject any shoes the distributor ships. D is incorrect because of the perfect tender rule. It is irrelevant how substantial the deficiency is under the perfect tender rule; if even one pair of shoes is missing, the recipient (here, the shoe store) may reject the entire shipment.

43. A is correct. This contract deals with brochures, which are goods. Therefore, the U.C.C. governs this contract. U.C.C §2-601 provides that a buyer may accept a non-conforming tender. Under §2-714, buyer's acceptance of partial tender does not operate as a waiver, and the buyer can still recover damages. Here, the law school (the buyer) accepted the delivery of 900 brochures, and it can still sue for damages for the remaining 100 brochures that were not delivered. B is incorrect because the materiality of seller's (i.e., the printer's) breach is not decisive. The buyer (here, the law school) is entitled to recover damages for any unexcused failure on the part of the seller to perform in full under the contract. C is incorrect because acceptance of partial tender does not operate as a waiver, as discussed in Answer A. D is incorrect because a non-conforming shipment constitutes a breach under the perfect tender rule.

Thus, it is irrelevant that the printer shipped all the brochures that it had.

44. D is the correct answer. Normally, the Statute of Frauds requires that a writing be signed by the party to be charged (i.e., the paying party, here, the retailer). However, when both parties are merchants, the Statute of Frauds is satisfied if one party (either the party to be charged or the other party) sends a signed written confirmation, and the receiving party does not object to it within ten days. Here, both parties are merchants. Therefore, the merchants' confirmatory memo rule applies. The facts show that there was no objection within ten days; the receiving party (the retailer) waited a month to object. A, B and C are incorrect statements of law. A is incorrect because, as discussed, the merchants confirmatory memo rule applies here, and it does not require that the memo be signed by the party to be charged. B is incorrect because the omission of a price term under the U.C.C. is not fatal to the validity of a contract. Only a quantity term is required. C is incorrect because the receiver of a merchant's confirming memo is not required to verify the contract terms within 10 days (or ever).

45. C is the correct answer. U.C.C. §2-313 provides that any affirmation of fact or promise, relating to the goods upon which a buyer could rely, creates an express warranty. Here, the salesman assured the woman that the truck comes with an intregal rollbar built into the cab structure, as shown in the truck company's brochure, and the brochure stated that the cab provides complete rollover protection. However, the woman had actual knowledge that when her friend used the same type of truck one week prior, her friend's truck rolled over and the friend was severely injured. The woman therefore should not have relied on the express affirmations by the truck company in its brochure, nor should she have relied upon the affirmations of the salesman as to the truck's safety from rollovers. Answers A and D are incorrect because neither the brochure nor the salesman's affirmations should have been relied upon by the woman for the reasons discussed above. B is incorrect because the truck did not have to be totaled for the woman to have a cause of action; rolling over would be sufficient, if she had had a sufficient basis to rely on the affirmations.

46. C is the correct answer. An offer of reward is an offer for performance (a unilateral contract – a promise in return for performance). Since the woman did not deliver the brief case, and the man effectively revoked the offer when he informed her that he was canceling the reward, no contract was formed because he revoked the contract before performance (i.e., acceptance) occurred. Merely calling the man did not constitute acceptance because the flyer specifically stated that the reward would only be paid for the return of the brief case, not for a telephone call about the brief case. A is incorrect because the

woman cannot orally accept the reward – as discussed, a unilateral contract can only be accepted by performance and she has not returned the brief case. B is incorrect for the reasons stated in correct answer C. If the woman had performed by returning the brief case, then B would have been the correct answer. However, as discussed above in C, she did not return it, and, thus, the unilateral offer had not yet been accepted at the time the man revoked it. Offers may generally be revoked prior to acceptance. D is incorrect because the man effectively revoked the offer before the woman could accept by returning the brief case.

47. C is the correct answer. The woman's offer called for acceptance by performance (a unilateral contract). In this case, the offer called for the man to walk across the Brooklyn Bridge. It did not call for him to merely promise to do so. Thus, the mailing of the letter by the man (a promise to perform) had no legal effect. The mailbox rule (whereby an offer is accepted upon dispatch of the acceptance letter) only applies to bilateral contracts (in which the offer calls for acceptance by a promise to perform). Before the man could perform (by walking across the Brooklyn Bridge), the woman revoked her offer. Thus, no contract was formed. A is incorrect for the reasons stated in Answer C. Thus, the man could only accept by an act, not by a promise to act. B is incorrect because the mailbox rule does not apply to unilateral contracts, as explained in Answer C. D is incorrect because the man's May 17 letter is not an acceptance, whether or not the woman received it. As discussed in Answer C, the man could only accept through the act of walking across the Brooklyn Bridge.

48. D is the correct answer. This is a contract for the sale of a home, which is a service covered under the common law. An offeree's power of acceptance is terminated when the offeror takes definite action inconsistent with an intent to enter into the proposed contract, and the offeree has reliable information to that effect. Revocations are effective upon receipt. Here, when the potential buyer received the homeowner's letter, which stated that the homeowner had sold to someone else, the potential buyer's power of acceptance was terminated because the homeowner took an action inconsistent with his original intention to sell to the potential buyer and informed the potential buyer. A is incorrect. Offers at common law are freely revocable, unless coupled with an interest (an option). Option contracts require consideration. Here, the homeowner's promise to the potential buyer to hold the offer open until January 30 did not create an option contract, since nothing was paid, so there was no consideration for the offer to be held open. Therefore, the homeowner did not breach by selling to another party because at common law, offers are freely revocable. C is an incorrect answer because revocations are effective upon

receipt. Here, although the homeowner acted inconsistently with the terms of the original offer by selling to another party, the potential buyer must be aware of that sale for it to be a valid revocation of that offer. Thus, Answer C is incorrect, and Answer D is correct.

49. D is the correct answer. An agreement to build a swimming pool is a service agreement and is, thus, governed by the common law. Under the common law, the Statute of Frauds (which requires agreements to be in writing to be enforceable) applies to contracts that cannot be completed within one year. Here, however, although the contract was oral, by its terms, it could be completed within one year (it was signed on March 10, and the completion date was June 15), and it otherwise does not fall within the Statute of Frauds. Thus, the Statute of Frauds defense does not apply here. Therefore, A is incorrect. B is incorrect both because, as discussed, this contract is governed by the common law (rather than the U.C.C.) and because the U.C.C. has no such provision in any case. C is incorrect because, although the woman could claim frustration of purpose since she sold the home and no longer needs the pool, her intention to sell was not indicated to the man at the time of the contract. Therefore, there are no defenses, making D the correct answer.

50. C is the correct answer. The agreement between the supplier and the store calls for performance in separate installments, making the contract divisible. Upon the supplier's performance of sending the first delivery and store's performance of paying $10,000, the first installment was complete. By the store repudiating the contract and failing to pay the second installment, the supplier may also sue for the damages caused by the store's repudiation of the remainder of the contract. The supplier would be excused from any further obligation under the contract. D is incorrect for the reasons stated in the explanation to Answer C.

51. B is the correct answer. The Parol Evidence Rule provides that when parties have placed their agreement into a writing, which they both agree and assent to as their full and complete integrated agreement, evidence of prior or contemporaneous oral or written terms will not be admitted to change or vary the terms of the writing. However, where the parties reduce their agreement to a writing, without language that the writing is fully integrated, parol evidence is admissible to show there is a condition precedent to the legal effectiveness of the writing. Here there are no facts indicating that the bar candidate and the student agreed that the written contract would be the full and integrated agreement. Since the parties orally agreed prior to the written agreement that the sale would occur only upon the bar candidate passing the Bar Examination (condition precedent), and the oral agreement was not made a part of the written agreement, the parol evidence of that condition precedent is admissible. A, C and D

are incorrect for the stated reasons to answer B. A is a correct factual answer because the bar candidate's purpose of the contract would be frustrated if he had to sell to the student, even though he failed the Bar Examination. However, even though the purpose of the contract would be frustrated, the bar candidate would not have been allowed to introduce evidence of the condition precedent if the written contract had been fully integrated. Therefore, B is the correct answer. C is an incorrect answer because there was a written contract satisfying the Statute of Frauds. D is incorrect because, although the written agreement did not include the oral agreement's condition precedent, the oral agreement does not contradict the written agreement; the written agreement merely fails to include the oral agreement. Under the Parol Evidence Rule, additional yet consistent terms may be admitted, while contradictory terms are barred.

52. D is the correct answer. U.C.C. §2-508 states that where any tender or delivery by the seller is rejected because of non-conformance, and the time for performance has expired, the buyer may properly reject the non-conforming tender. Here, the buyer properly rejected the seller's tender of the milk that was short 1,000 cartons because the time for the seller's performance had expired. Specifically, performance was due on May 1, and it was May 1 at the time the seller tendered the 9,000 cartons of milk (as opposed to the 10,000 called for in the contract). A is incorrect because the contract is not objectively impossible to perform because the seller could have obtained the additional 1,000 cartons of milk from other sources. B is incorrect because in contracts for the sale of goods (such as cartons of milk in this case), the seller is required to deliver perfect tender (here, all 10,000 cartons of milk) on the performance date set in the contract (here, May 1), under U.C.C. §2-601. C is incorrect because the seller has not indicated that the shipping of 9,000 cartons was an accommodation, which the seller would have been required to do before the performance date (May 1). Since the performance date (May 1) has now arrived, the buyer is no longer required to allow the seller to cure.

53. D is the correct answer. A liquidated damages clause will be upheld where the stipulated sum bears a reasonable relation to the actual loss, actual damages are uncertain or difficult to ascertain at the time of the contract, and the contract as a whole evidences a conscious intention of the parties to consider and adjust the damages that might flow from the breach. Note, liquidated damages are not punitive. None of the factors is present for the liquidated damages clause to be upheld, particularly since the lessor was able to resell the equipment before seeking liquidated damages, and, thus, was able to ascertain its actual damages. Consequently, the liquidated damages clause will not be upheld here. A is incorrect because a meeting of the minds

is not a requirement of a liquidated damages clause. B is incorrect because that is not the purpose of a liquidated damages clause. C is incorrect because a 10% liquidated damages clause may be conscionable in some cases; this is determined on a case-by-case basis.

54. A is the correct answer. A shipment contract was formed, since the contract required the manufacturer to deliver the chairs. Once the manufacturer placed the chairs upon the carrier, the risk of loss passed to the store owner because the contract provided F.O.B. (free on board) at the manufacturer's place of business. Since the risk of loss was on the store owner and the manufacturer placed the chairs upon the carrier, the third party, who was assigned all of the manufacturer's rights under the contract, is entitled to the contract price. Despite the language in the contract, the manufacturer could assign its right to collect from the store owner because a non-assignment clause takes away the right of the assignor to assign the contract but not the power to assign. In other words, although the store owner could sue the manufacturer for the breach of this provision of the contract, the store owner cannot prohibit the manufacturer from assigning its rights under the contract. B is incorrect because, since the risk of loss passed to the store owner when the chairs were delivered to the carrier, the store owner is responsible for the entire contract price. C is incorrect because, as discussed above, the risk of loss passed to the store owner when the chairs were delivered to the carrier. D is incorrect because the store owner could assign its rights, despite the language in the contract, as discussed in Answer A.

55. C is the correct answer. The risk of loss passed to the dealership when the manufacturer placed the automobiles upon the carrier. The contract included a clause that stated "F.O.B., at the manufacturer's place of business." The dealership signed the contract, thus, acknowledging that the risk of loss shifted to the dealership once the automobiles were on the carrier. Therefore, the dealership is responsible to pay the contract price. A is an incorrect statement of fact, as discussed above. B deals with "Acts of God" or force majeure. However, the risk of loss had already passed before the force majeure occurred, as discussed above. D is incorrect because it was not impossible for the manufacturer to perform because if risk had stayed with the manufacturer, the manufacturer would have been forced to find substitute automobiles. However, as discussed, the manufacturer completed its performance once the automobiles were delivered to the carrier. Thus, with or without the F.O.B. clause, it was not impossible for the manufacturer to perform under these facts.

56. C is the correct answer. The woman will not be limited to receiving only damages; she can rescind the contract because the man misrepresented a fact that relates to an essential part of

the bargain, namely that the land was properly zoned for building a tourist attraction. A, B and D are incorrect for the reasons stated in correct answer C.

57. A is the correct answer. The shareholder is a third party beneficiary. A third party beneficiary is known to the two contracting parties at the time of the contract, and in order for that person to recover for a promisor's breach of contract, the person must be either a donee or creditor beneficiary whose rights have vested. Here, the shareholder merely guaranteed repayment of the loan at the time that the bank lent the money to the corporation. When the corporation defaulted and the bank promised to sell the corporate assets at the highest possible price, this repayment agreement did not reference the shareholder's personal guarantee. Thus, at best, she would be an incidental beneficiary of the bank's promise to the corporation, rather than a donee or a creditor. Thus, the shareholder is not entitled to recover here. B is incorrect because there are two agreements in these facts. The initial agreement was between the bank and the corporation, and the bank lent money to the corporation on condition that the shareholder agrees to personally guarantee the loan. The second agreement occurred after the corporation defaulted on the loan, and bank decided rather than pursuing a remedy with the shareholder (guarantor), it would instead enter into a repayment agreement with the corporation, in which the bank would sell the corporation's assets to discharge the debt. The shareholder was not part of this second agreement, as discussed in answer A. Thus, the bank's sale of the assets would not discharge any contractual relationship between the shareholder and the bank. C is incorrect because while the corporation may have been able to raise the issue that the bank breached the repayment agreement by not realizing the highest possible price for the sale of the assets, a third party incidental beneficiary cannot prevail under this theory. Here, as discussed, the shareholder is a third party incidental beneficiary. Thus, she will be unable to prevail under this theory. D is incorrect because as discussed, the shareholder is a third party incidental beneficiary, and, thus, the bank had no fiduciary duty to her.

58. C is the correct answer. U.C.C. §2-601 requires perfect tender such that if the goods or tender of delivery are nonconforming in any respect, the buyer may reject the whole delivery, accept the whole, or accept part of the delivery and reject the rest. Since the shutters were nonconforming, the shipment was properly refused by the builder. A is incorrect because the Perfect Tender Rule requires perfect tender in every respect. Here, while the number of shutters shipped was correct (500), the size was incorrect (4' x 8' versus 4' x 6'.) B is incorrect because while a correct statement of law, a shipment of nonconforming goods is both an acceptance and a breach. Therefore, the builder is still able to reject the

nonconforming tender. D is incorrect because the builder still could reject non-conforming goods even if sent as an accommodation.

59. B is the correct answer. This contract is for teddy bears, which are goods. Therefore, the U.C.C. governs this contract. Under U.C.C. §2-508, a seller may seasonably notify the buyer of an intention to cure and may make a conforming delivery within the contract time, if a non-conforming tender or delivery is rejected. Here, the supplier notified the retailer of its intention to send the conforming tender (5,000 teddy bears dressed in Christmas outfits) by the December 1 deadline, and it did send them on November 28 (which was before the December 1 deadline). A is incorrect because, although the U.C.C. does not require consideration for modification of contracts for the sale of goods, the supplier's shipment on November 15 of nonconforming tender was not an attempted modification, but rather, a breach of contract, which was then cured by the conforming shipment on November 28. C is incorrect because the supplier's shipment on November 15 of nonconforming tender was not an anticipatory breach, but rather an actual breach of contract, which was then cured by the conforming shipment on November 28. D is incorrect because, although the November 15 shipment was a breach, the supplier timely cured this breach by sending conforming tender prior to the contract deadline of December 1.

60. A is the correct answer. The supplier accepted the grocery store's offer at the price of $5,000, creating a contract for that amount. The supplier bore the risk that it would be able to obtain the oranges at the wholesale price that had formed the basis of its $5,000 bid. B is incorrect because an unanticipated change of circumstances is not grounds for increasing a contract price because impracticability of performance requires an extreme change in circumstances, not merely an increase in price. C is incorrect because the supplier will not recover in quantum meruit because there is an actual contract and also, as explained in Answer A, the supplier bore the risk that it would have to operate at a loss. D is incorrect because the demand for $6,000 was an attempt to get more money, not to repudiate. Furthermore, the supplier did, in fact, end up delivering the oranges. Therefore, there was no repudiation here.

61. D is the correct answer. Based on the Doctrine of Promissory Estoppel, when a contractor detrimentally relies on the bid of a subcontractor in making its own bid on a project, the subcontractor is estopped from denying that an option contract was created, to the extent necessary to avoid injustice, when the contractor was induced to rely on the subcontractor's bid. Because the first wholesaler (subcontractor) failed to perform, the security company (contractor) may enforce its right to obtain the amount of its loss (the additional $1,000), based on the security com-

pany's reliance on the first wholesaler's promise to supply the burglar alarm component for $1,000. A, B and C are incorrect because D is the security company's best argument for the additional $1,000 for the reasons explained above.

62. A is the correct answer. There must be a meeting of the minds (mutual assent) between the parties in order to have a binding contract. Here, the contract merely stipulated that the bar owner would pay for all the "usual sponsoring fees." The facts indicate that the law student and the bar owner had different interpretations of what the "usual sponsoring fees" were. Hence, there was no meeting of the minds. Consequently, there was no contract. B, C and D are incorrect because they all indicate that a contract existed.

63. A is the correct answer. This offer is to sell fans, which are goods. It is, therefore, governed by the U.C.C. The U.C.C. §2-205 "firm offer" rule provides that where a merchant makes a signed, written offer to buy or sell goods that gives assurances that it will be held open, the offer is irrevocable, absent consideration, during the stated period or, if no time is stated, for a reasonable time (not to exceed three months). Here, the offer was made by a fan wholesaler, which is a merchant. The offer was made in a signed letter, and it promised to hold the offer open until June 1, which was less than three months later. Therefore, the offer could not be revoked until June 1. B is incorrect because being a merchant is not enough. As discussed in Answer A, the offer must not only be made by a merchant, but also must be a signed, written offer to buy or sell goods that gives assurances that it will be held open; such an offer is irrevocable, absent consideration, during the stated period or, if no time is stated, for a reasonable time (not to exceed three months). C is incorrect because the fan wholesaler's offer was a firm offer under the U.C.C. and not an option contract under the common law. Under the U.C.C.'s merchant's firm offer rule, the merchant's good faith serves as the consideration to hold the offer open. D is incorrect because the fan wholesaler made a firm offer that had to be held open until June 1, as discussed in Answer A. It is irrelevant whether or not the hardware store detrimentally relied on the offer.

64. D is the correct answer. This offer is to sell olives, which are goods. It is, therefore, governed by the U.C.C. U.C.C §2-207 provides that between merchants, additional terms become part of the contract, unless they materially alter it. Here, both the olive wholesaler and the restaurant owner are merchants because they regularly deal in goods of the kind (here, olives). Therefore, U.C.C. §2-207 is applicable here. In this case, requesting delivery of 150 pounds of fresh olives that could spoil in November instead of October, materially altered the terms of the contract. Thus, the court will give effect to the original terms of the offer (300 pounds of olives

for October delivery) and not add the proposed additional terms. A is incorrect because, under the U.C.C., any reasonable means of acceptance is allowed. B is incorrect because, as described in Answer D, the proposal of additional terms will not operate as a rejection or a counteroffer. However because they materially altered the terms of the contract in this case, the proposed additional terms here will not become part of the contract. C is incorrect for the reasons stated in the explanation to Answer D.

65. B is the correct answer. This offer is for mattresses, which are goods. It is, therefore, governed by the U.C.C. Under U.C.C. §2-607(3), a buyer who accepts tender of goods from a seller, must notify the seller of any breach within a reasonable time after he discovers or should have discovered the breach, or he is barred from any remedy. Since the mattress store accepted the nonconforming mattresses, it must notify the wholesaler that the mattresses do not conform to the mattress store's order in order to have any remedy against the wholesaler. A is incorrect for the reasons discussed in Answer B. C is incorrect because acceptance of nonconforming goods does not constitute a waiver of remedies. D is incorrect because risk of loss is not at issue in these facts.

66. B is the correct answer. Where a party expressed a future inability to perform, he has not repudiated the contract. Anticipatory repudiation occurs where one party to an executory bilateral contract repudiates the contract in advance of the time set for performance, by stating unequivocally that he will not perform the contract. Here, the contractor did not breach the contract by repudiation when he stated he did not think he could perform the remodeling work at the original contracting price. The contractor's statement was not unequivocal (merely "I think"). Therefore, the contractor will prevail because he attempted to perform the original contracting work as contractually agreed. A is incorrect because the hotel owner was not required to inform the contractor that he was hiring another contractor because as discussed in Answer B, the contractor did not commit an anticipatory repudiation of the contract. C is incorrect because the original contractor had not yet breached, as discussed in Answer B. Therefore, the hotel owner was obligated to allow the original contractor to perform. D is incorrect because the letter was not an anticipatory breach, for the reasons discussed in Answer B.

67. A is the correct answer. The bar candidate is entitled to the damages he suffered as a result of the loss of his bargain with the original tutor. Loss of bargain damages are measured by the difference between contract price and the price to receive replacement services. Here, the bar candidate was forced to hire another tutor. Since the new tutor charged $7,500 (an additional $2,500) the bar candidate is entitled to the $2,500 difference. B is incorrect because the bar candidate never paid

the $5,000 to the original tutor. The bar candidate's dissatisfaction with the second tutor is irrelevant here. C is incorrect both because he never paid the first tutor and because to give him both the $5,000 he would have paid the first tutor and the $7,500 that he paid to the second tutor would cause the bar candidate to be unjustly enriched. D is incorrect because the payment for tutoring services is not contingent upon passage of the bar exam, unless so specified in the contract. Here, the facts do not indicate that there was such a provision in the contract.

68. C is the correct answer. The buyer and the owner made a contract that was expressed in a writing. By signing, they both agreed that writing was a complete and accurate integration of all terms. ("All terms are incorporated.") The Parol Evidence Rule prohibits the introduction of any terms made prior to or contemporaneously with the signing of a fully integrated contract to vary or contradict the terms of the writing. Here, the buyer seeks to introduce the fact that the buyer and the owner orally agreed on December 1 that upon the buyer's payment of $1,000 to the owner, the offer to sell the ranch would remain open for thirty days. The December 5 written agreement made no reference to either the oral agreement for the buyer to pay $1,000 to hold the offer open, or to the owner's agreement to hold the offer open for thirty days. As discussed, by its own terms, the written agreement was a full integration.

Therefore, since the buyer signed this fully integrated written agreement, the buyer cannot now cite the oral agreement because the oral agreement (December 1) occurred prior to the written agreement (December 5), and the written agreement made no mention of the terms of the oral agreement. To allow the buyer's testimony would be a direct violation of the Parol Evidence Rule.

A is incorrect for the reasons stated in C. The Parol Evidence Rule does not permit the introduction of prior or contemporaneous oral terms that contradict the terms of the parties' fully integrated written agreement. B is an incorrect statement of law. The Parol Evidence Rule only applies to prior or contemporaneous terms, not subsequent oral modification. D is irrelevant to the facts as stated. The buyer has taken no actions to his detriment in reliance on the agreement. Even his attempt to tender $150,000 was refused by the owner, and the $1,000 was refunded, so the buyer did not lose this money. Furthermore, the facts do not indicate that the buyer passed up opportunities to purchase other properties in reliance on the owner's promise to sell him the ranch. Therefore, there was no promissory estoppel issue here.

69. B is the correct answer. A mutual mistake is grounds for rescission of a contract. Here both parties erroneously thought there would not be any change to the highway during the term of the ten-year lease (a mutual mistake). However, the

city's reconstruction of the highway was not anticipated by either the tenant or the owner at the time of the contract. Therefore, when the city reconstructed the highway and it caused substantial loss of business to the tenant, the tenant should not be held liable for rent for the remaining term. The tenant should be able to rescind the original contract due to this mutual mistake. Here, the tenant attempted to renegotiate the contract, but the building owner refused. Thus, the building owner is not entitled to rent for the remaining term. A is incorrect because it is not objectively impossible to pay the rent. C is incorrect because the tenant did not assume the risk where, as here, there was a mutual mistake as to a significant fact (in this case, that the highway would continue to lead to the shop). D is incorrect because there was a mutual mistake, which would allow the tenant to rescind the balance of the contract.

70. D is the correct answer. Since the first actress failed to perform first, if the court finds that her failure was not a material breach, the producer's duties to fulfill the contract and allow the first actress to return to work would not be excused. Here, the first actress' inability to perform for one week of a six-week contract would probably not be considered to be a material failure of performance by the first actress. A is incorrect because the contract called for performance as a whole, not weekly units. B is incorrect because her performance is not objectively impossible. She was merely sick for one of the six weeks. C is incorrect because reliance and promissory estoppel are only applicable when there is no contract. Because there is a contract here, these doctrines do not apply under these facts.

71. A is the correct answer. A contract for the sale of an interest in land must be in writing to be enforceable. Here, the agreement between the buyer and the seller was for an interest in land. However, it was oral. Thus, it is not enforceable and the buyer will prevail. B is incorrect because there is nothing in the facts to indicate that the price of the land was unconscionable here. C is incorrect because, as discussed in Answer A, the agreement here had to be in writing to be enforceable. Therefore, the buyer was not in breach by refusing to purchase the land. D is incorrect because there is nothing in the facts to indicate that the seller detrimentally relied on the buyer's promise to purchase the land.

72. C is the correct answer. The Parol Evidence Rule provides when a written contract is entered into between parties where the writing is intended to be the full and complete integration of their agreement, evidence of prior or written terms will not be permitted for the purpose of changing or altering the written terms. However, there are exceptions to the rule: fraud, duress, mistake, illegality and lack of consideration. Here, the typist mistakenly put in the term $1,000 instead of $10,000. Thus, parol evidence could be introduced to show the actual price for the water because of the

mistake. A is incorrect because the writing was intended as a full integration, not as a sham. B is incorrect because this contract was a full and not a partial integration, since it contained a merger clause, as discussed in the facts. D is incorrect because there was no misunderstanding between the supplier and the grocery store owner concerning the purchase price; there was a mistake in the written contract of which neither was aware at the time the contract was signed.

73. B is the correct answer. A contract is not enforceable, unless it is supported by consideration. Since the facts do not indicate that the woman gave any consideration in exchange for the man's promise to pay for her expenses in connection with the accident, no contract was formed based upon these facts. A is incorrect because the Statute of Frauds does not apply to promises that can be performed in less than one year. Here, the man's payment to the woman could be made in less than one year. Consequently, the Statute of Frauds does not apply here. C is incorrect because there is nothing in the facts to indicate that the woman relied on the man's promise. D is incorrect because there is no such thing as a "mere promise" in contract law; some promises are enforceable, while others are not. Here, for the reasons discussed in Answer B, this particular promise was not enforceable due to lack of consideration.

74. C is the correct answer because the father told the tutor he would pay her fees before she began tutoring the law student. This constituted consideration because it is a bargained for exchange (tutoring in exchange for the father's payment). A is incorrect because there was consideration here, as discussed in Answer C. B is incorrect because there was no provision in the contract between the father and the tutor that made payment contingent upon the father's personal satisfaction with the tutoring services. D is incorrect because unjust enrichment is an equitable remedy and, here, there are legal remedies (monetary damages that the tutor would recover in the lawsuit). Therefore, a court would never need to reach the issue of unjust enrichment of the law student.

75. A is the correct answer. Since the man performed his services in mowing the neighbor's lawn, the neighbor received a benefit. To allow the neighbor not to pay would, therefore, cause the neighbor to be unjustly enriched. B is incorrect because previous course of dealing only applies under the U.C.C. The agreement here dealt with mowing a lawn, which is a service covered by the common law. C is incorrect because this was an act that could be completed in less than one year. Thus, it was not required to be in writing. D is incorrect because, while there may have been no consideration here and, thus, no legal remedies available, quasi-contractual relief is available here to prevent unjust enrichment, as discussed in Answer A.

76. A is the correct answer. This contract was for the sale of a car, which is a good. Therefore, the agreement is

governed by the U.C.C. Under the U.C.C., contracts for the sale of goods in excess of $500 must be in writing to be enforceable. The oral agreement here was for the sale of a car for $600 and, therefore, needed to be in writing to be enforced. Consequently, the oral agreement here was not enforceable, and the man did not have to sell the woman his car. B is incorrect because, although the man is a non-merchant, this would not be grounds for his refusal to sell the vehicle to the woman, since the U.C.C. governs the sale of goods by non-merchants, as well as by merchants. C is incorrect because, although the woman is a non-merchant, the U.C.C. Statute of Frauds applies to both merchants and non-merchants. D is incorrect because, although this contract could be performed in less than a year (in this case, in one day), the U.C.C. Statute of Frauds applies to the sale of goods in excess of $500, as discussed in Answer A.

77. B is the correct answer. The Statute of Frauds requires a contract for the sale of land to be in writing to be enforceable. However, partial performance by the buyer (entering the property and making improvements) takes the oral agreement outside of the Statute of Frauds. Therefore, the agreement here does not need to be in writing to be enforced. A is incorrect because detrimental reliance is not an exception to the Statute of Frauds. C is incorrect because, as discussed in Answer B, not all contracts for the sale of land must be in writing to be enforced. Partial performance by the buyer (entering the property and making improvements) takes this oral agreement outside of the Statute of Frauds. D is incorrect because the contract was supported by consideration and because, for the reasons discussed in Answer B, the buyer will prevail.

78. B is the correct answer. Where parties enter into a transaction under a mistake regarding a material fact assumed by each party, which is the basis of the bargain for which they enter into the contact, the contract is voidable by either party, if enforcement would materially alter that which was bargained for. Here, the collector bargained for an actual rare coin that turned out to be counterfeit. The dealer, having examined the coin prior to his purchase, also believed that the coin was a rare coin. Thus, both parties were mistaken as to the authenticity of the coin. Because both parties were mistaken as to the material fact of the coin's authenticity, the contract can be rescinded. A is incorrect because there was no misrepresentation here, since both parties believed the coin to legitimately be a rare coin. C is incorrect because a warranty was not required under these circumstances. D is incorrect because assumption of the risk does not apply when both parties are mistaken as to a material fact.

79. A is the correct answer. Contracts entered into by minors, except for necessities, are voidable at the election of the minor, and may be disaffirmed by

the minor during minority or within a reasonable time after reaching majority. The continuing payments and use of the television by the teenager after reaching the age of majority constituted affirmation of the contract. B is incorrect because, as discussed in Answer A, a minor can disaffirm a contract within a reasonable time after reaching the age of majority. C is incorrect because contracts entered into by minors are voidable, not void. This means that, as discussed in Answer A, the minor can disaffirm the contract within a reasonable time after reaching majority. However, if he fails to do so, the contract is affirmed and enforceable. D is incorrect because, under the majority rule, a minor does not have to return the merchandise to have a valid disaffirmance.

80. D is the correct answer. A contract entered into by a minor is voidable and can be disaffirmed up until majority or a reasonable time thereafter. Here, the boy was sixteen years old at the time of the contract, and he was still a minor at the time he disaffirmed. A is incorrect because the majority rule does not require the minor to return the merchandise. B is incorrect because, as discussed in Answer D, a contract entered into by a minor is voidable and can be disaffirmed up until majority or a reasonable time thereafter. Here, the boy disaffirmed the contract while still a minor and, therefore, did not have to make any payments. C is incorrect because there is no such law.

81. C is correct because a seller has a duty to disclose any information involving latent dangerous conditions on the property. The prior owner had knowledge of the contaminated well and failed to disclose this information to the woman. This amounted to a fraudulent misrepresentation. A and B are incorrect because it incorrectly states the law. A is incorrect because there is a duty to disclose information, whether or not it was discovered after the woman looked at the property, if the information deals with latent dangerous conditions on the property. B is incorrect because the close of escrow did not release the prior owner from the obligation to disclose. D is incorrect because fraudulent misrepresentation is a basis to rescind a contract.

82. A is the correct answer. The contractor's omission of a significant amount of money from the bid was a material, unilateral mistake. A unilateral mistake is grounds for rescission where the party that wishes to rescind has adequate legal grounds to rescind. A unilateral mistake is such a ground. A unilateral mistake means a mistake made by only one of the parties. Here, there was a unilateral mistake by the contractor. B is incorrect because it is an incorrect statement of law. Unjust enrichment refers to one party getting goods or services to which it is not legally entitled; the party is required to return the property it has unjustly obtained. Here, the city has not yet obtained any benefits or property from the contractor and has, thus, not

been unjustly enriched because the contractor has not performed. C is incorrect because it assumes facts not given in the question. D is incorrect because a submitted bid can be withdrawn prior to its acceptance, as here.

83. C is the correct answer. Under the U.C.C., when the contract requires buyer's payment before he inspects the goods, such payment does not impair the buyer's right of inspection or his remedies in the case of nonconforming goods. A is incorrect because when a contract calls for payment for goods prior to inspection of the goods, receipt and payment of the goods does not constitute an acceptance of the goods for the reasons explained in Answer C. B is incorrect because, as stated in Answer C, pre-inspection payment does not constitute a waiver of any of the buyer's remedies. Therefore, the buyer has retained his right to inspect the pinball machines, despite his payment for them. D is incorrect because pre-inspection payment clauses are not invalid.

84. C is the correct answer because it is a correct statement of the amount of damages recoverable to a buyer when the seller has tendered nonconforming goods. The fabric company will seek damages in the amount of the price paid, plus an amount for reimbursement of the price to purchase substitute (No. 1 quality) goods. A is incorrect because specific performance is an equitable remedy that is not available, if legal damages are adequate. Here, damages are an adequate remedy, as discussed in Answer C. B is incorrect, for the reasons discussed in answer C. D is incorrect because, under the U.C.C. Perfect Tender Rule, the goods tendered must conform perfectly to what is called for in the contract. It is irrelevant if the nonconforming goods are of equal value.

85. B is the correct answer. Under the U.C.C., if a seller does not give the buyer instructions on how to dispose of non-conforming goods, a buyer may resell the goods, store the goods, or reship the goods back to seller. If the buyer intends to resell the goods at a private sale, it must give the seller reasonable notice of its intention to do so. Here, the electronics store was not given instructions on how to dispose of the nonconforming printers. It is, therefore, within its rights to resell them at a private sale, so long as it gives reasonable notice to the wholesaler that this is how it will dispose of the nonconforming printers. A is incorrect because it does not address the requirement that notice be given to the seller of the nonconforming goods (here, the wholesaler). C is incorrect because the buyer (here, the electronics store) may sell at either a public or a private sale, so long as it gives reasonable notice to the seller (here, the wholesaler). D is incorrect because the claim that goods are nonconforming has no connection with the method by which the recipient of the nonconforming goods disposes

of them. Here, the electronics store has elected to dispose of the nonconforming printers by selling them, which it is allowed to do, as discussed in Answer B.

86. A is the correct answer. The woman's offer stated, "If you will pick up the computer at my office this coming Friday at five o'clock in the afternoon, I will sell it to you for $1,000." The woman's letter was an offer for a unilateral contract, which can only be accepted by the doing of the act requested in the offer and not by a return promise. Here, the man made a return promise only; he did not do the act requested (picking up the computer). B is incorrect because a unilateral contract would only be formed when the man performed the required act of coming to the office to pick up a computer, not by the man mailing a letter promising to do so. C is incorrect because notice is irrelevant here. As discussed in Answer A, the woman's offer could only be accepted by doing the act requested (picking up the computer). D is incorrect because as discussed in Answer A, this was an offer for a unilateral contract; the man's letter, thus, had no legal effect.

87. C is the correct answer. The woman's offer was to sell a typewriter, which is a good. Therefore, the offer is governed by the U.C.C. U.C.C. §2-205 states that an offer made by a merchant will be irrevocable for a period up to three months without any consideration (good faith serves as the consideration) under the firm offer rule. Here, however, the woman was not a merchant (she did not deal regularly in goods of the kind, namely, typewriters). Thus, the merchant's firm offer rule does not apply here. Hence, the only way that the woman's promise to keep the offer open could be binding would be if there were consideration. Since the man gave no consideration here, the woman's promise has no effect. A is incorrect because it does not prevent the woman from revoking the offer, for the reasons discussed in Answer C. B is incorrect both because the woman did state a date for termination (five o'clock that day) and because, as discussed in Answer C, stating a date would not make this promise binding on the woman. D is incorrect because, as discussed in Answer C, the woman was free to revoke the offer in any manner, express or implied.

88. B is the correct answer. The man had an option to purchase the mare for 60 days. A mare is considered a good. Thus, this contract is governed by the U.C.C. Since neither the woman nor the man are merchants, the offer would only be held open if consideration is given because the merchant's firm offer rule only applies to offers made by merchants. Here, the man gave the woman $100. In exchange, she agreed to hold the offer open for 60 days from April 1. Therefore, when the man wrote to her on April 5, (which was less than 60 days later) accepting the offer, the woman's offer was still open (even though she sold the mare to another party on April

4). Thus, the man could still accept the offer and successfully sue the woman for damages. A is incorrect because the woman could sell the mare to another party after sixty days, as discussed in Answer B. C is incorrect because any amount of money – even $1 – is sufficient consideration. D is incorrect because, as discussed in Answer B, her offer had to be held open for 60 days, and no action that the woman could take (including selling the mare) would revoke the offer.

89. D is the correct answer because a counteroffer in an option contract (here, the neighbor's offer to pay $400 instead of $500 for the piano) does not terminate the power to accept the offer in and of itself. However, if the offeror (the woman) detrimentally relies upon the counteroffer as a rejection of the original offer, the offeree (the neighbor) can no longer accept the original offer. Here, the woman detrimentally relied on the neighbor's counteroffer as a rejection of her original offer and sold the piano to another person. A is incorrect because, as discussed in Answer D, the neighbor's power to accept terminated when the woman detrimentally relied on his counteroffer as a rejection of the original offer by selling the piano to somebody else on March 15. B is incorrect because, as discussed in Answer D, the neighbor's power to accept the offer did not terminate on March 11 (when the neighbor made the counteroffer). Rather, it terminated on March 15, when the woman detrimentally relied on his counteroffer as a rejection of the original offer by selling the piano to somebody else. C is incorrect because the woman's receipt of the neighbor's counteroffer did not terminate the neighbor's power to accept. Rather, the neighbor's power to accept terminated on March 15, when the woman detrimentally relied on his counteroffer as a rejection of the original offer by selling the piano to somebody else.

90. C is the correct answer. The contract here is for the sale of ice chests, which are goods. Therefore, the U.C.C. governs this contract. Furthermore, the parties are both merchants (a convenience store owner and a grocery store owner). Under U.C.C. §2-207, proposed new terms in a contract between merchants do not terminate the offer and become part of that contract, unless: (1) the offer is limited to its own terms; (2) the terms materially alter the contract; and (3) the offeror objects within a reasonable time. Here, the offeror (the convenience store owner) did not limit the offer to its own terms. Also, the fact that the grocery store owner was willing to pay the storage fees does not appear to materially alter the contract. Finally, the offeror (the convenience store owner) did not object to the new terms. Therefore, the additional terms became part of the contract and the convenience store owner must store the ice chests. A is incorrect because this contract is governed by the U.C.C. Under the U.C.C., additional terms may be added to an offer without it being a

counteroffer, as discussed in Answer C. The acceptance does not have to be a mirror image, as is required under the common law. B is an incorrect statement of fact, since the additional terms were definite. D is incorrect because, as discussed in Answer C, the additional terms (regarding storage of the ice chests) did become part of the contract. Therefore, the convenience store owner may not refuse to store them.

91. B is the correct answer. A bilateral contract consists of a promise in exchange for a promise. Here, the original owners of the company agreed to give the man lifetime employment in exchange for a reduced wage (the bilateral promises) and the new owners agreed to honor all existing employment contracts, which would necessarily include this one. A is incorrect because in these facts, the new owners agreed to honor the existing contracts. C and D are incorrect because they misstate the common law. Under these facts, there was a bilateral contract, not a unilateral contract, and under the common law, someone may enter into a lifetime employment contract.

92. B is the correct answer. The glass manufacturer will be able to show that there is a valid contract because the signed letter that the window manufacturer sent to the glass manufacturer attempting to cancel the balance of the order contained all of the necessary terms needed to satisfy the Statute of Frauds' requirement of a sufficient memorandum under the U.C.C. Therefore, although the initial agreement was oral, the window manufacturer will not be able to successfully assert the Statute of Frauds in order to cancel the balance of the oral agreement because the signed letter satisfied the Statute of Frauds. A is incorrect because, without the memo, the window manufacturer is only liable for the panes it has accepted since that portion of the oral agreement has been performed by the glass manufacturer. C is incorrect because a repudiation by one party does not terminate a valid contract. D is incorrect because the note does satisfy the Statute of Frauds.

93. B is the correct answer. For the general contractor to win, it must be shown that he neither had actual nor constructive knowledge of the sub-contractor's miscalculation. Here, the sub-contractor had submitted a bill for $80,000 and the next lowest bill was $85,000, with other bids ranging as high as $87,500. It could be argued that since the sub-contractor's bid was so much lower, the general contractor was on constructive knowledge of the sub-contractor's miscalculation. However, the sub-contractor may just have been wanting the business and was willing to charge less. It, therefore, cannot be definitively said that the general contractor was on constructive notice of the sub-contractor's miscalculation. A is incorrect because the sub-contractor would not be bound by the contract, if the general contractor knew of the miscalculation. C is incorrect because there is no rule requiring

general contractors to accept higher bids. D is incorrect because there was an anticipatory breach of contract by the sub-contractor when he unequivocally refused to do the work for $80,000. Because the refusal was unequivocal, the general contractor was not required to wait until the performance due date, since the sub-contractor's anticipatory breach occurred at the moment he refused to do the work.

94. A is the correct answer. This was a contract for piano lessons, which are services. Thus, this contract is governed by the common law. The piano teacher was under a pre-existing duty to do the work for $500. A change in contract terms requires consideration under the common law. Here, there was no consideration to support the parent promising to pay the additional $100. B is incorrect because there is nothing in the facts to indicate that an additional $100 is unconscionable for piano lessons. C is incorrect because of the pre-existing duty, as discussed in Answer A. D is incorrect because, as discussed in Answer A, there was no consideration to support this change. Mutual agreement does not satisfy the common law's consideration requirement for changes to contract terms.

95. C is the correct answer. In order for a term in a contract to be considered a condition, the contract must contain words such as "condition," "on condition," "proviso," "if," etc. Here, although the contract included a provision stating that all records describing the coins were to be kept off the store premises in a place where they would not be stolen, the contract did not contain any of the above language. As a result, this provision did not constitute a condition and failure to comply with this term cannot in and of itself be used as a reason to deny an insurance claim here. Since the owner had no reason to expect that his shop would be burglarized, his leaving the records in the shop for one night essentially complied with the provision. A is incorrect because the coin dealer had attempted to fulfill his performance under the contract, and as discussed, this term was not a condition of the contract. Thus, the contract was not breached. B is incorrect because, while the contract did state this requirement, it was not a condition for the reasons discussed. D is an incorrect statement of law. Unfairness will not in and of itself relieve a party of the obligation to perform under a contract.

96. D is the correct answer. When the offeree dispatches an acceptance and changes his mind and dispatches a repudiation, when such repudiation reaches the offeror first, there is, nevertheless, a valid contract, unless the offeror relies to his detriment on the rejection. Here, the man signed and mailed the contract back to the woman. This is an acceptance. Under the mailbox rule, acceptances are effective upon dispatch. Therefore, when the man signed and mailed the contract back to the woman, a valid contract was

formed. Even though the man called the woman and told her to ignore the signed contract, by this time it was too late, since a valid contract had already been formed. There are no facts indicating that the woman relied to her detriment on the man's repudiation. In fact, she is attempting to enforce the contract by the lawsuit. A is incorrect because, as discussed in Answer D, acceptances are effective upon dispatch, not upon receipt. B is incorrect because as discussed in Answer D, the Mailbox Rule deems the mail an effective source of communication. C is incorrect because the telephone is a reasonable method of communication, under these circumstances. Furthermore, as discussed in Answer D, the telephone call was ineffective here because the call was made after the acceptance was dispatched.

97. A is the correct answer. The parties to a valid bilateral contract that is executory (unperformed) on each side may agree to a discharge of all contractual duties. The consideration is provided by each party's discharge of the other's duties. Here, when the woman contacted the man on March 5 and informed him that she no longer required the tutoring services, and the man accepted and stated that he no longer wished to perform the tutoring services for her, these actions constituted a mutual agreement to discharge all contractual duties. B is incorrect because there was mutual assent when the man accepted the woman's offer to pay him for tutoring. C is an incorrect statement of law.

As demonstrated in Answer A, contracts may be rescinded. D is incorrect for the reasons discussed in Answer A. There was mutual consideration for the discharge of the duties.

98. D is the correct answer. In these facts, there was a mistake in computation that was made by the painter's foreman. This mistake was unilateral because only one party (the painter, through his foreman) made the mistake. If the nonmistaken party (here, the homeowner) did not know or should not have known of the mistake, then the nonmistaken party can recover in a breach of contract action. Here, the homeowner was unaware that the painter's bid was made through error. Therefore, unless the homeowner should have known of the mistake (he had previously received bids for $6,000 to $7,500, and the painter's bid was $5,500), then the homeowner could recover for breach of contract because the prior bids may not have been enough to put the homeowner on notice. A is legally irrelevant because the painter contracted the homeowner on December 30 and stated that he could not do the work for less than $6,100. This would be considered to be an anticipatory repudiation because the painter unequivocally stated that he would not perform for less than $6,100, and he was already under a duty to perform for $5,500. Thus, since the painter would be breaching the contract, he would not be able to recover. The fact that the painter had not started painting yet is not relevant because he was committing

an anticipatory breach. B is incorrect because the painter's mistake would not be grounds for him to recover, if the homeowner was not aware (or should not have been aware) of the mistake, as discussed in Answer D. C is incorrect because whether or not the homeowner could still accept bids is irrelevant.

99. B is the correct answer. This contract is for extermination work in a home, which is a service. Thus, this contract is governed by the common law. Here, the exterminator was under a pre-existing duty to spray the homeowner's home for $2,000. The homeowner's promise to pay an additional $500 was not supported by consideration, as required by common law for modifications to contract terms. Thus, the homeowner will not be required to pay the additional $500. A is incorrect because there is no requirement that a promise to pay additional money must be in writing. As discussed in Answer B, this is a service contract, and the U.C.C. requirement that contracts for the sale of goods over $500 be in writing is not applicable to contracts for services over $500. C is incorrect because there was no detrimental reliance here, since the exterminator already had a duty to exterminate the homeowner's home, anyway, as per the original contract. D is incorrect because there is no such public policy requirement to enforce modifications of common law contracts without consideration, especially where, as here, the exterminator already had a duty to perform under the terms of the original contract, as discussed above.

100. C is the correct answer. This contract is for hauling goods, which is a service and is, thus, governed by the common law. At common law, there must be new consideration for a modification of a contract. Here, the shipper asked the truck driver to haul additional goods to Pennsylvania, in exchange for the additional payment of $500. The shipper and the truck driver had a bargained-for exchange: $500 for extra work. Therefore, the truck driver will prevail because there was a valid modification of the original contract. A is incorrect because the truck driver was only under a pre-existing duty to haul the original goods to New York. The duty to haul new goods to Pennsylvania was new and only came about through valid modification of the contract, as discussed in Answer C. B is incorrect because, as discussed in Answer C, this is a service contract, and the U.C.C. requirement that contracts for the sale of goods over $500 be in writing is not applicable to contracts for services over $500. D is incorrect because "detrimental reliance" is used where a substitute for consideration is required. Here, there was a valid modification supported by consideration, as discussed in Answer C.

101. A is the correct answer. The U.C.C. would not apply to this contract, since it involves services (namely, the installation of plumbing), rather than goods. Even though goods are partially involved in this contract (namely, the plumbing equipment being installed),

the primary purpose of this contract is the installation of the plumbing equipment, and installation is a service, rather than a good. Therefore, the common law is applied here. Although U.C.C. §2-609 permits a party to a sales contract to demand "assurance of performance," the U.C.C. would not apply to this fact pattern. Therefore, A is correct and D is incorrect. B is incorrect, both because there is nothing in this fact pattern to suggest that the subcontractor intended to do the work himself, and because it is irrelevant. C is incorrect because the first subcontractor was not in breach because the common law does not require the subcontractor to explain why his workers were on strike or to give assurances in advance that the work would still be done. Therefore, the contractor should not have hired another subcontractor.

102. B is the best answer. All contracts require consideration, which is a bargained-for exchange. Here, the woman did nothing in exchange for the man's promise to purchase the diamond ring. Therefore, there was no consideration here. A is incorrect because an illusory promise generally arises where one party makes a promise in exchange for a promise that does not limit the other's future options. Here, as discussed the woman made no promise in exchange for the man's promise, so no issue of illusory promise arises. C is incorrect because the Statute of Frauds is a defense to contract formation. Because there was no consideration here, as discussed in Answer B, there was no need to reach any defenses to formation (Statute of Frauds or otherwise). D is incorrect because mutual assent is irrelevant where there is no consideration to make it binding. As discussed in Answer B, there was no consideration here.

103. C is the correct answer. Here, the nursing home turned down other applicants in anticipation of the man's mother coming to live there. This is an example of detrimental reliance, which is a consideration substitute. Thus, the nursing home will prevail for this reason. A is incorrect because under common law, contracts that can be performed in less than one year do not have to be in writing. Here, no one knows how long the mother would end up living in the nursing home. It is possible that she could die in less than one year. This is equivalent to a lifetime contract, which does not have to be in writing. B is incorrect because this is a temporary frustration of purpose, not a complete frustration of purpose. Once the mother recovered, she still could move into the nursing home. D is incorrect because this is not a legal principal.

104. D is the correct answer. There is a bargained-for-exchange under these facts. Here, the father agreed to pay, if the creditor did not file a claim against the son's estate. The creditor did not file the claim. This is called a forbearance. Forbearance is a valid form of

consideration. Thus, the creditor will be successful in its lawsuit. A is incorrect both because the lawsuit is against the father - not against a deceased person – and because deceased people can be sued (through their estates). B is incorrect because, as discussed in Answer D, there was consideration here (forbearance). C is incorrect because detrimental reliance is a consideration substitute. As discussed in Answer D, there was consideration here. Thus, consideration substitutes were not needed under these facts.

105. D is the correct answer. Where the inducement of a party's promise is a past event or benefit, the past consideration is not sufficient to render the party's promise enforceable. Here, the woman's landscaping work was completed before the man ever promised to install the woman's water heater. It is, therefore, past consideration and does not form the basis for an enforceable right. A is incorrect because the consideration was past consideration, as discussed. B is an incorrect statement of fact because, as discussed the consideration was past consideration and, therefore, does not give rise to a duty to perform. C is an incorrect statement, as applied to these facts. Involuntary servitude requires forced labor for no payment. Here, the man voluntarily made a promise to install the water heater. Consequently, if he were to do so, it would not be involuntary servitude.

106. B is the correct answer. An assignee takes a contract subject to defenses against his assignor. If the roofer has not properly performed, this defense could be used by the building owner against the creditor (the assignee under these facts). A is incorrect because it is irrelevant whether or not the creditor is capable of applying a roof because under these facts, there is an assignment of rights (to receive payment), not a delegation of duties (to put on the roof). C is incorrect because an agreement not to assign destroys the right, but not the power to assign, e.g., the right to receive payment. In other words, by assigning, the roofer was in breach, but the creditor was not. Therefore, the creditor still has a right to receive payment as an assignee. D is incorrect because the creditor is not claiming to be a third party beneficiary, but rather, is claiming to be an assignee. A third party beneficiary is known to the two contracting parties at the time of the contract, and his rights must become vested before he can sue. An assignee is one who receives rights after the contract has been formed. Because the creditor received his rights to payment after the contract was formed, the creditor is an assignee rather than a third party beneficiary.

107. A is the correct answer. In order for a third party beneficiary to prevail in a lawsuit, her rights must have vested. Vesting occurs when the third party beneficiary becomes aware of the agreement that is meant to benefit that person.

Here, the wife learned of the fact that she had been a beneficiary of the man's life insurance policy only after the man had changed his beneficiary from the wife to the daughter. The insurance contract gave the insured (the man) the power to change his beneficiary. Thus, the wife had no vested rights under the policy. B is incorrect because the wife never was an incidental beneficiary; she was an intended beneficiary, until the man changed the beneficiary from the wife to the daughter, as discussed in Answer A. C is incorrect because a wife may be provided for in ways other than through a life insurance policy (such as through a will). Thus, public policy does not have to be invoked to require the wife to be provided for through a life insurance policy. D is incorrect because, although at one time she was a donee beneficiary, the man used his power to change beneficiaries and made his daughter the sole beneficiary.

108. D is the correct answer. In order for a third party beneficiary to prevail in a lawsuit, her rights must have vested. Vesting occurs when the third party beneficiary becomes aware of the agreement that is meant to benefit that person. Here, the painter originally told the woman to pay the $5,000 to the girlfriend and informed the girlfriend of this fact. Thus, the girlfriend's rights vested and she will be able to sue the woman for the $5,000. The girlfriend is a donee beneficiary of the original contract between the woman and the painter because the facts indicate that the painter was giving the girlfriend a $5,000 gift. A is incorrect because, even though the painter later told the woman to pay him directly after he broke up with the girlfriend, the girlfriend's rights had already vested, as discussed in Answer D above. Thus, the girlfriend will prevail in her lawsuit for the $5,000. B is incorrect because there is no such public policy. A person is entitled to name anyone he wants as a beneficiary. C is incorrect because there are no facts to indicate that the girlfriend detrimentally relied on the painter's promise that she would be paid.

109. C is the correct answer. In order for a third party beneficiary to prevail in a lawsuit, her rights must have vested. Vesting occurs when the third party beneficiary becomes aware of the agreement that is meant to benefit that person. Here, the actor informed his girlfriend about the contract with the film producer. As soon as he did so, her rights vested. Even though the contract was freely assignable and the film producer was free to assign the contract to a studio (or to anyone else), the girlfriend's rights had vested and whoever had the duty to pay was required to pay the girlfriend. Because the duty to pay was assigned to the studio, the studio had the obligation to pay the girlfriend as per the terms of the original contract. A is incorrect because there is no such law. B is incorrect because, while the Screen Actor's Guild may state that performance can only be by a Guild actor, it does

not have the ability to determine who can and cannot be paid. D is incorrect because the girlfriend was a donee beneficiary, not a creditor beneficiary, since she was receiving a gift from the actor; there is nothing in the facts indicating that the actor owed her money.

110. D is the correct answer. The general rule is that the assignee is subject to the same defenses that the obligor has against the assignee. If the wedding planner had not performed properly, the bride would have a defense against her and could use this defense against the florist. Although the facts do not stipulate this dereliction in performance, the answer does. As a general strategy with multistate questions, it is better that all of the facts appear in the fact pattern. Nevertheless, when the three remaining options are clearly incorrect, as here, this kind of answer is correct. A is incorrect because the florist is an assignee, not a third party beneficiary. An assignee is one who receives rights after the contract has been formed. Because the florist received her rights to payment after the contract was formed, the florist is an assignee rather than a third party beneficiary. B is incorrect because the florist is an assignee rather than a third party beneficiary. As such, she is not required to detrimentally rely on the promise in order to have her rights enforced. C is a correct statement of law; however, furnishing the flowers would not be deemed to be a personal service and, thus, the special services rule would not be applicable.

111. D is the correct answer. A new promise to perform an obligation that is voidable will be enforced, so long as the new promise is not voidable for the same reasons. Here, the buyer's initial obligations were voidable due to the seller's fraud (namely, lying about the condition of the cabin). However, the buyer, fully aware of the fraud, then made a new promise in writing to pay the seller, despite the seller's fraud. The new promise is called a ratification. A and B are incorrect for the same reasons that D is correct. C is incorrect because the writing itself is not at issue based upon these facts, since no one here is asserting the Statute of Frauds as a defense against any contractual obligations.

112. D is the correct answer. This contract is for the sale of automobiles, which are goods. Thus, the contract is governed by the U.C.C. The U.C.C. Statute of Frauds requires that the sale of goods priced at $500 or more be in writing to be enforceable. Although the original agreement was oral (the agreement was for the sale of vehicles for $90,000, far in excess of the $500 requirement), a written confirmation between merchants may be binding on the party to be charged, without signing, if the receiving party fails to object within 10 days of receipt. Here, after receiving the car manufacturer's invoice for $90,000, the car dealership sent a letter of protest, identifying the existence of the contract at the discounted rate. Thus, the car dealership correctly asserted that the protest let-

ter was a sufficient writing to comply with the Statute of Frauds. Therefore, the car manufacturer will not prevail in its suit for the additional money. A is incorrect because the normal course of dealing between merchants can help to resolve an issue over price. However because there was a written protest (as discussed in Answer D), price is not at issue. Thus, under these facts, the normal course of dealing is irrelevant. B is incorrect because, while a correct statement of law about the U.C.C.'s Statute of Frauds, there was a sufficient writing here, as discussed in Answer D. C is incorrect because the additional amount is not unconscionable, particularly given the fact that it is the normal price for the cars.

113. A is the correct answer. When a check marked "payment in full" is cashed for a disputed debt, the courts generally regard it as evidencing an accord and satisfaction with the debtor. Here, there is a disputed debt (the bookstore believes it owes $4,000 for the binders, while the supplier believes it is owed $5,000). The bookstore's check was marked "paid in full," and the supplier cashed it. Therefore, the bookstore's best argument is accord and satisfaction. Answer B is incorrect because the Doctrine of Promissory Estoppel applies as a consideration substitute when consideration is at issue. Here, the consideration was the money for the binders and is, therefore, not at issue. Answers C and D are incorrect because the Doctrine of Novation (implied or express) is not applicable in this fact pattern because novation involves the addition of a new party to a contract, and no new party was added here.

114. C is the correct answer. An implied novation occurs where: there has been (1) an effective delegation; (2) the obligor repudiates liability to the obligee; and (3) the obligee accepts performance of the delegatee, without reserving rights against the obligor. Here, there has been an effective delegation by the husband to the wife, and the estate seller is aware of this delegation. The wife is unable to pay more than $4,000 on her $5,000 obligation, and she repudiates her liability to the estate seller for the additional $1,000. The fact that the wife has paid and the estate seller has accepted $4,000 without reserving any rights against the husband indicates that obligee (here, the estate seller) has accepted performance from the delegatee (here, the wife) without reserving any rights against the husband. Thus, there is an implied novation, since all of the above elements have been met. This would be the husband's best argument that he does not owe the extra $1,000. A is incorrect because accord and satisfaction requires the wife to have written "paid in full" on the $4,000 check, which she did not do here. B is incorrect because the initial contract between the antique store and the estate seller was in writing. D is incorrect because, since C is correct (for the reasons discussed above) a "None of the above" answer cannot be correct here.

115. B is the correct answer. This contract is for Ming Vases, which are goods. Thus, this contract is governed by the U.C.C. The U.C.C. provides that a buyer may receive specific performance, where the goods are unique (or in other proper circumstances), if a buyer is unable to find substitute goods. Here, the museum will be entitled to "cover" damages. Thus, it can purchase substitute Ming Vases from another supplier, if it can find them, and recover the difference in price from the original supplier. In the alternative, the museum may demand specific performance, if Ming Vases are considered to be unique goods, and damages may not be sufficient to make the museum whole. Thus, the museum can elect between the remedy of specific performance or damages. A is incorrect because if the Ming Vases are considered to be unique, the museum may be entitled to specific performance, as discussed in Answer B. C is incorrect because, as discussed in Answer B, the museum may be entitled to damages if it is able to find substitute Ming Vases. D is incorrect because one must elect remedies and cannot reform the contract.

116. B is the correct answer. A contract consists of a valid offer, acceptance, and consideration. An oral contract can be enforceable, so long as it does not violate the Statute of Frauds. Here, the woman orally offered to pay for her medical services and the doctor responded to her unilateral offer by treating her (acceptance). The consideration for this unilateral contract was the woman's offer to pay in exchange for the doctor's performance of the medical services. Therefore, there was a valid oral contract. A is an irrelevant statement of law because there was no need to look for an implied contract (under the Good Samaritan Rule) because there was already a valid oral contract, as discussed. C is incorrect because moral consideration is not legally valid consideration. D is incorrect because there was sufficient consideration.

117. A is the correct answer because it presumes the man was not incapacitated by his drinking. A reasonable person would have found the man's statement to be an offer, whether or not he made it in jest because the offer contained the subject matter (the rug) and the price. Therefore, the court will find a valid contract and the woman can most likely sue for specific performance. B is incorrect because the court will enforce the contract- most likely through specific performance. As discussed under these facts, it appears that the man knew what he was doing at the time he made the offer and there was, therefore, no temporary incapacity here. C is incorrect because, as discussed, the man was not incapacitated here. The woman did not seem incapacitated either, inasmuch as she rationally discussed her purchase of the rug and even recalled the transaction later when she wrote the check to the

man. D is incorrect because, whether or not the man's statement was made in jest, a reasonable person would find his statement to be an offer and such is the correct legal standard.

118. A is the correct answer. This contract was for the sale of linen, which is a good. Thus, the contract is governed by the U.C.C. The U.C.C. remedy for non-conforming goods is damages measured by the difference between the price of replacement conforming goods (cover) and the contract price. In these facts, the designer received non-conforming goods (they were not number one linen), and he returned those goods to the supplier and purchased replacement conforming goods at an increased price. Thus, he is entitled to the difference between the price of replacement conforming goods (cover) and the contract price. B is incorrect, since it misstates the law, regarding the measure of damages. C is incorrect because specific performance would only be applicable where the goods were unique or where damages would be inadequate. Here, the goods were not unique. Furthermore, as discussed in Answer A, damages were an adequate remedy. D is incorrect because, as discussed in Answer A, there are remedies available here.

119. C is the correct answer. This contract is for coffee, which is a good. Thus, it is governed by the U.C.C. U.C.C. §§2-711(3) and 2-706(2), (3), state that when a buyer has paid for goods that are nonconforming and buyer demands a refund, the buyer may resell the goods either at a private or public sale. However, if it is a private sale, reasonable advance notice must be given to the original seller. A and B are incorrect because the resale can occur at either a private sale or a public sale, as discussed in Answer C. D is incorrect because even non-conforming goods may be resold, as discussed in Answer C.

120. D is the correct answer. The facts tell us that this is a contract for the sale of goods. It is, thus, governed by the U.C.C. Under U.C.C. §2-512(2), pre-inspection payment does not act as a waiver of inspection or remedies. Answers A, B and C are incorrect statements of law because payment in advance of inspection is a valid contract provision under the U.C.C. It does not waive remedies or constitute an acceptance of the goods.

121. B is the correct answer. This contract is for landscaping, which is a service. Thus, this contract is governed by the common law. While personal services contracts ordinarily may not be delegated, here the personal services appear to be routine rather than unique (landscaping), and the duty will be found delegable. Here, the landscaper's son has a comparable reputation and, thus, the landscaper could assign his rights and delegate his duties under the contract to his son. The homeowner must accept performance by the son. A is incorrect because a novation oc-

curs when a new party takes over for an original contracting party and both original contracting parties agree to the new party. Here, there are no facts to indicate that the homeowner agreed to the son as a new party. The son was merely an assignee and delegatee of the original contract between the homeowner and the landscaper. C is incorrect because, as discussed in Answer B, the homeowner must accept performance by the son. D is incorrect because the original contract had no provision regarding assignments and, thus, the landscaper was not in breach of contract by assigning to his son.

122. C is the correct answer because the author has a cause of action against either the original proofreader or the co-worker, following the assignment and delegation to the co-worker. However, the author must first exhaust her remedies against the co-worker for the co-worker's poor performance before she can pursue remedies against the original proofreader (assignor). Answers A and B are incorrect because they are incomplete. As discussed in Answer C, the author has a cause of action against either the co-worker or the original proofreader. D is a misstatement of the law because there was no waiver by the author when she accepted performance by the co-worker. As discussed in Answer C, the author still has a cause of action against the original proofreader, even after the assignment and delegation to the co-worker.

123. B is the correct answer. The offer was a manifestation of an intent to be bound. It was very specific. It described the subject matter (skis), the amount ($250), and was directed to a specific group, (first come first serve.) Therefore, when the woman appeared at the ski shop and she was the first to arrive, she accepted the owner's unilateral offer by her performance. A is incorrect, since it is an offer – not merely an invitation to deal, as discussed. C is an incorrect statement of law. Advertisements can be either an offer or an invitation to bid, depending on their specificity. When an advertisement is found to be an offer (as here), then an acceptance of that offer along with valid consideration creates a binding contract; advertisements are not allowed to mislead as a way to "lure" customers. D is incorrect, for the same reasons that B is correct.

124. D is the correct answer. This contract is for cell phone service. It is, thus, governed by the common law. Under the common law, contracts may be assigned, even if the contract states that there can be no assignment without the consent of each party. When a party assigns a contract that contains such a provision against assignment and the party does not obtain the consent of the other party, the assigning party is in breach, and the non-assigning party is entitled to damages. However, the non-assigning party must accept the new assignee. Here, the contract between the original telephone company

and the woman contained a provision stating that the contract could not be assigned without the consent of the other party. Nonetheless, the original telephone company assigned to another company, and the woman was unaware of the assignment. Subsequently, the woman failed to pay her bill. Therefore, the new company was entitled to the outstanding balance that the woman still owes because the assignment to the new company was valid. A is incorrect because, as discussed in Answer D, the fact that the woman was unaware of the assignment at the time it occurred (and, thus, did not consent to the assignments) demonstrates that the original telephone company was in breach, but the woman must still accept and pay her bill to the new assignee. B is incorrect because, as discussed in Answer D, the assignment constituted a breach, but was nonetheless valid, and the new company (assignee) was entitled to bring an action against the woman and collect the outstanding balance. C is incorrect because there is no such law. Furthermore, punitive damages are almost never imposed in contract law.

125. A is the correct answer. This contract is for the sale of boats, which are goods. Thus, the contract is governed by the U.C.C. The contract states that the seller is to deliver 50 boats at $500 each, FOB seller's place of business. Thus, as soon as the boats leave the seller's place of business, the risk of loss shifts to the buyer. Here, the seller has delivered the boats to a carrier and the boats are destroyed in transit. Therefore, since the destruction of the boats has occurred after the boats have left the seller's place of business, the risk of loss has shifted to the buyer. Consequently, the buyer may not recover against the seller in its breach of contract action. B is incorrect because the seller had already delivered the boats to the carrier. The impossibility doctrine does not apply because the seller has already performed. C is incorrect because the buyer has the risk of loss, as discussed in Answer A. D is incorrect because there is no such public policy. Parties are free to contract for the risk of loss to pass however they wish.

126. B is the correct answer. The typographical error was a unilateral mistake. Further, the music lover would have known of the mistake, since people who know music would know that a Stradivarius is worth over a million dollars and $10,000 would be a highly unlikely offer for such an instrument. A is incorrect, since it is not the best answer. Specific performance is equitable in certain situations. However, due to the mistake here, it would be inequitable to enforce this agreement through specific performance. C and D are incorrect for the reasons stated in correct answer B.

127. A is the correct answer. A valid contract was not formed. This was a contract to put in wiring, which is a service. It is,

therefore, governed by the common law. Under the common law, acceptances must be mirror images of the offers. Here, the builder's offer stated that he would pay $2,000 for the wiring. The subcontractor did not accept the builder's offer in an unequivocal manner (mirror image), and, therefore, when the subcontractor said he would only do the work for $2,500, this was a counteroffer. Therefore, on May 27, there was no contract between the parties. Even though the subcontractor attempted to accept on May 28, saying that he would do the work for $2,000, the initial offer was no longer valid. Therefore, on June 1, there was no contract. B is incorrect because acceptance must be made by a reply, not conduct. As discussed, there was no contract here. C is incorrect because, as discussed, the subcontractor's May 28 letter was ineffective for the reasons discussed in A. D is incorrect because at that stipulated time, the subcontractor no longer had the power to accept the original offer, as discussed above.

128. D is the best defense. The Statute of Frauds requires that contracts that cannot be performed within one year must be in writing to be enforceable. Here, the man made an oral promise to pay the cousin's law school tuition for three years. Thus, by its terms, the contract could not be performed within one year. Therefore, the oral promise was not enforceable and is, thus, the man's best defense. A is incorrect because the cousin incurred the legal detriment of attending law school. B is incorrect because there is nothing in these facts to indicate that the man was not serious about his promise. C is incorrect because the facts indicate that the man was serious about his promise and the cousin attended law school in reliance on the man's promise, thus, indicating a contractual intent on the part of both parties.

129. D is the correct answer. The son joining the army would constitute valid consideration because it was something the son was not legally obligated to do. Thus, by taking on this obligation, the son had a legal detriment, which is the definition of consideration. The father's promise to pay would likewise constitute consideration on the father's part. A is incorrect because, as discussed in Answer D, there was consideration. B is incorrect because, as discussed in Answer D, there was a bargained-for exchange here. The promise was, thus, not gratuitous. C is incorrect because promissory estoppel is a more appropriate argument when there is a lack of consideration.

130. B is the correct answer. The man is entitled to sue on the basis of his bilateral contract with the woman. A bilateral contract is one in which there was a promise for a promise. Here, the woman promised to pay and the man promised to paint her house. A is incorrect because in a bilateral contract, the offeree's acceptance is by promise rather than by performance. Answer

A would be a correct answer, if this were a unilateral contract (which by definition entails a promise in exchange for an act). C is incorrect because it is irrelevant. There was a bargained-for-exchange and there are no issues of fraud, etc. relevant here. D is incorrect because performance (whether substantial or otherwise) is not the issue here. Once both sides had made their respective promises (and consideration was given), a bilateral contract was formed.

131. A is the correct answer. This notice is for winning a moot court competition, which is an action and is, thus, covered by the common law. For an offer to be valid under the common law, it must contain the following terms: quantity, time, identity of the parties, price, and subject matter. Here, the notice had all of the elements: $1,000 (price), moot court brief (subject matter), one brief (quantity), "by April 20" (time), and the parties (the school and the winning contestant). Therefore, the notice was a valid offer, which created a power of acceptance. B is incorrect because, as discussed in Answer A, this is a valid offer, not just an invitation to deal. C is incorrect because notices that meet all of the requirements for an offer are not made invalid merely because a specific offeree is not named. D is incorrect because the notice was, in fact, bargaining by trying to encourage moot court participation. Furthermore, this was not a promise, but rather an offer that created a power of acceptance, as discussed in Answer A.

132. C is the correct answer. The health foundation's offer was an offer for an act (winning the marathon), and full performance could only occur on the day of the marathon. With a unilateral offer (a promise in exchange for an act), part performance can constitute detrimental reliance. Here, the runner contacted the health foundation in a timely fashion and increased her efforts in reliance on the health foundation's offer (detrimental reliance). She never had a chance to actually win the marathon, since the health foundation wrote "Revoked" prior to the marathon. Her intensified efforts would, however, constitute sufficient part performance. Therefore, her part performance would prevent a valid revocation. A is incorrect because the March 30 "Revoked" notice was ineffective, as discussed in Answer C. B is incorrect because it is legally irrelevant whether or not the health foundation was private or public. D is incorrect because it is irrelevant whether or not the runner read the "Revoked" notice, since it was ineffective, for the reasons discussed in Answer C.

133. C is the correct answer. A unilateral offer is a promise in exchange for an act. Here, the offer (the promise to pay $100) can only be accepted by an act (being the first customer to come to the store on Monday morning.) A is incorrect because a bilateral offer requires a promise in exchange for a promise. As discussed in Answer C, the offer here is a promise in exchange for an act and

is, therefore, unilateral, not bilateral. B is nonsensical because an offer must be either bilateral or unilateral; it cannot be both. D is incorrect because there is nothing here that would turn the unilateral offer into a bilateral offer.

134. A is the correct answer. The girl scout troop's promise was conditioned on the occurrence of a girl winning the spelling bee. The girl had to win the spelling bee before the girl scout troop's duty to pay the $500 matured. Thus, the girl's performance (winning the spelling bee) needed to precede the girl scout troop's duty to pay the money. This is a classic condition precedent situation. B is incorrect because the girl scout troop's promise to pay $500 was a bargained-for exchange for the girl winning the spelling bee, as discussed in Answer A. It was not an unenforceable gift. C is incorrect because there is nothing in the facts to indicate that the girl was under a preexisting duty to enter and win the spelling bee. D is incorrect for the same reasons that A is correct.

135. D is the correct answer. The diamond cutter's death would not terminate the offer because he has already performed (cut the diamond). A is incorrect because, while the death of a party would void unperformed or executory duties of the surviving parties if the deceased party had not performed, death would have no effect if the deceased party had performed prior to dying. Here, the diamond cutter cut the diamond prior to his death. Therefore, the executor of his estate may enforce the promise against the merchant. B is incorrect because the promise is enforceable, as discussed in Answer D. C is incorrect because, as discussed in Answer D, the merchant's offer had been properly accepted by the performance of the diamond cutter. There was, thus, a fully enforceable contract, so detrimental reliance is not an issue.

136. B is the correct answer. Anticipatory repudiation occurs where one party to an executory bilateral contract repudiates the contract in advance of the time set for performance by stating unequivocally that he will not perform the contract. Here, the singer's statement that he may not be ready to start would not constitute an "unequivocal" repudiation because "may not be ready to start" is not unequivocal (as opposed to "will not be able to start"). A is incorrect because a repudiation does not have to be in writing. C is incorrect because there was not an unequivocal repudiation, for the reasons discussed in Answer B. D is incorrect because it is speculative before the contract performance date whether or not the nightclub owner might suffer damages.

137. B is the correct answer. An aggrieved party is relieved of his obligation (and may, thus, cancel the contract) only where a material breach occurs. A ten-day delay would likely not constitute a material breach under these facts because this contract was for eight months and ten days in an eight-month

contract is a minimal delay. A is incorrect because notification, under these facts, does not constitute an anticipatory repudiation, but merely a ten-day delay, for the reasons discussed in Answer B. C is incorrect because the inconvenience is too minor to justify canceling the contract for the reasons discussed in Answer B. D is incorrect because, as discussed in Answer B, there was no material breach here.

138. B is the correct answer. The non-breaching party to a contract (here, the travel agency) is entitled to be placed in the position it would have been in had the breaching party (here, the original tour guide) followed through with the contract. Here, the travel agency was forced to hire another tour guide at $1,000 more per month than the original tour guide when the original tour guide failed to appear for the month of June. Thus, the travel agency is entitled to $1,000 for June and the present value of $1,000 per month salary difference for the remaining 11 months. A is incorrect because the travel agency's damages would not be limited to just $1,000, for the reasons discussed in Answer B. C is incorrect for the reasons stated in Answer B. D is incorrect because the damages are only the additional $1,000 a month it must pay the new tour guide, as discussed in Answer B, since the remaining $5,000 per month that is being paid to the new tour guide was money that the travel agency was already planning to pay anyway under the original contract.

139. A is the correct answer because, if a contract involves goods over $500, it must be in writing to be enforceable. Here, the contract involved both goods (the pool parts) and services (the installation) and the facts do not indicate that there was a written contract. It can be assumed that the materials exceeded $500 in this $10,000 contract. Therefore, the homeowner's Statute of Frauds defense would be applicable, if there were no written contract. B is incorrect because service contracts that cannot be performed within one year must be in writing to comply with the Statute of Frauds. Therefore, the fact that building a pool is a service does not automatically mean that no writing is required. C is incorrect because in a hybrid contract (i.e., one that involves both goods and services), if the value of the goods exceeds $500 and/or the service cannot be performed in under one year, the contract must be in writing to comply with the Statute of Frauds. Therefore, the fact that it is a hybrid contract does not automatically mean that no writing is required. D is incorrect because the fact that it is a hybrid contract does not automatically mean that a writing is required. A writing is only required if the value of the goods exceeds $500 and/or the service cannot be performed in under one year.

140. D is the correct answer. Under modern law, a contract can be rescinded orally. Here, when the man agreed to let the woman out of the deal, this was an oral

rescission of the contract. Thus, the man cannot later recover for breach because there was no longer a contract to be breached. A is incorrect for the reasons stated in correct answer D. B is an irrelevant factual statement because there was no breach at that time; before the contract could be breached, the man orally rescinded it. C is incorrect because it is legally irrelevant. If one party has no money, this may affect the prevailing party's ability to collect damages, but it does not affect the ability to prevail on a breach of contact claim in the first place.

141. A is the correct answer. A breaching party may still recover its expenditures, even if it has committed a material breach. The recovery will be based on quasi-contract principles. Here, although the original contractor is in material breach by failing to complete the last 50% of the work, he already had incurred $100,000 in expenses. Thus, he may recover these expenses in quasi-contract. B is incorrect because, although the original contractor went broke, he could have borrowed money or used other methods to get the funds to complete the work. Thus, performance was not impossible. C is incorrect because the original contractor was in material breach, not the farmer. This would, thus, not be a proper theory of recovery for the original contractor. D is incorrect for the same reasons that A is the correct answer.

142. C is the correct answer. A breaching party may still recover its expenditures, even if it has committed a material breach. The recovery will be based on quasi-contract principles. Here, although the auto repair company is in material breach by failing to complete the last 50% of the work, it already conferred a $150,000 benefit on the owner. Therefore, the auto repair company may recover the $150,000 in quasi-contract, minus any expenses borne by the owner due the auto repair company's breach. A is incorrect for the reasons discussed in Answer C. B is incorrect because, while the failure to complete performance is a material breach, the auto repair company is still entitled to recover, as discussed in Answer C. D is incorrect because the facts do not indicate that the auto repair company's breach was willful.

143. B is the correct answer because, under the implied warranty of merchantability, the vehicle should not have a brake failure twenty days after it is purchased. Such a warranty cannot be disclaimed and, therefore, the defendants' claim that there was a warranty disclaimer on the back of the contract is legally irrelevant. A is incorrect because the injury must have been caused by the defendants in order for the man to recover. The fact that the man has been injured does not in and of itself give him the right to recover against these particular defendants, unless they were the cause of his injuries. C is incorrect because the man has sued

under an implied warranty theory. Here, the defendants' claim that they have a valid disclaimer on the back of the contract in fine print is not a valid disclaimer. The disclaimer must be conspicuous and in bold print. D is incorrect because the bargaining power is not at issue in this lawsuit for breach of an implied warranty. If the implied warranty was breached, it does not matter whether or not the bargaining power was equal.

144. A is the correct answer. This is a contract for the sale of tennis balls, which are goods. Therefore, this contract is governed by the U.C.C. Under U.C.C. §2-206(1)(b), an offer to buy goods for prompt shipment can be accepted by notice or by actual shipment. Here, the manufacturer shipped immediately. Therefore, it has properly accepted, creating an enforceable contract. B is incorrect because the common law's mirror image rule is not applicable under the U.C.C., and also because no terms were added in any case. C is incorrect because, as discussed in Answer A, the contract became enforceable once the tennis balls were shipped. The buyer attempted to revoke his offer after this had occurred, but by then, it was too late to do so. D is incorrect because, since there is an enforceable contract, it is irrelevant whether or not the manufacturer can sell the balls to somebody else.

145. D is the correct answer. This is a contract for sandals, which are goods. Therefore, this contract is governed by the U.C.C. Under U.C.C. §2-206(1)(b), shipment is a legal acceptance, even if the goods shipped are non-conforming. However, the shipment of non-conforming goods is a breach of contract. Here, the manufacturer has shipped blue sandals, which are non-conforming, since the retailer has ordered green sandals. Thus, even though there is a contract, the retailer can pursue remedies against the manufacturer. A and B are incorrect because, as discussed in Answer D, the fact that the sandals were non-conforming does not mean that there was no contract, only that there was a breach. C is incorrect because the manufacturer did not state that the non-conforming goods were only accommodations.

146. C is the correct answer. U.C.C. §9-313 allows the store to prevail over any person becoming a lien creditor after the security interest became perfected by the store's timely filing of the security interest in the air conditioning system. A is incorrect because it does not provide for a system of priority of filing. As discussed in Answer C, the store has priority over general creditors. B is incorrect because a secured interest is not automatically perfected, absent a filing. D is incorrect because, upon a proper filing of a secured interest in fixtures, that party is protected from other creditors claiming an interest in the fixture, regardless of whether it became part of the real property.

147. D is the correct answer. The F.O.B. term is a delivery term, even if only used in conjunction with the price; thus, requiring delivery from the seller to the buyer's plant to shift the risk of loss. The risk of loss did not pass because the container was merely loaded, not delivered, at the time it was stolen. A is incorrect because the exporter did not deliver the goods by merely loading the food company's shipping container. It had to deliver the carrier to the buyer's plant, as discussed in Answer D. B is incorrect because there was no such agreement. In fact, the contract called for FOB FOOD COMPANY'S PLANT, as discussed in Answer D. C is incorrect because the goods being stolen do not change which party bears the risk of loss.

148. B is the correct answer. U.C.C. §9-313(2) provides that no security interest exists in ordinary building materials incorporated into an improvement on land. Once the man used the lumber to construct the garage, the hardware store was prevented from having a security interest in the goods (the lumber). A and C are incorrect for the reasons discussed in Answer B. D is an incorrect statement of law because there is no security interest in ordinary building materials such as lumber, drywall or window glass, as discussed in Answer B.

149. A is the correct answer. U.C.C. §9-313(4)(b) provides that between a fixture financier (the store) and a subsequent real estate interest (the bank), the first secured party to file or record prevails. Here, because the store filed its interest before the bank, the store prevails. B and C are incorrect because when the mortgage is not preexisting (as it was here, since it was a second mortgage, taken out AFTER the store filed its security interest), the issue is not filing within 21 days; it is a matter of which entity files first, which was the store here, as discussed in Answer A. D is incorrect because Article 9 permits fixture financiers to have a secured interest in chattels affixed to realty.

150. D is the correct answer. U.C.C. §9-313(4)(a) permits a fixture financier to defeat a pre-existing realty interest when: (1) the fixture security interest is a purchase money security interest, (2) the fixture security interest is perfected by a fixture filing, (3) the filing is made before the goods become fixtures or within twenty days thereafter, and (4) the debtor has a recorded interest or possession of the realty. Here, the store filed its security interest four months later, which was after the 20-day grace period, thereby failing to comply with element (3) above. Thus, the bank will prevail here. A is incorrect because the grace period is only 20 days, as discussed in Answer D. B and C are incorrect for the reasons discussed in Answer D.

151. C is the correct answer. U.C.C. §9-401(2) provides that an improper filing, which is made in good faith is effective: (1) to the extent of the col-

lateral for which the filing was proper and (2) against any person who actually knows the contents of the financing statement. Here, since part of the tanning salon owner's description was proper, the filing is effective as to the properly-described collateral. A, B and D are incorrect for the reasons discussed in Answer C.

152. C is the correct answer. Although a secured party may remove his collateral upon default without resort to the judicial process, unless otherwise agreed, he must do so without a breach of the peace. Here, the booth supplier's smashing of the cafe window was a breach of the peace, which is not permitted under Article 9. A, B, and D are incorrect for the reasons discussed in Answer C.

153. D is the correct answer. A secured creditor of fixtures may remove his collateral upon default, but he must reimburse any party, except the debtor, for the cost of repair for the physical damage caused by the fixture removal. Here, the plumber was a secured creditor and the hunting lodge was the debtor. Consequently, the hunting lodge did not need to be reimbursed for damage to the property in removing the toilets it had purchased on credit. A, B and C are incorrect for the reasons discussed in Answer D.

154. A is the correct answer. The implied warranty of merchantability must be disclaimed by use of the term "merchantability." The language in the pet shop's contract made no mention of disclaiming the implied warranty of merchantability. Therefore, the woman is entitled to recover under the implied warranty of merchantability because a bird that dies in three weeks is not merchantable and because the pet shop failed to properly disclaim the warranty. B is incorrect because, even though a 72-hour period to determine the health of the bird may seem unreasonable, it was conspicuously stated in the bill of sale. Therefore, the woman will not prevail for this reason. However, she will prevail for the reasons discussed in A. C is incorrect because the woman is not required to prove the cause of the bird's death. D is incorrect because, as discussed, the implied warranty of merchantability was not disclaimed. There was also no language that expressly disclaimed the implied warranty of fitness for a particular purpose.

155. D is the correct answer. Under U.C.C. §2-312, a seller of goods warrants that she is conveying good title, that her title is rightful, and that the goods will be delivered free of security interest or other liens. Here, the woman was a bona fide purchaser of the CD player from the thief. A bona fide purchaser is someone who pays value and is unaware of any defects in title. Here, the woman paid for the CD player and was unaware that the CD player was stolen and was, thus, a bona fide purchaser. As a bona fide purchaser,

she was able to convey good title to man. A is incorrect because a seller of goods need not be a merchant to be required to convey good title. All sellers of goods are protected under the U.C.C. B is incorrect for the reasons stated in the explanation to answer D. C is incorrect because, as discussed, the woman was a bona fide purchaser and, therefore, could pass good title.

END OF ANSWERS

A
CONTRACTS

CRIMINAL LAW – QUESTION BREAKDOWN

1. Status Crimes
2. Malum in Se Crime – Mens Rea
3. Inchoate Crimes – Solicitation
4. Theft Crimes
5. Burglary – Modern Law vs. Common Law
6. Larceny
7. Felony Murder Rule
8. Defenses – Necessity
9. Attempt – Substantial Step
10. Burglary – Common Law
11. Defenses – Infancy
12. Conspiracy
13. Felony Murder
14. Accomplice Liability
15. Defenses – Insanity
16. Misdemeanor – Battery
17. Assault/Battery
18. Murder
19. Murder/Mitigation
20. Burglary
21. Attempted Rape
22. Defenses – Crime by Arresting Officer
23. Larceny/Embezzlement
24. Defense – Claim of Right
25. Protection of Property – Deadly Force
26. Malicious Mischief
27. Mistake of Fact
28. Battery
29. Defenses – Infancy
30. Statutory Rape – Defense
31. Inchoate Crimes – Solicitation
32. Actus Reus
33. Inchoate Crimes
34. Defenses/Year and a Day Rule
35. Voluntary Manslaughter
36. Embezzlement
37. Theft Crimes

38. Misprision

39. Assault/Battery

40. Inchoate Crimes – Conspiracy

41. Conspiracy/1st Degree Murder

42. Conspiracy/Murder

43. Theft Crimes

44. Larceny/Malicious Mischief

45. Larceny

46. Theft Crimes

47. Mayhem

48. Defenses – Intoxication

49. Miscellaneous Crimes

50. Burglary/Larceny

51. Battery

52. Involuntary Manslaughter

53. Attempt/Habitation Crimes

54. Arson

55. Year and a Day Rule

56. Defenses

57. Larceny

58. Larceny

59. Burglary – Mens Rea

60. Murder

61. Malice Mischief – Personal Property Element

62. Malice Mischief

63. Assault/Voluntary Manslaughter

64. Battery – Mens Rea

65. Involuntary Manslaughter

66. False Imprisonment

67. Battery

68. Malicious Mischief

69. Uttering/Larceny

70. Embezzlement

71. Burglary

72. Burglary, Forcible Entry, and Larceny

73. False Pretenses

74. False Pretenses

75. Embezzlement

76. Involuntary Manslaughter

77. Murder

78. Common Law Crimes

79. Vandalism

80. Rape – Defense of Consent

81. Malicious Mischief

82. Voluntary Manslaughter

83. Actus Reus/Mens Rea

84. Malicious Mischief

85. Larceny

86. Murder

87. Insanity

88. Defenses – Diminished Capacity

89. Mens Rea

90. False Pretenses

91. Theft

92. Theft

93. Involuntary Manslaughter

94. Murder – Causation

95. Conspiracy – Wharton's Rule

96. Mens Rea

97. Defenses – Necessity

98. Forcible Entry & Detainer

99. Defenses – Defense of Property

100. Defenses – Necessity

CRIMINAL LAW QUESTIONS

1. A State law makes it a crime to "be addicted to any illegal substance." The crime is a felony. A heroin addict is attending a rehab program. The police raid the program and arrest the heroin addict for violation of the State law. Can the man be charged under this law?

    A. Yes because it is a strict liability offense.

    B. No because involuntary intoxication and drug use is a defense to crimes.

    C. No because the law is unconstitutional for vagueness.

    D. No because the law is fundamentally unfair.

2. A man was convicted of false pretenses. The judge instructed the jury as follows: "The burden of proof is on the prosecution to prove each and every element of the crime beyond a reasonable doubt. Here, the prosecution must prove that the defendant obtained title to property of another by means of misstatement of past or existing fact. If you find each element proven by the facts, then the defendant is guilty." The man was convicted. His best ground of appeal, based on the preceding, is:

    A. The evidence was insufficient, as a matter of law.

    B. He has no grounds of appeal, since the instruction was perfect.

    C. The mens rea element was left out of "false pretenses," and since this is a malum en se crime, such omission violates due process.

    D. The instruction does not require the obtaining of documentary title.

3. A man spoke with a woman and asked her to help him rob a bank the following Tuesday. The woman said that she needed to think about it. Following the man's conversation with the woman, was either the man or the woman guilty of any crime?

    A. They were both guilty of conspiracy to commit robbery.

    B. The man was guilty of solicitation to commit robbery.

    C. The man and the woman were guilty of attempted robbery.

    D. No crimes were committed, since there was no actus reus.

4. A bank teller takes $500 home from her cash drawer at the bank. Is the teller guilty of any crime or crimes?

CRIMINAL LAW 171

A. Yes, she is guilty of embezzlement.

B. Yes, she is guilty of obtaining property by false pretenses.

C. Yes, she is guilty of malicious trespass.

D. Yes, she is guilty of larceny by trick.

5. A man and a woman agreed to steal a rare painting from a warehouse. At noon the following day, they drove to the warehouse, broke in, and stole the painting. Of which crime or crimes were the man and the woman guilty?

   A. At common law, they were guilty of burglary.

   B. Under most modern statutes, they were guilty of burglary.

   C. Under modern and common law, they were not guilty of burglary.

   D. None of the above.

6. A woman looked at a diamond ring in a store. While the salesperson was busy with another customer, the woman put the diamond ring into her pocket and walked out of the store. Was she guilty of any crime?

   A. She was guilty of embezzlement because she used no trick or force in the taking.

   B. She was guilty of false pretenses because she obtained both title and possession.

   C. She was guilty of larceny because there was a trespassory taking.

   D. None of the above.

7. A man rapes a woman. During the rape, the woman has a heart attack and dies. Other than rape, is the man guilty of any crimes?

   A. Involuntary manslaughter.

   B. No crime (other than rape).

   C. Voluntary manslaughter because there was a heat of passion.

   D. Murder, at common law, of the woman.

8. A starving man walked into an unoccupied house and saw some food on the table. He ate the food and left the house. As he was leaving, he was spotted by a patrol officer, who was driving by the house. The officer asked him what he was doing in the house. The man said that he was starving and that he broke into the house and ate the food. The man is charged with larceny of the food. Which of the following is the best defense to the charge of larceny of the food?

   A. There was no concurrence of mens rea and actus reus.

B. The man's taking the food was out of necessity.

C. The back door was wide open, he walked in without touching a tangible thing, and he did not take anything but the food.

D. It would violate due process to punish in this instance.

9. A woman was shopping in a dress store. She admired an expensive dress. She picked up the dress and started walking toward the store's exit. Before she got to the door, she turned around and put the dress back on the hanger. A security guard who witnessed this stopped her and held her until the police came and charged her with attempted larceny of the dress. Which of the following is the woman's best defense?

A. She had not taken a substantial step to commit larceny.

B. Larceny is a crime against possession and nobody was in possession of the dress at the time.

C. Since she never left the store with the dress, there was no "asportation" as defined by the common law.

D. The dress was damaged, and store would not have been been able to sell it anyway.

10. One night, a catburglar of limited intelligence climbed a ladder and entered a home through a completely open window with the intent to steal expensive silverware. While he was in the home, a policeman in patrol car spotted the catburglar climbing into the house through the window. He arrested the catburglar and charged him with burglary. Which of the following would be the catburglar's best common law defense?

A. The catburglar had diminished capacity.

B. Burglary is a crime against habitation, and nobody lived in the house at the time.

C. There was no "breaking."

D. The catburglar was under a compulsion to illegally enter homes.

11. A mentally disturbed five-year-old stabbed his neighbor to death. He was charged with murder. What is his best defense at common law?

A. His mental state prevented him from forming the requisite mens rea for murder.

B. He should have been charged with manslaughter.

C. Self-defense.

D. Infancy.

12. Three men agreed to rob a bank. The next day, one of the men broke his leg skiing and was in the hospital on the day that the bank robbery was to occur. The other two men robbed the bank but were arrested and charged with robbery. If the man with the broken leg is charged with conspiracy to commit robbery, what is his best defense?

    A. There was no agreement to commit robbery.

    B. Conspiracy merges with robbery. Since the man was in the hospital, he was unable to commit the robbery.

    C. The man effectively withdrew from the conspiracy.

    D. There is no defense.

13. One evening, a man drove to a woman's house, intending to steal the woman's computer. Pushing open the already slightly-opened ground floor window, he entered the house. When the woman arrived home, the man leaped out at her. Startled by the man's actions, the woman stepped backward, fell, hit her head, and died as a result of the fall. If the man is apprehended and charged with the death of the woman, he would most probably be found:

    A. Guilty of felony murder.

    B. Guilty of first-degree murder at common law.

    C. Guilty of voluntary manslaughter because of the heat of passion.

    D. Not guilty of homicide, based on the accidental manner of the woman's death.

14. A man kidnaps a young girl and hides her in a warehouse. The man goes to his mother and tells her, "I've kidnapped a girl. Please hide me." The police find the girl, and she implicates the man in the crime. The police go to the man's mother's house where they inquire if the man is there, as he is wanted for investigation of a kidnapping. The man's mother states that she does not know where the man is, despite the fact that the man, at the moment, is hiding in the closet. Modernly, the man's mother may be guilty:

    A. Of conspiracy.

    B. Of obstruction of justice.

    C. As a principal, in the second degree.

    D. As an accessory before the fact.

15. A man has suffered from chronic alcoholism for twenty years. One night while sober, he shot and killed a woman he claimed had been sent by the Devil. At his trial for murder, a psychiatrist testified the man knew what he was doing, but because of chronic alcohol-induced mental illness, he did not know it was wrong. The man should be found:

A. Guilty because voluntary intoxication is no excuse.

B. Guilty because he knew the nature and quality of his acts.

C. Not guilty because he was legally insane.

D. Not guilty because of a good faith unreasonable mistake of fact.

16. A man came home from work and saw his wife and their neighbor in the living room. He locked all the doors and windows and said, "Neither of you is leaving." He then proceeded to severely beat his wife. When the man beat his wife, the least serious crime he committed was:

    A. False imprisonment.

    B. Battery.

    C. Kidnapping.

    D. Negligent infliction of emotional distress.

17. One night, a woman went to a nightclub. Before she could enter, however, a bouncer shoved her for no apparent reason. The woman fell hard. As she was getting back to her feet, the bouncer shoved her again. The bouncer then tried to slap the woman in the face, but she turned away and he missed. The bouncer committed which of the following crimes?

    A. One count of battery and one count of assault.

    B. Two counts of battery and one count of assault.

    C. One count of battery and one count of assault.

    D. Assault only.

18. Two men were out gambling one night. The man who lost was very angry. The following night, he returned and stabbed the other man (the winner) to death. At common law, the man's killing of the winner would be:

    A. Murder.

    B. First-degree murder.

    C. Voluntary manslaughter.

    D. Involuntary manslaughter.

19. A woman has been beaten by her husband for many years. One night while the man is sleeping, the woman hits him over the head with an ax, instantly killing him. The woman is charged with murder. In a jurisdiction following modern rules, the woman's best argument in mitigation would be:

    A. Self-defense.

    B. Insanity.

    C. Imperfect right of self-defense.

D. None of the above.

20. One day at noon, a man went to a woman's house intending to rape the woman who lived there. He pushed her front window open with a crow bar. He put one foot through and alarms went off. While running away, he was apprehended by a police officer who was investigating the alarms. The man's best argument in defense of common law burglary is:

   A. He lacked the mens rea necessary.

   B. He did not intend to rape.

   C. The crime occurred during the day.

   D. The entry element was lacking.

21. A man tried to steal a woman's purse by attempting to pull it off her arm. Before he succeeded in getting the purse, he saw a policeman walking down the street. The woman screamed, and the policeman came and arrested the man for attempted larceny. The man will be found:

   A. Not guilty because he lacked the mental ability to form the mens rea to steal the purse.

   B. Not guilty because he did not take a substantial step toward the commission of the larceny.

   C. Guilty because he took a substantial step toward the commission of the larceny.

   D. Guilty because a gentleman would not steal a lady's purse.

22. A police officer stopped a driver who was weaving in and out of traffic. A field sobriety test was performed, and the officer determined that the man's blood-alcohol level was far above the legal limit. The officer informed the driver of his Miranda rights and charged him with Driving Under the Influence of alcohol (DUI). The officer then got mad and punched the driver. The officer's punching of the driver is:

   A. A complete defense to a charge of DUI.

   B. A partial defense to the charge of DUI.

   C. Relevant in the penalty phase of the driver's trial.

   D. Irrelevant to the prosecution of the driver.

23. A man walked into a tobacco store and purchased some tobacco that cost $3.12. He handed the clerk $100. The store manager then gave him back $6.88 from the cash register and said, "Thank you, sir." The man left. The store manager then pocketed the $100 bill. Has the store manager committed any crime or crimes?

A. Yes, the store manager has committed embezzlement against the store of $110 and larceny against the man for $100 (minus the $6.88 the clerk gave the man in change).

B. Yes, the store manager has committed embezzlement against the store for $6.88 and larceny against the man for $93.12.

C. Yes, the store manager has committed embezzlement against the store of $110.

D. No, the store manager has committed no crime because he made a mistake and thought that the man gave him $10.

24. A teenager lent his bicycle to his next-door neighbor, who was the same age. When the neighbor refused to return the bicycle, the teenager broke into the neighbor's house during the school lunch break and took the bicycle back. Which crime has the teenager committed?

    A. Robbery.

    B. Burglary.

    C. Larceny.

    D. None of the above.

25. A cattle rancher had a problem with people stealing his cattle. One night, he caught some men attempting to steal his prize bull. He shot and wounded one of the men. The rancher's shooting of the man was:

    A. Not an aggravated battery because it was the man's fault for trying to steal the bull.

    B. Not an aggravated battery because a man is allowed to protect his property.

    C. An aggravated battery because the theft of the rancher's cattle caused him to become aggravated.

    D. An aggravated battery because deadly force, in this situation, is impermissible.

26. A talented artist decides that she does not like the ugly art mural in the downtown district of the city in which she lives. One night, she brings a can of paint downtown and repaints the mural, making it look much nicer. What crime, if any, has the artist committed?

    A. Mayhem.

    B. Malicious mischief.

    C. Larceny.

    D. None because she improved the mural.

27. A seventeen-year-old girl wanted to have an affair with her married 40-year-old neighbor. One night, she broke into his house and secreted herself in his bed. The neighbor's wife was out. He man went to bed and had sex with the girl, thinking her to be his wife. The girl bragged to her friends about having sex with her neighbor. The police found out and the man was arrested for statutory rape. His best defense would be:

   A. Consent because he thought he was having sex with his wife.

   B. Privilege because he was married.

   C. Mistake of fact.

   D. None of these.

28. A woman approached a man and asked him for $100. When he refused, she grabbed some money out of the man's back pocket and punched him in the stomach. The man called the police, and the woman was arrested. Of which crime or crimes is the woman guilty at common law?

   A. Battery only.

   B. Battery and robbery.

   C. Robbery only.

   D. Larceny and robbery.

29. A 17-year-old boy hacked into the computer system of the Federal Bureau of Investigation (FBI) because he believed that all government agencies posed a threat to him. He was arrested and charged with hacking into a classified government computer system. What is his best defense?

   A. Infancy.

   B. Public Policy.

   C. Mistake of fact.

   D. Self-defense.

30. A man went to Las Vegas for his bachelor party. Unknown to the man, a stripper slipped a drug into his orange juice. Under the influence of the drug, the man began to hallucinate and thought that the stripper was going to steal from him. He hit her over the head with a lamp and killed her. He was charged with murder. What is his best defense?

   A. Self-defense.

   B. Mistake of fact.

   C. Voluntary intoxication.

   D. Involuntary intoxication.

31. A dying woman with no hope of recovery asked her brother to help her die by turning off her life support system. The brother refused. A policeman in the next room overheard the conversation and

arrested her. For which crimes, if any, can the woman be prosecuted?

A. Solicitation.

B. Attempt.

C. Conspiracy.

D. None of the above.

32. A man hated his next door neighbor, and he really wished the neighbor would die. The man even said to many people, "I would kill my neighbor if I could." The other people got concerned and called the police. With which crimes, if any, can the man be charged?

A. Solicitation.

B. Attempt.

C. Conspiracy.

D. None of the above.

33. A man hated his wife and decided to poison her by putting rat poison into her coffee. The man went to the store and stole some rat poison. He came home and put the rat poison into the coffee. He grabbed his wife and forced the coffee down her throat. He then had second thoughts and called an ambulance. The wife was taken to a hospital and survived. Of which crime or crimes is the man guilty?

A. Battery only.

B. Battery and attempted murder.

C. Battery, larceny and attempted murder.

D. Larceny only.

34. A man and his wife are on trial for tax evasion. The prosecutor keeps pointing his finger at the man's wife while she is on the witness stand. The man becomes enraged at the prosecutor, leaps out of his chair, and begins to strangle the prosecutor. The prosecutor falls, hits his head on the corner of a table, and goes into a coma. The prosecutor dies 13 months later. What would be the man's best defense to a charge of murder?

A. Provocation.

B. Insanity.

C. The year and a day rule.

D. Defense of others.

35. A Mexican man was in a bar. A Caucasian woman made racial slurs against the Mexican man. The man became enraged and picked up a glass and smashed it over the woman's head. She died instantly. He was charged with murder. Does he have any defenses?

A. Diminished capacity.

B. Insanity.

C. Provocation.

D. Mistake of Fact.

36. A store manager would on occasion pocket cash from the store's accounts received, rather than report it as store income. He figured that he was entitled to this money because he was underpaid. Which crime has he committed at common law?

 A. Larceny.

 B. Embezzlement.

 C. Larceny by trick.

 D. False pretenses.

37. A museum curator got angry at the museum administration and decided he deserved to have some of the artifacts with which he came into contact daily. He thus took some ancient jewelry home with him from the museum without obtaining permission from the museum. Which crime has he committed modernly?

 A. Receiving stolen property.

 B. Fraud.

 C. Petty theft.

 D. Grand theft.

38. A mob money launderer told his accountant not to show the laundered money in his tax return. The accountant, in order to help his client avoid tax fraud charges, agreed and did not show the laundered money on the tax return. If the accountant is charged with misprison, will he be found guilty?

 A. Yes.

 B. No because this transaction is protected by the accountant-client privilege.

 C. No because the mob launderer did not commit a crime.

 D. None of the above.

39. A law school hired a new dean in an effort to boost its rankings. The new dean was very unhappy with the law school's bar results and after careful consideration, proceeded to fire all the old staff and professors. Which crime or crimes did the dean commit?

 A. Assault and battery.

 B. Wrongful termination and intentional infliction of emotional distress.

 C. Assault only.

 D. None of the above.

40. A mob boss asked his hitman to take care of (kill) an enemy of the mob boss. The hitman agreed to do it for his usual fee. The hitman attempted to kill the

mob boss' enemy by sneaking up on him and strangling him with piano wire. However, unknown to the hitman, the enemy survived. He then approached the mob boss for his fee, which the mob boss paid. What crime or crimes has the mob boss committed?

A. Solicitation.

B. Conspiracy.

C. Robbery.

D. Murder.

41. A terrorist hired a bomber to construct a bomb and place it under a government building on April 15. Since the government building contained an office of the Internal Revenue Service (IRS), the terrorist knew that the building would be quite full that day. The bomber did as instructed. The bomb exploded and killed 5,000 people. Under the modern law, the terrorist is guilty of which crimes?

A. First-degree murder and conspiracy.

B. Second-degree murder and conspiracy.

C. First-degree murder only.

D. Second-degree murder only.

42. A movie producer wanted to kill his wife because it was cheaper than divorce. He asked an aspiring actor to break into his home and to kill his wife. The actor agreed in order to get a part in the producer's next film. The next day at noon, the actor broke into the producer's home and found the wife lounging at the indoor pool. He threw her into the pool and drowned her. At modern law, which crime or crimes did the actor commit?

A. Conspiracy to commit first-degree murder.

B. First-degree murder.

C. Conspiracy to commit first-degree murder, first-degree murder, and burglary.

D. Conspiracy to commit first-degree murder and first-degree murder.

43. A depressed man who had recently lost his job was sitting on a park bench, contemplating suicide when he looked down and spotted a wallet underneath the bench. He picked it up. Although he wanted to keep the wallet, his conscience demanded he surrender it to the local police. He filled out some forms, left the wallet at the police station, and walked out. When the man picked up the wallet, he committed which of the following crimes?

A. Larceny.

B. Embezzlement.

C. Trespass.

D. No crime.

44. One night, a woman threw a rock and broke the window of a car dealership. She crawled in, found some keys, and drove off in one of the cars in the showroom. She crashed the car, and it could not be repaired. When she drove off in the car, which of the following common law crimes were committed?

   A. Larceny.

   B. Malicious mischief.

   C. Larceny and malicious mischief.

   D. Larceny, malicious mischief, and burglary.

45. A college student took his professor's car without permission, intending to go on a ride to the local nightclub, impress a few girls there, and then return the car before the professor even knew that the car was missing. However, the professor noticed that his car was missing almost immediately after the college student took it. The professor called the police, who found and arrested and charged the college student with larceny. What would be the college student's best defense to the crime?

   A. The car was lost.

   B. The car was not owned by the professor; it was leased.

   C. The car was not personal property.

   D. The college student planned to return the car before the professor even knew that it was missing.

46. A woman took her grandmother's one-of-a-kind dress that the grandmother had worn in a film for which the grandmother had won an Academy Award. The woman sold the dress online for several hundred thousand dollars (since it was a collector's item). Were this jurisdiction to follow the modern law, which crimes did the woman commit?

   A. Larceny and grand theft.

   B. Larceny only.

   C. Conversion only.

   D. Grand theft only.

47. During a wrestling match a wrestler put his famous "sleeper" hold on his opponent. The wrestler and the opponent had actually rehearsed this move prior to the match, but the wrestler decided to do it for real. The wrestler won the match, but his opponent was hospitalized with neck injuries and permanent partial paralysis. The wrestler's use of the real sleeper hold on his opponent was:

   A. Battery only.

B. Not battery because the opponent consented.

C. Mayhem and battery.

D. Not mayhem because the opponent consented.

48. A male contestant on a reality show slipped a drug into a soda that was being consumed by a female contestant. The female contestant then killed the TV host, thinking that he was trying to sleep with her. Her belief was delusional and due to the drug. What crime or crimes has she committed, and does she have any defenses?

A. Murder, with no defenses.

B. Not murder because of involuntary intoxication.

C. Voluntary manslaughter, with no defenses.

D. Not voluntary manslaughter because of self-defense.

49. A man purchased a semi-automatic Uzi submachine gun at the local gun shop. Even though he knew it to be illegal, he modified the gun to be fully automatic. The law of this jurisdiction includes the following statute:

The willful modification of a semi-automatic weapon so that it is fully automatic, absent State permit, is a misdemeanor. Any unnecessary death or injury caused by this weapon shall not be excused by the uncontrollable nature of the weapon. At the common law, the man's modification of the gun was:

A. Malicious mischief.

B. Murder.

C. Lawful because it was for the defense of his property.

D. None of the above.

50. A woman kept a collection of swords in her home. One night, a man smashed a window and climbed into the woman's home, intending to steal some of the swords. The woman slept through the entire incident. The man was able to leave with some of the woman's favorite swords. What crimes, if any, has the man committed under the common law?

A. Burglary.

B. Larceny.

C. Burglary and larceny.

D. None of the above.

51. A woman loved her dog and considered the dog to be like her own child. One day, a man climbed the fence into the woman's backyard and started beating the woman's dog. The woman was horrified to see this. She picked up her rifle and shot the man to save her dog's life. The man was severely injured, but he

survived. The woman's use of deadly force on the man was:

A. Reasonable, thus, justifiable.

B. Unreasonable, thus, a battery.

C. Reasonable, thus, a battery.

D. Unreasonable, thus, a second-degree murder.

52. One night, a man broke into his neighbor's home to retrieve a blender that he had lent to the neighbor. Unknown to the man, a homeless trespasser had also broken into the neighbor's home and was asleep in the living room. The man went into the kitchen and was not aware that the trespasser was in the home. When the man grabbed the blender, he inadvertently knocked over a lit candle. The man did not realize what he had done, and he left the house. The candle ignited a fire, and the home was burned to the ground. The homeless trespasser was burned to death. At common law, the man's actions amounted to:

A. Burglary and involuntary manslaughter.

B. Burglary and murder.

C. Involuntary manslaughter.

D. Burglary.

53. One night, a woman broke into a man's home to steal some silverware. The man confronted her, and she threw a makeshift torch at him. The man ducked out of the way. The torch ignited the curtains and burned down the man's house. Both the man and the woman were able to flee before the house burned down. At common law, which crimes did the woman commit?

A. Arson, burglary, and attempted murder.

B. Arson and burglary.

C. Burglary and attempted murder.

D. Burglary.

54. A fire ignited in a woman's home. She called the fire department. The fire captain came to the scene. Because the woman had rejected his sexual advances, he purposely took his time in setting up the hoses. His willful delay, in fact, caused the woman's house to burn down. The fire captain committed which of the following crimes?

A. Willful delay.

B. Culpable omission.

C. Negative omission.

D. Arson.

55. A woman was raped and severely injured. While in the hospital, she went into a coma and remained in the coma for over two years. She woke up sud-

denly, but then died. At the common law, is the rapist guilty of any crime other than rape?

A. Yes, he is guilty of first-degree murder.

B. Yes, he is guilty of second-degree murder.

C. Yes, he is guilty of manslaughter.

D. No, he is not guilty of any crimes, other than rape.

56. One night, a man came upon two women engaged in a fight. Both women were in plain clothes, but unknown to the man, one of the women was an undercover police officer who was actually attempting to arrest the other woman, who was resisting. The man mistakenly thought that the police officer was attempting to rob the other woman. He, therefore, knocked the police officer to the ground and the other woman escaped. The man was charged with battery of the police officer. What is his best defense under these circumstances?

A. Defense of others.

B. Crime prevention.

C. Self-defense.

D. The man has no defense.

57. A woman borrowed her friend's car without consent. Once on the road, she decided to keep the car. She drove 200 miles and then decided to rest. What crime, if any, has the woman committed?

A. Larceny.

B. Larceny by trick.

C. Embezzlement.

D. No crime.

58. A homeless person was starving late one night. He broke into a convenience store and ate some food out of the store's refrigerator section. He fell asleep. The next morning, the manager found him there and called the police. At common law, which crimes has the homeless person committed?

A. Burglary only.

B. Burglary and larceny only.

C. Burglary and embezzlement only.

D. Larceny only.

59. One New Year's Eve, a man celebrated by shooting his gun into the sky. The bullet fell through the roof of a neighbor's house, killing the neighbor. The man was aware that someone could get hurt when he shot his gun, but thought that the likelihood of that happening was very slim. At common law, has the man committed a burglary?

    A. Yes, there was a burglary, by way of instrumentality used to consummate the crime.

    B. Yes, there was a burglary because a felony was committed therein.

    C. No, there was not a burglary because there was no entry by the man.

    D. No, there was not a burglary because there was no specific intent to commit a felony therein.

60. On one very hot day, a very strong woman became frustrated because her window air conditioner would not work. She, therefore, threw the air conditioner out from her twenty-first floor apartment window. The air conditioner hit and killed a pedestrian who was passing by on the sidewalk below. At the common law, the killing of the pedestrian is:

    A. Second-degree murder.

    B. Reckless homicide.

    C. Murder.

    D. Involuntary manslaughter.

61. At a fraternity party, a fraternity member decided that it would be cool to give an excessive amount of alcohol to the fraternity's mascot, a dog. The dog ingested the alcohol and died instantly. At the common law, the killing of the dog was:

    A. Malicious mischief.

    B. Cruelty to dogs.

    C. Canine homicide.

    D. None of the above.

62. A man and a woman were in the process of getting a divorce. One night, the man used his key and entered his former home that he had shared with the woman. He found the woman's wedding dress and cut it to shreds. Which of the following common law crimes has the man committed?

    A. Burglary and malicious mischief.

    B. Vandalism.

    C. Malicious mischief only.

    D. Trespass to chattel.

63. A man caught his girlfriend kissing her former boyfriend. Enraged, the man strangled the former boyfriend to death. He then made a threatening gesture toward his girlfriend and said, "I ought to strangle you, too." The girlfriend screamed and ran away. The man chased her, but was apprehended by several onlookers. Which of the following common law crimes did the man commit?

    A. Murder in the second degree of the former boyfriend and assault of the girlfriend.

B. Voluntary manslaughter of the former boyfriend and battery of the girlfriend.

C. Voluntary manslaughter of the former boyfriend and assault of the girlfriend.

D. Murder in the second degree of the former boyfriend and battery of the girlfriend.

64. A man was at a bar drinking a beer and having a sandwich. A woman sat down next to him and asked if she could have a taste of his beer. The man replied, "Yes," and she reached for the bottle. She inadvertently spilled the beer on him. Of which crime or crimes is she guilty?

A. Assault.

B. Battery.

C. Malicious mischief.

D. None of the above.

65. A woman was shopping at her favorite store when she saw an old friend of hers who she had not seen in years. The woman was so excited at seeing her old friend that she grabbed her friend to hug her. The friend fell backward, hit her head on the floor, and died. Which crime or crimes did the woman commit at common law?

A. Involuntary manslaughter only.

B. Assault only.

C. Second-degree murder only.

D. Battery only.

66. A college student was attending a homecoming party with his girlfriend. He asked the girlfriend to go upstairs so that they could have some quiet time to talk, but he was really expecting to have sex with her. He locked the door to the room upstairs and told his girlfriend to undress. She started to undress, but she changed her mind and tried to exit the room. However, the college student blocked the door and said, "You're not going anywhere." After a few minutes, he had a change of heart and opened the door. Which of the following crimes has the college student committed at common law?

A. Rape.

B. False imprisonment.

C. Battery.

D. He has committed no crime. The girlfriend led him on.

67. A college student started playing with the hair of the girl who sat in front of him in class. The girl told him to stop, but he did not. When the college student touched the girl's hair, what, if any crimes at common law did he commit?

A. He committed no crime because the touching was not offensive.

B. He committed no crime because this was the tort of battery.

C. He committed battery because there was no consent.

D. None of the above, but it would be a crime modernly.

68. One day, during the lunch hour, a secretary who was upset because she did not get a raise, saw her boss' car in the parking lot. She took out her own car keys, then "keyed" the boss' car. It left a nasty scratch. When she "keyed" the boss' car, what if any crimes did she commit?

A. She committed no crimes because the car could be repaired.

B. She committed the intentional infliction of emotional distress.

C. She committed a theft of movables.

D. She committed malicious mischief.

69. A man parked his car in a paid parking garage. Later, when it was time to leave, he exited the parking garage, using a token from a local arcade, which was the same size as the tokens from the parking garage because he believed that parking should always be free. He placed the token in the gate-exit slot, the gate pulled up, and he drove off. When the man used the token from the arcade, which, if any modern crimes, did he commit?

A. Forgery and theft by false pretenses.

B. Uttering.

C. Theft by embezzlement.

D. Forgery and theft by embezzlement.

70. A patron at a fancy restaurant checked her mink coat with the coat checker when she arrived at the restaurant. When the patron finished her meal, she went to retrieve her coat, but the coat checker accidentally gave her the wrong one. The patron did not notice this mistake until she got home. She thought about returning the coat but then realized that this coat was nicer than her own coat, so she kept it instead. Which crime, if any, did the woman commit?

A. Larceny.

B. Embezzlement.

C. False pretenses.

D. None of the above.

71. One night, a woman broke into an abandoned house with the intent to steal anything of value that she might find

inside. In the end, she found nothing of any value, so she left. If she is charged with common law burglary, what is her best argument in defense?

A. She did not actually take anything from the house.

B. It was not a "dwelling."

C. There was no one there.

D. None of the above.

72. One day during lunch, a locksmith decided that he wanted to use his skills to steal some valuables from a nearby home. He, therefore, came to the home and picked the lock and took a television set. At common law, did the locksmith commit any felonies?

A. Yes, there was burglary.

B. No because trespass was only a tort.

C. Yes, there was conversion.

D. Yes, there was a forcible entry and larceny.

73. A man went into a liquor store and picked out a $175 bottle of Single Malt Scotch. While no one was looking, he scraped off the price tag and put on a price tag from a bottle of cheap Scotch. That price tag read $7.99. The man paid the clerk $7.99 for the Scotch, put the receipt in the bag and left. At the common law, did he commit a crime when obtaining the Scotch?

A. Yes, it was a larceny.

B. Yes, it was a larceny by trick.

C. Yes, it was a false pretenses.

D. Yes, it was an embezzlement.

74. A man came to a pawnshop and saw a nice antique ring. He said to the pawnshop owner, "Don't you remember, I brought this ring in to you last week?" The owner of the pawnshop knew that the man had not pawned the ring but that the ring, in fact, belonged to someone else. Nonetheless, the pawnshop owner said, "Go ahead and take it. I don't think the rightful owner of the ring will return to claim it." Does the statement of the pawnshop owner relieve the man of liability for the crime of false pretenses?

A. Yes because the pawnshop owner gave the man consent.

B. Yes because the pawnshop owner was in lawful possession of the ring.

C. Yes because the man did not make any false statements.

D. No because the pawnshop owner did not have the right to give the ring to the man.

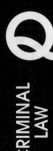

75. A car salesman who worked in a car dealership took home a car from the lot, intending to return it the next morning, which he was permitted to do as part of his job at the dealership. However, after he got home, he decided that he really did not like working at that dealership, so he took that car and drove out-of-state, never returning to that dealership again. Has he committed any crime against the dealership?

    A. Yes, he has committed embezzlement.

    B. Yes, he has committed larceny.

    C. Yes, he has committed conversion.

    D. No. It was good business, since no one would have bought the car anyway.

76. A woman was in a rush to get to work, so she got into her car and quickly backed out of her driveway without properly checking her mirrors. She ran over a small child who was playing behind the car. The child was severely injured and died in the hospital two weeks later. Under the common law, what crime did the woman commit?

    A. Vehicular manslaughter.

    B. Murder.

    C. Involuntary manslaughter.

    D. Reckless driving.

77. As part of his gang initiation, a young man severely beat an eight-year-old girl. The girl was taken to a hospital, where she spent the next thirteen months trying to recover from her injuries. However, she stopped breathing and died before she could be released from the hospital. At common law, is the young man guilty of criminal homicide?

    A. Yes because it is stipulated he was the proximate cause.

    B. No because the young man had no intent to kill the child.

    C. Yes because of the year and a day rule.

    D. No because of the year and a day rule.

78. A woman phoned her boyfriend and told him to come over immediately because she had a surprise for him. Excited, the boyfriend jumped into the car and made it to her apartment quickly. When he arrived, he gave her some flowers and a box of chocolates. She said, "Thanks, but the surprise is that I have another boyfriend, and I have to break up with you." Under the common law, which crime or crimes has the woman committed.

    A. Obtaining property through fraud.

B. Negligent infliction of emotional distress.

C. Intentional infliction of emotional distress.

D. No crime.

79. A man had a friend in the hospital. The friend asked the man to pick up some clothes for him at the friend's house, believing that the man had a key to the house. The man went to the house, but then he realized he was missing the key. So, rather than going back to the hospital, he smashed a window and went in the house. He took the clothes, as his friend had requested, and left by way of the front door (since it was unlocked from the inside). Under modern law, which crime has the man committed?

A. Vandalism.

B. Malicious mischief.

C. Burglary.

D. Forcible entry and detainer.

80. A man went to his girlfriend's bedroom and found her naked. She said, "Let's make love right now." He proceeded to have sexual relations with her. However, soon after genital penetration, the girlfriend said, "Stop. You're a heel and I'm done with you. Get out of my house now!" The man did not stop having sex. Three minutes later, after the girlfriend again told him to leave, he did. If the man is charged with common law rape, he will:

A. Be convicted, since consent was withdrawn.

B. Be convicted, since the girlfriend was not his wife.

C. Be acquitted, since the girlfriend's consent was binding.

D. Be acquitted because there was not complete carnal knowledge.

81. A woman went to her friend's house. When the friend was in the bathroom, the woman explored the house and found a picture of the friend and the woman's husband displayed in the friend's bedroom. Furious, the woman smashed the picture and left the house. At common law, which crime did the woman commit?

A. Malicious larceny.

B. Malicious mischief.

C. Vandalism.

D. Uttering.

82. A man caught his girlfriend in bed with his best friend. Enraged, he picked up a lamp and smashed the heads of his best friend and his girlfriend. Both died instantly. What crime did the man commit?

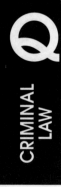

A. Murder.

B. Voluntary manslaughter.

C. Involuntary manslaughter.

D. No crime because the girlfriend deserved what happened to her.

83. A man lost his home to foreclosure. Angry, he followed his mortgage broker home. The next day, he took his gun out of his storage locker and contemplated going to the mortgage broker's house to kill the mortgage broker. (The man had passed the required gun training course and had a permit for the gun.) However, he had a change of heart and decided to borrow money from his parents to buy back the home. He put the gun back in the storage locker and went to his parents' house to borrow the money. Under these facts, what crime, if any, did the man commit when he picked up the gun?

A. Battery.

B. Assault.

C. Illegal firearms possession.

D. None of the above.

84. A drunken cowboy got into a barroom brawl with another cowboy in a saloon. The first cowboy ran out of the saloon and kicked and beat the second cowboy's horse. The horse suffered injuries so severe that he had to be put to sleep. When the first cowboy kicked and hurt the horse, what crime, if any, did he commit at common law?

A. Malicious mischief.

B. Cruelty to animals.

C. Murder.

D. Battery.

85. A teenage boy took his father's car out for a joyride because he was angry with his father. The boy decided to run away from home and keep the car. He, thus, drove off into the sunset and was never heard from again. What crime, if any, did the teenager commit at common law?

A. No crime because he was only trying to vent his anger at his father.

B. Malicious mischief.

C. Larceny by false pretenses.

D. Larceny.

86. A man walked into a bar and saw his second grade teacher. Years of bent up frustration from his horrible second grade year came to the forefront of his mind, and he ran up to the second grade teacher and hit her over the head with a barstool, killing her instantly. What crime is the man most likely to have committed?

A. First-degree murder.

B. Second-degree murder.

C. Voluntary manslaughter.

D. Involuntary manslaughter.

87. A man was walking down the street when he heard a voice that told him that the woman who was approaching was really Satan in a woman's body and needed to be killed immediately in order to eradicate evil from the world. The man turned around and punched the woman. She fell to the pavement and died instantly. What is the man's best complete common law defense to the killing of the woman?

    A. Insanity.

    B. Intoxication.

    C. Mistake of fact.

    D. Diminished capacity.

88. The mayor fired a man from his job at city hall. The man went home and stuffed himself with sugary snacks and milk. Still on a sugar high, he then returned to city hall and shot and killed the mayor. What is the man's best modern defense to the killing of the mayor?

    A. The Rule of Provocation.

    B. Insanity.

    C. Imperfect self-defense.

    D. Diminished capacity.

89. A man was smoking a cigarette by the railroad tracks when he noticed a small child was stuck on the track. A train was rapidly approaching. The man hated children, so he finished his cigarette and walked away. The child was hit by the train and killed instantly. The man's not giving aid to the child was:

    A. Battery.

    B. Assault.

    C. Misprision.

    D. None of these.

90. A man sat down in a restaurant and ordered a sandwich and a soft drink. The waiter miscalculated the amount owed. The food should have totaled $4.88, but the waiter totaled it as $3.59. The waiter gave the man the bill along with the food. The man at once observed that the bill was too low and pondered whether he would bother to correct it with the waiter. In the end, he decided that he would not bother to correct the error. He paid the $3.59 and left a dollar tip. The man's under-payment to the restaurant of the food bill was which crime?

    A. Larceny.

    B. Larceny by trick.

C. Robbery.

D. False pretenses.

91. An actress who was short on funds went into a local dress shop, placed one of the scarves that the store was selling for $100 into her purse, and snuck it out of the store. Under the modern law, what crime did the actress commit?

    A. Larceny.

    B. Petty theft.

    C. Grand theft.

    D. None of the above.

92. One night, a man returned to his home very drunk. He accidentally left his car door open and went into the house and went to sleep. A woman came along and hotwired the car and took it on a long trip, never intending to return it. The woman's taking of the car, modernly, was which, if any crime?

    A. Grand theft.

    B. Petty theft.

    C. Vandalism.

    D. No crime because she had constructive consent, since the man left the door open.

93. A man decided to steal a helicopter. He started it and expertly began to take off. However, a huge gust of wind blew the helicopter off course. The helicopter passed over a balcony, where a woman was standing admiring the city view. The woman's head was instantly chopped off by the propeller blades. If the man is convicted of involuntary manslaughter, which theory will, most likely, have been utilized by the prosecution?

    A. Malum in se unlawful act.

    B. Criminal negligence.

    C. Negligence.

    D. Depraved heart.

94. A homicidal maniac broke into a farmer's toolshed and stole a chainsaw, which he used to murder several people. Is there any theory under which the farmer could be charged with the criminal homicide of these people?

    A. Yes, he was a substantial factor.

    B. Unclean hands.

    C. Depraved heart.

    D. None of the above.

95. A law states the following:

The purposeful assembly of four or more individuals in public with the intent or with reckless disregard for the tranquility of others present is a Breach of the Peace.

If four friends light off firecrackers in Central Park in the presence of a huge crowd, their best defense to charges of Conspiracy to Breach the Peace and Breach of the Peace is:

A. There was no proof that anyone else was present.

B. This crime has multiple intent requirements, and these have not been proven.

C. Wharton's Rule.

D. Firecrackers in Central Park are no big deal.

96. At a party one night, a man offers his neighbor a marijuana cigarette. The neighbor believes it is a regular cigarette and puts it away to smoke later. The man leaves the party and immediately calls the police and tells them the neighbor is in illegal possession of marijuana. The police arrive 10 minutes later with a fully proper telephonic search warrant, and find the marijuana in the neighbor's coat pocket. What is the neighbor's best defense to a charge of "Knowing possession of marijuana?"

A. He was not in true possession.

B. He was entrapped, as a matter of law.

C. He lacked knowledge or scienter.

D. He lacked evil motives, and was a creature of circumstance.

97. A man drove through two red lights at 100 MPH in a school zone. A police officer pulled him over and could see that the man's wife (who was in the passenger seat) was visibly pregnant and in labor. The police officer gave the man a police escort to the hospital but, nonetheless, charged the man with violating the relevant traffic laws. Under modern majority rules, what is the man's best defense to violating the traffic laws?

A. Necessity.

B. Duress.

C. Emotional distress.

D. Unclean hands.

98. During a severe storm, a man docked his boat in a woman's boat dock. The woman ran out to the dock with a gun, pointed it at the man, and demanded that he leave her dock at once. The man explained to the woman that he needed to get out of a life-threatening storm, so that he would not drown. Nevertheless, the woman called the police and had the man charged with forcible entry and detainer. Is the man guilty under the common law?

A. Yes because he trespassed onto woman's property.

B. No because the woman used

excessive force.

C. No because he used no force in the trespass.

D. No because this was not a common law crime.

99. There was a series of burglaries in a suburban neighborhood. One man rigged up a gun so that it would fire automatically if someone tried to enter his home without first entering a code to disarm it. One evening when the man was out at a party, a burglar attempted to break into his home. The automatic gun discharged and killed the burglar instantly. Under the modern law, if the man is charged with murder, he will most likely:

A. Be found guilty, since deadly force cannot be used to protect property.

B. Be found guilty because burglars deserve to be shot.

C. Be found not guilty, based on the habitation defense.

D. Be found not guilty because the burglar was unlawfully present.

100. A man and his girlfriend were in a car kissing. A vigilante, who did not approve of men and women kissing in a car, smashed the window with his gun and pointed it at the man and the woman. The man was able to get out of the car and grab the gun. The vigilante ran away. The man threw the gun in a garbage can. A police officer saw the whole event and charged the man with criminal battery and robbery of the gun. What is the man's best defense?

A. Defense of property (the man's car).

B. Necessity.

C. The man did not intend to permanently deprive.

D. Diminished capacity.

END OF QUESTIONS

CRIMINAL LAW ANSWERS

1. Answer A is the correct answer because strict liability offenses require only the actus reas to be committed. There is no mens rea requirement. Here, the statute punishes substance addiction, with no mens rea requirement. Thus, the fact that the man is a heroin addict makes him guilty of the offense. (Remember to choose the right answer for the law involved, regardless of its fairness or unfairness.) Answer B is incorrect. Even though involuntary intoxication is usually a defense to strict liability crimes, it is irrelevant because the crime here has already been committed simply by virtue of the man being addicted to an illegal substance (here, heroin). Furthermore, there is nothing in the facts to indicate that the man was intoxicated at that moment, anyway. Answer C is incorrect because the unconstitutionality or constitutionality of the law needs to be tested in court. The man can still be charged with the crime in the meantime. Furthermore, there is nothing vague about the law here; it says "any illegal substance," which clearly applies to any substance that is illegal. Answer D is incorrect because it is irrelevant if the law is unfair.

2. C is correct. The jury instruction defined a basic crime (false pretenses), but left out any mens rea requirement. All crimes require an actus reas (criminal act), and most crimes also require mens rea (mental state) (other than strict liability crimes). As a general rule, crimes should include a mens rea. If they do not, there is a possible due process violation. Here, false pretenses is a specific intent crime, so the man had to have intended to obtain the title to the property, along with the rest of the elements of false pretenses. Without a mens rea requirement in the jury instructions, the jurors would not have considered whether the man had this specific intent in their decision to find him guilty of the crime. A is incorrect because no facts whatsoever were set out regarding evidence. Thus, one cannot reasonably conclude whether the evidence was sufficient or insufficient. B is incorrect for the same reason that C is correct. D is incorrect because false pretenses requires obtaining title, not "documentary title." Documentary title is, in fact, not a legal term of significance.

3. B is the correct answer. Solicitation to commit robbery is enticing another to commit robbery with the intent that the other commit robbery. The facts stipulate that the man tried to get the woman to commit robbery, and the woman said that she had to think about it. Since there was a serious request to commit robbery, both elements of solicitation are established. A is incorrect because conspiracy is the agreement by two or more parties to commit a crime. Here, since the woman did not explicitly agree – but instead said that she had to think about it - there was no meeting of the minds and no agreement on the part of

the woman. C is incorrect because attempt requires that there be a substantial step (dangerous proximity to success). Here, at the time of the solicitation by the man, the parties were not nearly close enough to commission of the crime for robbery, since the woman did not even agree to participate and there are no facts indicating that the man went any further. D is incorrect for the same reason that B is correct – solicitation is a crime and the enticement is a sufficient actus reus (guilty action).

4. A is the correct answer. Embezzlement is a crime committed when a person is in rightful possession of an item and converts it to his own use. Here, the bank teller had rightful possession of money in her cash drawer, and she converted it to her own use by taking the $500 home. This fraudulent taking of the $500 is an embezzlement. Answer B is wrong because she did not have title to the money, one of the elements of false pretenses. Answer C is wrong because there is no such crime as "malicious trespass." Answer D is incorrect because there are no facts to demonstrate that the woman did not intend to return the $500 or permanently deprive the bank of the money (the last element of larceny by trick). Therefore, D is incorrect. However, there is still an embezzlement for the reasons discussed in Answer A.

5. B is correct. At common law, a burglary required a trespassory breaking and entering into the dwelling of another at night with intent to commit a felony therein. All elements had to be met for a person to be found guilty of common law burglary. Under most modern statutes, burglary has been defined merely as the unlawful entering into a structure (not necessary a dwelling) with the intent to commit a crime therein (not necessarily at night, and not necessarily a felony). Here, the man and the woman broke into a warehouse (not a dwelling of another). They broke in during the daytime (not at night). Therefore, they could not be found guilty of common law burglary, but they could be found guilty under most modern statutes. Thus, Answer B is the correct answer. Answer A is incorrect because, as discussed in Answer B, common law burglary requires the breaking and entry occur at night and to a dwelling house. Those two elements are lacking here because the incident occurred during the day and at a warehouse (not a dwelling). C and D are incorrect because, as discussed in Answer A, they were not guilty under common law, but, as discussed in Answer B, they were guilty under most modern statutes.

6. C is correct. Larceny is the trespassory taking (stealing) and carrying away (stolen from a store) of the personal property of another (here the diamond ring) with the intent to permanently deprive (there is nothing in the facts to indicate that the woman intended to return the diamond ring). The facts indicate that all of the elements are present. Thus, a larceny has been committed. A is incorrect because, for there to be an embezzlement, the defendant must be in lawful possession

of the property. Here, the woman did not have lawful possession of the diamond ring. B is incorrect because false pretenses requires that the defendant obtain title to the property. Here, the woman did not get title to the diamond ring. D is incorrect for the same reason that C is correct.

7. D is the correct answer. Under common law, malice (one of the elements of murder) can be found if a person dies during the commission of a "particularly dangerous felony." Rape is considered to be such a "particularly dangerous felony." Here, the woman died during the commission of the rape. Therefore, the man is guilty of felony murder under the common law. A is incorrect because involuntary manslaughter requires no malice. However, as discussed in Answer D, when a person dies during the commission of a "particularly dangerous felony," there is malice at common law. B is incorrect because, as discussed in Answer D, the man is guilty of a crime other than rape – namely, felony murder under the common law. C is incorrect because voluntary manslaughter also requires there be "legally adequate provocation." Rape is not legally adequate, and the rapist was not provoked; he was the one engaging in the provoking action.

8. B is the correct answer. Larceny is the trespassory taking and carrying away of the personal property of another with intent to permanently deprive. Here, the man took and ate food (taking and carrying away) that was not his own without permission (trespassory) and, by eating it, intended to permanently deprive the food's owner of the food. Thus, the man committed a larceny of the food. However, necessity is a complete defense to all crimes, except murder and rape. Necessity allows doing a criminal act in order to avoid a greater calamity. Here, since the man was starving, stealing some food (larceny) was better than his own death. A is incorrect because when the man took the food (the actus reas), he intended to steal it (the mens rea), for the reasons discussed in Answer B. Thus, the mens rea and actus reas of larceny did concur. C simply misreads the question. Breaking and entering are elements of burglary and this question asked for the man's best defense to larceny of the food. D is incorrect because it is imprecise. Due process or "fundamental fairness" may be violated by punishing here, but the defense of necessity is the best defense, which is what this question is asking for.

9. A is the correct answer. Larceny is the trespassory taking and carrying away of the personal property of another with intent to permanently deprive. An attempted crime requires there be a substantial step and that intent to do the crime be present. Here, the fact that the woman had an original intent to take and carry away the dress without paying for it (which would satisfy both the "trespassory" and "permanently deprive" elements) would have resulted in a completed larceny, if the woman had not changed her mind and returned the dress

to the hanger without leaving the store. However, after she formed the intent, she returned the dress before she ever made it to the exit of the store. Thus, there was not a substantial step, and the first element of attempt was lacking. B is incorrect because the store was in possession of the dress. C is incorrect because "asportation" (movement of the item in question) was met when the woman started taking the dress toward the exit. However, she was charged with attempted larceny, and an element of attempt was missing, as discussed in Answer A. D is irrelevant, since the condition of the dress is not at issue.

10. C is correct. Burglary, at common law, requires there be a breaking and entering into the dwelling of another, at night, with intent to commit a felony therein. Here, the catburglar entered the home through a completely open window. The "breaking" element is satisfied when there is any movement into the dwelling. Here, the facts stipulate that the window (where the catburglar entered) was completely open. Thus, there was no breaking. This would be the catburglar's best defense. A is incorrect because diminished capacity was not a common law defense. B is incorrect because burglary is a crime against the dwelling of another. It is not necessary that there be any person home at the time of the burglary. It just has to be used as a habitation. D is incorrect because the defense of compulsion (or duress) requires that another human threaten the defendant with imminent violence, so that the defendant will commit a crime. There was no compulsion here.

11. D is the correct answer. Infancy refers to any person under the age of 18. At common law, a person under the age of seven years was irrebuttably presumed incapable of committing a crime. Here, the boy was only five years old at the time he stabbed his neighbor to death. Therefore, infancy is the boy's best defense, as it completely absolves him of any crime. A is incorrect because even mentally disturbed people can form the requisite mens rea for murder. B is incorrect because there are no facts to mitigate the charge to manslaughter. C is incorrect because there are no facts to indicate that the boy was acting in self-defense.

12. D is the correct answer. At common law, conspiracy was defined as an agreement between two or more parties to commit an unlawful act. The crime of conspiracy was complete at common law as soon as the agreement was reached. Therefore, one may never withdraw from the conspiracy itself once the agreement has been reached. Here, although the man could not go to the bank to participate in the robbery, he is still guilty of conspiracy because he made an agreement with the other two men to rob the bank (an unlawful act). Therefore, he has no defense. A is incorrect because, as discussed in Answer D, there was an agreement. B is incorrect because conspiracy never merges. It is a separate crime, not

a lesser included offense. C is incorrect because, as discussed in Answer D, one can never withdraw from a conspiracy, only from the crimes in furtherance of the conspiracy.

13. A is the correct answer. Under common law, malice (one of the elements of murder) can be found if a person dies during the commission of a "particularly dangerous felony." Burglary is considered to be such a "particularly dangerous felony." At common law, a burglary required a trespassory breaking and entering into the dwelling of another at night with intent to commit a felony therein. All elements had to be met for a person to be found guilty of common law burglary. Here, the man pushed open "the already slightly-opened ground floor window" in order to enter the house (breaking and entering). The facts tell us that this occurred at night and that he intended to steal the woman's computer (a felony). Thus, all of the elements of burglary have been met. Since the woman's death occurred during the commission of the burglary (a "particularly dangerous felony," as discussed above), the man is guilty of felony murder. B is incorrect because there was no first-degree murder at common law. C is incorrect because there are no facts to indicate heat of passion. Furthermore, the man is guilty of felony murder, not voluntary manslaughter, for the reasons discussed in Answer A. D is incorrect because accidental killings certainly can lead to criminal homicide convictions. Felony-murder is one such example.

14. B is the correct answer. A person with knowledge of the existence of a completed crime, who helps to hinder the arrest of the perpetrator, is guilty of obstruction of justice. Here, the man's mother knew of the man's crime, but hid him anyway and lied to the police when he inquired as to the man's whereabouts. She is, thus, guilty of obstruction of justice. A is incorrect because a conspiracy is an agreement between two or more people to commit an unlawful act. Here, the man's mother did not agree with the man or anyone else to commit a crime. C is incorrect because the man's mother was not a perpetrator of the kidnapping. She was, thus, an accessory after the fact (as discussed in Answer B), not a principal in the second degree. D is incorrect because there are no facts to indicate that the man's mother was involved in the planning of the kidnapping.

15. C is correct. If a defendant commits a crime while under the influence of drugs or alcohol, even if the drugs make him delusional, insanity is not available. Only voluntary intoxication is relevant. However, if the defendant has caused himself brain damage by chronic use of drugs – and is not then under the influence – insanity is relevant. Here, the psychiatrist has stated that the man has chronic alcohol-induced mental illness. Thus, the man has caused his brain damage through the chronic use of drugs (here, alcohol). The man killed the woman while he was sober. However, under the prevailing majority and

common law M'Naghten insanity test (not knowing the difference between right and wrong), the man had a mental illness, a defect of reason (the devil message) and did not know this killing was wrong. Therefore, M'Naghten is satisfied, and the man is legally insane, assuming that this is a M'Naghten jurisdiction. Thus, he would be found not guilty by reason of insanity. A is incorrect because the facts state that the man was not intoxicated at the time of the killing. B is incorrect. Although the man did know what he was doing (the nature and quality of his acts), this element is only an option in the M'Naghten test. M'Naghten can also be satisfied if the defendant does not know what he is doing is wrong, as discussed in Answer C. D is incorrect because the mistake of fact defense, for a malice crime like common law murder, requires the mistake to be objectively reasonable. D is incorrect because believing that the woman was sent by the Devil is not objectively reasonable.

16. B is the correct answer. A battery is the use of force against another, resulting in harmful or offensive contact. Battery is generally a low-grade misdemeanor. Here, the battery occurred when the man beat his wife. Of the crimes described in the answer choices, battery was the least serious. A is incorrect because, although the man locked the woman and the neighbor in the house (and he may, thus, be guilty of false imprisonment), this is a more serious crime than battery. C is incorrect because, while the man may have kidnapped the neighbor, kidnapping is a more serious crime than battery. D is incorrect because the negligent infliction of emotional distress is not a crime. It is a tort.

17. B is the correct answer. A battery is the use of force against another, resulting in harmful or offensive contact. An assault is an attempted battery. Here, the Bouncer committed two batteries: the first shove and the second shove. When he tried to slap the woman in the face but missed, this was an attempted battery, which is the definition of assault. A, C, and D are incorrect for the reasons that B is correct.

18. A is the correct answer. At common law, murder required the killing of a human being by another human being with malice aforethought. The mental state of malice aforethought is found by intent to kill, intent to do serious bodily harm, wanton or depraved heart, or felony murder. Here, the facts demonstrate that the loser intended to kill the winner and did so. Thus, he would be guilty of common law murder. B is incorrect because first-degree murder was not a crime at common law. C is incorrect because a requirement of voluntary manslaughter is that the killing follow immediately upon the passion-provoking incident. Here, he waited until the following day, which is too long for voluntary manslaughter. D is incorrect because involuntary manslaughter covers only unintentional killings, and this killing was on purpose.

19. C is the correct answer. The woman had a good faith but unreasonable belief that the killing was necessary to protect herself – the exact requirement of this partial defense. It is only a partial defense here because the husband was not in the process of beating or otherwise hurting her at the time of the killing; he was asleep. A is incorrect because, as discussed in Answer C, the husband was not in the process of beating or otherwise hurting her at the time of the killing; he was asleep. B is incorrect because there are no facts to indicate that the woman was insane. D is incorrect because C is correct.

20. C is the correct answer. At common law, burglary was the breaking and entering into the dwelling of another at night with the intent to commit a felony therein. Here, the man broke into the woman's home at noon. Therefore, the nighttime element has not been satisfied, so this is the man's best defense to common law burglary. A is incorrect because the facts state that he intended to commit a rape inside the house, which is a felony. As discussed in Answer C, the proper mens rea for common law burglary is the intent to commit a felony inside of the dwelling. Thus, the man had the proper mens rea for common law burglary here. B is incorrect because the facts state that the man did intend to rape the woman. D is incorrect because the entry element of burglary is satisfied when any part of the perpetrator's body penetrates the dwelling. Since the man's foot penetrated, the entry requirement was satisfied here.

21. C is the correct answer. Larceny is the trespassory taking and carrying away of the personal property of another with intent to permanently deprive. Attempt requires that there be a substantial step (dangerous proximity to success). Here, the man was in the zone of perpetration (dangerous proximity to success) because he was in the process of pulling the purse from the woman's arm, intending to permanently deprive her of it, and would have completed the act but for the fact that he saw the policeman. Thus, he is guilty of attempted larceny. A is incorrect because there are no facts to indicate that the man lacked the mental ability to form the mens rea to steal the purse. B is incorrect because, as discussed in Answer C, the man did take a substantial step toward the commission of the larceny. D is incorrect because it is irrelevant.

22. D is the correct answer. After a crime has been committed, a crime by an officer does not retroactively limit the guilt of the original perpetrator. Thus, the police officer's punching of the driver (a possible criminal battery) is irrelevant. A, B and C are incorrect for the same reason that D is correct.

23. A is the correct answer. This is a very tricky question. Embezzlement is a crime committed when a person is in rightful possession of an item and converts it to his own use. Here, the store manager was in more than mere custody of the money. Thus, when he pocketed the man's $100, he commit-

ted embezzlement. Since he did not put the man's money into the register, the $100 he took out was the store's, along with the $6.88 that he removed from the register as change for the man. Further, he deprived the store of the $3.12 item. Thus, he embezzled a total of $110. Larceny is the trespassory taking and carrying of the personal property of another with intent to permanently deprive. Here, the store manager took the man's $100 for a $3.12 item and only gave him $6.88 change. Thus, the store manager committed a larceny against the man by depriving the man of his accurate change. Answer B is incorrect because the amounts are wrong, for the reasons discussed in Answer A. Answer C is incorrect because it does not include the larceny against the man, as discussed in Answer A. Answer D is incorrect because it misstates the facts. Here, the store manager deliberately took the $100; there was no mistake here.

24. D is the correct answer. In a slim majority of jurisdictions, an honest claim of right negates the intent element of the theft crimes. Here, the teenager thought that he was entitled to retrieve his bicycle and that he had a claim of right. For that reason A, B and C are incorrect because all of the crimes in A, B, and C require specific intent.

25. D is the correct answer. A battery is the use of force against another, resulting in harmful or offensive contact. Battery is generally a low-grade misdemeanor. An aggravated battery is a more serious form of battery and generally involves the use of a deadly weapon. Thus, when the rancher shot the man with a gun (a deadly weapon), he committed an aggravated battery. Deadly force is never permissible when used merely to protect property, even living property (such as cattle). Here, the man's attempt to steal the cattle was merely a crime against the rancher's property (his cattle). Thus, the rancher impermissibly used deadly force in shooting at the man to defend the property. Thus, he is guilty of an aggravated battery and has no excuse for this crime. A is incorrect because, as discussed in Answer D, the fact that the man was attempting to steal the bull would not permit the rancher to use deadly force. B is incorrect because it misstates the law. As discussed in Answer D, a person is not permitted to use deadly force to protect property. C is incorrect because it is nonsensical.

26. B is the correct answer. Malicious mischief is the willful or wanton destruction of the property of another. Here, the artist's repainting of the mural was without permission and was, thus, the wanton destruction of the property (the mural) of another (likely the city). A is incorrect because mayhem requires the dismembering of a person, not an inanimate object (the mural). C is incorrect because larceny is the trespassory taking and carrying away of the personal property of another with intent to permanently deprive. Here, the artist did not take the mural. Thus, she

did not commit a larceny. D is incorrect because this is not an adequate defense to a crime.

27. D is the correct answer. Rape is defined as unlawful carnal knowledge of a woman (not the wife) by a man without her consent. Statutory rape is considered to be strict liability offense. It occurs when a man over the age of majority has carnal knowledge of a girl under the age of majority (which in most jurisdictions is 18). Because it is a strict liability offense, there are virtually no defenses to statutory rape. Here, the girl was 17, and the neighbor was over age of majority. Thus, there are no defenses. A is incorrect because consent is not an element of this crime, and his mistaken belief that the girl was his wife is not a defense to statutory rape. B is incorrect because the girl was not the neighbor's wife. C is incorrect because the mistaken belief that the girl was the neighbor's wife would not be a defense to statutory rape, as discussed above.

28. C is the correct answer. At common law, robbery was larceny with force or threat of force. Larceny was defined as the trespassory taking and carrying away of the personal property of another with intent to permanently deprive. Since robbery required force or threats of force, the force needed for battery merged with robbery. Also, larceny was a lesser included offense of robbery and, thus, merged with robbery, as well. Here, the woman took the man's money (larceny) and punched him in the stomach (battery). Thus, the woman was guilty of larceny and battery, which, as discussed above, is the definition of robbery. A, B, and D, are incorrect because, as discussed in C, larceny and battery merge with robbery.

29. A is the best answer. Modernly, infancy can be defined as under 18 years of age. Here, the boy is 17, so he might have such a defense. B is incorrect since, literally, public policy is not a defense. C is incorrect because whatever mistaken reason the boy hacked into the computer, since he hacked into the computer, it is highly unlikely that he did not realize that he was viewing restricted material. D is incorrect because, regardless of what the boy may have thought about the FBI, no one was immediately threatening him at the time. Thus, self-defense is not a valid defense under these facts.

30. D is the correct answer. Involuntary intoxication occurs when a person is unaware that he is under the influence of a drug or controlled substance. If a person, unaware that he is under the influence, commits a crime, he may raise the defense of involuntary intoxication, and it will be viewed as a form of temporary insanity. Here, the man was given a drug by the stripper, and he was unaware of this fact. During his delusional state as a result of the drug, he thought that the stripper was going to steal from him and, therefore, hit her over the head and killed her. Thus, since the man was drugged and could

not form the mens rea for the crime of murder, this would be his best defense. A is incorrect because, although the man believed he was acting in self-defense, his belief was delusional. Also, there is nothing to indicate that the man believed that the stripper was threatening the man with force, which would be necessary for self-defense. B is incorrect because, even though the man was mistaken in his belief that stripper was going to steal from him, this mistaken belief is not as good a defense as involuntary intoxication, which is a far stronger defense to any crime. C is incorrect because, as discussed in Answer D, the man's intoxication was involuntary.

31. A is the correct answer. Solicitation occurs when a person asks another person to commit a crime. Here, when the woman asked her brother to turn off the life support system, in essence she was asking him to commit a murder. Thus, there was a solicitation. Consent of the victim is no defense to murder. B is incorrect because the woman completed her solicitation when she asked her brother to turn off the life support system. C is incorrect. A conspiracy requires an agreement between two or more people to commit a crime. Here, the brother did not agree. Thus, there was no conspiracy. D is incorrect for the same reasons that A is correct.

32. D is the correct answer. A crime requires actus reas (an act), mens rea (the requisite mental state), and causation. Here, since the man only thought about killing his neighbor, but took no actions in furtherance of this, there was neither actus reas nor causation. Thus, there was no crime, since mens rea alone cannot be punished. A is incorrect because the man did not solicit anyone to commit a crime. B is incorrect because the man did not attempt a crime, as discussed in Answer D. C is incorrect because the man did not enter into an agreement with anyone to commit a crime.

33. C is the correct answer. A battery is the use of force against another, resulting in harmful or offensive contact. Larceny is the trespassory taking and carrying away of the personal property of another with the intent to permanently deprive the owner of the property. Murder is the killing of a human being by a human being with malice aforethought. Attempt requires that there be a substantial step toward the completed crime (dangerous proximity to success). Here, the man grabbed his wife and forced her to drink the coffee. This was harmful and offensive and, therefore, met the elements of battery. The man forced woman to drink the coffee containing the rat poison with the intent of killing her. But for the fact that he called the ambulance and she survived, she likely would have died, in which case he would have been guilty of murder. Therefore, he is guilty of attempted murder because his actions were in the zone of perpetration. Finally, he took the rat poison from the store without permission, thereby indicating an intent

to permanently deprive the store of the rat poison. He carried the rat poison away from the store when he took it home with him. Thus, he is also guilty of larceny. A, B, and D are incorrect because the man is guilty of all three crimes, as discussed in Answer C.

34. C is the correct answer. A murder requires the killing of a human being by a human being with malice aforethought. Like all crimes, murder requires actus reas (here, the strangling), mens rea (here, malice aforethought), and causation. At common law, there was a year and a day rule, which required that the victim die within a year and a day of the act. This was a means of cutting off the liability for the chain of causation. Here, the prosecutor died 13 months after the act. Thus, this would be the best defense. A is incorrect because, although a murder may be mitigated to a manslaughter if there is adequate provocation, a reasonable person would not have strangled the prosecutor for pointing his finger at the man's wife. B is incorrect because there are no facts to indicate that the man was insane. D is incorrect because one may only use an amount of force equal to the amount of force that is threatening others. Here, the prosecutor was merely pointing; he was not using any force. Thus, no force could be used against the prosecutor, making D the incorrect answer.

35. C is the correct answer. Murder is the killing of a human being by a human being with malice aforethought. Murder may be mitigated down to voluntary manslaughter, if there is adequate provocation. When an individual is reasonably provoked (here by the racial slur), is actually upset (stipulated in the facts), and has insufficient time to "cool down" (the attack occurred immediately after the racial slur was made), the rule of provocation will mitigate murder to voluntary manslaughter. A and B, and D are incorrect because there are no facts to indicate diminished capacity, insanity, or mistake of fact.

36. B is the correct answer. Embezzlement is a crime committed when a person is in rightful possession of an item and converts it to his own use. Here, since he was in a managerial position, the store manager had "lawful possession" of the money – not mere custody. When he pocketed the money, he converted it to his own use. Thus, he committed embezzlement. It is irrelevant that he did not report it as store income. A is incorrect because larceny is the trespassory taking and carrying away of the property of another. Here, as discussed in Answer B, the store manager had lawful possession of the money. Thus, when he pocketed the money, it was a conversion, but not a trespassory taking. C is incorrect. A larceny by trick occurs when one takes possession to the property of another by intentional false statement of past or existing fact with intent to defraud. Here, as discussed in Answer B, the store manager had lawful possession of the money; he did not obtain the possession by making

any false statements. D is incorrect. A larceny by false pretenses occurs when one takes title to the property of another by intentional false statement of past or existing fact with intent to defraud. Here, the store manager did not obtain title to the money, nor did he make any false statements; he simply pocketed the money.

37. D is the correct answer. Embezzlement is a crime committed when a person is in rightful possession of an item and converts it to his own use. Here, the museum curator was in lawful possession of the jewelry. However, he was not entitled to take it home with him. By doing so, he converted it to his own use and, thus, committed the crime of embezzlement at common law. Modernly, grand versus petty theft is determined by fair market value of what is stolen. A typical cut-off figure is $400. Although the facts are unclear as to the amount stolen, a reasonable inference is that the ancient jewelry was worth more than $400. Thus, Answer D is the correct answer. A is incorrect because no facts indicate that the jewelry was stolen property. B is incorrect because fraud is not a crime. C is incorrect because this was a grand theft, not a petty theft, as discussed in Answer D.

38. A is the correct answer. Misprison is the knowing concealment of the felony of another. Here, the money launderer committed the felony of money laundering and, by not showing it on the tax return, the accountant was knowingly concealing this felony. B is incorrect because there generally is no such privilege and, in any case, there is no privilege to cover up a crime. C is incorrect because, as discussed in Answer A, the money launderer did commit the crime of money laundering. D is incorrect for the same reasons that A is correct.

39. D is the correct answer. The dean did not commit any of the crimes listed, for the reasons discussed below. Answer A is incorrect because a criminal battery is the use of force against another, resulting in harmful or offensive contact, and assault is an attempted battery. Here, the dean neither assaulted nor battered the staff and the professors; he merely fired them. Answer B is incorrect because, although the dean may have committed both wrongful termination and intentional infliction of emotional distress, these are torts, not crimes. Answer C is incorrect because, as discussed in Answer A, the dean did not commit an assault here.

40. B is the correct answer. Conspiracy at common law was defined as an agreement between two or more people to commit a crime or unlawful act. Modernly, an overt act is also required. Here, when the mob boss and the hitman agreed to a killing, all of the elements of common law conspiracy have been met and, thus, the mob boss is guilty of conspiracy. Answer A is incorrect because, although the mob boss solicited the hitman to do the killing, solicitation (asking another to commit a crime)

merges into conspiracy. Answer C is incorrect because there are no facts to indicate that the hitman committed a robbery. Answer D is incorrect because the enemy did not die.

41. A is the correct answer. First-degree murder is a premeditated and deliberated killing of a human being by a human being with malice aforethought. Malice aforethought is the intent to kill, intent to do serious bodily harm, wanton or depraved heart, or felony murder. By statute, first-degree murder has added the element of premeditation and deliberation. Here, the terrorist intended to kill the people in the government building, and he hired the bomber to do so, showing his premeditation and deliberation to kill. It is irrelevant that the terrorist did not carry out the bombing himself; by hiring someone to carry it out on his behalf, it is considered to be as if the terrorist did the bombing himself. The terrorist is also guilty of conspiracy. Conspiracy is defined as an agreement between two or more parties to commit an unlawful act. Since the bomber carried out the action of placing the bomb in the government building, this shows implied agreement to do the unlawful act (the bombing). Answers B, C, and D are incorrect for the reasons discussed in Answer A.

42. C is the correct answer. At common law, conspiracy was defined as an agreement between two or more parties to commit an unlawful act. The crime of conspiracy was complete at common law as soon as the agreement was reached. Modernly, an overt act in furtherance of the conspiracy is also required. Conspiracy is a separate crime and it never merges with the completed crime itself. First-degree murder is a premeditated and deliberated killing of a human being by a human being with malice aforethought. Malice aforethought is the intent to kill, intent to do serious bodily harm, wanton or depraved heart, or felony murder. By statute, first-degree murder has added the element of premeditation and deliberation. Burglary at common law was the breaking and entering into the dwelling of another at night with the intent to commit a felony therein. Modernly, the unlawful entering into any structure (whether or not a dwelling) satisfies the "structure" requirement. Furthermore, modern law has eliminated the nighttime requirement; burglary may now be committed at any time of the day. Finally, modern law has eliminated the felony requirement; now the intent to commit any crime inside the structure will suffice for burglary.

Here, the actor expressly agreed with the producer to kill the producer's wife and broke into the producer's home to do so. Thus, there was a conspiracy to kill the producer's wife. Furthermore, the producer and the actor premeditated and deliberated regarding this killing, indicating their intent to kill the wife, demonstrating malice aforethought. Thus, the killing was a first-degree murder. Finally, the actor broke into the producer's home (a structure) with the intent to commit the crime of murder. Thus, the actor is guilty of burglary. Consequently, since he did in fact kill the producer's wife, the actor is guilty of all three crimes. Answers A, B, and D are incorrect for the reasons discussed in Answer C.

43. D is the correct answer. A crime requires an actus reas, mens rea, and causation. Here, the man intended to deliver the wallet to the police, which he did. Therefore, he did not have the mens rea necessary for a crime, since when he picked up the wallet, his intent was neither to steal (larceny) nor to defraud (embezzlement). Answers, A and B are incorrect for the reasons discussed in Answer D. Answer C is incorrect for two reasons: first, trespass is not a crime; and second, even if it were, there is no trespass when finding lost property (here, the wallet), provided one's intent is to turn it in, as the man did here.

44. C is the correct answer. Larceny is the trespassory taking and carrying away of the personal property of another with the intent to permanently deprive the owner of the property. Here, the woman drove off in the car with no apparent intent to return it. Thus, her driving off was both trespassory (since the car did not belong to her), and by driving it off, she carried away the property of another (the car dealership). Malicious mischief is the willful or wanton destruction of the property of another. Here because there was damage to the property of another (the window and the car), there was a malicious mischief. At common law, burglary was the breaking and entering into the dwelling of another at night with the intent to commit a felony therein. As always, if any of the elements of a crime are not met, the crime in question has not been committed. Here, since the breaking and entering was not of a dwelling (it was into a car dealership), there was no burglary. Thus, the woman was guilty of larceny and malicious mischief, but not burglary. Hence, Answer D is incorrect. Answers A and B are incorrect because they do not state both crimes (larceny and malicious mischief).

45. D is the correct answer. A larceny is the trespassory taking and carrying away of the personal property of another with the intent to permanently deprive the owner of possession thereof. Here, the college student intended to return the car to the professor. Thus, he did not intend to permanently deprive the owner (the professor or possibly the leasing agency) of possession of the car. Thus, this is his best defense to a charge of larceny, since negating even one element of a crime completely absolves a person of guilt. A is incorrect because the facts indicate that the car belonged to the professor and was not lost. Furthermore, taking away lost property is still a larceny, since the property still belongs to someone. B is incorrect because larceny is the crime of depriving someone of possession, not ownership, of property. Therefore,

it does not matter if the car was leased, since the professor was in lawful possession of the car either way. Thus, this would not be a good defense. C is incorrect because there are only two types of property: real and personal. Real property includes land and buildings, while personal property includes virtually anything else that can be owned. Thus, the car was personal property.

46. D is the correct answer. In modern law, grand theft is the intentional taking of the property of others in an amount exceeding the State statutory amount (which is generally a few hundred dollars). Grand theft has replaced the common law crime of larceny. Here, the woman's taking of the grandmother's dress (which was certainly worth well above the State statutory amount), which was then in lawful possession of the grandmother, would amount to a grand theft modernly (not a larceny – the common law term). Answers A, B, and C are incorrect for the reasons discussed in Answer D. Furthermore, Answer C is also incorrect because conversion is a tort, not a crime.

47. C is the correct answer. Mayhem includes not only disfigurement, but also any permanent damage to the body interfering with self-defense abilities. Paralysis qualifies as such. Here, the opponent suffered neck injuries and permanent partial paralysis. Thus, the wrestler committed mayhem. In addition, he committed a battery. Criminal battery is defined as a harmful or offensive touching through the use of force. Here, the sleeper hold constituted a touching. Since it resulted in the opponent's serious injuries, it was harmful and, thus, a battery. Answer A is incorrect because there was also a mayhem, as discussed in Answer C. Answers B and D are incorrect because the opponent gave a conditional consent – only and such is limited to the condition allowed. He did not consent to the sleeper hold – he consented to faking the sleeper hold.

48. B is the correct answer. Involuntary intoxication occurs when a person is unaware that he is under the influence of a drug or controlled substance. If a person, unaware that he is under the influence, commits a crime, he may raise the defense of involuntary intoxication. It will be viewed as a form of temporary insanity. Here, the male contestant slipped the drug into the female contestant's drink, and she was unaware of it. Her reaction to the drug was, thus, involuntary intoxication, and this would alleviate her guilt, since the drug created a mental disorder (her delusional belief that the TV host was trying to sleep with her). Answers A and C are incorrect for the reasons discussed in Answer B, namely, even if she committed a murder or voluntary manslaughter, the defense of involuntary intoxication relieves her of any guilt. Answer D is incorrect because in order to utilize self-defense, there must be an imminent attack and only reasonable force may be used. Neither situation existed here.

49. D is the correct answer because there was no common law crime committed here. Under the common law, a person was free to modify a gun any way he chose. Here, there is a statute, which the man appeared to have violated. However, the question asks what crime, if any, he committed at common law. Thus, D is the correct answer because the man did not commit any crime at common law. Answer A is incorrect. Malicious mischief is the willful or wanton destruction of the property of another. Here, the man altered (arguably destroyed) his own property (his gun). Thus, he did nothing to "the property of another" and, consequently, is not guilty of malicious mischief. Answer B is incorrect because no one was killed in this fact pattern, which is a basic requirement of murder. Answer C is incorrect because one may not use deadly force to protect his property.

50. C is the correct answer. Burglary at common law was the breaking and entering into the dwelling of another at night with the intent to commit a felony therein. Here, the man fulfilled all the elements of burglary. He broke and entered into the woman's home (the dwelling of another) at night with the intent to steal the swords, which is a felony. Larceny was a felony at common law. It consisted of the trespassory taking and carrying away of the personal property of another with the intent to permanently deprive the owner of possession. Here, the man took and carried away the swords (the personal property of another) with no intent to return them. Thus, all of the elements of larceny have been met. Answers A and B are incorrect because the man committed both larceny and burglary. Answer D is incorrect because Answer C is correct.

51. B is the correct answer. A battery is the use of force against another, resulting in harmful or offensive contact. Here, the woman's shooting of the man met the elements of battery, since the man was harmed (he was severely injured). The woman used excessive force (a rifle) under these facts to protect her dog, which at common law is considered property. Therefore, the woman's use of excessive force was legally unreasonable because there was no tumultuous entry into her dwelling, which would allow her to use deadly force. Answer A is incorrect because although the woman thought of her dog as a child, at common law, dogs were property. Thus, the woman's use of deadly force was neither reasonable nor justified under the law. Answer C is incorrect because, although the woman committed a battery, her use of deadly force was unreasonable, as discussed above. Answer D is incorrect because the man is still alive, so there is no second-degree murder (or any other type of murder).

52. C is the correct answer. Involuntary manslaughter is an unintentional killing that results from recklessness or criminal negligence. Here, the man's behavior was both reckless and crimi-

nally negligent in leaving a home after he had knocked over a lit candle. Thus, he is guilty of involuntary manslaughter because of the unintentional death of the trespasser. Answer A is incorrect because burglary at common law was the breaking and entering into the dwelling of another at night with the intent to commit a felony therein. Here, while the man broke and entered into the dwelling of another (his neighbor) at night, it was for the purpose of retrieving his own property (his blender). Thus, he did not have the intent to commit a felony therein and is not guilty of common law burglary. Therefore, Answer A is incorrect because, while he is guilty of involuntary manslaughter (as discussed in Answer C), he is not guilty of burglary. Answer B is incorrect because the man was guilty of involuntary manslaughter, not murder, as discussed in Answer C. Also, as discussed in Answer A, he was not guilty of burglary. Answer D is incorrect because, as discussed in Answer A, the man is not guilty of burglary.

53. A is the correct answer. At common law, arson was the malicious and willful burning of the dwelling of another. Here, the woman deliberately threw the torch at the man. This was a willful action that resulted in the burning of the man's house (the dwelling of another). Burglary at common law was the breaking and entering into the dwelling of another at night with the intent to commit a felony therein. Here, the woman broke and entered into the man's home (the dwelling of another) at night with the intent to steal (a felony). Attempted murder occurs when there would have been a murder, if the victim had died. Here, as discussed, the woman committed a burglary. If the man had died as a result of the woman's burglary, this would have been felony murder. Thus, the fact that the man survived means that the woman is guilty of attempted murder. Consequently, the woman is guilty of arson, burglary, and attempted murder. Answers B, C, and D are incorrect because the woman committed all three crimes.

54. D is the correct answer. At common law, arson was the malicious and willful burning of the dwelling of another. Here, although the fire captain did not maliciously start the fire, he had a duty to put out the fire. His deliberate delay was tantamount to the willful burning of the dwelling of another (the woman) because his delay resulted in the burning of the woman's home. Answer A is incorrect because "willful delay" is not a crime. Answer B is incorrect because "culpable omission" is not a crime; it is merely a method of proving causation. Answer C is incorrect because negative omission is not a crime.

55. D is the correct answer. At the common law, the inflicted wound must result in death within "a year and a day." As stipulated, the death here took two years. Thus, all of the homicides in Answers A, B and C are incorrect. At common law, the man would be considered to have not committed any crimes (other than rape).

56. B is the correct answer. A person is allowed to use non-deadly force to prevent the commission of a crime. Here, the man reasonably believed that a woman was being robbed by another woman, and he needed to prevent the crime. The man's belief was reasonable because the undercover police officer was not in uniform. Thus, the man's best defense would be crime prevention. Answer A is incorrect because, although it would be a correct defense, the call of the question asked for the best defense, which is given in Answer B. Answer C is incorrect because the undercover police officer was not threatening the man. Thus, he could not claim self-defense. Answer D is incorrect because Answer B is correct.

57. A is the correct answer. A larceny is the trespassory taking and carrying away of the personal property of another with intent to permanently deprive the owner of the property. Since the woman's initial taking of the vehicle was without permission, the taking was trespassory. However, she did not initially have the intent to permanently deprive her friend (the owner) of the vehicle. (She was at first only borrowing the car.) Later, while on the road, she decided to keep the vehicle, and it was at this point that she formed the intent to permanently deprive the owner of the car. Thus, the intent to permanently deprive formed after the taking, constituting a continuing trespass larceny. Thus, she is guilty of larceny. B is incorrect. A larceny by trick occurs when one takes possession to the property of another by intentional false statement of past or existing fact with intent to defraud. Here, there are no facts to indicate that the woman got possession by trick. She merely took the car. C is incorrect, as well. Embezzlement is a crime committed when a person is in rightful possession of an item and converts it to his own use. Here, there are no facts indicating that the woman was entrusted (lawful possession of the friend's car). In fact, she drove the car away without permission. D is incorrect for the reasons discussed in Answer A.

58. D is the correct answer. A larceny at common law was the trespassory taking and carrying away of the personal property of another with intent to permanently deprive the owner of the property. Here, the homeless person took the food belonging to the store without permission. When he ate it, he demonstrated his intent to permanently deprive the store of possession of the food. Thus, he is guilty of larceny at common law. Answer A is incorrect. At common law, a burglary required a trespassory breaking and entering into the dwelling of another at night with intent to commit a felony therein. Here, the homeless person broke into the store, which is not a dwelling. Thus, there was no common law burglary. Answer B is incorrect for the same reasons that Answer A is incorrect; namely that while he committed a larceny (as discussed in Answer D), he did not commit a burglary (as discussed in Answer A). Answer C is incorrect.

Embezzlement is a crime committed when a person is in rightful possession of an item and converts it to his own use. Here, the homeless person was not in rightful possession of the food and, thus, did not commit embezzlement. Also, as discussed in Answer A, he did not commit burglary.

59. D is the correct answer. For there to be a burglary at common law, there must be a breaking and entering into the dwelling of another at night with the intent to commit a felony in the dwelling. Here, the bullet broke and entered into the roof of the neighbor's house (a dwelling) on New Year's Eve (at night). When the bullet broke and entered into the neighbor's house, it was as though the man himself did so because the bullet was an instrumentality under the man's control. However, there was a missing element. The man did not have the specific intent to commit a felony in the neighbor's house. He was merely celebrating New Year's Eve. Thus, D is the correct answer, and he is not guilty of common law burglary because of the lack of specific intent. Answer A is incorrect because, although there was a breaking and entering by way of instrumentality, into a dwelling, at night (as discussed in Answer D), the specific intent to commit a felony therein was missing, as discussed above. B is incorrect because the issue is not whether a felony was actually committed, but rather, whether there was specific intent to commit the felony. C is incorrect because entry by instrumentality is valid if, as here, the instrumentality is used to complete the felony, as discussed in Answer D. In this case, the bullet was used to kill. However, because the man did not have the specific intent, there was no common law burglary. Therefore, Answer D is correct, and Answer C is incorrect.

60. C is the correct answer. At common law, murder was defined as the killing of a human being by a human being with malice aforethought. Malice aforethought is intent to kill, intent to do serious bodily harm, wanton or depraved heart, or felony murder. Here, the woman was aware of the substantial risk to human life and, nevertheless, threw the air conditioner out from the twenty-first floor window. A and B are incorrect because they are modern crimes, not common law crimes. D is incorrect because, even though the killing was accidental, the woman demonstrated indifference to human life and a depraved heart by throwing the air conditioner out the window, as discussed in Answer C.

61. A is the correct answer. At common law, the crime of malicious mischief was defined as the "wanton or reckless destruction of the personal property of another." The question then turns on the characterization of a dog, i.e., is a pet considered the chattel of the owner? The answer to that is yes, and there is a breadth of authority at common law dealing with pets as chattel, e.g., a lost pet and the rights of the true owner

to possession of his or her personal property. "Cruelty to dogs" was not, per se, a common law crime, therefore, B is incorrect. Homicide is the killing of a human being by another human being. Here, a human killed a dog, a non-human. Therefore, the fraternity member is not guilty of any homicide (including murder) and C is incorrect. As the elements of malicious mischief appear on the face of the facts, D is incorrect. Caveat: Where you see an option that is not internally logical or consistent, you must eliminate it from consideration. "Canine homicide" is such a contradiction.

62. C is the correct answer. Malicious mischief is the willful or wanton destruction of the property of another. Here, the man willfully destroyed the woman's wedding dress, which was her personal property. Thus, at common law, he was guilty of malicious mischief. Answer A is incorrect. At common law, burglary was the trespassory breaking and entering into the dwelling of another at night with intent to commit a felony therein. Here, the man entered with a key. Thus, there was no breaking. Also, he had no intent to commit a felony therein because malicious mischief was not a felony. Thus, there was no burglary, although there was a malicious mischief, as discussed in correct Answer C. B is incorrect because vandalism was not a common law crime. D is incorrect because trespass to chattel is a tort, not a crime.

63. C is the correct answer. Murder is the killing of a human being by a human being with malice aforethought. Murder may be mitigated down to voluntary manslaughter, if there is adequate provocation (heat of passion) and insufficient time to cool down. Here, there was adequate provocation (the girlfriend kissing the former boyfriend), passion (the man's anger), and insufficient time to cool down (the man immediately strangled the former boyfriend to death). Thus, the man is guilty of voluntary manslaughter of the former boyfriend. A battery is the use of force against another, resulting in harmful or offensive contact. An assault is an attempted battery. Here, when the man threatened and chased the girlfriend, there was an assault. However, since there was no application of force, there was not a battery. Consequently, C is the correct answer. Answer A is incorrect because, although there was an assault of the girlfriend (as discussed in Answer C), murder in the second degree was not a common law crime. Also, it was mitigated down to voluntary manslaughter, as discussed in Answer C. Answer B is incorrect because, as discussed in Answer C, there was no battery because there was no application of force, since the girlfriend ran away and the man was apprehended before he could catch her. Answer D is incorrect because there was neither second-degree murder nor battery here, for the reasons discussed above.

64. D is the correct answer. A crime requires an actus reas (voluntary act), mens rea (the requisite mental state), and causa-

tion. Here, the woman did not have the mens rea to commit any crime; she spilled the beer inadvertently. Answers A and B are incorrect. An assault is an attempted battery. A criminal battery is the use of force against another, resulting in harmful or offensive contact. Here, as discussed in Answer D, the woman inadvertently spilled the beer. She, thus, lacked the mental state (mens rea) to commit either assault or battery. C is incorrect, as well. Malicious mischief is the willful or wanton destruction of the property of another. Here, as discussed above, the woman's spilling of the beer was neither willful nor wanton. Thus, no crime was committed, and Answer D is the correct answer.

65. A is the correct answer. Involuntary manslaughter is the act of unintentionally and unlawfully killing another human being. In most states, involuntary manslaughter results from an improper use of reasonable care or skill while performing a legal act, or while committing an act that is unlawful, but not felonious. Here, the woman was performing a legal act (attempting to hug her friend). However, the fact that the friend fell and struck her head and died seems to indicate that the woman did not use reasonable care or skill in attempting to hug her friend. Therefore, the woman is guilty of involuntary manslaughter only. B and D are incorrect. An assault is an attempted battery, while a criminal battery is the use of force against another, resulting in harmful or offensive contact. Here, the woman did not possess the mental state to commit either an assault or a battery; she was merely trying to hug her friend. Also, Answer C is incorrect because second-degree murder was not a common law crime.

66. B is the correct answer. False imprisonment was a common law felony that consisted of the restraint of a person in a bounded area without justification or consent. Here, the college student locked the door and told the girlfriend to have sex with him. Although she started to undress, she changed her mind, which destroys the consent. Thus, the college student is guilty of false imprisonment at common law. A is incorrect. Rape at common law was the unlawful carnal knowledge of a woman by a man not her husband without her consent. Rape also required sexual penetration. Here, although the girlfriend was not the college student's wife, there was no sexual penetration. Thus, he was not guilty of rape. C is incorrect, as well. A criminal battery is the use of force against another, resulting in harmful or offensive contact. Here, the facts do not indicate that the college student used any force or that he even touched his girlfriend in any way. Thus, there was no battery. Answer D is incorrect because it is irrelevant whether or not the girlfriend led the college student on; it does not excuse any crimes that he may have committed.

67. C is the correct answer. A battery is the use of force against another, resulting in harmful or offensive contact. Here,

the college student's touching of the girl's hair was purposeful and certainly unapproved or offensive. In the facts, the girl said to stop. Therefore, the college student is guilty of criminal battery. Answer A is incorrect because the girl told the college student to stop. Therefore, it was offensive. Answer B is incorrect because legally a given act can be both a tort and a crime. Such are entirely separate issues. Answer D is incorrect for the same reason that C is correct, since battery is both a modern and a common law crime.

68. D is the correct answer. Malicious mischief is the willful or wanton destruction of the property of another. Here, the secretary scratched (damaged) the boss' car purposely (thereby satisfying the malice element). Thus, all the elements for malicious mischief are met. She is, therefore, guilty of this crime. Answer A is incorrect because nothing in the common law crime of malicious mischief requires the vandalism to be irreparable. Answer B is incorrect because intentional infliction of emotional distress is a tort, not a crime. Answer C is incorrect because there was no taking or carrying away of any personal property here.

69. B is the correct answer. Uttering requires the use of a forged instrument, knowing it to be such. Although an arcade token, in the context of going to the arcade, is not false, using it as a token of value somewhere else probably is. Moreover, it was used to defraud the parking garage. Thus, there probably was an uttering here. Answer A is incorrect because forgery requires the making of a false document. Although it is arguable that the man's arcade token constituted a document, it is quite clear that he did not make it. Therefore, since one element is missing, this crime is lacking. A theft by false pretenses occurs when one takes title to the property of another by intentional false statement of past or existing fact with intent to defraud. Here, there is nothing indicating that the man obtained title to the arcade token fraudulently. Answer D is incorrect because, as discussed in Answer A, there was no forgery. Also, embezzlement is a crime committed when a person is in rightful possession of an item and converts it to his own use. Here, the man was in lawful possession of the parking space, so long as he paid for it upon exiting the garage. However, if the intent to steal (defraud) was formed prior to obtaining possession of the parking space, then the possession of the parking space was not lawful and there can be no embezzlement. In that instance, the crime is larceny. Here, the facts indicated that the man believed that parking should be free and, therefore, never intended to pay for the space with a token from the parking garage. Therefore, his possession of the parking space was obtained fraudulently. Consequently, there was no embezzlement here. Answer C is incorrect because there was no embezzlement, as discussed in Answer D.

70. B is the correct answer. Embezzlement is a crime committed when a person is

in rightful possession of an item and converts it to his own use. Here, the woman accidentally received the wrong coat. Because she thought it was her own coat, she was in lawful possession. When she later realized that it was not her coat and decided to keep it anyway, she committed embezzlement. A is incorrect. Larceny is the trespassory taking of the personal property of another with intent to permanently deprive the owner of possession. Here, there was no initial "trespassory taking" because the woman took the coat believing it to be her own. Consequently, she did not commit larceny. C is incorrect, as well. False pretenses occurs when one takes title to the property of another by the intentional false statement of past or existing fact, with intent to defraud. Here, there was no passing of title, nor was there an intentional false statement of past or existing fact by the woman. Thus, the woman did not commit the crime of false pretenses. D is incorrect because, as discussed in Answer B, she committed the crime of embezzlement.

71. B is the correct answer. Common law burglary was the breaking and entering into the dwelling of another at night with the intent to commit a felony therein. Here, the woman broke and entered into an abandoned house. Under the common law, abandoned houses are not considered to be dwellings. Thus, since no one lived in this house, it was not a dwelling, which negates one of the elements of common law burglary. Hence, this is a complete defense to common law burglary. Answer A is incorrect because at common law, burglary required the intent to commit a felony therein (i.e., inside the dwelling). Here, the woman had the intent to steal (a felony); it is irrelevant that she did not actually end up stealing anything. Therefore, this is not a good defense to common law burglary. Answer C is incorrect because common law burglary does not contain an element that someone (other than the burglar) be present at the time of the breaking and entering. Answer D is incorrect for the reasons discussed in Answer B.

72. D is the correct answer. Forcible entry entails the willful trespass onto the land of another by force. The force required is not necessarily destructive force. Here, the locksmith picked the lock to enter the house, which satisfies this element. Moreover, he was clearly trespassing onto land, so all of the elements are met. At common law, a larceny was the taking and carrying away of the property of another with the intent to permanently deprive the owner of possession. Here, the locksmith took the television, which was the property of another and, thus, committed a larceny. Answer A is incorrect. At common law, burglary was the breaking and entering into the dwelling of another at night with the intent to commit a felony therein. Here, the facts state that the locksmith broke and entered during lunch, which was during the day, rather than at night. Hence, at common law, there was no burglary. Answer B

is a correct statement of fact, but still irrelevant because, as discussed in Answer D, the man did commit crimes at common law. Answer C is incorrect because conversion was not a common law felony; it is a tort.

73. C is the correct answer. False pretenses occurs when one takes title to the property of another by the intentional false statement of past or existing fact with intent to defraud. Here, the false statement was in the act of changing price-tags, and title passed with the passing of the receipt. Answer A is incorrect because common law larceny required the trespassory taking and carrying away of the property of another with the intent to deprive the owner of possession. Here, the man paid for the Scotch, albeit the wrong amount. Thus, his taking of the Scotch was not trespassory. Answer B is incorrect. Larceny by trick occurs when one takes possession of the property of another by the intentional false statement of past or existing fact with intent to defraud. Here, the man obtained full title to the Scotch, not mere possession. Answer D is incorrect, as well. Embezzlement is a crime committed when a person is in rightful possession of an item and converts it to his own use. Here, the man did not have rightful possession of the Scotch when he took it; rather, he paid for it (albeit the wrong amount) prior to taking it. Thus, there was no embezzlement here.

74. D is the correct answer. False pretenses occurs when one takes title to the property of another by the intentional false statement of past or existing fact with intent to defraud. Only the lawful owner of a piece of property has the right to consent to give it to somebody else. Here, although the pawnshop owner was in lawful possession of the ring, he did not own it. Thus, he did not have the right to give it to the man and, thus, the man is not relieved of liability for the crime of false pretenses. The man committed the crime of false pretenses because he made a false statement with the intent to obtain title to the ring. The fact that the pawnshop owner was an accomplice does not alleviate the man's guilt. Answer A is incorrect because, as discussed in Answer D, the pawnshop owner did not have the right to give consent. Answer B is incorrect because, as discussed in Answer D, mere possession is not enough to be able to give consent; only the owner can give consent. Answer C is an incorrect statement of fact; the man did make a false statement when he attempted to pass the ring off as his own.

75. A is the correct answer. Embezzlement is a crime committed when a person is in rightful possession of an item and converts it to his own use. Here, the car salesman had the right to go to and from work in the dealership's cars. However, he did not have the right to take the cars out-of-state and not return them. In so doing, he converted the car to his own use, something he did not have permission to do. Thus, he committed embezzlement. Answer B is incorrect.

Larceny is the trespassory taking and carrying away of the personal property of another with intent to permanently deprive. Here, the salesman's initial taking of the vehicle was not trespassory because he had permission to take the car to and from work. Thus, he did not commit larceny. Answer C is incorrect because conversion is a tort, not a crime. Answer D is incorrect because the salesman's actions satisfied all of the elements of embezzlement. It is irrelevant whether it was good business.

76. C is the correct answer. Involuntary manslaughter is an unintentional killing that results from recklessness or criminal negligence. Here, the woman's killing of the child was unintentional. However, her failure to properly check her mirrors prior to backing out of her driveway was a deviation from the reasonable standard of care owed. Thus, her actions were either reckless or criminally negligent, making involuntary manslaughter the correct answer. Answers A and D are incorrect because they were not crimes at common law (which is the stipulated jurisdiction). Answer B is incorrect because murder requires malice aforethought. This mens rea can be proven by an intent to kill (not present here), intent to cause serious bodily injury (also not present here), reckless/depraved heart (not present here because the woman was unaware of the risk to life), or felony-murder (not present because she was not in perpetration of an inherently dangerous felony).

77. D is the correct answer. At common law, the inflicted wound must produce death within a year and day. This specific rule of causation was called the "year and a day" rule. Here, the death occurred 13 months later. Therefore, the man is not guilty of criminal homicide under the common law. Answer A is incorrect because after a year and a day have passed, the chain of causation is cut off. Answer B is incorrect because malice (the mens rea for murder) is defined as, among other things, intent to commit serious bodily harm, (which the young man demonstrated through the beating). Answer C is incorrect because, as discussed in Answer D, the "year and a day" rule means that the young man is not guilty here because the death occurred more than a year and a day after the beating.

78. D is the correct answer because A, B, and C were not crimes at common law.

79. A is the correct answer. Vandalism is the willful damage or defacement of the property of another. Here, the man broke the window of his friend's house, which was clearly damaging the property of another. Even though he had consent to enter the friend's house, he did not have consent to break the window. Thus, he is guilty of vandalism. Answers B and D are incorrect because they were only crimes at common law, and the call of the question stipulated modern law crimes. Answer C is incorrect, as well. Burglary at modern law is the unlawful entering into a

structure with the intent to commit a crime therein. Here, the man broke and entered his friend's house, but he had no intent to commit a crime inside the house; he was there to pick up his friend's clothes, as requested. Thus, he is not guilty of burglary.

80. A is correct. Common law rape was the carnal knowledge of a woman by a man not her husband without her consent. Under both the modern and common law, the consent to engage in sex can be withdrawn at any time, even after sexual intercourse has commenced. Here, the girlfriend withdrew her consent, telling the man to stop. Because he did not stop immediately, his sexual actions after the girlfriend withdrew her consent amounted to rape. Thus, he can be convicted of rape. Answer B is a correct statement of fact, but is irrelevant because the primary issue with rape is consent, which was withdrawn here, as discussed in Answer A. Answer C is incorrect, because, as discussed in Answer A, consent can be withdrawn at any time; it is never binding. Answer D is incorrect legally because genital penetration is all that is required for carnal knowledge.

81. B is the correct answer. Malicious mischief at common law was the willful or wanton destruction of the property of another. Here, the woman smashed her friend's picture. Since the picture was the property of her friend (another), and the smashing constituted damage to the picture, the elements of malicious mis-chief have been met. Thus, she is guilty of malicious mischief at common law. Answers A and C are incorrect because they were not crimes at the common law. Answer D is incorrect because uttering entails offering a forged instrument - facts totally irrelevant here.

82. B is the correct answer. Voluntary manslaughter is a killing that immediately follows a passion-provoking incident. Here, the man killed his girlfriend and best friend immediately after finding them in bed together (a passion-provoking incident). Thus, the man is guilty of voluntary manslaughter. Answer A is incorrect because while the man killed both the girlfriend and the best friend, this killing was mitigated to voluntary manslaughter, for the reasons discussed in Answer B. Answer C is incorrect because this crime requires the killing to be unintentional. Here, the man's actions were intentional. Answer D is incorrect both legally and ethically.

83. D is the correct answer. Criminal battery is the use of force against another, resulting in harmful or offensive contact. Here, there was no touching; the man was apparently alone when he picked up the gun at the storage locker. Thus, there was no battery here. An assault is an attempted battery. As discussed above, there was no battery. Furthermore, since the man was apparently alone at the storage locker when he picked up the gun and put the gun back before leaving the storage locker, there was neither a substantial step toward battery (there

was only preparation), nor was there an intent to scare anyone. Thus, there was no assault here, either. Hence, Answers A and B are incorrect for the reasons discussed in Answer D. Answer C is incorrect because it was his gun, and he had the proper permit for it.

84. A is the correct answer. At common law, malicious mischief was the willful or wanton destruction of the property of another. At common law, malicious mischief included the damaging of another's animal. Here, the first cowboy hurt another cowboy's horse so severely that the horse had to be put to sleep. This qualifies as willful and wanton destruction. Therefore, at common law, the first cowboy was guilty of malicious mischief. Answer B is incorrect because it was not a common law crime. Answer C is incorrect because murder is the killing of a human being by a human being with malice aforethought. Here, although a human being committed the action that led to a death, the death was to an animal (a horse), not another human being. Thus, at common law, no murder took place here. Answer D is incorrect because, like murder, battery can only occur to a human being, not to a horse or other animal.

85. D is the correct answer. At common law, larceny was the trespassory taking and carrying away of the personal property of another with the intent to permanently deprive the owner of possession. Here, the teenager initially did not have the intent to permanently deprive his father of possession of the car, since he was just taking it out for a joyride. However, when the teenager drove off into the sunset, he permanently deprived his father of possession of the car. In so doing, he took and carried away the car, which was the personal property of another (the teenager's father) with the intent to permanently deprive the owner (his father) of possession of the car. This was trespassory because the teenager did not have permission to take the car. Thus, the teenager was guilty of larceny. Answer A is incorrect for the reasons discussed in Answer D. Answer B is incorrect. At common law, malicious mischief was the willful or wanton destruction of the property of another. Here, the boy did not destroy his father's car; he merely took it. Thus, the teenager did not commit malicious mischief. Answer C is incorrect, as well. At common law, larceny by false pretenses occurred when one took title to the property of another by intentional false statement of past or existing fact, with the intent to defraud. Here, the teenager had mere possession of the car; he never obtained title. Furthermore, there is nothing in the facts indicating that the teenager made a false statement, intentional or otherwise. Thus, there was no larceny by false pretenses here.

86. B is the correct answer. Second-degree murder is the killing of a human being by a human being with malice aforethought. Malice aforethought is found by intent to kill, intent to commit serious bodily harm, a wanton or depraved

heart, or felony murder. Here, the man's actions indicated an intent to kill or do serious bodily harm. Thus, he is guilty of second-degree murder. Thus, he had the requisite mens rea for second-degree murder (malice). Answer A is incorrect because first-degree murder includes all of the elements of second-degree murder, plus premeditation and deliberation. Here, the man simply reacted when he saw his second grade teacher; he did not have time to premeditate or deliberate on the killing. Thus, he is not guilty of first-degree murder. Answer C is also incorrect. Voluntary manslaughter is a mitigated murder. A requirement of voluntary manslaughter is that the killing follow immediately upon a passion-provoking incident. Here, merely seeing one's second grade teacher after many years could not reasonably be considered a passion-provoking incident. Thus, his killing of the second grade teacher cannot be mitigated to voluntary manslaughter. Answer D is incorrect because involuntary manslaughter is an unintentional or accidental death. Here, the man intended to kill or at least injure the second grade teacher. Thus, this was not an involuntary manslaughter.

87. A is the correct answer. All four insanity defenses require that the person raising the defense suffer from a mental disease or defect that affects his actions. Here, the man was clearly delusional because he heard a voice that told him that the woman needed to be killed, and he acted upon this. It is reasonable to conclude that acting upon such a stimulus could only be the result of a mental disease or defect. Thus, insanity will be a complete defense to the killing here. Answer B is incorrect because there are no facts to indicate that the man was intoxicated. Answer C is incorrect because the man's belief that the woman was Satan was obviously delusional. Furthermore, even if he were correct in his belief, this would not give the man the right to kill her. Answer D is incorrect because this was not a common law defense, and also because it is only a partial defense, whereas insanity is a complete defense.

88. D is the correct answer. Diminished capacity is an alteration to a defendant's mental state or a reduced ability to understand, usually the result of mental retardation or the influence of a substance, that exists at the time of the commission of a crime. Here, the man's mental faculties were diminished because of the sugar high. Thus, this is his best defense. Answer A is incorrect because the provocation that would reduce a murder to voluntary manslaughter must occur immediately before the killing. Here, the man had enough time to go home, stuff himself with sugary snacks and milk, and then return to city hall. Thus, there was no immediacy here. Answer B is incorrect because there is no indication that the man suffered from a mental disease or defect, as required by all four forms of insanity. Answer C is incorrect because there is nothing in the facts to indicate that the man believed he was in imminent physical danger.

89. D is the correct answer. The criminal law does not require good behavior. It simply prohibits bad conduct. The man's leaving the child alone was unethical, but not illegal in any way, unless the man had a duty to the child. Here, the man did not place the child in danger, nor did he have any relationship to the child. Thus, he committed no crime here. As a result, the crimes offered in answers A, B and C are incorrect.

90. D is the correct answer. A larceny by false pretenses occurs when one takes title to the property of another by intentional false statement of past or existing fact with intent to defraud. Here, the man paid his bill. He made a statement through his conduct (paying) that the bill was for the correct amount. Because he knew that the food actually cost more than this, his false statement was intentional. Thus because he obtained title to the food through an intentional false statement of fact (the incorrect price of the food), he committed larceny by false pretenses. Answer A is incorrect because larceny requires a trespass in the taking, and here the man received the food consensually. Answer B is incorrect because larceny by trick occurs when one takes possession of the property of another by intentional false statement of past or existing fact, with intent to defraud. Here, as discussed in Answer D, the man obtained full title to the food, not mere possession. Answer C is incorrect because robbery is a larceny with force or threat of force. Here, as discussed in Answer A, there was no larceny. Furthermore, there was neither force nor threat of force.

91. B is the correct answer. Under the modern law, petty theft is the fraudulent misappropriation of property worth, as a general rule, under $400. Here, the actress fraudulently misappropriated the property (the scarf) of the store when she snuck it out of the store. The facts stipulate that the scarf was worth less than $400 (since it was selling for $100). Thus, she committed petty theft. Answer A is incorrect because larceny was a common law crime, not a modern crime. Answer C is incorrect because grand theft entails misappropriation of property worth over $400. Here, as discussed in Answer B, the scarf was worth less than $400. Answer D is incorrect for the same reasons that Answer B is correct.

92. A is the correct answer. Under the modern law, grand theft is the fraudulent misappropriation of property valued at, as a general rule, over $400. Here, the man's car most likely exceeded that amount, and the woman fraudulently misappropriated the car by taking it and not returning it. Answer B is incorrect because petty theft covers stealing property of value under $400, and here, as discussed in Answer A, the car most likely exceeded $400 in value. Answer C is incorrect because vandalism requires damage to property, and there are no facts here to indicate that the woman damaged the car. Answer D is incorrect

because merely leaving a car door open does not constructively give someone constructive consent to take the car.

93. A is the correct answer. Involuntary manslaughter can be proven by showing that the defendant's killing occurred while perpetrating a "malum in se" (bad in itself) crime. Here, the man was in perpetration of a larceny (theft of the helicopter), which is bad in itself (i.e., "malum in se"). Answer B is incorrect because no facts indicate the piloting of the helicopter was a gross deviation from the reasonable standard of care owed. Answer C is incorrect. Mere negligence by itself is a tort action, not a criminal action. Furthermore, as discussed in Answer B, there is nothing in the facts here indicating a deviation from the reasonable standard of care. Answer D is incorrect because "depraved heart" is a method of proving malice aforethought. It is not an element of involuntary manslaughter and is, thus, irrelevant to this question.

94. D is the correct answer. A crime requires actus reas and mens rea. Here, the farmer took no criminal actions, nor did he have any criminal mental state. Thus, the farmer committed no crime, and there is no theory under which the farmer could be held criminally responsible for the deaths. Answer A is incorrect because the farmer was not a substantial factor. The homicidal maniac broke into the farmer's toolshed and stole the chainsaw. This was not the farmer's fault. B is incorrect because unclean hands is an equitable defense and is irrelevant in a criminal case. C is incorrect because it goes to the mental state of taking a reckless risk to human life. As discussed in Answer D, the farmer did not have a depraved heart or any other criminal mental state.

95. C is the correct answer. Wharton's Rule indicates that if a crime requires a set and necessary number of perpetrators, if only that minimum number is involved, then the perpetrators cannot be convicted of both the conspiracy and the target crime. The definition that was given for Breach of the Peace requires four individuals. Here, there were four individuals involved (the minimum number under the law), so there cannot be conviction for both the Breach of the Peace and the conspiracy to commit Breach of the Peace. A is incorrect because it contradicts the facts, since there were others present here. Answer B is incorrect because the four friends agreed to set off the fireworks in the park, which would be a Breach of the Peace under the law, and they did so. Answer D is irrelevant, since the law says that it is a "big deal" to disturb the peace.

96. C is the correct answer. The crime requires the knowing possession of marijuana. Here, the neighbor possessed the marijuana cigarette that was given to him by the man, but he did not know that it was a marijuana cigarette; he thought that it was a regular cigarette. Therefore, the man did not meet the "knowing" element, so lack of knowledge or sci-

enter is his best defense. Answer A is incorrect because the man was in true possession of the marijuana cigarette; he simply did not know that it was marijuana. Answer B is legally incorrect because, for entrapment to occur, the inducement to commit a crime must be from a government agent, not a private party, as here. Answer D is also legally incorrect because evil motives are not a requirement for conviction of crimes.

97. A is the correct answer. Necessity, or "choice of evils," is a defense when a criminal act is performed, so as to avoid a greater harm to the perpetrator. Here, if the man had not violated the traffic laws, his wife may have had to give birth in a car, without the medical attention that she needed. Answer B is incorrect because duress is only relevant when one performs a crime at the imminent threat of another. Here, there was no one threatening the man. Both Answers C and D are incorrect because neither are defenses at criminal law.

98. C is the correct answer. Forcible entry requires there be force used in the trespass. No force was evident here. Answer A is incorrect for the same reason that Answer C is correct. Answer B is incorrect because the guilt of the victim is not a criminal law defense. Answer D is legally incorrect; this was a crime at common law.

99. A is the correct answer. On the facts given, it appeared that in no way was the burglar attempting a crime against the man's person; the burglar was only trying to break into the man's home. Thus, the man utilized deadly force just to protect his property. The criminal law does not allow this. [Note: The mere threat of physical force is, however, allowed.] Answer B is incorrect because, as discussed in Answer A, using deadly force against a burglar who is only threatening property is not justified under these circumstances. Answer C is incorrect for the same reasons that Answer A is correct. Since the man was not home, he was not defending his person at the time; he was only defending his property, and deadly force is not permitted to merely defend property. Answer D is incorrect because the guilt of the victim does not allow an excessive use of force against that victim.

100. B is the man's best defense. The question did not ask for reasons. Instead, it asked for "affirmative defenses." Here, the vigilante's deadly assault was averted by the man grabbing the gun. Although the man ordinarily would have had no right to forcibly take the vigilante's gun, under these circumstances, it was acceptable. For the same reasons, the incidental battery that occurred when the man grabbed the gun out of the vigilante's hand would also be excused by the defense of necessity. Answer A is incorrect because, even though the man's car window was smashed by the vigilante, this would not be the best defense to battery (of the vigilante) and robbery (of the gun) because once the

car window was smashed, there was no further threat to the car. Answer C is incorrect because, although it is a defense to robbery, the defense of necessity is a defense to both robbery and battery. Thus, answer C is incorrect, and Answer B is correct. Answer D is incorrect because there are no facts to indicate that the man's mental clarity was impaired, so as to give him diminished capacity.

END OF ANSWERS

TORTS – QUESTION BREAKDOWN

1. Nuisance – Private
2. Nuisance – Private
3. Nuisance
4. Deceit
5. Deceit – Reliance
6. Negligent Misrepresentation
7. Negligent Misrepresentation – Liability
8. Deceit – Reliance
9. Deceit – Concealment
10. Trade Libel
11. Trade Libel – Special Damages
12. Invasion of Privacy – Misappropriation
13. Abuse of Process
14. Abuse of Process
15. Interference with Contract
16. Interference with Prospective Advantage
17. Assault
18. Transferred Intent
19. Trespass to Land
20. Defense of Property
21. Negligence Per Se
22. Causation
23. Negligence – Duty
24. Duty – Cardozo's View
25. Joint and Several Liability
26. Duty – Licensee
27. Licensee – Duty Owed
28. Contributory Negligence
29. Last Clear Chance
30. Comparative Negligence
31. Strict Liability
32. Strict Liability
33. Strict Liability – Defenses
34. Strict Liability – Causation
35. Duty Owed to Rescuer
36. Duty Invitee

37. Res Ipsa Loquitur

38. Res Ipsa Loquitur

39. Respondeat Superior

40. Negligence – Attractive Nuisance Doctrine

41. Negligence – Contributory Negligence

42. Causation

43. Battery

44. Battery – Social Standards

45. Shopkeepers Privilege

46. Products Liability

47. Pre-existing Condition

48. Strict Liability

49. Assault – Apprehension

50. Trespass to Chattels

51. Battery

52. Res Ipsa Loquitur

53. Duty – National Standard of Care

54. Negligence – Omission to Act

55. Intentional Infliction of Emotional Distress

56. Intentional Infliction of Emotional Distress

57. Intentional Infliction of Emotional Distress- Damages

58. Negligence Per Se

59. Causation

60. Causation

61. Joint & Several Liability

62. Contribution

63. Guest Statute

64. Battery

65. Implied Consent

66. Negligence – Duty

67. Negligence – Duty

68. Intervening Acts

69. Thin Skull Plaintiff

70. Survival Action – Common Law

71. Wrongful Death

72. Respondeat Superior

73. Vicarious Liability – Course and Scope of Employment

74. Federal Torts Claims Act

75. Defamation – Libel
76. Defamation – Common Law
77. Defamation – Libel
78. Defamation – Slander v. Libel
79. Defamation – Republication
80. Defamation – Malice
81. Defamation – Burden of Proof
82. Defamation – Slander Per Quod
83. Defamation – Falsity
84. Privileges
85. Defamation – Republication
86. Strict Liability in Tort
87. Strict Liability – Foreseeable Bystanders
88. Strict Liability in Tort
89. Products Liability
90. Strict Liability in Tort – Warning
91. Negligence
92. Vicarious Liability
93. Products Liability
94. Products Liability
95. Duty to Act
96. Good Samaritan Statute
97. Wrongful Life
98. Wrongful Death – Defenses
99. Wrongful Life – Damages
100. Professional Negligence – Privity Requirements
101. Strict Liability in Tort
102. Products Liability – Design Defect
103. Products Liability – Defenses
104. Concurrent Tortfeasors
105. Strict Liability in Tort – Damages
106. Implied Warranty of Merchantability
107. Causation
108. Products Liability – Recoverable Damages
109. Landowner Occupier Rule
110. Indemnity
111. Warning Defect
112. Causation
113. Causation

TORTS 233

114. Negligence

115. Causation – Substantial Factor

116. Causation – But for

117. Implied Warranty

118. Warranty

119. Express Warranty

120. Negligence - Res Ipsa Loquitur

121. Strict Liability in Tort

TORTS QUESTIONS

1. An oil company owns an oil refinery in a sparsely populated area. Although the refinery is a "state of the art" operation, it occasionally releases noxious, but harmless, gas into the atmosphere.

    A man recently leased land adjoining the oil company's refinery and occupies a home on the property. The man started complaining that the gas released by the refinery sometimes makes him nauseous and that, as a result, he cannot mow his lawn or have picnics on the lawn. If the man sues the oil company over the gas, his best theory of recovery will be for:

    A. Strict liability for abnormally dangerous activities.

    B. Private nuisance.

    C. Public nuisance.

    D. Negligence.

2. A tenant leases an apartment in a large apartment complex. His upstairs neighbor plays loud music on his stereo after midnight every night. Although the tenant has complained to the landlord, the neighbor continues to play the music every night. If the tenant sues the neighbor for private nuisance, and the neighbor challenges the tenant's standing to sue, the court should:

    A. Dismiss the action because the tenant, as lessee, has no standing to sue over a private nuisance.

    B. Dismiss the action because a private citizen never has standing to sue over a public nuisance.

    C. Allow the action because the tenant is a resident of the area.

    D. Allow the action because the tenant is lessee of the apartment.

3. A cell phone company sets up cell towers throughout a city. Shortly thereafter, a woman rents an apartment near one of the towers. She develops headaches, which she blames on the radiation emitted from the towers. She sues the cell phone company for private nuisance. What is the cell phone company's best defense to enjoin the law lawsuit?

    A. The woman moved to the nuisance and, thus, cannot complain.

    B. The cell phone towers are a social necessity, which are operated in a proper place and in a proper manner.

    C. No one else has ever complained about the cell phone towers or the radiation that they emit.

    D. The woman's cause of action is against her landlord, not the cell phone company.

4. A stockbroker was responsible for the portfolio of one of his clients. The stockbroker believed that shares in a particular company would be a good investment for the client. In order to convince the client to purchase shares in the company, the stockbroker told the client that he had heard that the company had an unannounced major government contract. The stockbroker knew this statement was untrue when he made it. The client purchased 100 shares of stock for $10 each. The client recently learned that the company is now insolvent. If the client sues the stockbroker for common law deceit:

   A. The client will recover, even though the stockbroker had his best interest in mind when he made the statement about the company.

   B. The client will recover because the stockbroker's negligence caused the client's actual injury.

   C. The client will not recover because the malicious intent element required for common law deceit is absent.

   D. The client will not recover because he assumed the risk that the stock would fall in value.

5. When a student graduated from college, he had thought about going to law school. His mentor, a lawyer, tried to further convince the student to go to law school by saying that the student would have a job in the mentor's law firm when he graduated from law school and passed the Bar Examination. At the time, the mentor, a mere associate at the law firm, had no power to make such a promise on behalf of the firm, and the mentor was aware of this fact. Furthermore, the mentor knew that the firm had implemented a hiring freeze, although the mentor believed that the firm would resume hiring by the time the student graduated. The student went to law school, graduated with honors, and passed the Bar Examination. However, due to the poor economy, the mentor's law firm was unable to hire the student. The student sues the mentor for common law deceit. The mentor's best defense to the lawsuit would be:

   A. The mentor acted in good faith when he made the statement.

   B. The student was planning to go to law school anyway.

   C. The student has suffered no out-of-pocket damages.

   D. The inability of the law firm to hire the student was not reasonably foreseeable when the mentor made the statement.

6. In the course of conducting an audit for a company, an accountant carelessly computed the company's total assets. As a result, the audit report stated that the company was substantially stronger financially than it really was. A bank

relied on the audit when it approved a $1 million loan to the company. The company is now insolvent and unable to repay the $1 million loan to the bank. If the bank sues the accountant, what would be its best cause of action?

A. Common law deceit.

B. Negligent misrepresentation.

C. Innocent misrepresentation.

D. None of the above.

7. A homeowner requests an appraisal of his home without telling the appraiser the reason for the appraisal. The appraiser accidentally miscalculates the value of a home. The appraiser's valuation of the home is $100,000 higher than the home's actual value. Relying on the appraiser's valuation, a homeowner puts his house up for sale, at the price given by the appraiser. A buyer who knows little about the neighborhood takes an interest in the home. The buyer asks the homeowner the source of the selling price, to which the owner replies, "I got this price from the appraiser." The buyer then purchases the home at the selling price. The buyer later finds out that the home was actually worth $100,000 less than what he had paid for it. In the majority of American jurisdictions, if the buyer sues the appraiser for negligent misrepresentation:

A. The buyer will not recover because the appraiser did not owe a duty of care to the buyer.

B. The buyer will not recover because it did not justifiably rely on the appraiser's valuation of the home.

C. The buyer will recover because it is a reasonably foreseeable plaintiff.

D. The buyer will recover, but only if it can establish gross negligence on the appraiser's part.

8. A woman went to a car dealership to purchase a used car. The car salesman showed the woman a used car and stated that it was, "A honey of a car, a one of a kind steal for the money." The woman relied on the car salesman's statements and purchased the vehicle from the car dealership "as is." The car's engine failed soon after the woman purchased it. If the woman sues the car dealership for common law deceit, the result will be:

A. The woman will recover because the car dealership is vicariously liable for the fraud of its salesman.

B. The woman will recover because it is fraud to sell a car "as is."

C. The woman will not recover because she could not justifiably rely on the car salesman's opinion.

D. The woman will not recover because the "as is" clause in the contract insulates a car dealership from liability for a deceit action.

9. A homeowner was attempting to sell his home. He knew that the floorboards were rotted, so he placed expensive Persian rugs on top of the floorboards to cover up the floorboards. He told a perspective buyer that he would throw in the rugs without additional charge. The buyer purchased the home with the rugs. One day, when he was cleaning, the buyer lifted the rugs and discovered the rotted floorboards. In an action by the buyer against the homeowner:

A. The buyer will have no cause of action for common law deceit, since the element of a false statement of fact has not been met.

B. The buyer will have no cause of action, since he should have hired a professional home inspector to inspect the home, in which case the home inspector would have discovered the rotted floorboards.

C. The buyer will have a cause of action, since active concealment constitutes common law deceit.

D. The buyer will not have a cause of action for deceit because the homeowner acted reasonably.

10. A manufacturer, in an effort to cut into its competitor's sales, distributed a brochure to potential customers of the competitor. In the brochure, the manufacturer made numerous false and derogatory statements of fact about the competitor's product. Six months after the brochure was distributed, the competitor began experiencing a drop in profits. If the competitor sues the manufacturer, the most appropriate cause of action would be for:

A. Interference with contractual relations.

B. Trade libel.

C. Trade slander.

D. Common law deceit.

11. A new bar review company was struggling to get customers. A well-known review company posted fliers that stated that the new company's tutors were all disbarred attorneys and were terrible teachers. None of these statements was true, and the well-known company was aware of the falsity of the statements. The new company lost significant profits as a result of the statements in the fliers. The new company sues the well-known company for trade libel. The well-known company is found liable. Under common law rules, what, if anything, will the new company recover?

A. The new company will recover because it has sustained a loss in profits.

B. The new company will recover for general lost profits, plus punitive damages.

C. The new company will recover, if it can show loss of specific customers as special damages.

D. The new company will not recover because the well-known company's activity is an accepted business practice.

12. A reputable sporting goods equipment store used a photo of a famous basketball player in a newspaper advertisement for its products. The equipment store did not have the player's permission to use the picture. In an action by the basketball player against the store, the basketball player will have a cause of action for invasion of privacy under which of the following theories:

    A. Public disclosure of private facts.

    B. Misappropriation.

    C. Intrusion on seclusion.

    D. False light.

13. A woman obtained a civil judgment against a man for $100. The man refused to pay the award. In an effort to "teach the man a lesson," the woman had writs of attachment issued against the man's real property, personal property and bank accounts, which had a total value of $500,000. As a result of the woman's actions, the man suffered financial loss and considerable embarrassment. The man is most likely to succeed against the woman under which of the following theories?

    A. Malicious civil prosecution.

    B. Malicious criminal prosecution.

    C. Abuse of process.

    D. Conversion.

14. A man is acquitted for the murder of his wife and a waiter from a nearby restaurant. The wife's family institutes a civil action for wrongful death against the man in which it attaches thousands of pieces of the man's property. The man countersues for abuse of process. In order to recover for abuse of process, the man is not required to establish:

    A. The prior proceeding was terminated in the man's favor.

    B. The family had an ulterior motive for bringing the multiple attachments.

    C. The man suffered damages as a result of the family's actions.

    D. The family's excessive attachments were intentional.

15. A popular professor entered into a contract with X College in which she agreed to teach for one year. Under the

contract's terms, the professor agreed that she would not teach at another college in the same city during the contract term.

Y College, which is located in the same city as X College, learned about the contract and decided to offer the professor more money to teach the same courses. The professor decided to accept Y College's offer. When Y College made public the fact that the professor would be teaching there, enrollments at X College's programs dropped dramatically. If X College sues Y College for damages resulting from Y College's actions:

   A. X College will not recover because the professor has the right to an efficient breach of the contract.

   B. X College will not recover because Y College did not breach any agreement.

   C. X College will recover, but only if Y College intentionally interfered with the contract between the professor and X College.

   D. X College will recover, whether Y College acted intentionally or otherwise, when it interfered with the contract between X College and the professor.

16. A famous chef was in negotiations with the producers of a reality television show to enter into a contract for him to cook on the show. A gourmet restaurant contacted the chef and offered him an extremely large salary to come and work for the restaurant if he would agree not to appear on the reality show. The producers of the reality show sue the restaurant. Will the producers prevail in their lawsuit?

   A. No, they will not prevail because the restaurant did not have a contract with the producers of the reality television show.

   B. Yes, they will prevail under a breach of contract theory.

   C. Yes, they will prevail under a theory of interference with contractual relations.

   D. Yes, they will prevail under a theory of interference with prospective economic advantage.

17. Two college students were conversing loudly during a professor's lecture. The professor threw a pen at them to stop them from talking. The students saw the pen and ducked, thus, avoiding being hit by the pen. If the two college students sue the professor, the most likely outcome will be:

   A. The two college students will recover for intentional infliction of emotional distress.

   B. The two college students will recover for assault.

C. The two college students will not recover because the pen did not strike them.

D. The two college students will not recover because the professor did not intend to hit them with the pen.

18. During a barroom fight, one man attempted to slice the throat of the bartender with a piece of glass from a bottle. The glass slipped out of the man's hand. Just at that moment, an elderly woman walked into the bar. The glass sliced off her head. The woman's estate sued the man for wrongful death. Will the woman's estate recover?

    A. The woman's estate will not recover because the man did not intend to hurt the woman.

    B. The woman's estate will not recover because the extent of the injury and death were not reasonably foreseeable.

    C. The woman's estate will not recover because the transferred intent doctrine does not apply where a person attempts to batter one individual but ends up committing a battery on another.

    D. The woman's estate will recover.

19. A local land surveyor was retained to survey the parcel of land adjoining a woman's property. While conducting the survey, the land surveyor inadvertently walked onto the woman's property, even though the woman had posted several "No Trespassing!" signs throughout her property. In an action by the woman against the land surveyor for trespass to land, the likely outcome will be:

    A. The woman will recover because the land surveyor is a licensee who has exceeded the scope of his license.

    B. The woman will recover, even if the land was not damaged.

    C. The woman will not recover because the land surveyor did not intend to trespass.

    D. The woman will not recover, unless she can prove some actual damage.

20. A farmer was having a problem with people stealing his cattle. He therefore placed an electrified fence around his property, so that any person trying to steal cattle would get an electric shock. The farmer posted signs throughout the property warning people of the electrified fence. A cattle thief attempted to get into the farmer's property one night. He received an electric shock from the fence. If the thief sues the farmer for his injuries, will he recover?

    A. No because he was a trespasser and signs were properly posted.

B. No because it is illegal to steal cattle.

C. No because the farmer was justified in protecting his property.

D. The thief will recover.

21. There is a State law that requires the use of hands-free devices when talking on cell phones while driving. Violation of this law is a misdemeanor. A woman was talking on her cell phone while driving. She was not using a hands-free device. She got into a heated discussion and was not paying attention to the road. The car in front of her stopped at a traffic signal and the woman crashed her car into the car in front, severely injuring the driver. In a negligence suit against the woman, if the driver raises the claim of negligence per se, the court should:

A. Apply the doctrine because the thing speaks for itself.

B. Apply the doctrine because the driver was within the class of persons the statute was designed to protect.

C. Reject the doctrine because the reasonably prudent person test is the universal standard of care in negligence cases.

D. Reject the doctrine because the driver was contributorily negligent.

22. A construction worker is hit by debris and his leg is almost severed. The worker is rushed to the hospital and prepared for surgery. The doctor determines that the leg cannot be saved and that amputation is required. However, at the last minute, a substitute surgeon is called into the procedure. Distracted by a football game on the television set in the operating room, the surgeon inadvertently amputates the wrong leg. The worker sues the owner of the construction site for negligence. The construction site's best defense is:

A. The worker had the last clear chance to avoid being hit by the debris.

B. The surgeon's actions were a superseding cause of the worker's injuries.

C. Surgeons are protected by statute, and this protection is imputed to the owner of the construction site, as well.

D. The owner's liability insurance policy does not cover injuries committed by a negligent surgeon.

23. A twelve-year-old boy jumped started a car and drove it away. After driving for about a mile, the boy lost control of the vehicle. The car jumped the curb and struck a pedestrian. The pedestrian suffered extensive injuries. If the pedestrian sues the boy for his injuries, the likely result will be:

A. The boy will be liable because the pedestrian's injuries were suffered because the boy stole the car.

B. The boy will be liable, if he failed to exercise the care expected of a reasonable, prudent twelve-year-old when he drove the car.

C. The boy will be liable, if he failed to exercise the care expected of a reasonable, prudent person when he drove the car.

D. The boy will not be liable because a twelve-year-old does not have the capacity to be negligent.

24. A man was walking across the street in a crosswalk with his sister when a car approached. The driver accidentally stepped on the accelerator instead of the brake pedal, causing his vehicle to lurch forward. The car struck the sister, and she sustained serious physical injuries. As a result of witnessing the accident, the man went into shock and suffered serious emotional distress. He has incurred substantial expenses for psychiatric treatment.

In most jurisdictions, if the man sues the driver for negligent infliction of emotional distress:

A. The man will recover because he was within the zone of danger and the injuries were inflicted upon his sister.

B. The man will not recover because he did not sustain a physical impact.

C. The man will not recover because he is not closely related to the injured party.

D. The man will not recover because his injuries were not reasonably foreseeable.

25. A bicyclist was injured when a man lost control of his automobile while rounding a curve on a local highway. In a single lawsuit, the bicyclist sued the man for negligently operating his automobile and also sued the State Highway Department for negligent design of the curve. In a special verdict, the jury found the man to be 75% responsible for the bicyclist's injuries and the State Highway Department 25% responsible. The State Highway Department is not immune from a damages judgment.

In a state that follows common law principles, if the man is insolvent:

A. The bicyclist can recover the entire judgment from the State Highway Department.

B. The bicyclist can recover only 25% of the judgment from the State Highway Department because of the rule of indemnification.

C. The bicyclist can recover only 25% of the judgment from the

State Highway Department because of the rule of contribution.

D. The bicyclist cannot recover anything from the State Highway Department on the judgment.

26. A man's house was robbed, so he called the police to come investigate the robbery. A police officer entered the man's house to conduct an investigation. While in the man's house, the law would characterize the police officer as:

   A. Trespasser.

   B. Business invitee.

   C. Social guest.

   D. Licensee.

27. A woman recently purchased a farm subject to an easement by a power company. The easement included the authority to trim trees that might interfere with the power company's electrical lines. An employee of the power company entered the woman's property to check the electrical lines. The employee fell into an abandoned well and suffered numerous injuries. The well had been overgrown with brush, so the employee could not see it. The woman was not aware of the abandoned well. If the employee sues the woman for negligence, a court applying common law rules will find:

   A. The woman owed no duty of care to the employee.

   B. The woman's duty of care was limited to warning the employee of dangers known by the woman.

   C. The woman's duty of care was to warn the employee of dangers known by the woman and to inspect her property for unknown dangers.

   D. The woman's duty of care was that of the reasonable, prudent landowner under the same or similar circumstances.

28. A man had car trouble and pulled his van to the side of the road. However, the van's rear bumper extended one half foot onto the highway. A woman was driving an automobile in the same direction and approached the van from the rear. She was traveling at an excessive rate of speed and was not paying attention to her driving. Her vehicle struck the rear of the man's van, and he was severely injured. In a jurisdiction that has not adopted comparative fault and still follows common law principles, the man will:

   A. Recover $100,000 from the woman.

   B. Recover $95,000 from the woman.

   C. Not recover anything from the woman because the man was contributorily negligent.

D. Not recover anything from the woman because the man assumed the risk.

29. A man had a fight with his wife and drove off angrily. Distracted, he drove at an excessive rate. A woman who was late to take her children to school backed out of her driveway without checking to see if the road was clear. The man could have applied his brakes and avoided hitting the woman's car. However, he was so distracted that he did not notice her car until it was too late. His car collided with her car, causing damage to both automobiles and injuries to both drivers, as well as the woman's children. The woman sued the man for negligence. The man countersued for the woman's negligence. If this is a jurisdiction that follows common law principles, and the woman can show that the man had the last clear chance to avoid the accident, will she recover?

   A. Yes, the woman will recover because the man had the last clear chance to avoid the accident.

   B. The woman will recover because the man was negligent.

   C. The woman will not recover because she was negligent.

   D. None of the above.

30. A state has enacted a comparative negligence statute that provides: "The negligence of the injured party will not bar recovery against another person, so long as the injured party's negligence was not greater than the negligence of the person against whom recovery is sought. Any damages shall be diminished in proportion to the amount of negligence attributable to the injured party." A man and a woman were involved in an automobile accident in that state in which the woman sustained personal injury damages totaling $100,000. She sued the man for negligence. The jury returned a special verdict in which it found the man 40% at fault and the woman 60% at fault, respectively, for the accident. Under the State's comparative negligence statute, the woman will recover from the man:

   A. $100,000.

   B. $60,000.

   C. $40,000.

   D. Nothing.

31. A company stores and manufactures acid gas on its premises. Early one morning, a leak developed in the connecting lines between the tanks. The leak was not the fault of the company. The escaping gas formed a greenish cloud. Before the greenish cloud of acid gas reached the point of dispersal, it made contact with a cable repairman who was repairing a cable atop a telephone pole. The repairman did not see the cloud and he inhaled the gas, which caused him to black out

and fall from the pole, sustaining severe injuries. In a suit by the cable repairman against the company, on which of the following legal theories should he base his cause of action?

A. Battery

B. Private nuisance.

C. Strict liability.

D. Negligence.

32. A utility company had a high voltage electricity power substation near a housing project. The company took every possible precaution to prevent any harm to any children who might try to climb the fence and get near the electricity power substation. If a homeless man receives an electric shock after climbing the fence and getting near the electricity power substation, even though the company posted "No Trespassing" and "Warning!" signs, will the company be liable to that man?

A. No because the exercise of extreme care was used.

B. No because there is no fault.

C. Yes because the electricity power substation was negligently maintained.

D. Yes because this was an activity involving a serious degree of danger.

33. A man was visiting a wild animal park. He let his arm reach out from the bus that was carrying him around. The man attempted to feed one of the lions. The lion accepted the food, along with the man's hand, which the lion bit off and swallowed in one gulp. When the man recovered, he sued the wild animal park for failure to control the animals. The wild animal park raised the defense of contributory negligence. The wild animal park will:

A. Win because the man was reckless.

B. Win because the man was negligent.

C. Lose because contributory negligence is not a defense to strict liability.

D. Lose because the man was not negligent.

34. A woman purchased a blender and went home to make smoothies for her family. Unknown to the woman, the blender had a defective blade. When the woman placed several pieces of fruit into the blender to make the smoothie and turned on the blender, it exploded, spewing pieces of fruit all over her kitchen counter. The woman took a damp rag and wiped up the mess. Suddenly, her telephone rang, so she went into the other room to answer it. She did not see the damp rag fall off the counter and onto the floor. Just then,

her five-year-old entered the kitchen and slipped on the damp rag. The child broke her arm. The woman sued the blender manufacturer for strict liability on behalf of her child. Will the woman recover on behalf of her child?

A. No, if this type of injury is unforeseeable from the use of the blender.

B. No because the child was contributorily negligent.

C. Yes because the woman purchased the blender.

D. Yes because a parent can sue on behalf of a child.

35. A man was driving a new car that he had just purchased when, for no apparent reason, the engine exploded and set the car aflame. A passerby attempted to pull the man from the burning car, but as the passerby was trying to free the man, the passerby slipped on some oil left in the road and sustained injuries. Will the passerby prevail in an action against the car manufacturer?

A. No because the passerby assumed the risk.

B. No because the passerby's conduct was unforeseeable.

C. Yes because the car manufacturer was engaging in abnormally dangerous activities.

D. Yes, since the car manufacturer put the man in peril, it is responsible to any foreseeable rescuer.

36. A woman went into a yogurt shop to purchase some yogurt. As the woman entered the shop, the door closer snapped and struck the woman on the head, rendering her unconscious. In a cause of action for negligence, the woman's best theory would be?

A. Res ipsa loquitur.

B. She was owed a duty of care as a business invitee.

C. She was owed a duty of care as a licensee.

D. None of the above.

37. A man was a passenger in a car driven by a woman. The woman suddenly lost control of the car and swerved off the shoulder of the road. The car then overturned and rolled down the embankment. The man was killed on impact. The woman stated that loose rocks and gravel on the road might have caused her to lose control of the car, but she could not be definite. A subsequent investigation revealed that there were, in fact, no loose rocks or gravel, nor any other abnormal road conditions at the time of the accident. The man's estate sues the woman. What is the estate's best theory of recovery?

A. Res ipsa loquitur.

B. Wrongful death.

C. Survival statute.

D. Substantial factor.

38. If the court finds res ipsa loquitur in a particular lawsuit, what would be the result?

    A. Binding on the jury.

    B. The defendant would win.

    C. The plaintiff would win.

    D. An inference of negligence is created.

39. A clerk at a hardware store negligently stacked a number of rolled window shades behind the customer service counter. The area behind the customer service counter was not open to the public. A woman entered the store one afternoon to make some purchases. She was accompanied by her 6-year-old daughter. While the woman's back was turned, the daughter walked unseen behind the counter and tried to climb atop of the pile of rolled window shades. Because of how the window shades were stacked, they fell. Several of the heavy shades landed on the daughter, causing serious injuries to her. The woman sued the owner of the store on her daughter's behalf. In order for the daughter to recover for her injuries, an appropriate action would be:

    A. Recklessness.

    B. Doctrine of respondeat superior.

    C. Strict liability.

    D. There is no appropriate action because the owner of the store was not negligent.

40. A homeowner had a swimming pool in his back yard. Normally, he would keep the gate to the pool locked, so that neighboring children could not get in. However, one day, he was busy and forgot to lock the gate. The five-year-old son of a neighbor entered the gate and jumped into the pool. Because he could not swim, he drowned. The neighbor sues the homeowner. What is the best theory of recovery in holding the homeowner liable for the son's death:

    A. The son was a business invitee.

    B. Strict liability in torts.

    C. Attractive nuisance doctrine.

    D. The son was owed a duty as a licensee.

41. A woman was driving down the road at an excessive speed. A twelve-year-old boy darted out into the road to catch a ball. The woman was unable to stop in time and hit and severely injured the boy. The boy's parents bring a lawsuit against the woman on the boy's behalf. In a common law jurisdiction, will the boy prevail?

A. Yes because the woman was negligent.

B. Yes because this type of accident could have only occurred if the woman were negligent.

C. No because the boy was negligent in darting out into the road.

D. No because the boy's negligence is imputed to the parents.

42. A and B are hunting in the forest. Each, at the same time, fires his shotgun. A pellet from one of the shotguns strikes C in the leg. What is C's best theory of recovery?

   A. Substantial factor.

   B. Joint and several liability.

   C. "But for."

   D. None of the above.

43. A girl loved to play practical jokes on her classmates. One morning, as one of her classmates was about to sit in his chair, the girl pulled the chair from under him. Surprised by the girl's conduct, the classmate fell down and was humiliated by the incident. The classmate can most likely make a claim against the girl for:

   A. Battery.

   B. Assault.

   C. Assault and battery.

   D. Infliction of emotional distress.

44. While jogging down a crowded street, a jogger noticed a beautiful brunette ahead. At that moment, the jogger was not watching where he was going. He stepped in a pot hole and lost his balance. In order to keep from falling, the jogger grabbed the brunette by the arm. If the brunette brings a cause of action against the jogger, the jogger will most likely be found:

   A. Not liable because the brunette was not hurt.

   B. Not liable because the jogger's conduct was acceptable under the circumstances.

   C. Liable for battery.

   D. Liable for assault.

45. Two teenage girls went into a department store. The security guard, who was always suspicious of teenage shoppers, asked the girls to remove their coats and to empty their purses. After about 10 minutes, the guard, convinced that the girls had not taken anything, apologized and let the girls leave. If the girls bring a cause of action for false imprisonment, the department store will most likely:

   A. Win, since the store had a privilege to detain them.

B. Win because the girls were, at all times, free to leave.

C. Not win, since the girls took nothing.

D. Not win, since the guard had no reasonable grounds for suspicion.

46. A woman saw a demonstration of a hair dryer that dried hair in three minutes. The woman purchased the dryer directly from the manufacturer. After several uses, she noticed that the dryer took longer than three minutes to dry her hair and that the dryer made a loud noise. She called the manufacturer, which assured her that some dryers were just louder than others. Several days later, while using the dryer, the woman received a severe shock that caused her physical injury. In an action against the manufacturer, the woman will most likely:

A. Prevail because the dryer was defective.

B. Prevail because the manufacturer should have warned the woman of the danger when she called.

C. Not prevail because an intelligent person would not have continued to use the dryer.

D. None of the above.

47. A man was hit by an automobile, negligently driven by a woman. He was immediately taken to the hospital for treatment. At the hospital, he developed severe uncontrolled internal bleeding, as a result of pre-existing hemophilia. He died the next day from the bleeding. What effect will the man's pre-existing hemophilia have on recovery of damages in a lawsuit against the woman by his estate?

A. The woman is liable for all damages resulting from her negligent conduct.

B. The man's hemophilia is an intervening independent cause of death. Thus, the woman is only responsible for those damages that would have occurred if the man were not a hemophiliac.

C. The man's estate will not recover any damages from the woman.

D. None of the above.

48. A woman decides to have a garage sale at her home. She buys signs from a sign company to advertise her garage sale. The signs are made of thin sheet metal and have rough edges. She places the signs in her front yard. A teenager is skateboarding in the street when a driver, driving his pickup truck, fails to see the teenager and collides his front bumper with him. The teenager goes flying through the air and lands on the garage sale signs, one of which beheads him. In an action by the teenager's estate against the sign manufacturer, the estate's best theory of recovery is?

A. Strict liability.

B. Battery.

C. Recklessness.

D. Negligence of the driver.

49. A large 6'2" man was at a sports bar watching a sporting event. The man was excitedly cheering for his preferred team. A small man who was a fan of the opposing team became enraged at the large man's exuberance. The small man raised his fist and shouted to the large man, "If you weren't such a large pig, I would knock you down." The large man brings a suit against the small man for assault. The large man will most likely:

    A. Win, since he felt apprehension when the small man was shaking his fist at him.

    B. Win, since the small man was shaking his fist.

    C. Lose, since in light of the small man's statement, his conduct was not sufficient to create immediate apprehension in the large man.

    D. Lose because the small man was not big enough to assault the large man.

50. A man lived in a remote area of town. One evening, he heard a noise outside. He grabbed his gun and proceeded to look around his front yard. Thinking he saw a wolf, he fired a shot and killed the animal. It turned out that the animal was the neighbor's dog. Which of the following propositions is most correct?

    A. The neighbor will have a cause of action for trespass to chattel.

    B. The man will not be liable to the neighbor because the man made a reasonable mistake.

    C. The neighbor will have a cause of action for battery.

    D. The man will be found guilty of cruelty to animals.

51. A brunette woman went to the hairdresser for a wash and blow dry. While the hairdresser was shampooing the woman's hair, the hairdresser decided to use a color shampoo because "blondes have more fun." When the hairdresser finished drying the woman's hair, the woman was surprised and unhappy to see that her hair had turned blonde. The woman received a lot of compliments from her friends on her new hair color but, nonetheless, sued the hairdresser. What is the woman's best cause of action in this lawsuit?

    A. There is no cause of action because the woman's friends thought that she looked better with the hair color.

    B. There is no cause of action because the woman impliedly consented to the hairdresser's artistic discretion, which includes hair coloring.

C. Battery.

D. Negligence.

52. A doctor performed a surgery around a man's eyes after obtaining informed consent from the man. When the man awoke, he found that he had no sensation on the left side of his face. If the man contends that the doctor was responsible for the man's loss of sensation in his face, the likely outcome will be:

A. The man will recover, if he can show that the doctor had exclusive control of his person during the surgery and that the injury suffered usually would not occur in the absence of negligence.

B. The man will recover because a doctor is always responsible for a patient's injuries during surgery.

C. The man will not recover, unless a percipient witness testifies that the doctor's negligence was the cause in fact of the injury.

D. None of the above.

53. If a person sues an orthopedic surgeon for negligence, what is the applicable standard of care the court should apply?

A. The reasonable, prudent physician.

B. The reasonable, prudent orthopedic surgeon in the surgeon's locality.

C. The reasonable, prudent orthopedic surgeon as determined by national standards.

D. The reasonable, prudent orthopedic surgeon with education and experience similar to that of the defendant.

54. A man, as a joke, pushed his girlfriend into a swimming pool. She yelled out, "Save me! I can't swim!" The man wanted to break up with her anyway, since she had cheated on him, so he walked away, hoping that she would drown. At the last minute, a bystander jumped into the pool and saved her. The girlfriend suffered injuries and sued the man. Will she prevail?

A. Yes because the rescuer actually caused the girlfriend's injury.

B. Yes because the man had a duty to save his girlfriend.

C. No because the girlfriend had cheated on the man and deserved to drown.

D. No because a person never has a duty to act. Since the man did not save her, he did nothing wrong.

55. A motivated telemarketer begins calling a man's home every night between the

hours of 11:00 p.m. and 6:00 a.m. The man has placed a "Do not call" on his phone. Nonetheless, the telemarketer continues to make these calls for one week. The man has such sleep deprivation that when he is able to sleep at all, he suffers disturbing dreams and is forced to visit a psychiatrist. He locates and sues the telemarketer. The man is most likely to recover for his injuries under which of the following theories:

A. Intentional infliction of emotional distress.

B. Assault.

C. Negligence.

D. False light invasion of privacy.

56. A collection agent visited a man's home and told him in the presence of the man's wife that the man would suffer "serious consequences to his health" if he did not pay the debt within 24 hours. The man paid the debt later that day. If the man's wife sues the collection agent for intentional infliction of emotional distress, will she recover?

A. No because the collection agent had no intent to cause her emotional distress.

B. Yes because the doctrine of transferred intent applies.

C. No because she has not suffered pecuniary loss.

D. Yes, if she can show that the collection agent should have reasonably foreseen that the wife would suffer emotional distress.

57. To recover for intentional infliction of emotional distress, most jurisdictions require a plaintiff to prove, in addition to an intentional and outrageous act, that the act has caused:

A. Plaintiff a physical impact that caused the emotional distress.

B. Plaintiff physical consequences from the emotional distress.

C. Plaintiff severe emotional distress only.

D. Plaintiff's emotional distress by an assault, battery, or false imprisonment by defendant.

58. A state law requires that one is not permitted to talk on a cellular telephone while driving unless a hands-free device is being used. A lady was talking on her cellular phone without the use of a hand-free device, when she drove her car into another automobile that was stopped at a red light. The driver of the other automobile sued the lady. The judge should instruct the jury that the state law regarding the use of cellular telephones while driving:

A. Establishes the duty of care.

B. Is a factor that the jury can accept

or reject when it determines the duty of care.

C. Is of no relevance in establishing the duty of care.

D. Sets the duty of care under the theory of res ipsa loquitur.

59. A woman operates a restaurant in a part of the city that is notorious as a high-crime area. The restaurant opens every day at 11:00 a.m. and closes at midnight. Customers park their automobiles in a lot, which the woman also owns, and that is adjacent to the restaurant. Although she has considered it, the woman has never gotten around to installing lighting in the parking lot.

One evening, a customer was beaten and robbed in the lot by an unknown assailant at 10:00 p.m. This was the first time that anyone had been the victim of a crime in the lot. If the customer sues woman for negligence due to injuries caused by the robber, and it is determined that the woman breached her duty of care by failing to keep the parking lot lighted:

A. The woman should prevail because the intentional act of a felon is always a superseding cause.

B. The woman should prevail because no one had ever been beaten or robbed in her parking lot before.

C. The customer should prevail if, given the fact that the woman's establishment is in a high-crime area, he can prove that it was reasonably foreseeable that he might be robbed in the unlighted parking lot.

D. The customer should prevail because the owner of a restaurant owes a higher duty of care to a patron that results in strict liability.

60. A driver's license had expired, but because he needed to get to work, he drove carefully on his way to his job. An intoxicated man stumbled into the roadway. Although the driver applied his brakes and did everything he could to avoid having his car collide with the intoxicated man, nonetheless, the intoxicated man was hit and suffered a broken arm. If the intoxicated man sues the driver for negligence, will he prevail?

A. Yes because the driver was negligent per se.

B. Yes because the intoxicated man's injuries were a reasonably foreseeable result of the driver's negligence.

C. No because the driver's breach of the duty of care was not the cause of the intoxicated man's injury.

D. No because the intoxicated man had the last clear chance of preventing the injury.

61. A woman was a passenger in a man's automobile. As the man drove the car through the mountains, a heavy snow storm suddenly came up. The man, who was driving too fast for the conditions, failed to see a tractor trailer that was blocking the road. The owner of the tractor trailer had stopped the tractor trailer to install snow chains, but had carelessly failed to pull off the road. The man was unable to stop his car, and it struck the tractor trailer. The woman was injured in the accident. If the woman sues the man and the owner of the tractor trailer in negligence to recover damages for her injuries:

   A. The woman will recover only those damages that she can prove each defendant caused.

   B. The man and the owner of the tractor trailer will each be liable to the woman for the full amount of her damages.

   C. The man and the owner of the tractor trailer will each be liable for fifty percent of the woman's damages.

   D. The woman will recover nothing because she assumed the risk.

62. If a jury determines that two tortfeasors are responsible for a plaintiff's damages, and one tortfeasor pays the plaintiff the entire amount, that tortfeasor's best recovery against the non-paying tortfeasor is:

   A. Satisfaction.

   B. Indemnification.

   C. Vicarious liability.

   D. Contribution.

63. A woman gives a ride to a hitchhiker. Although the woman is driving within the speed limit, a flash flood occurs, causing her to lose control of the car. The car goes down an embankment. The hitchhiker is severely injured. The hitchhiker sues the woman for negligence. In a jurisdiction that has adopted an automobile guest statute, will the hitchhiker recover?

   A. Yes because the woman was negligent.

   B. Yes, but only if the hitchhiker can show that the woman's conduct amounted to gross negligence.

   C. Yes, but only if he can show that the woman's conduct amounted to an intentional act.

   D. The hitchhiker will only recover if it can be demonstrated that the woman acted with malice.

64. During the course of a baseball game, a player decided to make a hard slide into

the shortstop. As a result, he broke the shortstop's ankle. If the shortstop sues the player for the ankle injury, his most likely cause of action will be for:

A. Assault.

B. Battery.

C. Intentional infliction of emotional distress.

D. Strict liability.

65. At rush hour on a crowded subway train, a man accidentally bumped into a woman and bruised her arm. If the woman sues the man for her injuries, the man's best defense to the woman's lawsuit would be:

A. Contributory negligence.

B. Justification.

C. Implied consent.

D. Private necessity.

66. A man is walking his dog on the public sidewalk next to a woman's property. He trips and falls on a crack in the sidewalk. He sues the woman for his injuries. At common law, most courts would classify the man as:

A. A trespasser.

B. A licensee.

C. An invitee.

D. None of the above.

67. A man owns a furniture store with a large neon sign attached to the building. The sign, which extends out over a public sidewalk approximately 15 feet from the ground, is anchored by two large cables.

The man had not checked the condition of the cables in years, so he was unaware that they were severely corroded. During an unusually violent windstorm, the cables broke and the sign fell, striking a pedestrian. If the pedestrian sues the man for negligence for her injuries, a court will likely find that the man:

A. Had a duty of care to keep the cables in good repair.

B. Had a duty of care to warn the pedestrian only of known, latent defects.

C. Had a duty of care to warn the pedestrian only of dangerous active operations on his property.

D. Had no duty of care to the pedestrian.

68. A woman engaged contractors to do work on her roof and the inside of the second floor of her house. One day, when the contractors were ready to leave for the day, they left a window open on the second floor with their ladder leading up to that window. In the

middle of that night, a burglar broke into that woman's home and stole her jewelry. The woman sued the contractors for the loss of her jewelry. The effect of the burglar's actions on the woman's negligence suit against the contractors will likely be to:

A. Prevent the woman from recovering from the contractors because the burglary was an intervening criminal act.

B. Prevent the woman from recovering from the contractors because a burglar breaking into the woman's home is not a reasonably foreseeable event.

C. Not adversely affect the woman's suit, as a defendant is liable for all injuries directly caused by him.

D. Not adversely affect the woman's suit because the burglary was a reasonably foreseeable intervening criminal act.

69. A grandmother pinches the cheek of her lovely grandson. Unknown to the grandmother, the grandson is a hemophiliac (one who can easily start bleeding from the slightest touch). Although he survives, he suffers severe injuries from the pinch. The grandson's parents, on behalf of the grandson, sue the grandmother. They will be able to recover:

A. Only those damages that the grandmother could have reasonably foreseen under the circumstances.

B. Only those damages that an ordinary person would have suffered because the grandmother was not responsible for the grandson's preexisting condition.

C. All damages that the grandson sustained, even though the grandson had a rare condition that made him more susceptible to injury.

D. None of the above.

70. A woman was swimming at a private beach owned by a wealthy man when she was attacked by a shark. The shark bit off her leg. She was in the hospital for four weeks recovering. The stump where her leg was bitten became infected. The infection spread to her heart, and she died. At common law, if her estate sued man to recover for medical expenses incurred between the date of the accident and the date of the woman's death, the result would be:

A. The woman's estate would recover medical expenses in a wrongful death action.

B. The woman's estate would recover medical expenses in a survival action.

C. The woman's estate would recover nothing because her right of action against the man ended with her death.

D. None of the above.

71. While her husband and minor children were away on a fishing trip, a woman decided to go for a swim. She left her apartment unit and started walking toward the apartment complex's common swimming pool. Forty stories directly above her, some other tenants were moving a safe by a cable into their apartment window. Suddenly, the cable snapped and the safe came crashing down on the woman, instantly crushing her to death. In most states today, if the woman's husband and minor children wish to recover for lost financial support, services, and society suffered as a result of her death, their claim against the apartment owner will be:

A. A wrongful death action.

B. A survival action.

C. A negligent infliction of emotional distress action.

D. A simple negligence action.

72. One day, a pizza delivery boy who was employed by a local Italian restaurant was driving on a public highway and, because he was anxious to make sure that he delivered all of his pizzas within thirty minutes or less, he was speeding and lost control of his van. The vehicle jumped the curb and struck a pedestrian. The pedestrian was seriously injured in the accident. Under what doctrine could the pedestrian bring a cause of action against the restaurant that employed the pizza delivery boy?

A. Negligent hiring.

B. Respondeat superior.

C. Nondelegable duty.

D. Independent contractor.

73. A garbage collector was trying to improve his lot in life and was attending night school. One day, while he was driving his garbage truck, he stopped at the local library and got some books for his night courses. As soon as he returned to the garbage truck and attempted to drive the truck out of the parking space, his truck struck and hit an elderly man. If the man sues the garbage company that employed the garbage collector, the garbage company's best defense will be:

A. The garbage collector was acting within the scope of his employment.

B. The garbage collector's actions were a superseding cause.

C. The garbage collector was engaged in a frolic and detour.

D. The garbage company's duty was nondelegable.

74. A civilian employee of the United States Army was responsible for delivering packages between military bases. He drove a small government-owned van when making his deliveries. One day, he was driving on a public highway and, because he was careless, he lost control of the van. The vehicle jumped the curb and struck a pedestrian.

The pedestrian was seriously injured in the accident. She sued the Army for her injuries. It was determined that the civilian employee was negligent, and the Army was vicariously liable. If the Army raises the defense of sovereign immunity, the result will be:

A. The Army will be liable because sovereign immunity violates the Equal Protection Clause of the Fourteenth Amendment.

B. The Army will be liable because Congress waived sovereign immunity in negligence cases through the Federal Tort Claims Act.

C. The Army will be liable because agencies of the United States government have never enjoyed sovereign immunity.

D. The Army will not be liable.

75. In a recent issue, a local newspaper ran an item stating: "Local resident Sally Smith, age 21, gave birth to twins last week." There is one resident in the town named Sally Smith and she is 21, but she is not married and has never had a child. Smith suffered ridicule and embarrassment because of the news item. At common law, if Sally Smith sued the local newspaper for libel based on the news item:

A. She would recover because the statement is libel per se.

B. She would not recover because there has been no publication.

C. She would not recover because she has not established the colloquium.

D. She would recover, so long as she produced sufficient evidence to show reasonable innuendo.

76. A well-meaning woman sent letters to her bridge club, asking them to bring food and clothing to a particular street corner so that it could be given to a man who had been seen at that corner pushing a basket and who the woman believed was homeless. The letters referred to the man by name. It turned out that the man was not homeless, but rather, owned a business at that location and was bringing supplies to that business in his shopping cart. When the well-meaning bridge club members attempted to deliver the food and clothing to the man, the man became incensed and sued the woman who had sent the letters. If the woman can prove that the letters were written and sent as a result of an innocent mistake, at common law the effect on the man's libel suit would be:

    A. His suit would fail because libel required malicious intent at common law.

    B. His suit would fail because libel required at least reckless conduct at common law.

    C. His suit would fail because libel required at least negligence at common law.

    D. His suit would succeed.

77. A man was running for political office. He wrote an editorial in the local newspaper, alleging that his opponent had received campaign contributions from a racist group. It turned out that this was completely untrue. The opponent sued the man for libel. The man then issued a written retraction and a public apology for his false statements about the opponent. The effect of the man's retraction and apology would be:

    A. To limit damages the man must pay because of the mitigation rule.

    B. To limit damages the man must pay because of the collateral source rule.

    C. To limit damages the man must pay because of the offsetting benefit rule.

    D. To prevent the opponent from recovering any damages from the man.

78. At his seminars, a motivational speaker sells tapes in which he gives anecdotes about real people in order teach and inspire others to better their own lives. In one of his tapes, there is an anecdote about a specific woman who attended the seminar when she was drunk. It turns out that the woman never drinks alcohol. She sues the motivational speaker for defamation. The most appropriate cause of action would be:

    A. Slander.

    B. Libel.

C. Slander per se.

D. Libel per quod.

79. A large bookstore sells several kinds of books. One of the books it sells turns out to contain libelous material against a particular individual. The owner of the bookstore has never read this particular book, but the bookstore has sold several copies of the book. If the individual against whom the libelous statements were made brings a defamation action against the bookstore, the result will be:

A. The bookstore will be liable for republishing the defamatory statement.

B. The bookstore will be vicariously liable.

C. The bookstore will not be liable because it is a secondary publisher.

D. The bookstore will be liable, but it may seek indemnification from the author of the book.

80. On a nationally syndicated talk radio show, a controversial talk show host alleged that a female United States senator had worked as a dancer in a topless bar while she was in college. The talk show host had heard this "rumor" from an ex-convict with a very poor reputation for the truth, but he did no further investigation before going on the air with this allegation. In fact, the story was a complete fabrication. The senator, a very conservative individual, was distressed and embarrassed when she learned of the story. If she sues the talk show host for libel, the rulings of the United States Supreme Court require that she must prove:

A. "Actual malice," meaning that the talk show host acted willfully and wantonly in publishing the defamatory statement.

B. "Actual malice," meaning that the talk show host acted with knowledge that the defamatory statement was false or with reckless disregard for the truth.

C. The talk show host was at least negligent and the senator suffered "actual injury."

D. The talk show host intended to make the defamatory statement.

81. In a defamation action by a public official, the public official's burden of proof, according to rulings of the United States Supreme Court, is:

A. Preponderance of the evidence.

B. Clear and convincing evidence.

C. Beyond a reasonable doubt.

D. None of the above.

82. At a local Bar Association meeting, a lawyer told everyone present that his former partner comingled client trust funds with personal assets. This allegation was untrue in all respects. At common law, if the former partner sues the lawyer for defamation with respect to these statements, the appropriate cause of action would be:

   A. Slander per se.

   B. Slander per quod.

   C. Simple slander.

   D. Intentional interference with prospective business advantage.

83. A student who was dissatisfied with his grades told all his friends that his professor was a "was a real clown, who wouldn't recognize a book if one fell on his head."

   Modernly, if the professor sues the student for defamation with respect this statement, the likely result would be:

   A. The professor will not recover because the statement is the student's opinion and all opinions are constitutionally protected under the Gertz v. Welch decision.

   B. The professor will not recover because professors are always public figures under New York Times v. Sullivan.

   C. The professor will not recover because the student's statement is an opinion that does not appear to be founded on underlying false facts.

   D. The professor will recover.

84. During a lawsuit against a man for the battery of his daughter, a witness testified that the man sexually abused his daughter numerous times. The man sued the witness for defamation for the statements about the abuse, which turned out to be false. The witness' best defense will be:

   A. Privileges do not apply to lawsuits for battery.

   B. The witness' statement is protected by a conditional privilege.

   C. The witness' statement is protected by an absolute privilege.

   D. One is never liable for damages for statements made on the witness stand in a civil suit.

85. A man and a famous actress were having dinner in a restaurant. A waitress overheard the man refer to the actress as a prostitute. The waitress recognized the actress immediately and quickly ran to a phone and to call her best friend, in order to inform her of the "fact" that this particular actress was a prostitute. It turned out that the actress was not a prostitute and had never been one. If the

actress sues the waitress for defamation, the result will be:

A. The waitress will prevail because she is protected by the waitress' privilege.

B. The actress will prevail because the waitress has republished the defamatory statement.

C. The actress will prevail because waitress has exceeded the scope of her conditional privilege.

D. The waitress will prevail if her best friend did not believe the statement.

86. A woman purchased a new toaster over from a department store. The following day, while making breakfast for her family, the toaster oven overheated and burned her. If the woman sues the manufacturer of the toaster oven under modern law for her injuries, the likely result will be:

A. She will not recover because she is not in privity of contract with the manufacturer of the toaster oven.

B. She will not recover, unless she can prove that the manufacturer of the toaster oven was negligent.

C. She will recover under a strict liability in tort theory because the manufacturer of the toaster oven is responsible for the design defect.

D. She will recover under a strict liability in tort theory because the manufacturer of the toaster oven is responsible for the manufacturing defect.

87. A man purchased a snowmobile from a retailer. The very first time he operated the vehicle, the steering mechanism malfunctioned, causing the snowmobile to overturn. The snowmobile struck a bystander. The man and the bystander both suffered serious injuries. Accident investigators determined that a critical bolt in the steering mechanism was missing and that the accident resulted from this defect. Furthermore, the retailer had not properly inspected the snowmobile's steering mechanism before it sold the snowmobile to the man. If the bystander sues the retailer for his injuries under a strict liability in tort theory, in most jurisdictions today:

A. The bystander will not recover because the retailer did not cause the manufacturing defect.

B. The bystander will recover, so long as he was a reasonably foreseeable plaintiff.

C. The bystander will not recover because he was not in privity with the retailer or the manufacturer of the snowmobile.

D. The bystander will recover, but only if he was related to the man.

88. Which of the following statements would constitute a manufacturer's best defense to a strict liability in tort action?

   A. The evidence shows that the plaintiff (consumer) tampered with the product before using it.

   B. The evidence shows that the plaintiff was contributorily negligent.

   C. The plaintiff had never used a similar product before the incident in question.

   D. In the manufacturer's industry, this manufacturer has the most elaborate quality control checks during the manufacturing process.

89. A manufacturer made children's pajamas. After thorough testing, the manufacturer determined that in 1% of the tests that it performed, the pajamas spontaneously ignited if the room temperature was above a certain threshold. Nonetheless, the manufacturer sold the pajamas to retail stores. A woman purchases the pajamas and puts them on her child. The child is burned when the pajamas spontaneously ignite. The woman sues the manufacturer of the pajamas under a strict liability in tort theory for her child's injuries. The likely result will be:

   A. The woman will recover because the manufacturer is responsible for the manufacturing defect.

   B. The woman will recover because the manufacturer is responsible for the design defect.

   C. The woman will not recover because the product was unavoidably unsafe.

   D. The woman will not recover because clothing manufacturers are exempt from strict liability rules.

90. A drug manufacturer developed a new allergy pill that could be purchased by a consumer without a prescription. Laboratory tests revealed, however, that a side effect of the drug was deafness in very small percentage of patients who were treated with the medication. Despite diligent efforts, the drug manufacturer's scientists were unable to completely eliminate the deafness side effect associated with the drug. Nonetheless, the manufacturer did not place a warning on the pill bottle because the drug caused deafness in such a small percentage of people. A woman purchased the pills for her allergies. She took the pills and became completely deaf. If the woman sues the manufacturer under a strict liability in tort theory for her deafness, the result will be:

A. The woman will not recover because her lawsuit should have only been in negligence.

B. The woman will recover because the drug manufacturer is responsible for all personal injuries caused by its drug.

C. The woman will recover because the drug manufacturer failed to warn her of the deafness side effect.

D. The woman will not recover because drug manufacturers are exempt from strict liability rules.

91. An employee of a company that manufactures explosives carelessly left a container of liquid nitroglycerin in the aisle of an unlighted section of the company's warehouse. An inspector from the State Department of Safety tripped over the container. Fortunately, it did not explode, but she broke her arm when she fell. If she sues the company for injuries she suffered when she broke her arm:

A. The company should be held strictly liable because it is engaged in abnormally dangerous activity.

B. The company should be held liable because its employee was negligent.

C. The company should not be liable because the injury was not reasonably foreseeable.

D. The company should not be liable because the inspector's injury is covered by worker's compensation.

92. A school bus driver was operating his bus negligently while driving students to school. His bus hit a car and he was cited by the police for negligent driving. Several students received injuries. The school system had a strict safety policy that required the summary dismissal of any employees who were cited for negligent driving. The injured students sued the school system for negligence. The school system's safety controls and its policy of summarily dismissing careless employees will:

A. Prevent the students from recovering from the school system because the driver was engaged in a frolic and detour.

B. Prevent the students from recovering from the school system because the driver was acting beyond the scope of his employment.

C. Enable the students to recover from the driver only.

D. Enable the students to recover from both the school system and the driver.

93. A woman purchased a food processor. The first time she used it, a wire shorted and caused a fire. The woman received minor burns in attempting to extinguish the blaze. An investigation revealed that the type of wire in question that was used in all food processors of this model was inadequate to safely conduct normal household electrical current.

    If the woman sues the manufacturer of the food processor for her injuries, the most appropriate cause of action would be:

    A. A suit for strict liability in tort because the food processor had a manufacturing defect.

    B. A suit for strict liability in tort because the food processor had a design defect.

    C. A suit for strict liability in tort because the manufacturer failed to warn of the danger.

    D. A suit for strict liability in tort, provided she can demonstrate that she and the manufacturer were in privity.

94. A bar exam tutor purchased a new computer. Five minutes after turning it on for the first time, the computer overheated and caught on fire. Although the tutor received no injuries, the computer stopped working altogether as a result of the overheating and the fire. If the tutor sues the computer manufacturer in strict liability in tort, alleging a manufacturing defect, in order to recover the cost of a replacement computer, the result will be:

    A. The tutor will recover because the computer had a manufacturing defect.

    B. The tutor will recover because the computer had a design defect.

    C. The tutor will not recover.

    D. The tutor will not recover, unless she sues the computer manufacturer for breaching its implied warranty of merchantability.

95. A man was standing near a railroad track smoking a cigarette. He noticed a small child caught on the track. A train was approaching, and the child called out to the man to help him. Instead, the man laughed, finished his cigarette, and walked off. The train ran over the child, killing him. If the child's parents sue the man for wrongful death:

    A. They will recover because there is a common law duty to rescue someone in peril.

    B. They will recover because most states modernly require people to rescue others who are in peril.

C. They will recover because, while there is no duty to rescue adults in peril, there is a duty to rescue children in peril.

D. They will not recover.

96. A physician was with a friend. A car driven by a man had overturned on the road ahead, and the man was severely injured. Emergency paramedics had not arrived on the scene. The physician stopped to assist the man, but her treatment was below the professional standard of care, and the man died. If the man's wife sues the physician for wrongful death, in a state that has a Good Samaritan statute:

A. She will recover because the physician undertook a duty and performed it negligently.

B. She will recover because Good Samaritan statutes provide physician liability for negligent acts.

C. She will recover, assuming she can prove that the physician acted recklessly in the circumstances.

D. She will not recover, unless the physician caused the man's car to overturn in the first place.

97. A woman was pregnant with her first child. Her family had a history of congenital birth defects, so she went to her doctor for tests to determine if her fetus would likely be born in an impaired state. The doctor performed various tests to make this determination. The doctor negligently misread the test results and informed the woman that the fetus was normal. The woman carried the fetus to term. Her child was born with severe birth defects and will require expensive medical care and special education for the rest of his life.

If the child through a guardian ad litem sues the doctor for damages, in most jurisdictions, his cause of action would be called a suit for:

A. Wrongful birth.

B. Wrongful life.

C. Wrongful death.

D. None of the above.

98. A man was severely injured when his motorcycle was struck by a car. The doctor informed the man's wife that an operation was necessary immediately, in order to save the man's life. The wife refused, for religious reasons, to give consent for the operation. The man died. The wife sued the hospital for wrongful death. If the hospital prevails, it will be because:

A. Hospitals are shielded from wrongful death actions.

B. The wife's religion forbade the operation.

C. The man drove his motorcycle without a helmet.

D. The wife signed a form agreeing not to sue the hospital for negligence.

99. A woman came into an emergency room when she was in labor. Her regular doctor was not available to deliver the twins that she was expecting. After the woman was prepared for a caesarian section and was under sedation, the doctor on call delivered one baby. After a few minutes, it became apparent that there was another baby in the woman's womb. The doctor delivered the second baby, but because of the lack of oxygen during the time delay, the baby suffered severe birth defects. If the baby through a guardian ad litem sues the on call doctor for wrongful life, his recovery would include:

A. General damages only.

B. Special damages only.

C. General and special damages only.

D. General damages, special damages, and punitive damages.

100. A man retained an attorney to write his will. They entered into a standard written retainer agreement, and the man paid the fee that the attorney charged. The man instructed the attorney that he wished to leave his real property to his favorite nephew. The attorney prepared the will, but carelessly overlooked a relevant section of the Probate Act.

When the man died and the will was offered for probate, the nephew and the other heirs learned of the attorney's error. As a direct result of the error, the devise to the nephew was adeemed, and the nephew received nothing from the man's estate.

If the nephew sues the attorney for professional negligence in the preparation of the man's will, in most jurisdictions today, the likely outcome will be:

A. The nephew will not recover because he was not in privity of contract with the attorney.

B. The nephew will not recover because an attorney does not owe a duty of care to anyone but his client.

C. The nephew will recover because he is a third party beneficiary of the contract between the attorney and the man.

D. The nephew will recover, but his damages will be limited to the fee that the man paid to the attorney.

101. In a products liability suit for strict liability in tort, the plaintiff has the burden of proving:

A. The manufacturer was unreasonable.

B. The product was defective.

C. That he has privity with the manufacturer.

D. That he did not misuse the product.

102. A man purchased an MP3 player (a device that plays music). The device exploded because of faulty wiring found in all MP3 players of this particular model and caused a person who was using it to become permanently deaf in one ear. If the person sues for products liability in strict liability in tort, he must prove that the product has the following defect:

    A. A design defect because it created an avoidable hazard.

    B. A manufacturing defect because it was made as intended.

    C. A marketing defect because it was advertised as a safe MP3 player.

    D. A fabrication defect because the wire was faulty.

103. A woman bought a glass thermometer. On the box that contained the thermometer, there was a warning stating that there was a slight danger that the mercury inside the thermometer could leak. The woman threw away the box without reading the warning. Upon using the thermometer, the mercury leaked and she got mercury poisoning. If the woman sues the manufacturer of the thermometer, the best defense that the manufacturer could offer is:

    A. That this was the first time this had happened and the manufacturer was not aware of the danger.

    B. That thermometers are necessary for health and, as such, thermometer manufacturers are shielded from liability.

    C. That the woman was contributorily negligent.

    D. That the woman failed to read the warning and this constituted an assumption of the risk by the woman.

104. A woman and a man were racing their new cars on a public street. A small child darted into the road. Neither of the drivers was able to stop his car in time to avoid having his car hit the child. Both cars ran over the child. The child survived, but suffered severe injuries as a result of the accident. The child sues both the woman and the man for his damages. The woman contends that she is only 40% liable and that the man should be liable for all other damages. This argument is:

A. Incorrect because the woman was a substantial factor in causing the child's damages.

B. Correct because some damage to the child would have occurred, even if the man's car had not run over the boy.

C. Correct, but the woman has the burden of apportioning the damages.

D. Correct and the child must prove what portion of his damages were caused by the woman in order to recover.

105. The commercial freezer at a store that sold ice cream and other products suddenly stopped working. As a result, all of the ice cream had to be moved to a freezer at another location, where it was stored until the store's freezer was fixed. As a result of the freezer malfunction, the store believes it lost profits because it could not sell ice cream during the time that the freezer was not working. If the store sues the freezer manufacturer on a theory of negligence, it will probably:

A. Not recover for lost profit because this is pure economic loss.

B. Recover for expense of storing the ice cream at the temporary facility.

C. Recover for profits lost while the freezer was being repaired.

D. Both B and C.

106. A carpet manufacturer advertised and promoted one of its carpets mainly as a good carpet for hotels and motels because of its long-wearing qualities. A hotel purchased that carpet and had it installed in the halls and lobby, having to close the hotel down in order to rip up the old carpet and install the new. This job was accomplished just prior to the opening of the summer season, a time during which the hotel could expect full occupancy and make a good profit. Before reopening, the hotel had to get a certificate from the local fire inspector. The fire inspector tested a sample of the carpet and found it was highly flammable, so he refused to certify the hotel for occupancy.

The hotel had to remain closed, rip up the carpet and install new, fire retardant carpet, and lost all profits from the first month of the summer season.

On these facts, if the hotel sues the carpet manufacturer, the best theory of recovery for the hotel is:

A. Negligence.

B. Breach of contract.

C. Express warranty.

D. Implied warranty of merchantability.

107. A group of people was watching a movie at a movie theater, located in a neighborhood where there had been several incidents of arson in the past. An arsonist came and set the front lobby on fire. Due to a malfunction in the exit doors, the people were unable to escape and perished in the fire. If the estates of the people who died at the movie theater sue the movie theater for wrongful death, what is the movie theater's best defense?

   A. The estates lack privity and cannot sue the movie theater.

   B. Causes of action for negligence do not survive the death of the injured party.

   C. The arsonist was a superseding cause of the people's deaths.

   D. The people (and their estates) are unforeseeable plaintiffs and barred under the rule enunciated by Justice Cardozo in <u>Palsgraff</u>.

108. A plaintiff in a products liability action may recover the following damages:

   A. Compensation for medical expenses and compensation for lost wages and earning capacity only.

   B. Compensation for medical expenses and compensation for pain and suffering only.

   C. No recovery.

   D. Compensation for medical expenses, compensation for lost wages and earning capacity, and compensation for pain and suffering.

109. A man went into a convenience store late at night to purchase a soda. As the man attempted to retrieve the soda from the shelf, he was <u>hit on the head</u> by <u>one of the soda cans</u>. If he sues the convenience store in negligence, what is his legal status in relation to the store?

   A. A licensee.

   B. An invitee.

   C. A foreseeable trespasser.

   D. An unforeseeable trespasser.

110. A driver was delivering flowers for a florist. He failed to stop his car at a stop sign. As a result, his car collided with another vehicle and injured the passengers in the second vehicle. The passengers from the second vehicle sue the florist and recover in full against the florist. If the florist then sues the driver, it will be entitled to sue for:

   A. Indemnity.

   B. Contribution.

   C. Equitable apportionment.

   D. None of the above.

111. A drug company manufactured a drug used for the treatment of multiple sclerosis (MS), which also contained an ingredient that was effective in treating MS in virtually everyone who took the drug, but had a side effect of causing complete blindness in a small percentage of patients. The drug company continued to market the drug for five years without a warning of the side effect, even though it knew or should have known of the side effect throughout this time. In the sixth year, the drug company began publishing a warning of the side effect in the Physician's Desk Reference and also in package inserts. Before the drug company began putting the warnings in the packages, a doctor prescribed the drug to his patient. Due to taking the drug, the patient went blind. The patient sued the drug company on a theory of strict products liability. On these facts, the patient will probably be able to prove that the drug is defective under a theory of:

    A. Manufacturing defect.

    B. Design defect.

    C. Warning defect.

    D. She can't prove defectiveness.

112. A man was driving his car and failed to stop at a stop sign. His car collided with a pedestrian, who happened to be a hemophiliac (a person who bleeds easily and does not clot). The pedestrian was rushed to the hospital with a broken leg that required surgery. However, the pedestrian's wife refused to give consent to the surgery for religious reasons. Rather than getting a court order so that the surgery could be performed anyway, the hospital merely left the pedestrian to bleed out and die. The pedestrian's wife sued the hospital for negligence. In attempting to prove that the hospital's actions were the cause in fact of the pedestrian's death, his wife must rely on:

    A. The sine qua non test.

    B. The substantial factor test.

    C. Alternative liability.

    D. Market share liability.

113. A five-year-old child was in the care of a babysitter. The babysitter was talking on the telephone and did not notice that the child had left the house and gone to a neighbor's yard. The child sprayed himself with an insecticide that the neighbor had accidentally left in the yard. The child brought the can of insecticide to the babysitter and said, "The can made me sick." The babysitter read a label on the can of insecticide that said, "If insecticide comes into contact with skin, immediately wash affected area with soap and water." However, since the babysitter wanted to finish her telephone conversation, she did not wash the child's arm until an hour later. The child developed a

severe rash on his arm, which could have been prevented if the babysitter had immediately washed the child's arm with soap. The child's parents sued the neighbor for negligently leaving the insecticide in his yard, resulting in the child's rash. The neighbor's best defense is:

A. The child had no choice but to spray the insecticide because of the pretty roses on the bottle.

B. The child assumed the risk.

C. The child was a trespasser, so the neighbor owed the child no duty.

D. The babysitter's failure to administer soap and water to the child's arm immediately was an intervening, superseding, unforeseeable cause of the child's injuries.

114. A woman went to a doctor who was a fertility expert because she was having trouble getting pregnant. The doctor suggested that she take a series of fertility treatments. The doctor failed to inform her that the treatments might result in multiple pregnancies. The woman became pregnant and gave birth to eight children. If the woman sues the doctor for prescribing the treatments without warning her, she may prevail under the following theory:

A. Negligent failure to obtain her informed consent.

B. Strict liability in tort.

C. Breach of implied warranty of merchantability.

D. Battery.

115. A man became ill at age 55 and was diagnosed as suffering from Asbestosis, a disease caused by exposure to small asbestos speckles that lodge in the lungs and, after a long incubation period of 10 to 20 years, results in asbestosis. Although the asbestos industry had been aware of the hazards of asbestos dust and particles to workers using insulation for more than 50 years, no warnings had ever been issued by the asbestos manufacturers. The man knows that his employer purchased asbestos insulation from one particular company during the man's tenure working for the employer and he also knows that his employer has purchased insulation from at least 10 other manufacturers while he worked there. He is unable to discover the identity of the other asbestos suppliers.

The man sues the one asbestos manufacturer of which he is aware. In order to get a complete recovery for his damages in the case, he should use:

A. The sine qua non test for causation in fact.

B. The substantial factor test for causation in fact.

C. Alternative liability.

D. Market share liability.

116. An astronaut was in flight when he ate some of the prepackaged astronaut food. Although the food was prepared in accordance with the Food and Drug Administration's standards, nevertheless, the astronaut suffered severe stomach cramps after he ate the food. None of the other astronauts on board the ship became ill after eating the food. The astronaut sues the manufacturer of the food for products negligence. During the course of the trial, it was revealed that the plaintiff had a unique stomach ailment and that, no matter what he ate, he would have developed the stomach cramps. What is the food manufacturer's best defense here?

A. The food was prepared in accordance with the Food and Drug Administration's standards.

B. There was no design defect with the food.

C. The manufacturer was not the cause in fact of the astronaut's stomach cramps.

D. All of the above.

117. A woman went to a hardware store and asked the salesman to give her some picture hangers that would hold pictures weighing at least 20 pounds. The salesman gave the woman standard picture hangers. When the woman attempted to use the picture hangers to hang a 15-pound picture, the hanger broke, and the picture fell and broke. If the woman sues the hardware store (vicarious liability for the salesman's advice to purchase these particular picture hangers), what would be her best theory of recovery?

A. Express warranty.

B. Implied warranty of merchantability.

C. Design defect.

D. Implied warranty of fitness for a particular purpose.

118. A woman purchased a hair dye from her local drugstore. The woman used the product as directed but, nevertheless, she lost all of her hair. She sued the manufacturer of the hair dye. On these facts, her best chance for a full recovery would be a suit based on:

A. Battery.

B. Intentional infliction of emotional distress.

C. Warranty.

D. All of the above.

119. A man bought a chainsaw from a store. He took it home and attempted

to behead his wife. However, he was unable to behead his wife because the chainsaw malfunctioned. He sued the store for breach of express warranty. The store's best defense would be:

A. It made no express warranty.

B. The man was engaged in a criminal activity.

C. The man should have sued the chainsaw manufacturer.

D. All chainsaws come with an express warranty.

120. A woman bought a car and took it up into the rugged mountains near her home. As she was driving, the steering wheel fell off. She lost control of the car, and both she and the vehicle went over an embankment. The woman did not die, but was severely injured. She took the car to a mechanic to determine the cause of the accident. Because the steering column had been destroyed in the crash, he was unable to determine if there was any kind of defect, but he said it was extremely likely that a spring was not properly fastened that would have prevented the steering wheel from falling off.

If the woman sues the car manufacturer for negligence, the best way she can prove her case is by use of:

A. Manufacturing defect.

B. Design defect.

C. Warning defect.

D. Res ipsa loquitur.

121. An earthquake occurred and the gates at the local zoo were broken. A ferocious lion escaped, and it bit off the arm of a man who was visiting the zoo. If the man brings a negligence action against the zoo for his injuries, will he recover?

A. No because the lion was hungry.

B. Yes, if the zoo could have taken reasonable steps to prevent the attack.

C. Yes, in strict liability in tort.

D. No, zoos are protected from lawsuits for the actions of their animals.

END OF QUESTIONS

TORTS ANSWERS

1. B is the correct answer. Private nuisance is the interference with the use and enjoyment of one's property. Here, the gas that is being omitted by the oil company interferes with the man's use and enjoyment of his property, since he cannot mow his lawn or have picnics on the lawn, due to the effects of the gas. Thus, the man's best theory of recovery is private nuisance. Answer A is incorrect because there is nothing in the facts to suggest that the refinery's activities are abnormally dangerous; the fact that one man may become nauseous as a result of the gas does not indicate that this happens to everyone. Answer C is incorrect. In order to sue for public nuisance, one must demonstrate that other members of the public are affected by the gas, and the person bringing the suit must suffer specialized harm (i.e., harm that is different from that suffered by other members of the public). Here, there is no indication that other members of the public are affected by the gas. Thus, public nuisance is not the best theory of recovery under these facts. Answer D is incorrect, as well. Negligence is a breach of a duty, causing harm. Here, there is no indication that the oil company breached any duties in its operation of the refinery, especially in light of the fact that the refinery was state-of-the-art, showing that, if anything, the oil company was not careless.

2. D is the correct answer, since a person in lawful possession of land has standing to bring suit to abate a private nuisance. Here, the tenant was in lawful possession of the apartment and, thus, he had standing to bring a suit to abate the private nuisance (the loud music). Answer A is incorrect because, as discussed in Answer D, a lessee does have standing to sue for private nuisance; one need not be an owner to sue for private nuisance. Answer B is incorrect, since a private citizen can bring suit to abate a public nuisance when he has an injury different in kind from the general public. However, there is no indication that the music is bothering anybody else (the public). Thus, public nuisance would not be an appropriate theory under which to bring the lawsuit. Answer C is incorrect because mere residency in the area does not confer standing; as discussed in Answer D, one must be in lawful possession of land in the area, as well.

3. B is the correct answer. An equity court, when considering whether to abate a private nuisance, will balance the hardships. Here, it will likely find that the value of the cell phone towers as operated outweighs occasional inconvenience to the woman. The woman, of course, can still recover damages, but her suit here is for an injunction. The cell phone company's best defense to the suit is the social necessity of the cell phone towers, since the cell phone company appears to operate the towers in a proper place in a proper manner.

Answer A is incorrect because coming to the nuisance is not a complete defense, but rather, one factor the court will consider on the abatement issue. Answer C is incorrect because it is not relevant to the woman's individual claim for private nuisance. Answer D is an incorrect statement of law.

4. A is the correct answer because one who intentionally deceives another, even for a good motive, is liable for common law deceit. Answer B is incorrect, since the stockbroker's act was intentional, not negligent; the facts indicate that the stockbroker knew that the statement was false when he made it. Answer C is incorrect because it confuses malicious intent with common law deceit; malice is not an element for common law deceit. Answer D is incorrect because the client was justified in relying on the statement of a trusted financial advisor.

5. B is the correct answer because the student must show that he was induced by the mentor's statement when he went to law school, as an element of common law deceit. If the student planned to go to law school anyway, he was not induced by the mentor's statement and has, thus, not met this element of common law deceit. Answer A is incorrect because the mentor knowingly made a false statement of fact. It was, thus, not in good faith. Answer C is incorrect because the facts show that the student has incurred significant has out-of-pocket damages; law school and the Bar Examination cost a great deal of money. Answer D is incorrect because it was reasonably foreseeable that the firm would not hire the student, both because the mentor had no power to make such a promise on behalf of the firm and because the firm had implemented a hiring freeze at the time the mentor made the statement to the student.

6. B is the correct answer. Negligent misrepresentation occurs when the defendant carelessly makes a representation while having no reasonable basis to believe it to be true. Here, the facts stipulate that the accountant was careless in computing the company's total assets, and he misrepresented the financial status of the company. Therefore, since the bank relied on the accountant's representations in the audit in making its loan to the company, the bank has a cause of action against the accountant for negligent misrepresentation. Answer A is incorrect because the accountant did not intend to deceive anyone, as is required for common law deceit. Rather, as discussed in Answer B, the accountant was merely careless. Answer C is incorrect because the accountant's representations were not innocent; they were careless and negligent, as discussed in Answer B. Answer D is incorrect because Answer B is correct.

7. A is the correct answer. Under the majority rule of <u>Ultramares v. Touche</u>, one making a negligent misrepresentation is liable to third parties only in situations approaching privity of contract. Since the appraiser did not know of the exis-

tence of any potential buyer (as the facts state that the appraiser is unaware of the reason why the home owner requested the appraisal), the privity-like requirement has not been met here because the appraiser did not owe any duties to the buyer. Answer B is incorrect because the buyer did rely on the appraiser's valuation in making the purchase. However, as discussed in Answer A, the appraiser was unaware of the buyer and, therefore, owed the buyer no duty. Answer C is incorrect because, as discussed in Answer A, the buyer is not a reasonably foreseeable plaintiff because the appraiser was unaware of why the appraisal was requested. Also, Answer C states the minority rule, and the call of the question asked what would happen in the majority of American jurisdictions. Answer D is an incorrect statement under these facts because there is nothing here indicating that the appraiser was grossly negligent.

8. C is the correct answer. Common law deceit is a misrepresentation made with the express intention of inducing reliance upon the fraudulent statement and that subsequently causes injury to the person who relies on the fraudulent statement. One cannot justifiably rely on statements of opinion of quality and value when entering into a contract. Here, the car salesman's statements that it was a honey of a car, a one of a kind steal for the money are not statements upon which a reasonable person would rely as to the condition of a car. Therefore, the woman will not recover for common law deceit under these facts. A is incorrect, since the car salesman did not commit common law deceit, as discussed in Answer C. Therefore, the car dealership cannot be vicariously liable. Answer B is an incorrect statement of law. As is clauses are legally permissible. Answer D is also an incorrect statement of law, as deceit is a tort action and is not based on contract. Any contractual waiver of fraud liability would violate public policy.

9. C is the correct answer. Common law deceit is a misrepresentation made with the express intention of inducing reliance upon the fraudulent statement and that subsequently causes injury to the person who relies on the fraudulent statement. Courts have long recognized that active concealment constitutes common law deceit. Here, the homeowner actively concealed the condition of the floorboards by covering them up with Persian rugs. Thus, the buyer will have a cause of action for common law deceit. Answer A is incorrect because a false statement is not necessary in concealment cases. Answer B is incorrect because the concealment was designed to cover the rotted floorboards and to discourage the buyer from making further inspection. Answer D is incorrect because the homeowner's actions were unreasonable, since it is not reasonable to actively conceal known defects in a home one is attempting to sell.

10. B is the correct answer. Defamation is any intentional false communication, either written or spoken, that harms a person's reputation; decreases the respect,

regard, or confidence in which a person is held; or induces disparaging, hostile, or disagreeable opinions or feelings against a person. When the communication is written and involves products that one uses in its trade, it is known as trade libel. Here, the manufacturer distributed a brochure (a writing) in which it made false and derogatory comments about its competitor's product. Thus, the manufacturer's statement was false. In addition, the competitor suffered a drop in profits (evidence of harm against its reputation). Therefore, the manufacturer committed trade libel, and this would be the competitor's most appropriate cause of action. Answer A is incorrect because the facts only tell us that the competitor experienced a drop in profits, not that the competitor specifically lost certain contracts. Answer C is incorrect, both because this tort does not exist and because slander is oral defamation, and here, as discussed in Answer B, the defamation was written (through the brochure). Answer D is incorrect. Common law deceit is an intentional misrepresentation made with the express intention of inducing reliance upon the fraudulent statement and that subsequently causes injury to the person who relies on the fraudulent statement. Here, although the manufacturer made false statements, it was the competitor's customers who relied on these statements. There is nothing in the facts showing that the customers were harmed as a result of this reliance, only the competitor itself seems to have been harmed.

11. C is the correct answer, since the common law required a trade libel plaintiff to show special damages in the form of particular lost customers or profits. Here, if the new company can show loss of specific customers, it can recover for trade libel. Since the facts indicate that the well-known company was found liable, then the new company can recover. Answers A and B are incorrect because a general loss of profits is not enough to meet the special damages rule to recover for trade libel. Punitive damages would not meet the specific special damages rule either. Answer D is incorrect because it is a false statement of law, since the well-known company's actions exceeded the bounds of legal business competition.

12. B is the correct answer. The tort of invasion of privacy includes intrusion on solitude, publication of private facts, facts that place the plaintiff in a false light, and misappropriation of one's name or likeness for commercial advantage. If the defendant commits any of these causes of action, the plaintiff can recover for invasion of privacy. Here, the equipment store misappropriated a photograph of the basketball player, since it did not have the player's permission to use the photograph. In addition, the equipment store placed the photograph in a newspaper advertisement, which presumably would give the equipment store a commercial advantage in selling its products. Thus, the basketball player can recover for invasion of privacy (misappropriation

of his name or likeness for commercial advantage). Answer A is incorrect, since there has been no disclosure of private facts about the basketball player. Answer C is incorrect, since publication of the photograph did not invade on the basketball player's seclusion. Answer D is incorrect, since picturing the basketball player in a reputable sporting goods ad did not place him in a false light.

13. C is the correct answer because the woman has used an appropriate civil process for an unlawful purpose. She is not merely collecting on a valid judgment, but is attempting to punish the man through her excessive executions (having writs of attachment issued against the man's real property, personal property, and bank accounts). Answer A is incorrect because the woman had probable cause to bring the executions of the writs and is entitled to attach the man's property up to the $100 judgment amount. Answer B is incorrect because this is not a criminal case. Answer D is incorrect. Conversion is the unlawful turning or applying the personal goods of another to the use of the taker, or of some person other than the owner; or the unlawful destroying or altering of their nature. Here, the woman has not taken any of the man's property unlawfully. Thus, there has been no conversion.

14. A is the correct answer, since it is not a prerequisite for an abuse of process action that the prior proceeding be terminated in plaintiff's favor. Rather, this is an element of malicious prosecution, a criminal action, whereas abuse of process is a civil action. Here, although the criminal proceeding did terminate in the man's favor, it is still not an element for his abuse of process action. Answers B, C, and D are incorrect because they are all elements of an abuse of process action, and the call of the question asked which was not something that the man needed to show in his action.

15. C is the correct answer because the tort of intentional interference with contractual relations requires intentional, purposeful conduct that interferes with an existing contractual relationship. Here, the professor had a contract with X College, and Y College intentionally interfered with the professor's contractual relationship with X College by offering the professor more money to teach at Y College. A is incorrect because there is no such right. Furthermore, the professor is not being sued here; X College is suing Y College B is incorrect, since the suit is based on tort, not on breach of any agreement between the colleges. D is incorrect because, as discussed in Answer C, the tort of intentional interference with contractual relations is an intentional tort that requires intentional action.

16. D is the correct answer because there is a tort action for interference with prospective economic advantage. This tort requires that one party's conduct intentionally cause a second party to not enter into a business relationship

with a third party that otherwise would probably have occurred. Here, the restaurant offered the chef a much higher salary to come and work for it, knowing that the chef was in contractual negotiations with the reality television show. The restaurant went further and made acceptance of the restaurant's offer conditional upon the chef not appearing on the reality television show. Therefore, the restaurant is liable for interference with prospective economic advantage. A is incorrect because this is a tort action, not a contract action; as discussed in Answer D, the restaurant is liable for interference with prospective economic advantage even though there was no contract between the restaurant and the producers of the television reality show. Answer B is incorrect because, as discussed in Answer D, this is a tort action for interference with prospective economic advantage, so no contract was required. Furthermore, no contract had yet been signed in any case. Answer C is incorrect because there was no contract as of yet; the chef and the producers of the reality television show were merely in negotiations.

17. B is the correct answer. Assault occurs when one intentionally places another in apprehension of an imminent harmful or offensive contact. Here, the professor intentionally threw the pen. The two college students apprehended an imminent contact with the pen, which is why they ducked to avoid it. Answer A is incorrect because the facts do not show that the two college students suf-

fered any emotional distress. Answer C is incorrect because contact is a requirement for battery, not assault. Answer D is incorrect because the professor should have known that his act would cause an apprehension of an imminent harmful or offensive contact.

18. D is the correct answer since, under the doctrine of transferred intent, the man is held to have intended to commit the battery and ultimate death of the woman because his intent to batter the bartender transferred to the battery and death of the woman. Answer A is incorrect because, as discussed in Answer D, the man is held to have intended to commit the battery and ultimate death of the woman because his intent to batter the bartender transferred to the battery and death of the woman. Answer B is incorrect because a defendant is responsible for all personal injuries, including death resulting from a tort. Answer C is an incorrect statement of the transferred intent doctrine. If one intends to commit a battery on one person but batters another, the transferred intent doctrine applies.

19. B is the correct answer. Trespass to land is the unlawful entry onto the property of another. Every unlawful entry onto the property of another is a trespass, even if no harm is done to the property because damages are presumed in trespass cases. Even if the woman cannot show actual damage, the law will allow nominal damages. Answer A is incorrect because the facts show that

the land surveyor was a trespasser, not a licensee. Answer C is incorrect because the only intent necessary for trespass is to walk on the land, an intent that the land surveyor had. It is irrelevant if the surveyor thought that he was on the neighbor's land when he walked onto the woman's property. Answer D is incorrect for the same reason stated in B.

20. D is the correct answer because the farmer (as a land owner/occupier) owes a duty to an undiscovered trespasser not to set traps for him. Here, even though the farmer posted warning signs about the electrified fence, using an electrified fence is an improper way to defend ones property. Answer A is incorrect for the reason stated above. The fact that signs were posted is irrelevant. Answer B is incorrect because even though it is illegal to steal cattle, this is irrelevant here because, as discussed in Answer D, the farmer used excessive force to defend his property; he had a duty to undiscovered trespassers to not set traps for them. Answer C is incorrect because, as discussed in Answer D, the farmer was not allowed to protect his property by use of a trap or any other excessive force.

21. B is the correct answer because the negligence per se rule provides that when a statute sets the duty of care, and the plaintiff is within the protected class whom the statute was designed to protect and suffered the type of injury that the statute was designed to prevent, then the plaintiff will prevail on a negligence per se claim. Here, the cell phone law is designed to protect other drivers from being hit by a car driven by a person who is distracted because of talking on a cell phone without using a hands-free device. This is precisely what the woman was doing. Thus, when her car hit the front car, this was the type of action that the statute was designed to prevent. Hence, the driver of that front car was in the class of people the statute was designed to protect. Further, the injuries that that driver suffered were the type of injuries that the statute was designed to prevent because they occurred as a result of a distracted driver. Answer A is incorrect because it states the res ipsa loquitor rule, not negligence per se. Answer C is incorrect because, although it states the general standard of care for drivers, the negligence per se statutory standard is a higher standard of care and trumps the ordinary negligence standard. Answer D is incorrect because the other driver was not negligent at all (he was merely stopped at a traffic signal), and because the negligence of the other driver has no bearing on the application of the negligence per se standard.

22. B is the correct answer, since the owner can argue that it was not reasonably foreseeable that a surgeon would negligently amputate the wrong leg. The surgeon's actions were gross negligence and, thus, a superseding cause of the worker's good leg being amputated. Therefore, this would be the owner's

best defense to the worker's negligence action. However, the owner would still be liable for the injuries to the worker's other leg (which occurred as a result of falling debris at the owner's construction site). Answer A is incorrect because the last clear chance doctrine is a rule designed to save the plaintiff's case when he is contributorily negligent. The facts here do not show any negligence on the part of the construction worker. Answer C is incorrect because it is an incorrect statement of law. Answer D is incorrect because the owner's insurance coverage is irrelevant; it only determines who pays, not who is negligent.

23. C is the correct answer because a child who engages in adult activity is held to the adult standard of the reasonable and prudent person (driver) under the same or similar circumstances. Here, although the boy was twelve years old (an infant under the law), he was engaging in an adult activity (driving a car) and will, thus, be held to the adult standard and will be liable for the injuries of the pedestrian. The boy failed to exercise the care of a reasonable and prudent person when he lost control of the car and is, thus, liable to the pedestrian for his injuries. Answer A is incorrect. Although the boy stole the car, his negligence was losing control of the car. The stealing of the car is not the cause of the pedestrian's injuries. Answer B is incorrect because the subjective standard for children does not apply when a minor is engaged in adult activity, as discussed in Answer C. Answer D is incorrect because anyone over the age of four years old can be liable for torts (such as negligence here).

24. A is the correct answer. Negligent infliction of emotional distress occurs when one violates his duty to use reasonable care to avoid causing emotional distress to another individual. If one fails in this duty and unreasonably causes emotional distress to another person, that person will be liable for monetary damages to the injured individual. The tort is to be contrasted with intentional infliction of emotional distress in that there is no need to prove intent to inflict distress. An accidental infliction, if negligent, is sufficient to support a cause of action. Here, the man was a reasonably foreseeable plaintiff (and, thus, within the zone of danger) because the driver was aware of the man's presence, and it is unlikely that the man will be feigning his injuries. Furthermore, the injured party was the man's sister and, thus, a close relative. Answer B is incorrect, since most jurisdictions do not require a physical impact. Answer C is incorrect because the injured party was a close relative; she was the man's sister. Answer D is incorrect for the reasons discussed in Answer A.

25. A is the correct answer. The common law recognized joint and several liability for joint tortfeasors. A plaintiff who has been injured due to the negligence of more than one tortfeasor can recover the entire amount from one of the joint tortfeasors. Following that, the joint

tortfeasor who pays can seek contribution from the other joint tortfeasor. Here, the bicyclist was injured due to the negligence of both the driver and the State Highway Department. Under the rule of joint and several liability, she can recover the entire amount from the State Highway Department. Answers B and C are incorrect because indemnity and contribution are concepts that affect the joint tortfeasors' liability to each other, not to the plaintiff. Answer D is an incorrect statement of law.

26. D is the correct answer. A licensee is a person who is on the property of another, despite the fact that the property is not open to the general public because the owner of the property has allowed the licensee to enter. Here, the police officer was invited into the man's house to conduct an investigation, even though the man's house was presumably not open to the public. Answer A is incorrect because the man invited the police officer into his house, so the police officer was not a trespasser. Answer B is incorrect. An invitee is a person who is invited onto land by the possessor of the land as a member of the public or one who is invited to the land for the purpose of business dealings with the possessor of the land. Here, the police officer was not in the man's house for the purposes of business dealings with the man. Thus, he was not an invitee. Answer C is incorrect, since the police officer was not the man's social guest.

27. B is the correct answer. A licensee is a person who is on the property of another, despite the fact that the property is not open to the general public because the owner of the property has allowed the licensee to enter. Here, the employee was allowed to enter the land because of the easement that his employer had. Thus, the employee was a licensee. The duty of care owed by a landowner to a licensee is only to warn of dangers known by the landowner. Here, the woman was not aware of the existence of the abandoned well and, thus, had no duty to warn the employee about it. Answer A is incorrect because the employee was not an undiscovered trespasser. Answer C is incorrect, since a landowner owes this more extensive duty to an invitee, not a licensee. An invitee is a person who is invited onto land by the possessor of the land as a member of the public or one who is invited to the land for the purpose of business dealings with the possessor of the land. Here, the employee was on the land for the purpose of checking the power lines, not for the purpose of engaging in business dealings with the woman (the owner of the land). Thus, as discussed in Answer B, the employee was a licensee, not an invitee, so the higher duty that is owed to an invitee did not apply in this situation. Answer D is incorrect because the duty owed by landowners relates to the status of the person coming onto the land, and there are different duties owed depending on this status. The reasonable and prudent person test is not applied when dealing

with the duties owed by landowners to people coming onto their land.

28. C is the correct answer in a common law jurisdiction, which is what the call of the question says we have here, because a plaintiff's contributory negligence, even if slight, totally bars recovery against a defendant at common law. Here, the man was slightly negligent in leaving part of his van's rear bumper protruding onto the highway. Thus, he will not recover. Answers A and B are incorrect because, as discussed in Answer C, the man's contributory negligence will totally bar his recovery. Answer D is incorrect because the facts do not show that the man voluntarily assumed the risk of a known danger.

29. Answer A is the correct answer. At common law, if a plaintiff were even slightly negligent, the plaintiff's negligence would bar any recovery in a lawsuit against a negligent defendant. However, the common law "last clear chance" rule "saves" the contributorily negligent plaintiff's case and puts the entire burden of loss on defendant. Here, although the woman was contributorily negligent in not checking to see if the road was clear, the man still had the "last clear chance" to avoid the accident by applying his brakes early enough to avoid the accident. Answer B is incorrect because, at common law, the woman would not recover (due to her own contributory negligence) were it not for the "last clear chance" doctrine discussed in Answer A. Answer C is incorrect for the reason discussed in Answer A. Answer D is incorrect for the same reason that Answer A is correct.

30. Answer D is the correct answer because under the state's modified comparative negligence statute, the woman will recover nothing because her negligence (60%) was greater than the man's (40%). Answers A, B, and C are incorrect for the reasons discussed in Answer D.

31. C is the correct answer. The Restatement Second of Torts establishes that one who carries on an abnormally dangerous activity is subject to liability for harm to the person, land or chattels of another resulting from the activity, although he has exercised the utmost care to prevent the harm. Here, the company, through the escaping gas, caused harm to the repairman because the gas caused him to black out and fall. Even though the escaping gas was not caused by any fault on the company's part, it will be subject to liability. Answer A is incorrect as there was no intentional touching (a requirement of battery). Answer B is incorrect because there was no invasion of the repairman's use and enjoyment of his land. Answer D is incorrect because there are no facts indicating that the company was negligent. The facts state that the company was not at fault, which is a requirement for negligence.

32. D is the correct answer. An ultrahazardous activity is one that is so inherently dangerous that a person engaged in such

an activity can be held strictly liable for injuries caused to another person, even if the person engaged in the activity took every reasonable precaution to prevent others from being injured. Where strict liability is applied for the ultrahazardous activity (transmission of extremely high voltage electricity in this instance), evidence that the company is without "fault" is of no consequence. Strict liability is absolute and is seen as liability without fault. Answers A and B are incorrect because the justification for strict liability is that, "useful but dangerous activities must pay their own way." In other words, where there is utility but also an unavoidable risk of harm, we may require someone in such a business to bear the loss as a cost of doing business. The fact that extreme care was used will not matter because duty is absolute. Answer C is incorrect because there is no evidence on the face of the facts that the utility failed to adhere to the standard of conduct that would be expected of that a utility similarly situated. Although a student may want to posit that electricity is so pervasive and common in today's society that it should not be construed as abnormally dangerous, D is the only response that addresses the unavoidable danger of transmitting electricity at extremely high voltage.

33. C is the correct answer. Strict liability in tort is applicable when, among other things, a wild animal inflicts injury upon a person. Here, although the lion was in a wild animal park, she was still a wild animal. Therefore, the wild animal park is strictly liable for the injuries inflicted by the lion. The man's contributory negligence in reaching his hand out is not a defense to strict liability in tort. Answers A and B are incorrect because, although the man was both reckless and contributorily negligent, these are not defenses to an action in strict liability in tort, as discussed in Answer C. Answer D is incorrect because the man was negligent. However, as discussed in Answer C, this is not a defense to strict liability in tort.

34. A is the correct answer. When a manufacturer places a product into the stream of commerce and that product causes a foreseeable injury, a plaintiff can recover for strict liability in tort. The problem here is that the injury to the child was not of a type that was foreseeable because the child was injured as a direct result of the woman's failure to secure the damp rag, not of the blender's blade issues. Therefore, the woman cannot recover on behalf of her child. The child's injuries were not a direct result of the failure of the blade on the blender to operate properly. Answer B is incorrect because there are no facts to indicate that the child was contributorily negligent. Furthermore, contributory negligence is not a defense to strict liability. Answer C is incorrect because while the woman did purchase the blender, as discussed in Answer A, the child's injuries were not foreseeable. Answer D is incorrect because, while this is true statement, it does not

affect the woman's ability to recover on behalf of a child for an unforeseeable injury.

35. D is the correct answer. Where one is responsible for putting another in peril, a duty is owed to one who attempts a rescue, as long as the rescuer is acting reasonably under the circumstances. Here, the passerby was acting reasonably in trying to assist the man. Since the car exploded because of an apparent defect on the part of the car manufacturer, it is responsible for putting the man in peril. The passerby was a foreseeable rescuer, so the car manufacturer was liable to the passerby for the injuries that he sustained while rescuing the man. Answer A is incorrect, as the passerby did not assume the risk, since danger invites rescue. Answer B is incorrect because the passerby's conduct does not have to be foreseeable, just reasonable under the circumstances, which it appears to have been here. Answer C is incorrect because there is nothing to indicate that the car manufacturer was engaged in abnormally dangerous activities.

36. B is the correct answer. The woman was a customer, since she came in to purchase some yogurt. Here, the woman, a business invitee, is owed a duty by the yogurt shop to inspect and remedy any defect on the premises. Answer A is incorrect. Res ipsa loquitur is relevant when there is a reasonable presumption that the defendant is the negligent actor. Here, however, the door could be defective without negligence. Thus, res ipsa loquitur is incorrect here. Answer C is not the best theory because, as discussed in Answer B, the woman was a business invitee, not a licensee. Answer D is incorrect for the reasons discussed in Answer B.

37. A is the correct answer. Res ipsa loquitur means that the thing speaks for itself and that the damage could only have occurred through negligence. Under the Restatement Second of Torts, it may be inferred that harm suffered by the plaintiff is caused by the negligence of the defendant when: 1) The event is of a kind that ordinarily does not occur in the absence of negligence; 2) The negligence must be within the scope of a duty that the defendant owes the plaintiff; 3) The plaintiff must not have contributed to his own injury. Here, cars do not ordinarily swerve off the shoulder of the road and roll over in the absence of negligence, when, as here, there were no abnormal conditions on the road. The woman owed a duty to her passenger, and the passenger did not contribute to his own injury and death. Therefore, the elements of res ipsa loquitur have been satisfied and would be the man's best theory of recovery. Answers B and C are not correct answers because they would and could not establish fault on the woman's part. Rather, they are causes of action brought by the estate. Answer D is an incorrect and irrelevant statement of law as applied to these facts. Causation is only one element of the required proof of a tort.

38. D is the correct answer. In most courts, res ipsa loquitur warrants an inference that the defendant is negligent. However, it is only an inference and not a conclusion that there was, in fact, negligence because causation and damages must still be proven. Answer A is incorrect. The jury may or may not agree on the inference that the defendant is negligent. Answer B is an incorrect statement as it would be up to the jury to decide whether or not they find the plaintiff negligent. Answer C is incorrect because, even if res ipsa loquitur is established, the jury may find that the defendant has sufficient evidence to rebut the presumption. If this were the case, the plaintiff would not win.

39. B is the correct answer. The doctrine of respondeat superior would cause the owner of the store to be liable for the negligence of his employee, which occurred during the course and scope of employment. Here, the clerk worked for the store and during the course of his employment, he negligently stacked the window shades. Thus, under respondeat superior, the owner of the store is liable for negligence. Answer A is incorrect because there is nothing in the facts indicating that either the owner of the store or any of his employees were reckless. Answer C is incorrect, as strict liability is not applicable to this fact pattern involving a non-inherently-dangerous-activity. Answer D is incorrect because, although the owner of the store was not personally negligent, he can still be held liable under respondeat superior, as discussed in Answer B.

40. C is the correct answer. The neighbor could establish the attractive nuisance doctrine since: 1) The son was only five years of age and could not appreciate the danger of an unguarded swimming pool. 2) The swimming pool was an artificial condition and would be attractive to children of the son's age. 3) The swimming pool could have been made safe with little effort by simply closing and locking the gate. 4) The homeowner should have been aware of the risk, as he should have known of the inquisitive nature of children and the likelihood that children would jump into the pool. Answer A is incorrect because the son was not on the neighbor's property to conduct business with the neighbor. Answer B is incorrect because this was not an inherently dangerous activity, nor did it involve wild animals. There was also no defective product involved here. Therefore, there would be no strict liability here. Answer D is incorrect because the son was not a licensee, since he was not invited onto the neighbor's property.

41. C is the correct answer. The call of the question stipulates that this is a common law jurisdiction. Under the common law, if the plaintiff is even slightly contributorily negligent, he is completely barred from recovery against the defendant. Here, the boy was negligent in darting out into the street. Thus, even though the woman's speeding most likely meant that she was also negligent, the boy will not be able to recover due to his own contributory

negligence. Answers A and B are incorrect because, regardless of whether the woman was negligent, the boy's contributory negligence will be a bar to his recovery, as discussed in Answer C. Answer D is an incorrect statement of law. Anyone over the age of four years is liable for his own negligence.

42. B is the correct answer. Each of the defendants has the burden of proving that it was not his gun that fired the damaging pellet. Since this burden is equally impossible for each defendant, they will be held jointly and severally liable. Answer A is incorrect because this test is used where each of the defendants' acts was a substantial factor in causing the damage. Here, it is impossible to determine whose acts were substantial factors. Thus, as discussed in Answer B, each will be jointly and severally liable. Answer C is incorrect because "but for" causation is not enough; one must also prove proximate causation (i.e., that the chain of causation is not cut off by a superseding, intervening event). Also, C will be unable to prove complete responsibility of either A or B, as discussed in Answer B. Answer D is incorrect for the same reason that Answer B is correct.

43. A is the correct answer. Battery is the intentional harmful or offensive touching of another without consent or privilege. Battery extends to any part of the body or anything attached to it. Thus, when the classmate's body contacted the floor, a "touching" occurred. This touching was offensive to the classmate, and the girl will be liable to him for battery. Answer B is incorrect, as assault requires the intentional placing of another in reasonable apprehension of a harmful or offensive touching without consent or privilege. The facts indicate that the classmate was surprised by the girl pulling out the chair. Therefore, no apprehension could have been created. Answer C is incorrect because assault does not exist in this fact pattern, as discussed in Answer B. Answer D is incorrect because the facts do not imply that the girl's conduct was extreme and outrageous and calculated to cause severe emotional distress. Rather, the facts state that the girl's actions were motivated simply by her desire to play practical jokes on her classmates.

44. B is the correct answer. Under the Restatement Second of Torts, "a bodily contact is offensive if it offends a reasonable sense of personal dignity." Here, the jogger's conduct would be acceptable under the circumstances because he needed to hold onto the brunette to keep from falling. Answer A is incorrect. Whether harm was caused to the brunette or not is not at issue. This was an emergency situation and, as discussed in Answer B, the jogger grabbed the brunette simply to keep from falling. Answer C is incorrect because, under the circumstances, the touching would not be considered harmful or offensive, since the jogger grabbed the brunette simply to keep from falling. Answer D is incorrect because the facts do not

indicate that the brunette felt any apprehension by the jogger's conduct, as is required for assault.

45. D is the correct answer. False imprisonment is the intentional placing of the plaintiff in a bounded area with no reasonable means of escape. A defense to a false imprisonment action by a shopkeeper is the shopkeeper's privilege, which allows a shopkeeper to detain a suspect for a reasonable time in a reasonable manner, if he has a reasonable suspicion of theft. Here, the security guard detained the girls, but had no reasonable grounds for suspicion. Thus, the department store would not prevail because the shopkeeper's privilege would not be applicable in this situation. Answer A is incorrect, since the store had no privilege to detain the girls, as discussed in Answer D. Answer B is incorrect because, under the facts, the girls were not free to leave. Answer C is incorrect because the suspicion need not be correct - it need only be reasonable. Therefore, although C's conclusion is correct, its reasoning is incorrect.

46. A is the correct answer. The Restatement Second of Torts §402A holds that one who sells any product in a defective condition unreasonably dangerous to the user or consumer or to his property is subject to strict liability for physical harm thereby caused to the ultimate user or consumer. Here, the manufacturer was engaged in the selling of the product (the hair dryer), and the product was defective because it caused the woman to receive a severe shock and physical injury. Answer B is incorrect because the manufacturer can be liable, even if it was unaware (and, therefore, could not warn) of the product defect, since this is a strict products liability action. Answer C is incorrect because, while misuse can be a defense to a strict products liability action, the woman's continued use of the dryer, even though it made a loud noise, is foreseeable since the manufacturer assured her that some dryers are just louder than others. Answer D is incorrect for the same reasons that Answer A is correct.

47. A is the correct answer. Under the "thin skull" (or "eggshell") plaintiff doctrine, which is recognized in all jurisdictions, a person injured by a defendant's negligent conduct may recover damages to the full extent of his injuries where his injuries are more severe (even if resulting in death) because of a pre-existing condition, such as hemophilia in this case. Note that damages in a wrongful death case may be reduced because of the decedent's lowered life expectancy due to the pre-existing condition. Here, the woman drove the car negligently, causing the car to hit the man. His pre-existing hemophilia exacerbated the injuries he received from being struck by the woman's car, ultimately resulting in his death. Thus, the woman would be liable to the full extent of his injuries, but the amount of recovery may be possibly reduced by the man's lower life expectancy, due to his hemophilia. Answers B, C and D are incorrect for the reasons that Answer A is correct.

48. A is the correct answer. When a manufacturer places a product into the stream of commerce and that product causes a foreseeable injury, a plaintiff can recover for strict liability in tort. Here, the facts state that the signs that the company manufactured and that the woman placed in her yard had rough edges, a defect, and the teenager was beheaded when he came into contact with the signs. Thus, the rough edge on the sign was the cause of the teenager's death. Consequently, the manufacturer is strictly liable. Answer B is incorrect because the intentional element is missing and would be needed to establish battery. Answer C is incorrect because there are no facts indicating that the sign manufacturer was reckless. Answer D is incorrect because, while the driver may have been negligent, this would not help the teenager's estate recover against the sign manufacturer.

49. C is the correct answer. Assault is the intentional placing of the plaintiff in apprehension of an imminent harmful or offensive touching or contact. Although the shaking of one's fist under the nose of another person can constitute an assault, where the fist shaking is accompanied by a statement that reasonably would remove the assaultive effect of the physical act, there is no assault (as in this fact situation). Here, the small man stated, "If you weren't such a large pig, I would knock you down." This qualifying statement indicated that the small man was not, in fact, about to harm the large man. Thus, the large man had no apprehension of an imminent touching or contact from the small man. Answer A is incorrect for the reasons discussed in Answer C. Answer B is incorrect because the statement of the small man removed the assaultive effect of the fist shaking, as discussed in Answer C. Answer D is incorrect because a small person can certainly assault a big person, but the small man's statement that he was not about to actually strike the large man is the reason why the large man had no apprehension of an imminent touching or contact, as discussed in Answer C.

50. A is the correct answer. According to the Restatement (Second) of Torts §217, a trespass to chattel is defined as "intentionally dispossessing another of the chattel or using or intermeddling with a chattel in the possession of another." Here, the man's actions in shooting what he thought was a wolf ultimately dispossessed the neighbor of his possession of the dog. The man can be liable for trespass to chattel, even though he did not intend to interfere with the neighbor's property. It is necessary only that he intended to deal with the chattel in the manner in which he did (namely, shooting). Answer B is incorrect because, for this tort, a reasonable good faith mistake is no defense. Answer C is incorrect because one cannot have a battery against an animal; battery is an intentional tort against humans only. Answer D is incorrect because cruelty to animals is a crime, not a tort. Furthermore, Answer D says that the man

will be found guilty. One can only be found liable for a tort - not guilty.

51. C is the correct answer. Battery is the intentional harmful or offensive touching of another without consent. Here, the hairdresser colored the woman's hair without consent. The woman considered the coloring offensive. Therefore, all the elements of battery have been met, and this would be her best cause of action. Answer A is incorrect because, even though the woman was complimented on her new hair color, the woman was not happy with the hair color and, thus, considered it offensive. It is irrelevant what others thought; only the woman's own views are relevant as to whether this was offensive. Answer B is incorrect because the facts do not reveal any consent beyond the shampoo and blow dry. Answer D is incorrect because the facts do not show that the hairdresser was negligent; there is nothing to show that the hairdresser acted in a manner inconsistent with the reasonable and prudent person standard.

52. A is the correct answer. Res ipsa loquitur means that the thing speaks for itself and that the damage could only have occurred through negligence. Under the Restatement Second of Torts, it may be inferred that harm suffered by the plaintiff is caused by the negligence of the defendant when: 1) The event is of a kind that ordinarily does not occur in the absence of negligence; 2) The negligence must be within the scope of a duty that the defendant owes the plaintiff; 3) The plaintiff must not have contributed to his own injury. Here, the loss of sensation in the man's face is the kind of injury that does not ordinarily happen in the absence of negligence. In addition, the doctor had a duty of care to the patient (the man). The man in no way contributed to his own injury. Therefore, the man will recover against the doctor for negligence under a res ipsa loquitur theory. Answer B is incorrect because a doctor is not responsible for an injury unless he is negligent. Answer C is incorrect because the doctrine of res ipsa loquitur creates an inference of negligence, as discussed in Answer A, even if there are no percipient witnesses. Answer D is incorrect for the same reasons that Answer A is correct.

53. C is the correct answer because, modernly, there is a national standard for most medical specialties. Answer A is incorrect because it does not take into account that the surgeon is an orthopedic surgeon. Answer B is incorrect because the national standard has replaced the local standard for doctors. Answer D is incorrect because it focuses on the surgeon's subjective qualifications rather than on those expected of all practitioners of orthopedic surgery.

54. B is the correct answer. Normally, a person has no duty to act. An exception to this rule is when the defendant put the plaintiff in harm's way. Here, the man pushed his girlfriend into the swimming pool. She begged him to save her, but he did not. Because he was responsible for

her predicament, since he had pushed her into the swimming pool, he had a duty to rescue her. By failing to do so, he breached a duty to her. Answer A is incorrect because there is nothing in the facts to indicate that the rescuer acted unreasonably, or that the rescuer was the cause of the girlfriend's injuries. C is incorrect because, even though the girlfriend may have cheated on the man, this does not relieve him of the duty to save her when her put her in harm's way, as he did here. Answer D is incorrect because, while there is generally no duty to act, an exception is when the defendant put the plaintiff in harm's way, as discussed in Answer B.

55. A is the correct answer. Intentional infliction of emotional distress has four elements: (1) the defendant must act intentionally or recklessly; (2) the defendant's conduct must be extreme and outrageous; and (3) the conduct must be the cause (4) of severe emotional distress. Here, the telemarketer intentionally called the man, the telemarketer's conduct was extreme and outrageous because of the late hours that he continually called him, and the man's sleep deprivation and nightmares were severe enough to have to cause the man to visit a psychiatrist. Thus, the telemarketer's conduct caused the man severe emotional distress. Consequently, the man will recover against the telemarketer for this cause of action. Answer B is incorrect. Assault occurs when one intentionally places another in apprehension of an imminent harmful or offensive contact. Here, the telemarketer did nothing to cause the man to apprehend an imminent harmful or offensive contact. Thus, there was no assault here. Answer C is incorrect because the telemarketer's acts were intentional, not negligent. Answer D is incorrect because the man has not been placed in a false light by the telemarketer.

56. D is the correct answer. Intentional infliction of emotional distress has four elements: (1) the defendant must act intentionally or recklessly; (2) the defendant's conduct must be extreme and outrageous; and (3) the conduct must be the cause (4) of severe emotional distress. The tort of intentional infliction of emotional distress encompasses conduct that might cause emotional distress to a reasonably foreseeable bystander. Here, the collection agent intentionally threatened the man with serious consequences to his health, which is an extreme and outrageous threat. It would be reasonable to assume that doing so in front of the man's wife would cause her emotional distress. Thus, the wife would be able to recover against the collection agent for intentional infliction of emotional distress. Answer A is incorrect because the collection agent's actions were intentional. It does not matter that the collection agent had no intent to cause the wife emotional distress, since threatening the man in the wife's presence would be reasonably likely to cause her such distress, as discussed in

Answer D. Answer B is incorrect because transferred intent does not apply in intentional infliction of emotional distress cases. What is important here is that it is reasonably likely that the wife would suffer emotional distress as a result of the collection agent's actions, which was the case here, as discussed in Answer D. Answer C is incorrect because intentional infliction of emotional distress is about emotional distress, not pecuniary loss.

57. C is the correct answer. Intentional infliction of emotional distress has four elements: (1) the defendant must act intentionally or recklessly; (2) the defendant's conduct must be extreme and outrageous; and (3) the conduct must be the cause (4) of severe emotional distress. The modern rule, as reflected in the Restatement of Torts (Second), allows for recovery of severe emotional distress without any physical injury. Answer A is not correct because a physical impact is not required. Answer B is incorrect because most states do not require a showing of physical consequences as a prerequisite for recovery. Answer D is incorrect because a plaintiff need not show another underlying intentional tort to recover for intentional infliction of emotional distress.

58. A is the correct answer because the negligence per se rule provides that where a law, ordinance, or administrative regulation is intended to protect a class of persons from a particular type of harm, the legislative body has impliedly established the duty of care. Here, the state law prohibits the use of cellular telephones while one is driving, in the absence of a hands-free device. The law appears to have been passed to protect others from harm that could be caused by drivers who are distracted by the use of cellular telephones while driving. Here, the lady failed to comply with this law and drove her car into another automobile that was stopped at a red light. The driver of the other car appears to have been in the class of people that this state law was meant to protect. Thus, the lady committed negligence per se because of the implied duty of care. Answer B is incorrect because if all the elements of negligence per se are met, the jury is not permitted to find no duty. Answer C is incorrect for the reasons discussed in Answer A. Answer D is incorrect. Res ipsa loquitur means that the thing speaks for itself and that the damage could only have occurred through negligence. Under the Restatement Second of Torts, it may be inferred that harm suffered by the plaintiff is caused by the negligence of the defendant when: 1) The event is of a kind that ordinarily does not occur in the absence of negligence; 2) The negligence must be within the scope of a duty that the defendant owes the plaintiff; 3) The plaintiff must not have contributed to his own injury. Here, the woman's negligence per se is clear, for the reasons discussed in Answer A. Thus, res ipsa loquitur is not at issue under these facts.

59. C is the correct answer. Negligence occurs when there is a duty, a breach of that duty, and the breach is both the actual and proximate cause of damages to the plaintiff. A negligent tortfeaser's liability may be cut short by an intervening, superseding, unforeseeable act, such as a criminal act, so long as that criminal act is unforeseeable. Here, the woman owed a duty to the customer (a foreseeable plaintiff in the parking lot of her restaurant). The woman breached her duty by failing to install lighting in the parking lot. Since the woman's restaurant and parking lot were in a high-crime area, it would be foreseeable that a criminal act could occur in her unlit parking lot. Thus, the man can recover for his injuries because the woman's negligence was both the actual and proximate cause of his harm. Answer A is incorrect because courts have found proprietors liable where the intentional acts of third parties are reasonably foreseeable, which was the case here, as described in Answer C. Answer B is incorrect because an act may be reasonably foreseeable, even if it has yet to occur. Answer D is incorrect. Strict liability can be found when dealing with an ultrahazardous activity, wild animals, or products liability. Here, none of these factors was present. Thus, the woman will not be strictly liable.

60. C is the correct answer. The negligence per se rule provides that when a statute sets the duty of care, and the plaintiff is within the protected class whom the statute was designed to protect and suffered the type of injury that the statute was designed to prevent, then the plaintiff will prevail on a negligence per se claim. Here, the law requiring drivers to have a valid, unexpired driver's license is for the protection of other drivers on the road. The driver in these facts was driving with an expired license, but he was not driving negligently, and he did everything in his power to avoid causing his car to hit the intoxicated man (who was also negligent). While negligence per se establishes a duty and a breach of that duty, the plaintiff in a negligence action must also prove causation and damages. Here, the driver's violation of the statute was not the proximate cause of the intoxicated man's harm because the facts indicate that the intoxicated man stumbled into the road, an unforeseeable act. Answer A is incorrect because, as discussed in Answer C, negligence per se relates to the duty and breach elements, not causation and damages. Answer B is incorrect because, as discussed in Answer C, the intoxicated man's injuries were not reasonably foreseeable. Answer D is an incorrect statement and application of the last clear chance rule. The last clear chance rule applies when a contributorily negligent plaintiff sues a negligent defendant and claims that the negligent defendant had the last clear chance to avoid the accident. Here, the intoxicated man was the contributorily negligent plaintiff, and he had the last clear chance to avoid the injuries. Thus, this is an incorrect application of the last clear chance rule.

61. B is the correct answer because, when the concurrent negligence of two or more tortfeasors results in an indivisible injury, they are jointly and severally liable for plaintiff's entire loss. Here, the man was driving too fast for the weather conditions and failed to see the tractor trailer that was blocking the road. The owner of the tractor trailer was negligent in failing to pull the tractor trailer off the road. Since both the man and the owner of the tractor trailer were responsible for the woman's injuries, both will be liable to her for the full amount of her damages. She must elect which defendant will actually pay, and that defendant will then be able to seek contribution (partial reimbursement) from the other defendant. Answer A is incorrect because the law does not require the woman to prove proportionate liability under the circumstances. Answer C is incorrect because each defendant is liable for the entire amount. Answer D is incorrect because there is no evidence that the woman voluntarily assumed any risk.

62. D is the correct answer because modern law allows contribution among joint tortfeasors. Answer A is incorrect because the satisfaction doctrine limits recovery by a plaintiff who has already recovered against another joint tortfeasor. Here, the tortfeasors are going against each other; the plaintiff is no longer a part of this legal action. Answer B is incorrect because the paying tortfeasor is not entitled to indemnification, but only to having the non-paying tortfeasor's share in paying the judgment. Answer C is incorrect because the tortfeasors are not necessarily in a relationship that would give rise to vicarious liability of one for the other.

63. B is the correct answer. An automobile guest statute requires that the plaintiff demonstrate gross negligence or reckless conduct, rather than the ordinary negligence that plaintiffs who are not guests in automobiles must demonstrate. Here, the hitchhiker was a guest in the woman's car. Thus, in order to recover, he will have to show gross negligence or recklessness on the part of the woman. However, in these facts, the woman was confronted with a flash flood and could not prevent the car from going down the embankment. Consequently, her conduct does not appear to be either grossly negligent or reckless under the circumstances. Answer A is incorrect because ordinary negligence is not actionable if there is a guest statute, as discussed in Answer B. Furthermore, the facts do not indicate that the woman was negligent. Answer C is incorrect because the woman's conduct need not be intentional, but rather, grossly negligent or reckless under an automobile guest statute. Answer D is incorrect because, as discussed in Answer B, the automobile guest statute requires only that the woman drove with gross negligence or recklessness, not with malice.

64. B is the correct answer. Battery is the intentional harmful or offensive contact of the plaintiff's person. Here,

the player made a hard slide into the shortstop (an intentional act) and broke the shortstop's ankle (which demonstrates that the contact was harmful). Thus, the player is liable for battery to the shortstop. Answer A is incorrect. Assault is the intentional placing of the plaintiff in apprehension of an imminent harmful or offensive contact. Here, the facts do not indicate that the shortstop was in apprehension of the contact before it occurred. Answer C is incorrect. Intentional infliction of emotional distress has four elements: (1) the defendant must act intentionally or recklessly; (2) the defendant's conduct must be extreme and outrageous; and (3) the conduct must be the cause (4) of severe emotional distress. Here, the facts do not indicate that the player intended to cause emotional distress or that the shortstop suffered any such distress. Answer D is incorrect. Strict liability can be found when dealing with an ultrahazardous activity, wild animals, or products liability. Here, none of these factors was present. Thus, the shortstop will not be able to recover in strict liability.

65. C is the correct answer because, by riding a crowded subway, the woman impliedly consented to possible harmful contact that could occur on the subway. Answer A is incorrect because contributory negligence is not a defense to an intentional tort (battery), and also because there is no evidence that the woman was negligent in any case. Answer B is incorrect because justification and private necessity are irrelevant under these circumstances.

66. D is the correct answer. Since the man has not entered the woman's property, his status is not that of a trespasser, licensee, or an invitee and, thus, the woman owes him no duty. Answers A, B and C are incorrect because they relate to categories of persons who are on a landowner's property for different reasons.

67. A is the correct answer because a landowner owes a person off the premises a duty of ordinary care with respect to artificial conditions the landowner maintains. Here, the pedestrian was off the premises on a public street, and the sign was an artificial condition. Therefore, the man had a duty to keep the cables on the sign from injuring anyone off of the premises, such as the pedestrian here. Answer B is incorrect because this is the duty owed a licensee. Here, the pedestrian was not physically on the man's property and was, thus, not a licensee. Answer C is incorrect because this is the duty owed a discovered trespasser. Here, the pedestrian was not on the man's property and was, thus, not a trespasser, discovered or otherwise. Answer D is incorrect for the same reasons that Answer A is correct.

68. D is the correct answer. A person is liable in negligence for a breach of duty that causes (both actual and proximate) foreseeable injury or loss. Here, the contractors' liability will not be cut off

because it was reasonably foreseeable that when the contractors left the ladder leading to an open window, a burglar could use the ladder to break into the woman's house. Thus, the criminal act of the burglar was a foreseeable act under the circumstances. Answer A is incorrect because an intervening criminal act does not automatically relieve one of liability for negligence. Answer B, which is really a rephrasing of Answer A, is incorrect for the same reason. Answer C is incorrect because it overstates the potential liability of a defendant by not taking foreseeability into account at all.

69. C is the correct answer. In personal injury cases, the adage "you take the plaintiff as you find him" is still the majority rule. This is known as the "thin skull" or "eggshell plaintiff" theory, and it prevents a tortfeasor from avoiding liability because of a preexisting medical condition on the part of the plaintiff. Therefore, the grandmother is liable for all of her grandson's injuries that resulted from her pinching his cheek. Answer A is incorrect because personal injury damages are not limited to what the defendant might reasonably foresee. Answer B is incorrect because this is not a preexisting injury case; it is a case of preexisting medical condition, which is not the same thing as a preexisting injury. Answer D is incorrect for the same reasons that C is correct.

70. C is the correct answer because, at common law, a cause of action personal to a plaintiff terminated when the person died. Here, had the woman lived, she would have had a cause of action in negligence against the man. However because the call of the question said that this suit was at common law, any right of recovery that the woman may have had terminated with her death. Answer A is incorrect because wrongful death actions were not recognized at common law. Answer B is incorrect because survival claims were not recognized at common law. Answer D is incorrect for the same reasons that Answer C is correct.

71. A is the correct answer because lost financial support, services and society are available to designated beneficiaries under a statutorily created wrongful death action. Here, the woman's death was wrongful, and the call of the question says that this suit is under the law of "most states today." Therefore, the husband and the minor children can recover in a wrongful death action. Answer B is incorrect because survival statutes typically allow an estate to recover for injuries sustained by the decedent only until the time of death. Here, the woman is dead. Thus, the proper cause of action would be wrongful death. Answer C is incorrect because the husband and children do not qualify for a negligent infliction of emotional distress claim because they did not witness the woman's death and, thus, could not recover the damages mentioned in the question in this type of action. Answer D is incorrect because, without the

wrongful death statute, the apartment owner would not have negligence liability to the husband and children; he would only have negligence liability to the woman's estate.

72. B is the correct answer because an employer is responsible for the negligence of an employee, so long as the employee was acting within the scope of his employment. Here, the pizza delivery boy was driving negligently while he was delivering pizzas as part of his employment for the restaurant. Thus, the restaurant will be held liable under the doctrine of respondeat superior. Answer A is incorrect, as the facts do not state the restaurant was negligent in hiring the delivery boy. Answer C is incorrect because the nondelegable duty rule applies to independent contractor cases. Here, the pizza delivery boy was an employee of the restaurant, not an independent contractor. Answer D is incorrect because the facts show that the pizza delivery boy was not an independent contractor; rather, he was an employee of the restaurant.

73. C is the correct answer because the garbage company will not be vicariously liable for garbage collector's negligence if his activity, when the accident occurred, was totally unrelated to the garbage company's business. Here, the garbage collector was on a personal errand getting library books when the accident occurred. Thus, the garbage company will not be liable. Answer A is incorrect because the garbage company would be liable if the garbage collector were acting within the scope of his employment, as discussed in Answer C, so this would not be a good defense. Answer B is incorrect because superseding cause is not an issue. Under the doctrine of respondeat superior, an employer is responsible for the negligence of an employee, so long as the employee was acting within the scope of his employment. Here, the issue is not a superseding cause, but rather, simply the fact that at the time of the accident, the garbage collector was not acting within the scope of his duties. Answer D is incorrect because the nondelegable duty rule applies in the independent contractor setting. Here, the garbage collector was an employee of the garbage company, not an independent contractor.

74. B is the correct answer because Congress waived sovereign immunity in numerous cases, including negligence, under the Federal Tort Claims Act of 1946. Here, the facts stipulate that the Army was vicariously liable for the civilian employee's negligence. Therefore, the Federal Tort Claims Act will operate to waive any sovereign immunity that the Army would have otherwise enjoyed. Answer A is incorrect because sovereign immunity has never been held to violate the Equal Protection Clause. Answer C is incorrect because until 1946, United States government agencies did enjoy sovereign immunity. Answer D is incorrect because Congress has waived sovereign

immunity in negligence cases, as discussed in Answer B.

75. D is the correct answer. Defamation is a defamatory statement of and concerning the plaintiff, published to a third party, causing injury to reputation. Libel is written defamation. Here, the statement is not libelous on its face because there is nothing inherently embarrassing about a woman giving birth to twins. Sally Smith must show facts that make the otherwise innocent statement actionable. (This fact would be that she is unmarried; a statement that she, as an unmarried woman gives birth to children, may cause harm to her reputation.) This is called a reasonable innuendo. Furthermore, the newspaper's statement was false because Sally Smith never had a child. Answer A is incorrect because the statement is not libelous on its face, as discussed in Answer D. Answer B is incorrect because there has been publication to others who read the newspaper. Answer C is incorrect because the statement clearly related to the only person named Sally Smith in the community.

76. D is the correct answer. Defamation is a defamatory statement of and concerning the plaintiff, published to a third party, causing injury to reputation. Libel is written defamation. Here, the woman's letters contained a false statement (that the man was homeless), the letters were sent to others (which constituted publication), they were in writing, and they could cause injury to the man's reputation (because being called homeless is not complimentary). At common law, libel was a strict liability tort. Defendants were liable for unintended and innocent defamation, as was the case here. The call of the question states that this was at common law. Thus, the woman's writing and sending of the letter, albeit innocent, was still actionable. Answers A, B and C are incorrect because they all state that some degree of fault was required in a common law libel action, which was not true.

77. A is the correct answer because retraction and apology are steps a libel defendant can take to limit the damages caused by a libelous statement. Here, when the man realized that he had printed a false statement about his opponent, he issued a retraction and an apology. This would limit his damages. Answer B is incorrect and irrelevant because the collateral source rule relates to payments made to a plaintiff from a source independent of the defendant. This doctrine is not raised by the facts, since the defendant himself is being asked to pay. Answer C is incorrect because the offsetting benefit rule applies when the plaintiff receives a benefit, however small, from the libelous statement. Here, the facts do not show that the opponent (the plaintiff) received any benefit from the libel. Answer D is incorrect because retraction and apology only mitigate damages and do not completely relieve a defendant of liability.

78. B is the correct answer. Defamation is a defamatory statement, of and concerning the plaintiff, published to a third party, causing injury to reputation. Libel is written defamation. Here, although the defamatory statement (that the woman was drunk) was "spoken" on the tape, it has been reduced to permanent physical form through the taping and, thus, would be libel. Answers A and C are incorrect because they relate to slander, which is spoken defamation. Here, for the reasons discussed in Answer B, the defamation is considered "written" because it is on tape and is, thus, libel. Answer D is incorrect because libel per quod is used when the statement is not libelous on its face; in these cases, the statement must be demonstrated to be libelous through the introduction of extrinsic evidence. Here, the statement (that the woman was drunk) is libelous on its face. Thus, there is no need for extrinsic evidence, so libel per quod is not the correct answer.

79. C is the correct answer because a bookseller who sells libelous matter without knowledge is not liable under the secondary publisher rule. For purposes of defamation and libel suits, "publication" means the communication of a defamatory statement to a third party. Here, the libelous material was initially "published" when the statements were made in the book and read by others. However, the bookstore is protected under the secondary publisher rule because it "published" (i.e., passed the statements on to those who purchased the book from it) innocently, since it had not read the book. Answer A is incorrect because it does not take into account the exception stated in Answer C. Answer B is incorrect because the bookstore and the author of the book did not have a relationship that would give rise to vicarious liability. Answer D is incorrect because, since the bookstore is not liable, as discussed in Answer C, an indemnification issue would not arise.

80. B is the correct answer. When a public official or figure sues for libel related to a matter of public concern, "actual malice" as defined in New York Times v. Sullivan becomes part of the plaintiff's prima facie case. "Actual malice" is a knowing falsity or reckless disregard for truth or falsity. Here, the female senator is a public official. Thus, the New York Times v. Sullivan standard applies here. Because the talk show host did not investigate the truth of the ex-convict's statements about the senator before making these statements on the air, he acted with reckless disregard for the truth. Answer A is incorrect because this definition is typically used for punitive damages by state courts. Here, the call of the question asks what the United States Supreme Court's rulings require. Answer C is incorrect, since this is the rule established in Gertz v. Robert Welch Co. for private persons defamed on matters of public concern. Here, as discussed in Answer B, the senator is a public official, not a private person. Thus, the rule stated in Answer C does not apply here. Answer D is incorrect

because it embodies the common law rule, before the Supreme Court decisions beginning with New York Times v. Sullivan.

81. B is the correct answer. The Supreme Court held in New York Times v. Sullivan that the burden of proof in defamation actions brought by public officials is "actual malice." "Actual malice" is demonstrated by clear and convincing evidence. Therefore, Answers A, C and D are incorrect.

82. A is the correct answer. Defamation is a defamatory statement of and concerning the plaintiff, published to a third party, causing injury to reputation. Slander is spoken defamation. Slander per se is an oral defamatory statement alleging unchastity of an unmarried woman, a loathsome disease, unethical business practices, and moral turpitude. Here, the lawyer has defamed his former partner by accusing him of unethical business practices and perhaps, also, the commission of a crime. Thus, the statement is slander per se for two reasons. Answer B is incorrect because there is no slander per quod theory of recovery. Answer C is incorrect because the statement goes beyond simple slander. It is slander per se, for the reasons discussed in Answer A. Answer D is incorrect because this tort does not protect a plaintiff's reputation interest.

83. C is correct, since the student's statement is an opinion that does not appear to be premised on false underlying facts. Clearly, calling the professor a "clown" is not meant to be taken literally. Answer A is incorrect because the Gertz holding regarding opinion has subsequently been interpreted in Malkovich as not protecting all opinions under a First Amendment umbrella. Answer B is incorrect because it does not address the opinion issue, and also because professors are not always public figures. Answer D is incorrect because, modernly, an opinion not based on underlying false facts is not defamation.

84. C is the correct answer. A witness testifying in a court proceeding has absolute immunity from defamation liability, provided the statements relate to issues in the trial. Here, the man is on trial for the battery of his daughter, and the statements relate to the sexual abuse of the daughter, which is a form of battery. Thus, the witness is immune from defamation liability. Answers A and D are incorrect statements of law. B is incorrect because, as discussed in Answer C, the privilege is absolute, not conditional.

85. B is the correct answer. The waitress is a republisher of the defamatory statement made by the man. The fact that the best friend may not have believed the statement is not required. It is sufficient that the friend understand the words as accusing the plaintiff (the actress) of some disgrace (in this case, being a prostitute). Answer A is incorrect because there is no waitress' privilege. Answer

C is incorrect because, as discussed in Answer A, there is no waitress' privilege, conditional or otherwise. Answer D is incorrect for the same reason that Answer B is correct.

86. D is the correct answer. Modernly, a manufacturer is strictly liable for a manufacturing defect (the breach of its duty) that causes injury to a foreseeable plaintiff. A manufacturing defect is a frailty or shortcoming in a product resulting from a departure from its design specifications during production. This is different from a design defect in that the latter is a defect in the entire line of products under that model name, rather than a defect in the individual unit, as seems to be the case here. In this case, the manufacturer of the toaster oven owed a duty of care to the woman as a foreseeable plaintiff (a consumer), and the manufacturer breached its duty through a manufacturing defect that caused the woman to be burned. Answer A is incorrect because privity of contract between a manufacturer and a purchaser is no longer required; here, the call of the question asked for the result under modern law. Answer B is incorrect because a purchaser need not prove negligence to recover for a personal injury caused by a dangerously defective product. As discussed in Answer D, the manufacturer is strictly liable for the woman's injuries here. Answer C is incorrect because a manufacturing defect, not a design defect, caused the injury, as discussed in Answer D.

87. B is the correct answer. Most states today allow bystanders to recover for personal injuries caused by dangerously defective products, so long as they were reasonably foreseeable bystanders. Here, the snowmobile overturned due to a manufacturing defect in the mechanism and it struck a bystander, causing his injuries. The bystander was foreseeable because it is foreseeable that snowmobiles will be used in an area where bystanders are located. Answer A is incorrect because every party in the manufacturing/marketing chain is liable for injuries caused by a dangerously defective product. Answer C is incorrect because privity is not required. D is incorrect because a bystander need not be a family member to recover for personal injuries.

88. A is the correct answer because a plaintiff may not recover in strict liability in tort, if the manufacturer can show that the product has been altered after it leaves the manufacturer's hands. Answer B is incorrect because contributory negligence is not a defense to a strict liability action. Answer C is incorrect because there is no requirement that the plaintiff use a similar product in the past. Answer D is incorrect because a manufacturer is strictly liable, even though it took all possible care to avoid manufacturing defects. Quality control is not valid defense to a strict liability action.

89. C is the correct answer. The Restatement of Torts and the courts recognize

that, although some products pose a risk of injury, where their utility outweighs the risk, they are not unreasonably dangerous. Here, the manufacturer's tests determined that the pajamas would ignite only 1% of the time. Since no product can be made 100% safe, a 1% risk is low enough as to shield the manufacturer from strict liability in this case. Answers A and B are incorrect because there is no manufacturing or design defect, for the reasons discussed in Answer C. Answer D is incorrect because clothing manufacturers do not have a blanket exemption from strict liability rules.

90. C is the correct answer. This is a strict liability in tort action. A manufacturer owes a duty to a foreseeable consumer. That duty is breached by either a manufacturing or a design defect, or a failure to warn or inadequate warning. If the product that the manufacturer produces causes injury to the plaintiff, then the manufacturer is liable in strict liability in tort. Here, the manufacturer of the allergy pills failed to place a warning on the pill bottle that the drug could cause deafness in a very small percentage of the population. The pill was sold over the counter. Thus, the woman was a foreseeable consumer. The woman became deaf as a result of using the drug. Therefore, she can recover from the manufacturer in strict liability in tort. Answer A is incorrect because a plaintiff may bring a lawsuit for a defective product under a strict liability in tort theory, a warranty theory, or a products negligence suit. The woman is not limited to bringing a products negligence action. Answer B is incorrect because it overstates the liability of a drug manufacturer. Answer D is incorrect because drug manufacturers do not have a blanket exemption from strict liability rules.

91. B is the correct answer. Negligence is the breach of a duty, causing damages. An employer is vicariously liable for the torts committed by its employees during the course of its employment. Here, the inspector's injury was caused by the carelessness of the company's employee during the course of his employment. Therefore, the company will be held liable for the negligence of its employee. Answer A is incorrect because, although the manufacturer of explosives may be considered to be engaged in an abnormally dangerous activity, the type of injury that the inspector sustained was not a result of the activity that was abnormally dangerous. (Had the container exploded, the result would be different.) Answer C is incorrect because injuries caused when a person falls over a container in a dark aisle are reasonably foreseeable. Answer D is incorrect because the facts do not mention a worker's compensation statute, and also because these laws usually affect only those in employer–employee relationships. Here, the inspector was not an employee of the company.

92. D is the correct answer. Negligence is the breach of a duty, causing damages.

An employer is vicariously liable for the torts committed by its employees during the course of its employment. Here, the driver was driving students when he drove recklessly and caused the students' injuries. The driver was, thus, engaged in the scope of his employment when he caused the students to be injured. Consequently, the students can recover from the driver because he was negligent and from the school system because it is vicariously liable for the negligence of its employee. Answers A and B are incorrect because, as discussed in Answer D, the driver was acting within the scope of his employment when he was negligent. Answer C is incorrect because it states that the students can recover from the driver only, and as discussed in Answer D, the students can also recover from the school system under a theory of vicarious liability.

93. B is the correct answer. Since the manufacturer used an inadequate wire in all food processors of this model, this is a design defect that created an unreasonable risk of danger. Therefore, the most appropriate cause of action would be a products liability action in strict liability in tort, and breach would be established because of the design defect. Answer A is incorrect because this is not a manufacturing defect, since the problem was with all food processors of this particular model, not with this individual food processor. Answer C is incorrect because there is nothing in the facts to indicate that the manufacturer was aware of the defect in order to warn consumers about it. Answer D is incorrect because privity is no longer required to bring an action in strict liability.

94. D is the correct answer. A plaintiff may bring a products liability action in strict liability in tort for breach of an express or implied warranty. Here, the facts do not indicate that the computer manufacturer gave any express warranties. However, all products are subject to the implied warranty of merchantability. Under the implied warranty of merchantability, a manufacturer who produces a computer that catches on fire and is completely destroyed within five minutes of its first use has produced a product that is not merchantable. Therefore, the tutor will not recover in strict liability for her economic losses (the loss of the computer) unless she sues under a warranty theory. Answers A and B are incorrect for the reasons discussed in Answer D. Answer C is incorrect because, as discussed in Answer D, the tutor can recover under an implied warranty of merchantability theory.

95. D is the correct answer. Generally, a person has no duty to come to the aid of one in distress, unless he has placed that person in peril. Here, although the man's actions appear very callous under the circumstances, there are no facts indicating that the man put the child in peril. The man, thus, had no duty to rescue the child. Consequently, the child's parents will not recover against

the man. Answer A is incorrect because the common law did not recognize a duty to rescue. Answer B is incorrect because most states have not changed the common law rule. Answer C is incorrect because there is no special duty to rescue children who are not related to the defendant. Here, there is nothing in the facts to indicate that the child was related to the man. Thus, the man had no duty to rescue the child.

96. C is the correct answer. In a jurisdiction with a Good Samaritan statute, a physician who administers aid in an emergency is not liable for mere negligence, but instead must have acted recklessly or willfully and wantonly in causing an injury. Answer A is incorrect because Good Samaritan statutes insulate physicians from liability for mere negligence in emergencies. Answer B is incorrect because it misstates the effect of Good Samaritan statutes. As discussed in Answer C, Good Samaritan statutes insulate physicians from liability for mere negligence. Answer D is incorrect because it is not necessary for the physician to have been the initial cause of the man's injuries.

97. B is the correct answer. When a child sues a health care provider for birth defects brought about because the provider negligently failed to discover a possible birth defect while the child was still a fetus, the claim is called a wrongful life claim. Here, the woman went to the doctor, and the doctor negligently misread the test results and told the woman that the child would be born normal. Instead, the child has severe birth defects and requires expensive medical care and special education, something the doctor would have been able to warn the woman about if the doctor has read the test results correctly. Thus, wrongful life is the correct answer. Answer A is incorrect because wrongful birth is the term used when a parent sues for damages in the same circumstances. Answer C is incorrect because this is plainly not a wrongful death claim, since the child is not dead. Answer D is incorrect for the same reason that B is correct.

98. B is the correct answer. Since the wife refused to give consent to the operation for religious reasons, and the man could have been saved if the operation had been performed, the hospital was neither the actual cause (the motorcycle accident was the initial cause of his injury) nor the proximate cause (because the hospital was not allowed to perform the operation to save the man's life) of the man's death. This would be the hospital's best defense to a wrongful death action. Answer A is an incorrect statement of law. Answer C is incorrect because this would not relieve the hospital of liability for the man's death; driving without a helmet is merely a factor that led to the injuries that brought the man to the hospital in the first place. Answer D is incorrect because a waiver of liability in a wrongful death case would not be enforced — it violates public policy.

99. B is the correct answer. Most jurisdictions that recognize a wrongful life claim limit recovery to special damages. Answer A is incorrect because general damages are not usually allowed. (This is because a jury cannot determine damages based on the difference between non-life and life in an impaired state.) Answer C is incorrect because it includes general damages. Answer D is incorrect because it includes general damages and punitive damages, which are generally not available in negligence cases.

100. C is the correct answer. Although an attorney usually does not owe a duty of care to a non-client, an exception has been recognized in cases where a specific person is an intended beneficiary of a will. Here, the nephew was a specific intended beneficiary of a will. Thus, under this exception, he will be able to recover for the attorney's negligence. Answers A and B are incorrect because privity is not universally required in attorney malpractice cases. Answer D is incorrect because the nephew's recovery will not be limited to the amount of the fee. He may recover all proximately caused damages from the attorney for his negligence.

101. B is the correct answer. A plaintiff in a products liability action in strict liability in tort must prove that the product causing his injury was defective. Answer A is incorrect, since it states one of the elements of negligence, which is not necessary in strict liability in tort. Answer C is incorrect because privity is no longer required in strict products liability lawsuits. Answer D is incorrect because misuse is a defense to a strict products liability in tort action and must be alleged by the defendant, not the plaintiff.

102. A is the correct answer. A design defect is found when the product is made as the maker intended, but a problem inherent to all products in that line causes an avoidable hazard to the user. Here, the faulty wiring was in all of the MP3 players of this particular model. If the manufacturer had avoided using faulty wiring, it would not have produced a defective product, and the plaintiff would not have become deaf from using it. Answer B is incorrect. A manufacturing defect is found when the product is not made as intended. Here, the MP3 player was made as intended, but the problem was inherent in the design itself. Thus, A is the correct answer, and Answer B is incorrect. Answer C is incorrect because a marketing defect is found when the maker has failed to warn the user of a danger known to the manufacturer. Here, the facts do not state that the manufacturer was aware of the danger. Answer D is incorrect because fabrication means the same as manufacturing and if the product was as intended, it is not a fabrication or manufacturing defect, as discussed in Answer B.

103. D is the correct answer. In a products liability lawsuit in strict liability in tort, the manufacturer's breach may

be established by lack of a warning or an inadequate warning. Here, the manufacturer had an adequate warning on the box that contained the thermometer. In addition, the woman's failure to read the warning constituted her assumption of the risk, which is a valid defense to a strict products liability action. Answer A is incorrect because the facts indicate that the manufacturer was aware that mercury poisoning could occur and warned accordingly. Answer B is incorrect because it is nonsensical and an incorrect statement of law; thermometer manufacturers are not shielded from liability. Answer C is incorrect because contributory negligence is not a defense to a strict products liability action.

104. C is the correct answer. Concurrent tortfeasors always bear the burden of apportioning loss, or they are jointly and severally liable for the entire loss. Here, both the woman and the man caused the child's injuries and are, thus, concurrent tortfeasors. When there is more than one tortfeasor, the plaintiff can sue one of them for the entire amount. Here, the child has done just that by suing the woman alone. It is the woman's burden to apportion the loss between she and the man. Answer A is incorrect because both the woman and the man were substantial factors in causing the child's injuries. As discussed in Answer C, the woman has the burden of apportioning the loss between herself and the man. Answer B is incorrect because this is not a valid argument when there are concurrent tortfeasors, since otherwise no one would be liable. D is incorrect because the child does not have the burden of apportioning damages caused by joint and concurrent tortfeasors at modern law, as discussed in Answer C.

105. A is the correct answer. The courts have consistently drawn a line at what type of damages may be recovered under a negligence theory. Damage caused to persons or property other than the defective product itself may be recovered, but any damages other than that are deemed part of the loss of the benefit of the bargain. Here, lost profits clearly are a pure economic loss, and the cost of storing the ice cream at the temporary facility is probably also not recoverable under a negligence theory. Answers B, C, and D are incorrect for the reasons discussed in Answer A.

106. D is the correct answer. There is an implied warranty of merchantability in the sale of any product. This warranty means that the manufacturer guarantees that the product will pass in the trade and will do what it is supposed to do. Although a sale is a contract theory of recovery, in products cases, a plaintiff may recover for a breach of the implied warranty of merchantability. Here, since the carpets could not pass the fire inspection, they were of no use to the hotel. Thus, there was a breach of the implied warranty of merchantability, which would permit recovery based on the "benefit of the bargain,"

lost profits and expenses of replacing the defective product fit within this concept. Answers A and B are incorrect for the reasons discussed in Answer D. Answer C is incorrect because there is nothing in the facts to indicate that an express warranty was given.

107. C is the correct answer because an intentional or criminal intervening act is normally unforeseeable as a matter of law. However, the defense will fail in this case, since the arsonist is within the risk created by having exit doors that did not operate in cases of fire, particularly where, as here, the neighborhood had experienced several incidents of arson in the past. Answer A is not an arguable defense, since lack of privity is no longer a defense in any of theory of strict liability in tort. Furthermore, the movie theater is being sued in negligence. Answer B is incorrect because modernly, estates do have the right to sue on behalf of the deceased under a survival action. Answer D is not arguable, since a movie-goer is clearly foreseeably at risk from the defective product (the malfunctioning exit doors).

108. D is the correct answer. A plaintiff in a products liability action may recover for lost wages, medical expenses, and pain and suffering. Answers A, B, and C are incorrect for the same reasons that Answer D is correct.

109. B is the correct answer. The man was in the store for commercial purposes, namely, to patronize the store by purchasing a soda. Consequently, he is an invitee. Answer A is incorrect because a licensee is someone who is there for social purposes. Here, as discussed in Answer B, the man was an invitee who was there for commercial purposes, not for social purposes. Answers C and D are incorrect because the man had permission to be there as a customer; he was, therefore, not a trespasser.

110. A is the correct answer. Since the passengers from the second vehicle have obtained a judgment against the florist, and florist has paid the judgment, the florist is now able to seek indemnity from the driver of its car. The florist is vicariously liable for the negligence of the driver that was committed in the course and scope of his employment. However, since the florist was not negligent itself, it is entitled to be indemnified (reimbursed) by the driver. Answers B, C, and D are incorrect for the reasons discussed in Answer A.

111. C is the correct answer. A manufacturer that is aware that its product has side effects (such as causing blindness here) has a duty to warn potential consumers of all side effects, even if the side effects only occur in a small percentage of the population. Here, the drug manufacturer was aware of the side effect, but failed to issue any warnings until the sixth year that it was manufacturing the drug. The patient took the drug before the warnings were issued and suffered complete

blindness as a result of using the drug. Thus, the patient can prove that the drug company owed her a duty, that that duty was breached when the drug company failed to warn her, and that the drug was the cause of her blindness. Thus, the patient's best theory of recovery is under a warning defect theory. Answer A is incorrect because there is nothing in the facts to indicate that the particular batch of pills that the patient took deviated from the norm. Thus, there is no manufacturing defect. Answer B is incorrect because, although causing blindness is a defect in the design of the drug, this only occurs in a small percentage of the population, while the drug effectively treats MS in virtually everyone who takes the drug. Thus, the benefit of the drug (treating MS) outweighs the cost (causing blindness in only a small percentage of the population). Thus, the patient would have a better chance of recovery under a warning theory because, if she proceeded under a design theory, she would be subject to the cost/benefit analysis. Answer D is incorrect because, as discussed in Answer C, the patient could prove a defective warning.

112. B is the correct answer. The substantial factor test is used where each of the defendants' acts was a substantial factor in causing the damage. Here, there were several factors contributing to the pedestrian's death. First, there was the negligent driver's causing of the accident, which resulted in the pedestrian having a broken leg. Second, there was the pedestrian's wife's refusal to consent to him having surgery. Third, there was the fact that since the surgery could not be performed, and the pedestrian was a hemophiliac, he bled out and died. Assuming that the patient would have recovered if the surgery had been performed, the hospital's failure to overrule the wife's refusal to consent and get a court order to perform the surgery anyway may have been a substantial factor leading to the pedestrian's ultimate death. Answer A is incorrect. The sine qua non test (but for causation) would not be effective here because it would eliminate all of the causes discussed in Answer B, since each one by itself was a cause of the pedestrian's death. Thus, the substantial factor test is the appropriate test to use here. Answers C and D are incorrect. Both alternative liability and market share are substitutes for causation when a plaintiff cannot prove that the defendant's act caused the injury, although it could have. Here, as discussed in Answer B, it can be proven that the defendant (the hospital) was a cause of the pedestrian's injury (death) through its failure to obtain a court order to perform the surgery.

113. D is the correct answer. The neighbor breached a duty to any foreseeable plaintiff by leaving the can of insecticide in his yard. When the child sprayed the insecticide, it was a cause of the child's injuries. However, a tortfeasor's liability may be cut off by an

intervening, superseding, unforeseeable act. Here, the babysitter's failure to immediately administer soap and water was gross negligence. Since the child showed the babysitter the can and the babysitter read the warning regarding soap and water, her failure to administer the soap and water for one hour was an action that superseded the neighbor's initial negligence. It was also unforeseeable that someone would act so callously as to leave an injured child without the required care for one hour. Therefore, the neighbor's liability would be cut off due to the babysitter's failure to act. Answer A is incorrect because a child's contributory negligence is determined by the child standard of care. Thus, the child will be judged against other five-year-olds of similar experience and intelligence. In light of that standard, the child's actions in spraying himself with the insecticide that he may have thought was perfume indicate that he was not contributorily negligent. Answer B is incorrect for the reasons discussed in Answer A; the child did not assume the risk. Answer C is incorrect because a discovered trespasser is owed a duty, and most likely a neighbor's child would be a discovered trespasser.

114. A is the correct answer because the woman has the right to decide for herself whether or not to accept the fertility treatments that could result in multiple pregnancies. Since the doctor failed to obtain her informed consent, he was negligent, so this would be the woman's best theory of recovery. Answers B and C are incorrect because they both require sales of products, something in which medical doctors do not engage. Answer D is incorrect because the woman gave consent for the doctor to touch her during the treatments. Since battery is an intentional harmful or offensive touching, the woman's consent means that the touching was not offensive. Consequently, the woman would not prevail under a battery theory.

115. B is the correct answer. The substantial factor test is used where each of the defendants' acts was a substantial factor in causing the damage. Here, there were several asbestos manufacturers whose asbestos contributed to the man's asbestosis. So long as the man can prove that the defendant's asbestos was a substantial factor in causing his disease, he will be able to prevail under this theory. Answer A is incorrect. The sine qua non test (but for causation) would not be effective here because it would eliminate all of the causes discussed in Answer B, since each one by itself was a cause of the man's asbestosis. Here, if the defendant's asbestos is removed from the factual equation, the man would have still probably gotten asbestosis, since exposure to any asbestos provided by any of the many suppliers over the years could be sufficient to produce asbestosis. Answer C is incorrect, since the man can prove that the defendant's asbestos was the cause of his injury, as discussed in

Answer B. Answer D is not correct, since the man can identify at least one of the suppliers. Answer D is also incorrect because it would not give the man a complete recovery. Each maker would only have to pay its percentage of the injury coincident with its market share. In the many decades of exposure, many of the suppliers will have gone out of business and cannot be held liable for their percentage.

116. C is the correct answer. In order to prevail in a products negligence action, a plaintiff must prove that the manufacturer owed him a duty of care, that the manufacturer breached that duty, and that the breach of the duty was both the actual (but for) and proximate cause of the plaintiff's injuries. Here, it was revealed at trial that the astronaut suffered from a unique stomach ailment that caused him to suffer stomach cramps after eating. Therefore, the ingestion of the food in question was not the cause in fact of the astronaut's stomach cramps. Thus, this is the manufacturer's best defense. Answer A is incorrect, since it refers to the defendant's knowledge of the hazard as a prerequisite to its duty to warn. Here, the manufacturer would not have been in a position to know about the astronaut's stomach cramps or to warn him about them, since the stomach cramps did not have any connection to the manufacturer's product. In addition, the fact that the food was prepared in accordance with the Food and Drug Administration's standards (state of the art) is not the best defense for a manufacturer of a food product because the Food and Drug Administration only provides minimal inspection of products. Passing their inspection does not relieve a defendant of liability for negligence. Answer B is incorrect because the astronaut is suing under a products negligence theory, not a design defect theory. Answer D is incorrect because, as discussed above, Answer C is the only correct answer.

117. D is the correct answer. The warranty of fitness for a particular purpose is implied when a buyer relies upon the seller to select the goods to fit a specific request. Here, the woman (the buyer) relied upon the seller's expertise to give her picture hangers that could hang pictures weighing up to 20 pounds (her specific request). The salesman failed to provide the woman with picture hangers that could fulfill this purpose, as demonstrated by the fact that the picture hangers could not hold up a picture weighing 15 pounds (which was within the 20-pound upper limit set by the woman's request). Thus, the salesman breached the implied warranty of fitness for a particular purpose, and the hardware store is vicariously liable for the salesman's breach because it occurred during the course and scope of his employment. Answer A is incorrect because the salesman merely gave the woman picture hangers and gave no express warranty that they would

properly perform. Answers B and C are incorrect because there is nothing in the facts demonstrating that the picture hangers did not work at all for lighter pictures; the facts only show that they could not hold up a picture that weighed 15 pounds. In addition, the breach of the implied warranty of fitness for a particular purpose is the best theory of recovery, for the reasons discussed in Answer D.

118. C is the correct answer because all products are subject to the implied warranty of merchantability. This product (the hair dye) is not considered to be merchantable, since it caused the woman to lose her hair. Therefore, this product would not pass in the trade, and the woman's best chance for a full recovery would be based on an implied warranty of merchantability theory. Answer A is incorrect because battery is an intentional tort involving a harmful or offensive touching, and there is nothing in the facts indicating that the manufacturer intended a harmful or offensive touching toward the woman. Answer B is incorrect because it, too, is an intentional tort, and there is nothing in the facts to indicate that the manufacturer intended to cause the woman emotional distress. Answer D is incorrect for the reasons discussed above.

119. A is the correct answer because there is nothing in these facts to indicate that the store made an express warranty. Answer B is incorrect because, while the man's criminal activity may have offered a defense in a negligence action, the man sued for breach of express warranty. Answer C is incorrect because a person may sue anyone in the chain of distribution; a lawsuit is not limited to the manufacturer of a product. Answer D is incorrect because an express warranty must be made affirmatively; only implied warranties are implied.

120. D is the correct answer. In a negligence case, the plaintiff must prove that the defendant owed her a duty of care and that the breach of that duty of care was the actual and proximate cause of her injuries. Here, the manufacturer owed a duty to everybody who purchased its automobiles, including the woman. The manufacturer's breach must be proven by the theory of res ipsa loquitur ("the facts speak for themselves"), since the mechanic was unable to determine the actual cause of the accident, but since steering wheels do not normally fall off of brand new cars in the absence of negligence, these facts show a classic res ipsa loquitur scenario. Answers A and B, and C are incorrect because the woman has sued under a products negligence theory, and not in strict liability in tort.

121. B is the correct answer. As a visitor to the zoo, he may properly be seen as an invitee at common law. Where dangers are so open, obvious and apparent, it may be expected that someone in the visitor's position will take such steps

as are reasonable to protect himself. A mere warning may suffice; however, this is not a fixed rule, and all of the circumstances must be taken into account. Where a landowner should anticipate an unreasonable risk of harm to an invitee, regardless of the invitee's awareness of danger, the landowner may be required to take greater steps to ensure the safety of an invitee. Answer choice B addresses this possibility. While strict liability in tort can be found in cases involving, among other things, wild animals, this item specifically requests a negligence action. This is one of the reasons why a careful reading of the lead-in is vital. Answer choice C is incorrect because it doesn't address the negligence action. Answer choice D is incorrect because there is no blanket immunity for zoos, either modernly or at common law.

END OF ANSWERS

A
TORTS

SIMULATED BAR QUESTIONS

1. A builder and a homeowner signed a contract providing that the homeowner's duty to pay would not arise, unless the home was constructed according to the construction plans, except to the extent of construction changes approved in writing.

   The builder began construction of a home, but determined that there was a shortage of roofing tile because of recent large-scale efforts to rebuild many local homes destroyed in seasonal fires. When contacted on the telephone, the homeowner agreed with the builder to the use of a different type of tile because of the tile shortage. After a week, the homeowner decided that his "dream home" must be completed as he originally planned and told the builder he wanted a roof made out of the originally specified tiles. The builder refused because he knew that those tiles would be difficult to obtain, although he had not yet purchased the new type of tiles. If the homeowner brings an action against the builder for breach of contract, the court will most likely find for:

   A. The builder because the homeowner waived his rights to have the original roofing tiles installed.

   B. The builder because the homeowner agreed to modify the contract.

   C. The homeowner because of the builder's pre-existing duty to use the original roofing tiles and the attempted modification was done over the telephone.

   D. The homeowner because the modification must be expressly agreed upon.

2. The Internal Revenue Service (IRS) notified a Bar Exam tutor of its intent to audit her. At the time, the tutor was tutoring a bar candidate who happened to be an accountant. When the accountant heard the tutor grumbling to herself about the upcoming audit, the accountant volunteered to meet with the IRS to resolve the tutor's problem. Fearing the worst, the tutor was ecstatic to learn that the accountant was able to reach a favorable resolution on her behalf. As a result, the tutor stated to the accountant, "I'll do all the rest of your bar exam tutoring for free." At the next tutorial session, the tutor changed her mind and refused to tutor the accountant, unless he paid the normal fee. The accountant sued the tutor for breach of contract. At common law, the court will find for:

   A. The tutor, since the accountant's gratuitous services were insufficient consideration for the tutor's promise.

B. The tutor, since the Parol Evidence Rule bars oral testimony of the tutor's promise.

C. The accountant, since the tutor's statement constituted an enforceable moral obligation.

D. The accountant, since the Doctrine of Promissory Estoppel is a substitute for the accountant's otherwise gratuitous services.

3. A garage door installer and a homeowner enter into a contract. The contract provides for the installation of an automatic garage door opener, but does not mention the type of door opener to be used. The installer has installed a 1/2 horsepower motor for the door opener. Garage doors of similar size and type to the homeowner's reasonably require a 1 horsepower motor. The homeowner has noticed the 1/2 horsepower motor and states, "You'll never get paid." If the installer files a lawsuit to obtain payment, the installer will recover:

A. Full price because he substantially performed the contract.

B. Full price because neither the contract nor plans specified the type of motor to be used.

C. Nothing because there was no meeting of the minds due to the failure of the installer and the homeowner to set forth each material term in the written contract.

D. Full price, but less any damages for the installer's breach of the implied duty to install a motor with the reasonably required amount of power.

4. A builder and a business enter into a contract for a warehouse to be built. The builder agrees to complete the warehouse by August 1. On July 15, when construction of the warehouse is about 80% complete, the warehouse is accidentally destroyed by fire, without fault of either the builder or the business owner. The builder seeks to recover for the work previously performed. Will the builder prevail?

A. Yes, for the reasonable value of his services less cost of completion of the home.

B Yes, for 80% of the contract price less the business' damages.

C. No because no benefit was conferred upon the business because of the destruction of the warehouse.

D. No, if the builder cannot complete the warehouse by August 1.

5. A jeweler and a diamond merchant entered into a contract for the purchase of expensive diamonds. The contract provided that the jeweler would pay the diamond merchant only upon receipt of a certification from an international agency that certifies the quality of diamonds. The jeweler hired a reputable international

agency to inspect the diamonds. After conducting the inspection, the agency refused to issue the certification because the diamonds were of low quality. The jeweler refused to pay the contract price. If the diamond merchant brings suit against the jeweler for the contract price, the court will most likely find for:

A. The diamond merchant, if the international agency has made a gross mistake in its decision.

B. The diamond merchant, unless the jeweler proves that the diamonds were, in fact, of low quality.

C. The jeweler because both the diamond merchant and the jeweler agreed to the condition that performance must be to the satisfaction of a third person.

D. The jeweler, unless the diamond merchant can prove another reputable international certification agency would have issued a certificate.

6. A landscaper and a museum enter into a contract for the landscaper to plant various plants around the museum's grounds. The landscaper assigned his rights under this contract to a university for the outstanding college tuition bills of his daughter. The university notified the museum of the assignment, but the landscaper only completed 50% of the landscaping work before abandoning the job. Although the museum makes several requests, the landscaper refuses to complete the job. What will be the result if the university files an action against the museum to recover the contract price?

A. The museum will prevail because the contract is not assignable.

B. The museum will prevail, but only because the landscaper did not complete the job.

C. The university will prevail, but will only receive the reasonable value of the services performed, less damages caused by the landscaper's failure to complete the job.

D. The university will prevail, but only the contract price, less the cost of completion of the contract.

7. A man was injured while skiing in a remote area. A retired nurse lived in a nearby cabin and was able to provide medical treatment to mend the man's arm. She was also starved for companionship and decided to keep the man from leaving by locking the door to the room where she had placed him. Exhausted from his injuries, the man had fallen fast asleep before the nurse had locked him in the room. After a night's sleep, the nurse realized what she was doing was wrong and unlocked the door. When the man later awoke, he

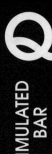

asked the nurse to telephone a relative for transportation home, and she complied. Is the nurse liable to the man for false imprisonment?

A. Yes because man was actually confined with no reasonable means of escape.

B. Yes because the nurse intended to confine the man within the room.

C. No because the nurse did not threaten or force the man into confinement.

D. No because the man was neither aware of nor harmed by his confinement.

8. A State passed a statute that requires that every facility where people may obtain money from an automatic teller machine must have a security guard posted during the period the machine is operative, or in the alternative, a 4' x 4' sign must be posted at the facility warning the consumer of the potential risk of robbery.

Despite the new law, a bank did not provide a security guard, nor did it post a sign at its automatic teller. A tourist who was visiting this city for the first time went to the bank's automatic teller machine to withdraw some money. The tourist was robbed and killed at the bank's automatic teller machine. His estate brings a wrongful death action against the bank.

Under which of the following theories is the bank likely to prevail?

A. The failure to comply with the statute was not the actual cause of the man's death.

B. None of the bank's customers had ever been killed before at any of its automatic teller machines.

C. The tourist was negligent for using an automatic teller in an unfamiliar city.

D. The statute is an ex post facto law.

9. A married man goes on a business trip. Shortly after the man's airplane was supposed to arrive in another city, the man's wife receives a phone call from the airline informing her that the plane has crashed and her husband is dead. She sues the airline for negligent infliction of emotional distress. The wife will:

A. Prevail because airlines are always per se liable for emotional distress suffered by the loved ones of victims of airplane crashes.

B. Prevail, but only because the wife suffered emotional distress.

C. Not prevail because the wife was not present at the scene when the man was killed.

D. Not prevail because the wife was not a foreseeable plaintiff.

10. A man "convinced" a woman to rob a bank by handcuffing a locked briefcase to her wrist, telling her it is full of plastic explosives that will be detonated by a remote control unit in the man's possession if the woman failed to follow the man's request. Unknown to the woman, the briefcase was actually full of cookie dough. The woman obtained $100,000.00 from the bank after threatening the bank teller with a loaded gun. The State's penal code makes it a crime to "obtain bank funds by use of a weapon or threat of injury." The woman was arrested before she could flee the bank. The State prosecutor charged both the woman and the man with conspiracy to violate the penal code section. The woman and the man will most likely be found:

   A. Guilty because the general rule is that withdrawal is not a defense to the crime of conspiracy.

   B. Guilty because the woman failed to thwart the completion of the crime.

   C. Not guilty because the woman was an unwilling participant to the crime.

   D. Not guilty because the man never agreed to the details of the woman's plan to carry out the crime.

11. As part of his initiation into a gang, a man was required to rob an old lady at gunpoint. His fellow gang member put a realistic-looking toy gun to the man's head and said, "Either you rob the old lady or you will never be part of this gang because I will kill you." The man believed that the toy gun was real, so he robbed the old lady by pointing an actual loaded gun at her and saying he would shoot her if she did not immediately give him her money, which she did. He ran off, intending to give the money to the gang, and not to keep any for himself. However, he was arrested while fleeing the scene. He was charged with robbery. Is he likely to be convicted?

   A. Yes because there was no defense of duress, since the gun used to threaten him was merely a toy.

   B. No because he robbed the old lady under the duress of the other gang member's threats.

   C. Yes because he threatened the old lady with injury if the money was not given to him.

   D. No because he never intended to keep the money.

12. A terrorist planned to blow up a building with a bomb hidden in a brief case. He went to a park near the building, where he spotted an employee from that building with an identical brief case. When the man was not looking,

the terrorist switched brief cases. The man got up to leave and grabbed the brief case containing the bomb, thinking it was actually his own brief case. The man returned to the building. The bomb detonated, and the building blew up. Since the man was away from the blast area at the time, he survived and was arrested and charged with terrorism. He was later acquitted because he did not know that he had brought the bomb into the building. Since he had gotten a look at the terrorist who left the brief case, he gave a description of the terrorist to the police. The terrorist was later located and arrested. Can the terrorist be convicted of terrorism, even though the man was acquitted?

A. No because only the party performing the prohibited act may be convicted of terrorism.

B. No because the man never made an agreement with the terrorist.

C. Yes because the man would not have entered the building if he had known that there was a bomb in the brief case.

D. Yes because the terrorist can commit the crime through an innocent agent.

13. A video game store ordered 5,000 copies of a popular video game from its supplier. The supplier, instead, tendered 5,000 copies of a competing video game that was not nearly as popular as the game that the video store had ordered. When the video game store manager tested out the video game, he discovered that this was not the game that the store had originally ordered. Since the store had paid upon delivery, it returned the games and immediately sued the supplier for breach of contract. Who will prevail?

A. The store because, although the supplier accepted the store's offer to buy the games when the supplier shipped the non-conforming games, this was also a breach.

B. The supplier because the store returned the games.

C. The supplier because it had the option of shipping non-conforming goods as an accommodation to the store.

D. The supplier because the store failed to inspect the goods at time of tender.

14. A man owned a home on 5 acres of land in an oil rich region of his home state. An oil company owned and operated a pipeline, delivering oil to its refineries, which, in part, passed across the man's property. The oil company was the state's largest employer. After two years of operation, the pipeline cracked with oil from the pipeline flooding the man's property with a black gooey mess. This did not present any danger to the man,

but caused substantial damage to his property. If the man brings an action against the oil company, under what theory will he most likely prevail?

A. Strict liability because the operation of a pipeline is an inherently dangerous activity.

B. Strict liability in tort, if the pipeline was defective.

C. Public nuisance because the man's use and enjoyment of his property was interfered with.

D. Negligence, if the pipeline was improperly maintained.

15. A man installed an electrical fence around his ranch. When the fence was touched, a mild shock was given. A boy inadvertently touched the fence when trying to retrieve his hat, which blew off as he was walking by. He received a mild shock. Although the shock would not ordinarily harm an adult, the boy died from the shock. The medical examiners determined that the boy had a heart condition that caused his death as a result of the shock. If the boy's estate brings suit against the man for wrongful death, the boy's estate will:

A. Prevail because the man's electrical fence was the cause in fact of the boy's death.

B. Prevail because the man cannot use deadly force to protect his property.

C. Not prevail because the boy was a trespasser.

D. Not prevail because the man was not using unreasonably excessive force to protect his property.

16. A man borrowed a woman's water pump and forgot to return it. The woman's basement flooded, and she needed the water pump. She remembered that she had loaned her pump to the man. By the time she went to his home, it was after dusk. She then remembered that the man was out of town. Not wanting to wait until the man returned home, she forced the man's back door open and went into his house. She promptly left upon finding her pump. Did she commit a common law burglary?

A. Yes because she forced the man's back door open.

B. Yes because the man had legal possession of the pump until he returned it.

C. No because the man did not return the pump.

D. No because the woman entered to retrieve her own property.

17. A company that transported jewelry hired a retired police detective to ride

in the truck when a shipment of particularly valuable jewels were being transported. The detective was instructed to "shoot to kill" if necessary, to prevent a robbery. While in transit with the jewels, a thief forced the truck off the road and approached the truck with an automatic rifle. When the detective saw the thief aim the rifle at him, he fired at the thief, killing him. The detective is charged with homicide. He will be found:

A. Guilty of murder in the first degree because he deliberately shot the thief.

B. Guilty of murder in the second degree because the detective believed the killing was necessary.

C. Guilty of involuntary manslaughter because deadly force was used to protect personal property.

D. Not guilty, if the detective reasonably believed deadly force was necessary to prevent the robbery.

18. A man hired a woman to take care of his horse for a week, until the following Friday when he returned home from a business trip. The woman secretly decided to keep the horse for herself before agreeing to the man's proposal. When the man returned on Friday, he discovered that the woman had not returned the horse. The woman was later arrested when the horse was discovered in her possession. If the woman is charged with larceny, she will most likely be found:

A. Guilty because the woman never returned the horse to the man.

B. Guilty because the woman had a secret intent to keep the horse when she took the horse from the man.

C. Not guilty because the woman had legal possession.

D. Not guilty because the woman was given possession of the horse without any fraudulent act or inducement.

19. A clothing retailer entered into a contract with a clothing wholesaler for the retailer to purchase all the clothes it required from the wholesaler at a fixed price for five years. On March 11 of the second year, the wholesaler notified the retailer that, because of a rise in the cost of thread, the wholesaler would no longer be able to supply the retailer with clothes. The retailer brought a breach of contract action against the wholesaler. If the wholesaler argues that the contract is not binding because it lacks consideration, the court will find for:

A. The wholesaler because all contracts must be supported by consideration.

B. The wholesaler because the contract is illusory.

C. The retailer because no consideration is needed for a requirements contract.

D. The retailer because the retailer's agreement to buy all the clothes that it requires, and the wholesaler's agreement to supply the same quantity, is sufficient consideration.

20. A catering company and its supplier entered into a requirements contract in which the supplier agreed to supply approximately seven dozen sandwiches per week to the catering company for the next four years. During the third year, the catering company expanded its business, and its sandwich requirements escalated to twenty dozen sandwiches per week. The catering company asked the supplier to supply the additional sandwiches. The supplier refused to supply the catering company with any more than seven dozen sandwiches per week. The catering company brings a breach of contract action against the supplier. The court will find for:

A. The supplier, if the normal requirements of the original contract are seven dozen sandwiches a week.

B. The supplier because the catering company's increase in its requirements was not contemplated by the parties at the time of contracting.

C. The catering company because a valid requirements contract was formed.

D. The catering company because the catering company's expansion was normal.

21. A florist and a grower entered into a requirements contract in which the grower agreed to supply the florist with its requirements for roses for ten years for a price of $20.00 per dozen. The next year, the florist realized that by paying $20.00 per dozen for the roses, the florist was unable to make a sufficient profit. The florist, thus, requested that the grower lower the price of the roses to $17.00 per dozen. When the grower refused to lower the price, the florist stopped selling roses altogether and, therefore, stopped purchasing roses from the grower. If the grower sues the florist for breach of contract, who will prevail?

A. The grower because the florist's action of not selling roses was not in good faith.

B. The grower because, under the contract, an agreement was formed for the florist to purchase roses.

C. The florist because the grower refused to lower the price to $17.00 per dozen when asked.

D. The florist because a buyer, under a requirements contract, can eliminate its requirements for any reason.

22. An office entered into a requirements contract with an office supplier for the supplier to supply the office with all of its requirements for ink at a set price for the next five years. Three years later, the office was sold to another company. The new company demanded that the office supplier continue to supply it with ink under the terms of the original contract. The office supplier refused. The new company then sued the office supplier for breach of contract. Who will prevail?

A. The new company, under the exact terms of the original contract.

B. The new company, and the office supplier must supply it with ink in an amount that it not unreasonable based on the amount that the previous office owner required just prior to the sale of the office to the new company.

C. The office supplier, which is not required to supply the new company with any ink.

D. The new company, which is entitled to be supplied with an increased number of ink that it requires as a contemplated result of the anticipated improvement in management of the business.

23. A man purchased a car from a car dealership. As part of the contract, the man was to receive free servicing for his car for the life of the vehicle. Eight years later, the car dealership was sold to a new owner. The man agreed that he would continue to get service for his car at the dealership under the new owner. However, when he went to get the car serviced, the car dealership refused to service the car. The man sues the car dealership for breach of contract. Who will prevail?

A. The dealership because man was not a third party beneficiary to the sale of the dealership to the new owner.

B. The dealership because the original owner of the dealership is still liable under the contract.

C. The man, under the implied warranty of serviceability.

D. The man because there was a novation.

24. A woman lent her sled to her boyfriend. As he was whipping in and out between trees, the metal runner on the sled snapped, causing him to fall off the sled and strike his head on a rock. He suffered severe head injuries from the accident.

It was determined that, although most sled manufacturers used steel runners, a much stronger metal than that used by the manufacturer of this sled, the use of steel would increase the manufacturing cost of each sled by about $2.25.

If the boyfriend brings an action against the sled manufacturer based on the theory of strict liability to recover for his injuries:

   A. He will recover because most sled manufacturers used a different metal to make the ski on the sled.

   B. He will recover, if use of the weaker metal used by this manufacturer resulted in the sled being unreasonably dangerous.

   C. He will not recover because he was not the purchaser of the sled.

   D. He will not recover because he was contributorily negligent.

25. A man purchased a fan from a drug store. The fan was manufactured by a third party. One hot day, he lent the fan to his female neighbor. The first time the woman attempted to use the fan in her home, a blade flew off and struck her in the eye. If the woman brings an action against the drug store based on the theory of strict liability, she will:

   A. Not prevail because the drug store was not the manufacturer of the product.

   B. Not prevail because the woman was not in privity of contract with the drug store.

   C. Prevail, only if the fan was defective.

   D. Prevail, but only if the drug store could have discovered the defect.

26. A woman bought a car from his local dealer. She lent the car to her son so that he could drive it to school. On the way to school, the car exploded, and the son suffered severe burns. If he brings an action against the car dealer based on the theory of negligence, he will:

   A. Prevail because the car was defective and unreasonably dangerous.

   B. Prevail, but only if the dealer could have discovered the defect by a reasonable inspection.

   C. Not prevail because the son was not an intended user of the car.

D. Not prevail because the dealer owed no duty of care to the son.

27. A man purchased a tricycle for his toddler. As the toddler rode the tricycle down the street, the wheel fell off, and the toddler struck her head on the sidewalk. She suffered severe injuries as a result. The man observed the toddler falling off of the tricycle and became physically ill and emotionally upset. If the man asserts a claim against the manufacturer of the tricycle for negligent infliction of emotional distress, who will prevail?

    A. The man because he witnessed the accident.

    B. The man because he suffered emotional and physical injury.

    C. The manufacturer because the man was not using the tricycle.

    D. The manufacturer, since the man suffered no harm other than becoming ill and severely upset.

28. A man was angry at a neighbor. One day, he overheard a couple of thieves planning to burglarize the neighbor's house. That afternoon, he went to the neighbor's house, allegedly to make amends. In reality, he had other plans. The man excused himself to go to the bathroom and left the bathroom window open to make it easier for the thieves to get into the house. That evening, the thieves entered the house through the open bathroom window and burglarized the house.

    The thieves are arrested, and they implicate the man. The man is arrested, as well, and charged with burglary. He should be found:

    A. Guilty because he opened the window to permit access to the neighbor's home.

    B. Not guilty because the actus reas was performed by the thieves.

    C. Not guilty because there was no conspiracy between the thieves and the man.

    D. Not guilty because the thieves, not the man, burglarized the house.

29. A nineteen-year old boy decided to break into a liquor store. One night, just before closing, the boy walked into the store carrying a gun, and he robbed the store attendant. If he is prosecuted for common law burglary, he should be found:

    A. Guilty because he committed a felony therein.

    B. Guilty because he committed the act at night.

    C. Guilty because he entered the store.

D. Not guilty.

30. A man went into the home of his ex-wife, intending to stab her to death. However, he was extremely nervous because it was his first murder and he could not stand the sight of blood. Instead of stabbing her, he took a broom laying outside the home, soaked it in gasoline, ignited it, and threw it through the open window. The ex-wife died while in a panic, trying to escape from the fire to her bed coverings that were ignited by the broom. After the fire was extinguished, the only damage to the structure was smoke discoloration to the walls in the bedroom.

    If the man is prosecuted for arson at common law, he should be found:

    A. Guilty, since he inserted the flaming broom into the house.

    B. Guilty, since he had the specific intent to commit a felony therein.

    C. Not guilty because there was no burning to the structure.

    D. Not guilty because arson is a specific intent crime.

31. A man telephoned an antique store to determine whether his fifteenth-century wooden table could be refurbished to its original condition. The store's owner asked the man to bring it by his shop for inspection. When the man came to the shop, the store clerk recognized the table as part of some antique furniture stolen from the inventory of a local auction warehouse. After telling the man that he knew the table was stolen, the store's owner agreed to refurbish the table for $500.00, payable upon the sale of the table. This was twice his regular price for similar work. The man and the store's owner were arrested after an undercover police officer "bought" the table at the man's garage sale for $2,000.00. If the store's owner is charged with the crime of conspiracy to sell stolen goods, the verdict will be:

    A. Not guilty because only the man had the table for sale.

    B. Not guilty because the store's business of refurbishing furniture is not illegal.

    C. Guilty because the store's owner had knowledge the table he was refurbishing was stolen.

    D. Guilty because the store's owner agreed to be paid $500.00 for the refurbishing of the table upon its sale.

32. A man and a woman were two of the top students at a medical school, each vying to be top of the class. The man succeeded in being named top of the class, which greatly enraged the woman. On graduation night, the woman physically confronted the man, and a fight ensued between them. As the man was about to punch the woman, she struck him

over the head with her diploma. The man suffered a concussion and lost consciousness. The man's attorney filed a lawsuit against the woman to recover for the man's injuries.

Will the man be successful in his claim against the woman?

A. Yes, if the woman intended to strike the man with the diploma.

B. Yes because the woman failed to retreat.

C. No, unless the woman used unreasonably excessive force.

D. No because most women are not strong enough to cause a man to suffer a concussion.

33. One night, while a woman was loading her groceries into her car in a store parking lot after shopping at the store, a man grabbed her purse and ran off. The woman sued the store for negligence. Who will prevail?

A. The store, if the woman did something to provoke the man to grab her purse.

B. The store, unless it did not use reasonable care in supervising its premises.

C. The woman because she was injured in the store's parking lot.

D. The woman because the incident in question took place outside of the store itself.

34. A reporter for a sleazy magazine obtained a picture of a nun drinking a beverage that appeared to be a beer. The reporter wrote a story with the nun's picture indicating that even nuns enjoy this type of beer. The magazine sold a lot of copies because people were happy to see a nun drinking beer. The nun was incensed and, in fact, had been drinking a soda. She sued the magazine for its use of her photograph. Who will prevail?

A. The nun, if she did not agree to the use of her picture in the magazine.

B. The nun, if her picture was taken without consent.

C. The magazine because the nun was already a public figure.

D. The magazine because it is not responsible for the acts of the reporter.

35. A paparazzi photographer photographed a celebrity driving an expensive convertible one sunny weekend. Because the top was down, the celebrity could be seen wearing a broad smile and appearing to be enjoying himself. The photographer sold the photograph to a publication devoted to photographs of famous people having fun, and the pho-

tograph appeared in the next edition.

The celebrity discovered the photographs in the publication and sued the publication for invasion of privacy under the theory of intrusion on solitude. Who will prevail?

A. The celebrity, if his picture was published without consent.

B. The celebrity because the publication profited from publishing the photograph of the celebrity.

C. The publication because the celebrity was photographed in a public place.

D. The publication, if the celebrity benefited from receiving commercial endorsements as a result of his photograph appearing in the publication.

36. A woman found an antique and obviously valuable book, with a bookmark between the pages containing the name and address of the book's owner. The woman threw away the bookmark, but she kept the book because she believed that she would make a lot of money selling the original version online. What crime, if any, did the woman commit?

A. No crime because the woman obtained possession of the book in a lawful manner.

B. Uttering because the woman did not believe the book was actually the original version, but instead, was a forgery.

C. Larceny because the woman intentionally kept the book instead of returning it to the owner.

D. Embezzlement because the woman's possession was lawful at the time she formed the intent to keep the book.

37. A man asked his friend to loan his bicycle to him for "a little exercise" on the weekend. Knowing that he could not return the bicycle until Monday, the man told the friend that he would return the bicycle on Sunday. The man never returned the friend's bicycle and never contacted the friend again for any reason. If the man is arrested and charged with larceny of the friend's bicycle, will he be convicted?

A. Yes because the man first lawfully obtained possession of property, then later converted it unlawfully.

B. Yes because the man never returned the bicycle.

C. No because the friend gave possession of the bicycle to the man voluntarily.

D. No because the actus reas and mens rea did not concur at the same time.

38. A famous comedian was scheduled to appear at a comedy club. Five days before his scheduled appearance, the comedian was struck on the head and suffered amnesia. The comedian's doctor advised the owner of the club that the comedian would not be able to perform because he had forgotten his entire act.

The owner of the club immediately overnight mailed a letter to another comedian, stating:

"I had a comedian scheduled to perform, but he is no longer able to do so. I have nobody to replace him. I need a comedy act right away and will pay your normal appearance fee. Be here by Sunday, so that I can see a dry run of your act before opening curtain.

signed . . . Club Owner"

The second comedian received the letter and sent the owner of the club a reply by way of telegram stating, "Thanks, I've just ended an appearance at Las Vegas and currently have no other commitments, but I hope you provide me limousine service during my stay this time. Will arrive at the club Saturday morning. Sincerely, Comedian."

After the club owner had sent the letter, but before he received the second comedian's reply, the first comedian called the club owner and told the club owner that his memory had returned and would be performing his act as scheduled. The club owner then telephoned the second comedian and told him that the second comedian would not have to fill in for the first comedian because the first comedian's memory had returned.

The second comedian brings an action against the club owner, and the club owner raises the defense that there was no valid acceptance of the club owner's offer. Will the second comedian prevail?

A. Yes because the club owner did not revoke his offer by the same method with which he communicated the offer.

B. Yes because the second comedian sent a telegram stating his acceptance prior to the club owner's attempt to revoke the offer.

C. No because there was uncertainty in the salary term.

D. No because the second comedian's request for a limousine constituted a counteroffer, which the club owner was free to reject.

39. A man sent a letter to his best friend, offering to sell him his motorcycle. He sent an identical letter to his girlfriend, offering to sell her the same motorcycle.

Because the man sent the identical letter to his best friend and his girlfriend, and he only had one motorcycle to sell, the man claims that the letter cannot be construed by the girlfriend to be an offer. Will he prevail on this argument?

A. No, if the girlfriend was unaware of the man's mailing of an identical letter to his best friend.

B. No, if the girlfriend and the best friend both insist purchasing the motorcycle.

C. Yes because the man's intent was to sell the motorcycle to only one person.

D. Yes because the man, as offeror, is the master of his offer.

40. A woman hired a painter to paint her house, at a rate of $15,000, as part of the renovations that she was having done on the house. Two weeks before work was to begin, a person who was installing windows had to raise his prices unexpectedly from $20,000 to $25,000. As a result, the woman told the painter that she could only pay him $2,500 for the painting job. The painter refused to do the work for less than $15,000.00. How much may the painter recover from the woman?

A. $25,000.00, plus any expected profits.

B. $15,000.00, plus any expected profits offset by the money he saved by not having to perform the contract.

C. $12,500.00, plus any expected profits.

D. $0.

41. A concert hall owner sent an offer to an opera singer, stating that he would like her to perform the following Saturday night, and that she should let him know if she could come for a dress rehearsal on Friday. The opera singer arrived at the concert hall on Saturday night, after receiving the letter. She was unaware that an identical letter had been sent to another opera singer and did not notify the concert hall owner in advance of her arrival at the concert hall of her intentions to perform. The concert hall owner said, "You're too little too late. The second opera singer is better than you, and she arrived last night, so she'll be performing at the concert hall. I only sent the letter to you because I was in a bind, and I didn't expect you to come without letting me know." Who will prevail if the opera singer sues the concert hall owner?

A. The concert hall owner because a return promise is the only valid method of accepting an offer.

B. The concert hall owner because a reasonable interpretation of his letter would be that the opera singer was required to accept by way of a timely return promise.

C. The opera singer because the concert hall owner's letter could be reasonably interpreted to invite acceptance by performance or return promise.

D. The opera singer because there was no revocation by the concert hall owner before the opera singer had commenced performance.

42. A woman was scheduled for a root canal with her dentist. On the day that the procedure was to occur, the dentist took ill. After the assistant administered the anesthesia, the woman became very groggy and did not realize that a different dentist had performed her root canal. Even though the woman suffered no injuries, she sued the second dentist. Who will prevail?

A. The second dentist, unless the woman establishes that the original dentist was negligent in substituting him for this procedure.

B. The second dentist because he was not responsible, since the first dentist became ill.

C. The woman, for battery.

D. The woman, for negligence, under the doctrine of res ipsa loquitur.

43. A man visited an outpatient clinic for a rhinoplasty (nose job) to be performed by a particular doctor. After he was given general anesthesia and became unconscious, the doctor performed a vasectomy instead. The vasectomy was performed because an unidentified employee of the clinic mixed up the man's chart with the chart of another patient. The mistake was not discovered until after the wrong procedure to the man was completed. When he woke up, the man was upset to discover that his nose looked exactly the same, but other parts of his body no longer functioned as they used to.

If the man asserts a personal injury claim against the clinic, who will prevail?

A. The clinic, unless the man can establish vicarious liability for the doctor's conduct.

B. The clinic because it is without fault.

C. The man, for battery.

D. The man, for negligence, under the doctrine of res ipsa loquitur.

44. A man took his violin to a violin shop to have the instrument restrung. After the work was completed, the shop's owner confused it with another instrument he had for sale, and the man's instrument was sold to a woman for $400.00. The woman believed the violin was owned

by shop's owner at the time of her purchase. When the man returned to pick up his violin, the shop's owner realized his mistake. If the man sues the shop's owner and the woman for conversion, the man will be successful against:

A. The woman only, due to her negligence in failing to verify ownership prior to her purchase.

B. The woman only because the act of the shop's owner is considered mere intermeddling with the violin.

C. The shop's owner only because the shop's owner was in the best position to authenticate ownership of the man's violin.

D. The shop's owner and the woman because they both have exercised dominion over the violin.

45. A man was traveling cross-country in his new motor home. Near the end of the first day of his trip, he came across a woman, who told him that her car had broken down and that she needed a ride. Not believing that the woman would reimburse him for the expense, the man refused to give her a ride to the nearest town, which was fifty miles away. The woman, therefore, had to walk. She almost died from exhaustion and hunger while walking to the town and required hospitalization for several weeks, in order to recover. If the woman sues the man to recover for her injuries and damages, who will prevail?

A. The man, if he reasonably believed that the woman would not reimburse him for the expense of driving her to town.

B. The man, unless there was a special relationship between him and the woman.

C. The woman, if the likelihood of harm to her was greater than the likelihood that she would not reimburse the man.

D. The woman, if she would not have been injured "but for" the man's refusal to drive her to town.

46. A woman is caught stealing a wallet from the pocket of an off-duty police officer. At time of trial on the charge of larceny, the woman testifies that she had been so intoxicated at the time she took the wallet that she could not have formed the intent to commit the crime. When the members of the jury are instructed on the burden of proof, they should be advised that:

A. The prosecution must establish beyond a reasonable doubt that the woman had the capacity to form the necessary intent.

B. The prosecution must establish by clear and convincing evidence that the woman had the capacity to form the necessary intent.

C. The defendant must establish diminished capacity by a preponderance of the evidence.

D. The defendant must establish diminished capacity by clear and convincing evidence.

47. On January 1, a woman entered into a written contract to buy a man's house for $2.5 million. The woman requested to delay the closing of the sale until March 15, at which time payment was to be made in exchange for the deed to the property.

On February 15, the man conveyed the house to his uncle. The woman now wants to take advantage of the man's conveyance to his uncle as a reason to get out of her contract with the man so that she can buy a much more modest home. Is the woman still obligated to perform her contract with the man?

A. Yes because the man could still purchase the property back from his uncle and be able to provide the deed to the woman on March 15.

B. Yes because the man is not due to perform until March 15, which means there is no breach until such date, and the woman must remain ready to perform on the contract until then.

C. No, if the man did not protect the woman's rights as part of the sale of the house.

D. No, but the woman must demand assurance from the man that he will perform on March 15.

48. On March 1, a woman entered a contract with a man to sell him her car. Delivery and payment of the purchase price were to occur on April 1. Instead, on March 15, the woman told the man she no longer intended to sell her car and that she would not go through with the sale on April 1. May the man assert an action for breach of contract on March 15?

A. Yes because the woman's statement was a repudiation of the contract, which permits the immediate filing of litigation by the man.

B. Yes, but only if the woman has contracted with a new buyer of the car.

C. No because the woman is not obligated to perform until April 1, so there can be no breach until that date.

D. No because the woman might retract her repudiation before April 1.

49. On December 25, a man entered into a contract with a woman for the woman to sell him her television set for $4,000. On December 25, the man arrived at the woman's home to get the television set. The woman, however, refused to part with the television set because it had been a Christmas gift the previous year from her husband. May the man bring an immediate action against the woman to recover for breach of contract?

    A. No because he must make a formal written demand for the woman's compliance with the contract terms.

    B. Yes, but the man must have paid the $4,000 on December 25.

    C. Yes, if the man tendered payment of the $4,000 on December 25.

    D. Yes, whether or not the man either tendered payment or actually paid the $4,000 on December 25.

50. An assassin obtained a job as a security guard in an office building because he knew that his intended target worked in the building. After determining the target's schedule, the assassin intended to kill the target as he left work one day. The assassin set up an ambush and fired his gun at the target, missing him and striking a passerby, but only causing a slight injury to him. Is the assassin guilty of attempted murder of the passerby?

    A. Yes because the assassin had the requisite malice aforethought and premeditation.

    B. Yes because the assassin attempted to kill the target.

    C. No because the assassin did not intend to kill the passerby.

    D. No because the passerby received only a slight injury.

51. A woman with poor vision mistakenly believed that a man was about to strike her with a knife. In fact, he was pointing a pen at her, intending to give it to her to write something down. The woman strikes the man on the head. Is she guilty of battery upon the man?

    A. Yes because the man had not committed any crime.

    B. Yes because she intentionally beat up the man.

    C. No, if the woman reasonably believed that the man was attempting to kill her.

    D. No because she her poor vision is a valid defense.

52. A man was involved in a motor vehicle accident with a truck, as a result of the man's negligence. The property damage

to the truck cost $10,000.00 to repair. At the time the truck's owner hired a collection agency to collect money for the property damage from the man, the president of the collection agency intended to use the money to extinguish a joint debt of the president of the collection agency and the collection agency that was incurred to purchase computers for the collection agency. An employee of the collection agency collected the $10,000.00, which was used by the president to extinguish the joint debt, less the collection agency's fees for collecting the money from the man. The president intended to pay the truck's owner when the president returned from his vacation three weeks later.

What, if any, theft crime was committed by the president of the collection agency?

A. No crime because the employee of the collection agency who collected the money was an innocent agent of the collection agency who did not have the necessary mens rea to commit a crime.

B. False pretenses from the man because the president of the collection agency intended to use the money for his own benefit at the time it was collected from the man.

C. Embezzlement from the truck's owner because the truck's owner entrusted his money to the collection agency.

D. Larceny from the truck's owner because the president of the collection agency intended to keep the money for his own use at the time it was collected from the man.

53. A board of directors of a big company told all officers and employees of the company to do whatever was necessary to "kill the competition." One night, the president of the company spotted the president of the company's largest competitor in a parking lot. In order to literally "kill the competition," the president of the first company pulled out a knife and beheaded the president of the competing company, which resulted in the death of the latter. If the president of the first company is convicted of murder, can the big company also be convicted of the same crime?

A. No because the company, as a corporation, is a fictitious business entity that cannot be sent to prison.

B. No because a corporation cannot form the specific intent necessary for conviction.

C. No, unless there is a contemporaneous conviction of the company's president for the same offense.

D. Yes because the crime was committed by the company's president.

54. A man hired an accountant to prepare his federal tax return. The accountant told the man that he could deduct certain business expenses from the operation of his bar, although she knew her advice was incorrect. The man signed and filed the erroneous tax return with the Internal Revenue Service. If the U.S. Attorney prosecutes the man for willful income tax evasion, does he have a valid defense for following his tax accountant's advice?

   A. No, if the accountant knew his advice was erroneous.

   B. Yes because the man only signed and filed the tax return.

   C. Yes because the income tax return was prepared by the man's tax accountant.

   D. Yes, if the man had a reasonable and good faith reliance upon the accountant's advice.

55. A man was hiking in the wilderness in the mountains near his home when he found a woman, apparently injured from exposure to the elements. He picked her up and carried her several miles before coming upon a hiker, who was using a cellular telephone to talk to his friends. The man asked the hiker to get off the phone and call emergency services. When the hiker refused, the man drew his knife and threatened to harm the hiker, unless the hiker agreed to let the man use the telephone. The hiker immediately hung up and permitted the man to call for assistance. The man is now being prosecuted for assault with a deadly weapon. Did the man have any privilege to threaten the hiker with harm?

   A. No, if the man did not know the woman.

   B. No, unless there was a special statute in the jurisdiction establishing such privilege.

   C. Yes because the man was privileged to use deadly force to rescue the woman, if necessary to save the woman's life.

   D. Yes because the man was privileged to threaten the use of deadly force, if reasonably necessary to save the woman's life.

56. A couple decided to purchase a new home. The couple signed a written contract to buy a particular home for $300,000.00 from a developer. The contract stated that the couple would purchase the home "as long as they are able sell their present home for $175,000.00 cash within the next 90 days."

Because the home the couple intended to purchase was a bargain price and because the developer decided against possibly waiting for 90 days to receive the sale proceeds, the developer told the couple that the sale was off the following day – before the couple had even put the present home up for sale. The couple filed a lawsuit against the developer for breach of contract, but the developer raised the defense that there was no consideration for the contract. Will the developer be successful with this defense?

A. No because the developer's promise to sell the new home was consideration for the couple's promise to sell the present home.

B. No because within the couple's promise to buy the home from the developer is a condition that the couple make a good faith effort to find a buyer for the present home.

C. Yes because the couple's promise to sell the present home within 90 days was not within the developer's nor the couple's control.

D. Yes because the couple had not changed its position in reliance on the developer's promise to sell.

57. A woman decided to move out-of-state and put her car up for sale, since she would not be needing it in the new city. She entered into a contract with a man to sell him the car for a set price the following Wednesday on the condition that the man obtain a bank loan by the close of business the following Tuesday (the day before the sale was to be finalized). On Wednesday, the man told the woman that he would not be purchasing her car because he had never contacted the bank to apply for the loan. The woman sued the man for breach of contract. Who will prevail?

A. The woman because the condition that the man obtain a bank loan was excused by his refusal to make it occur.

B. The woman because the term that the man obtain a bank loan was not a condition but a promise.

C. The man because the condition that he obtain a bank loan at the stated terms did not occur.

D. The man because he did not make any promise to actually obtain a bank loan.

58. A man entered into an employment contract with a company. During negotiations, the man and the company agreed upon a yearly salary for the man, along with certain other perks, including a gym membership. When the final contract was signed, there was no mention of the gym membership in the written contract. The man refused to begin work until he was given the gym membership. If the company sues

the man for breach of contract, and the man attempts to present evidence of the oral discussions regarding the gym membership during negotiations, and the company objects on the grounds of the Parol Evidence Rule, what is the man's best argument against the use of the Parol Evidence Rule to prevent introduction of the oral discussions regarding the gym membership?

A. The evidence was provided to show a modification of the written contract.

B. The evidence would be offered to clear up an ambiguity in the written contract.

C. Evidence of an oral agreement may be offered to establish an oral condition to an integrated written contract.

D. The written contract was not fully integrated.

59. One afternoon, a woman was jogging with her dog. Suddenly, the dog saw another big dog and lunged, causing the woman to drop the leash. Before the woman could pick up the leash, the dog spotted a passerby and bit him. If the passerby sues the woman for his injuries, who will prevail?

A. The woman, unless the dog had previously displayed a propensity to bite.

B. The woman, unless she was negligent in not preventing the dog's escape.

C. The passerby because he was bitten by the woman's dog.

D. The passerby because the dog escaped from the woman's control.

60. A state law requires that all vehicles that travel into areas that potentially have large snow falls be equipped with chains. One bright, sunny day when there was no snow fall, a woman was driving to the mountains and did not have chains on her vehicle. A tire blew out, and the car went off the road, striking and killing a pedestrian who was walking along the mountain road. If the pedestrian's estate sues the woman in negligence for her violation of the state law, who will prevail?

A. The woman because the tire blowout was an Act of God.

B. The woman because the harm that occurred to the pedestrian was not within the statutory purpose under these facts.

C. The estate because of the woman's violation of the statute.

D. The estate because, if she had had chains on her tires, they would not have blown out.

61. A police detective received a reliable tip that a well-known criminal was about to set up an operation in the city. In the past, this criminal had set up legitimate valet parking businesses, only to steal the owners' cars some time later. According to the tip, the criminal had set up a new valet parking service.

The police detective went to the parking business in uniform and left his private vehicle with the criminal. When he returned to pick up his vehicle, both the vehicle and the criminal were gone. The police detective was able to find and arrest the criminal using the vehicle's Global Positioning System (GPS). The police detective arrested the criminal for auto theft.

If the criminal claims the defense of entrapment, will he succeed?

A. No because the criminal's business was an ongoing criminal enterprise.

B. No because the criminal was predisposed to take the vehicle.

C. Yes because the police detective was in uniform.

D. Yes because it is not possible to steal a police officer's car.

62. An undercover police officer approached a known drug dealer and asked him how much it would cost to purchase a kilo of heroin. Even though the drug dealer thought that the undercover police officer might be a cop, he quoted a price and offered to sell the heroin to the undercover police officer. The drug dealer was immediately arrested and charged with attempt to distribute heroin. If the drug dealer claims the defense of entrapment under these facts, will he succeed?

A. No because the drug dealer agreed to sell the heroin.

B. Yes because the drug dealer's quote of a price constitutes an acceptance and consideration for the police officer's offer to purchase the heroin.

C. No because confidence in the police force would otherwise be undermined.

D. Yes because the violation of the drug dealer's due process rights, however slight, underlies the defense.

63. A man went into a restaurant one night to have dinner. At the door, he was requested to check his coat, obtaining a ticket in return. The man's coat, while not very valuable, had a lot of sentimental value to him. The ticket, which was read by the man, disclaimed liability for any loss or damage to the coat. By the time he had finished his dinner, the man decided to leave for home. When the man presented the ticket and requested his coat, the coat could not be located

by the coat clerk. If the man brings a conversion action against the restaurant, who will prevail?

A. The restaurant because the express disclaimer of liability resulted in a waiver of the man's rights.

B. The restaurant, if its method of coat check operations maintained reasonable procedures to prevent losses or theft of the checked coats.

C. The man, since the restaurant was unable to return the man's coat.

D. The man, unless there was no intrinsic value in the coat.

64. A five-year-old child movie star was to be a guest on a late night talk show. The movie star was brought to the studio by the movie star's mother. The host of the talk show requested that the movie star make his entrance by being lowered from the ceiling while inside a large cage and then stepping onto the set when the cage reached the ground. As the movie star was making his entrance, the cage rapidly dropped to the ground, injuring him.

The host quickly removed the movie star from the cage and telephoned for emergency medical care. The movie star brought an action for personal injury, through his guardian ad litem, against the host.

Will the movie star prevail against the host?

A. No because it was the primary duty of the movie star's mother to supervise him.

B. No, unless the host failed to exercise reasonable care removing the movie star from the cage.

C. Yes because the host had a nondelegable duty to make the cage safe.

D. Yes, because the movie star was a business invitee of the premises.

65. A magician was performing a trick on stage in which he sawed a person in half, only to have the person emerge, unharmed. The magician called for a volunteer and placed the volunteer in a wood box. The magician proceeded to saw the volunteer in half. However, to his horror, the volunteer remained sawed in half, and when he opened the box, the stage was filled with blood. The volunteer died. His estate brought an action against the manufacturer of the saw. Through discovery, it was revealed that the saw was improperly manufactured, which resulted in the volunteer really being sawed in half. On which theory or theories will the estate prevail against the manufacturer of the saw?

A. Negligence only.

B. Strict products liability only.

C. Strict products liability and strict liability for abnormally dangerous condition.

D. Negligence and strict products liability.

66. A woman drove her car in excess of the speed limit, causing her car to collide with a limousine. A passenger in the limousine was a famous tennis player. The tennis player suffered from a congenital bone defect (unknown to him) that rendered his skeleton susceptible to fracture. As a result of his congenital defect, the accident rendered him a paraplegic, which would not have occurred if he did not have the bone defect. As a result of the accident, the tennis player was unable to play in a match for which he was to be paid $2 million had he not become a paraplegic.

Will the tennis player be entitled to recover the $2 million as damages, if he sues the woman and she is found liable?

A. Yes, unless the tennis player's inability to play in the match was the result of an unforeseeable injury.

B. Yes, if the $2 million loss of income was the result of his injuries.

C. No because, as a "thin skull" plaintiff, the tennis player's loss of earnings must be reduced to reflect the probability of a shortened career.

D. No because the tennis player's congenital defect was a preexisting condition.

67. A man was shot by two hunters who mistakenly thought he was a deer. He sustained injuries, but survived. The man sued the two hunters and obtained a judgment against both of them. If one hunter pays the entire judgment, is that hunter entitled to recover any portion of the amount paid from the second hunter?

A. Yes because their guns were defectively manufactured.

B. Yes because both hunters were actively negligent.

C. Yes because, under the Hunter's Rule, hunters are always entitled to indemnification for the torts of other hunters, since their duties are non-delegable.

D. No because a plaintiff may choose against which, if any, of the "deep pocket" defendants he wants to proceed.

68. A woman and a man decided to steal several famous art works from a museum. The woman told the man that

she would have nothing to do with the actual heist, but would take him away on her boat once the job was completed. She told the man that she could earn her money legitimately this way, and would charge $10,000.00 for the service, payable at time of departure. The man stole the art works, immediately fencing one Renaissance master painting for $10,000.00 and using the money to pay for his passage on the woman's boat. Has the woman committed any crime?

A. Yes, as a principal in the first degree.

B. Yes, as a principal in the second degree.

C. Yes, as an accessory after the fact.

D. No because she did not participate in any stage of committing the theft.

69. A man receives a telephone call, telling him that his daughter has been taken hostage and that she will be killed unless the man goes to a bank, releases a can of toxic gas, and steals all the cash in a teller's cash drawer. The man had no reason to believe that the threat was not true, since his daughter had been missing since early that morning.

That afternoon, the man went to the bank with the toxic gas and threatened to release it, unless he was handed all the cash in the teller's cash drawer. A security guard at the bank drew his gun and pointed it at the man. The man gave the canister containing the gas to the security guard and was placed in custody until the police arrived to arrest him. The man is charged with robbery. He will be found:

A. Guilty because he intended to obtain the money.

B. Guilty because the threat of harm was to third parties.

C. Not guilty because he did not complete the robbery.

D. Not guilty because he was threatened with harm to a member of his family.

70. A man attempted to steal a woman's purse by putting a gun to her back. Before the man was able to take the purse, the woman, who happened to be a black belt in jiu-jitsu, got the man in a strangle hold and retrieved the gun. She held the man until the police came to arrest him. The man was charged with attempted robbery. He will be found:

A. Guilty because had the specific intent to commit robbery and took a significant step in furtherance of the crime.

B. Guilty because the woman, as a black belt, was not really in any danger.

C. Not guilty because the man never actually committed the act of robbery.

D. Not guilty, if the man was a brown belt in jiu-jitsu.

71. One morning, while on her way to work, a woman stopped at a fast food restaurant's drive-thru window to buy breakfast. After paying for her order, the cashier gave her a bag containing her food. As she drove away, the woman opened the bag and found not only her meal, but also, cash that was supposed to be deposited in the bank. The woman drove off without returning the money. What crime, if any, did the woman commit?

   A. Larceny.

   B. Larceny by trick.

   C. Embezzlement.

   D. None of the above.

72. A man purchased a home. Adjacent to his home was a sushi bar. In order to increase business, the owner of the sushi bar set up a Karaoke machine (which amplified both recorded music and the singer's voice) and marketed the Karaoke as "fabulous family entertainment."

The Karaoke resulted in bringing in a lot of business for the sushi bar. Although there were now long waits and large crowds at the sushi bar, it was the loud, off-key howling of the Karaoke singers that disrupted the man's solitude into the late hours each night.

Prior to the sushi bar's offering of the Karaoke, a local ordinance was passed, prohibiting amplified music in restaurants and bars within town limits. The man asked the owner of the sushi bar to cease the "entertainment." The owner refused to get rid of the Karaoke machine. If the man files a nuisance action against the sushi bar, will he prevail?

   A. Yes because the sushi bar is violating the ordinance.

   B. Yes because the man is suffering a substantial and unreasonable harm in the use and enjoyment of his land.

   C. No because the man assumed the risk of being annoyed by the operation of the sushi bar by coming to the nuisance.

   D. No, unless the annoying sounds are accompanied by trespass by the sushi bar's patrons.

73. A woman decided to scare her ex-boyfriend by shooting a gun near his head, but not actually striking him. One night, she spotted her ex-boyfriend in a park and saw her chance. She pulled out her gun and approached him. While he stood motionless, staring at the gun, she fired. As planned, the bullet did not strike her ex-boyfriend. However, the

bullet did knock his gym bag out of his hand. Which crimes did the woman commit?

A. Attempted murder, assault with a deadly weapon, and battery.

B. Attempted murder and assault with a deadly weapon.

C. Assault with a deadly weapon, and battery.

D. Battery.

74. After failing to obtain a promotion at work, a man was distraught when a recently hired woman got the very same promotion for which he had been working.

The next day, he saw the woman walking down the street. He immediately got into his car and drove straight at her, striking and killing her.

What is the most serious crime of which the man can be convicted?

A. Involuntary manslaughter.

B. Voluntary manslaughter.

C. Second-degree murder.

D. First-degree murder.

75. In a bar one night, a man stabbed a woman in the stomach because she would not have sexual relations with him. Unknown to him, the woman was pregnant. Although the woman survived, the fetus did not. Will the man be found guilty if charged with homicide of the fetus?

A. Yes, of first-degree murder since he intended to kill the woman.

B. Yes, of involuntary manslaughter based upon the transferred intent doctrine.

C. Yes, of first-degree murder since confirmation of the woman's pregnancy is medically feasible.

D. No because a fetus is not a living "human being."

76. An adult woman decided to sell the car she had owned since her sixteenth birthday. She placed an ad for the sale of the car online. A man responded and met her to take the car for a test drive. He noticed that the car bounced and vibrated severely at freeway speeds, but was told by the woman that the vibration merely meant that the tires needed to be balanced. What the woman failed to tell the man (and which was known to the woman) was that the vibration was from worn shocks and a bent frame, which were costly to repair.

Based on the facts available to him, the man agreed to buy the car for $2,500 and signed an agreement that, in part, stated that he would pay the woman and pick up the car the following Friday. In the meantime, the woman allowed the man

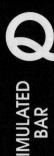

to take the car to a car repair shop for tire balancing. It was at this time that the man learned the true nature and cost of the problem. He drove the car back to the woman's house and told her that he would not go through with the purchase of the car.

If the woman sues the man for breach of contract because the man refused to follow through with the purchase, will she prevail?

- A. Yes because only the woman can void the contract based upon her infancy.
- B. Yes because the man's reliance on the woman's representations were unreasonable.
- C. No because the contract is voidable due to the woman's incapacity to contract.
- D. No because the woman materially misrepresented the car's condition.

77. A sixteen-year-old boy entered into a signed, written contract with a dealership to purchase a motorcycle. He was to pick up the motorcycle the following day and pay for it. When the boy told his parents what he was planning to do, they forbade him to follow through with the contract. The boy told the dealership that he could not purchase the motorcycle. The dealership sued the boy for breach of contract. Will the dealership prevail?

- A. Yes, if the dealership, in reliance on the contract with the boy, did not sell the motorcycle to another customer.
- B. Yes because the boy may not avoid the contract, since he signed it.
- C. No because the boy may avoid the contract because he is a minor.
- D. No because contracts with minors are null and void.

78. A baker entered into an oral contract with a cake supplier for 400 cakes, for $2,000. The transcriber mistakenly wrote down "40 cakes" instead of "400 cakes." The baker paid the supplier the $2,000, but only received 40 cakes from the supplier. As a result, the baker was short 360 cakes. The baker then asked the supplier to immediately send the additional cakes. The supplier refused, on the grounds that the written contract only said "40 cakes." The baker sued the supplier for specific performance. The supplier claimed that the baker could not bring in evidence of the oral agreement for 400 cakes, due to the Parol Evidence Rule. Who will prevail?

- A. The baker because the Parol Evidence Rule does not bar evidence that the baker actually intended to purchase 400 cakes.

B. The baker because the baker is not responsible for the transcription mistake.

C. The supplier because the Parol Evidence Rule prohibits evidence of oral negotiations prior to the signing of the written contract.

D. The supplier, if $2,000 was not a reasonable price for just 40 cakes.

79. A man entered into an oral contract with a computer dealer to purchase a mid-range laptop computer. Due to a transcription error, however, the written contract listed the most expensive laptop computer that the dealer had in stock, but at the same price as the mid-range laptop computer. The man was aware of the transcription error, but said nothing. He and the dealer then signed the written contract. Later, before shipping the computer, the dealer noticed the mistake and refused to ship the more expensive laptop computer. The man sued the dealer for breach of contract. Who will prevail?

A. The man because the Parol Evidence Rule bars evidence of the misidentification of the laptop computer that the dealer had put up for sale.

B. The man because the computer dealer was unaware of the unilateral mistake.

C. The computer dealer because there was no agreement to sell the more expensive laptop computer to the man.

D. The computer dealer because there was a mutual mistake.

80. Seller transferred title to his vacant lot in Sunny Ville to Buyer for $78,000. Buyer purchased land on the representation made by Seller that the property was unencumbered, except for a mortgage for $15,000. However, Seller did not disclose that the property was encumbered by an easement, which restricted the use of the land. The easement will not interfere with the use Buyer intends for the land. The lot subject to the encumbrance is worth $93,000, but without the encumbrance the worth is $98,000. If Buyer asserts a claim against Seller for damages, will Buyer prevail?

A. Yes because the land is worth $98,000 without the encumbrance.

B. Yes, unless Buyer reasonably could have discovered the easement against the property.

C. No because Buyer can make full use of the land as intended.

D. No, if the reasonable value of the property is $93,000.

81. A man was walking past his neighbor's house when he noticed that there was a fire in the house. The neighbor had been smoking a cigarette and had fallen asleep, which caused the fire. The man did not know if anybody was in the house at the time, but he attempted to rush into the house to save anybody who might be inside. In the process, he tripped over the neighbor's son's tricycle and sustained injury. If the man sues the neighbor on a negligence theory, will he prevail?

    A. Yes because of the Good Samaritan Rule.

    B. Yes because the man's conduct in attempting to put out the fire was foreseeable.

    C. No because the injury to the man was not a foreseeable risk posed by the neighbor's negligence.

    D. No because of the child's intervening negligence.

82. A woman had car trouble, and her car stalled out on a bridge. The man driving behind her did not have time to stop his vehicle before hitting the woman's car. The woman sustained injuries. If she sues the man on a negligence theory, and the man raises the affirmative defense of contributory negligence, which facts would be relevant in determining whether the man will prevail on his affirmative defense?

    A. Whether the woman had maintained her car properly and whether the woman was speeding before her car stalled.

    B. Whether the man had a last clear chance of avoiding the accident.

    C. Whether the woman was speeding before her car stalled.

    D. Whether the woman had maintained her car properly, whether the man had a last clear chance of avoiding the accident, and whether the woman was speeding before her car stalled.

83. A woman was attempting to purchase a cantaloupe at her local grocery store. As she reached for the cantaloupe, she slipped on a greasy substance that was on the floor. The woman did not see the substance before she fell. She sustained a broken arm as a result of the fall. If the woman sues the grocery store on a negligence theory, will the woman prevail in her action?

    A. No because the woman was not an invitee of the grocery store when she fell.

    B. No, if a customer of the grocery store spilled the grease moments before the woman's fall.

    C. Yes because the owner or operator of premises has the duty to inspect and correct defects thereon.

D. Yes because the risk of having spilled grease on the floor is outweighed by the utility of having frequent inspections of the premises.

84. A man was at the airport, rushing to get on a flight. He slipped and fell on some crushed ice that was on the floor on the way to the gate. The man sustained a broken ankle as a result of the fall. If he sues the airport on a negligence theory for failure to clean up the crushed ice and the airport asserts that the man assumed the risk of injury, will the man prevail in his action?

A. No, if the man saw the crushed ice.

B. No, if the man was a minor.

C. Yes, if the man should have seen the crushed ice.

D. Yes, if the man was in a hurry.

85. A man intended to hire a particular private investigator to break and enter the local prosecutor's office and recover a handgun that was being used as evidence in a murder trial. The man left a note intended for the intended private investigator, stating that he would have to break and enter the prosecutor's office and recover the handgun, but that care should be taken during the job to avoid detection by, and injury to, anybody who might discover the break-in activity. Instead of being found by the intended private investigator, the note was found by a rookie private investigator, who thought the note was intended for him. That evening, the rookie broke into the prosecutor's office to retrieve the gun.

Is the man guilty of soliciting the rookie to perform an unlawful act?

A. No because he did not intend that the rookie perform the act.

B. No, unless the rookie was reasonable in believing the note was intended for him.

C. Yes because the man asked that evidence from a murder trial be recovered.

D. Yes because the rookie performed the act as requested in the note.

86. A woman telephoned her boyfriend on his cell phone number to confirm that he had received a note that she had left for him in his office in which she asked him to obtain a handgun to rob a local bank and split the proceeds with her. The boyfriend told the woman that he had not been to his office, but based on their discussion the previous night, he would obtain handgun the following day and rob the bank, as she had stated in her note. Is the woman guilty of soliciting

her boyfriend to perform an unlawful act?

A. No because the boyfriend did not receive the note.

B. No because the boyfriend did not understand her instructions on the cell phone.

C. Yes, when the woman told her boyfriend over the telephone that she wanted him to rob a bank.

D. Yes because the woman's note was intended for the boyfriend.

87. A law student and his girlfriend decided to break into a professor's office and steal the professor's notes to help the student prepare for his examination. The following night, the law student and his girlfriend asked the girlfriend's mother to drive them to the campus, so that they could attend a late-night lecture there. When they got to the campus, the law student and his girlfriend broke into the professor's office, but were apprehended by the campus police. A short time later, the campus police also arrested the mother, who was waiting in her car in the campus parking lot. Was there a conspiracy to commit breaking and entering?

A. Yes, between the law student and the girlfriend's mother.

B. Yes, between the girlfriend and the law student.

C. Yes, between the law student, the girlfriend, and the girlfriend's mother.

D. No.

88. A woman badly in need of money asked her boyfriend to break into the woman's mother's house and steal the mother's jewelry, which the woman planned to sell to make some money. The boyfriend agreed and broke into the mother's home one night. He had expected that the home would be empty, as the woman had told him, but he was surprised to find the mother sitting at the dining room table. To make sure that there were no witnesses, he beheaded the mother and proceeded to steal her jewelry. May the woman be held criminally liable for the death of her mother?

A. No because the woman had told the boyfriend that no one would be home when he broke into the house.

B. No because the woman did not intend that anybody be killed during the break-in.

C. Yes because of Blackstone's Rule.

D. Yes because the woman's actions were the cause in fact of the boyfriend's presence at her mother's home.

89. A movie producer made a film that

purported that the Holocaust never occurred. In her review, a movie critic stated that the movie's premise was an intentional distortion of the truth, the producer's motives for making such propaganda were his bigotry and racism, and he was using the film as a springboard for his recently-announced candidacy for state congressman. Despite the critic's review, the film did very well at the box office. If the producer sues the critic for defamation, will he prevail?

A. No because the producer's film was doing very well.

B. No because the critic's review was merely an expression of her opinion.

C. No because the producer is a public figure.

D. No, unless the critic acted with reckless disregard of the truth.

90. In a recent article, an investigative reporter reported that the president of a national military defense company was being fired for his role in the manipulation of the company's stock for personal profit. In fact, he had left his position as president of the company to work for an organization dedicated to reversing environmental destruction that has occurred during the industrialization of the world during the 19th Century. If the former president files a defamation action against the reporter, will the former president prevail?

A. No, if the reporter used reasonable care in her investigation for the article on the former president.

B. No, if the reporter believed the article was true.

C. No, if the reporter promptly issued a retraction in the paper that reasonably would be seen by readers of the paper.

D. No, if the reporter did not intend ill will toward the former president.

91. A man placed the following advertisement on the local cable channel: "Special prices this weekend only. Furnish your home with our couches – $299.00." The man had no experience selling furniture, but was able to rent a temporary space in a vacant store located in the center of town, to display and sell the furniture.

A woman responded to the advertisement. When she arrived at the store, she saw three couches, one of which was of much higher quality than the other two. She handed the man $299.00 cash, telling him that she wanted the higher quality couch. The man refused to accept her money and told her she had chosen the couch with a price of $1,499.00. If the woman sues the man for breach of contract, who will prevail?

A. The man because $299.00 was not sufficient consideration for the couch.

B. The man because the advertisement did not constitute an offer.

C. The woman because she objectively manifested her intent to purchase the higher quality couch.

D. The woman because the man's advertisement was an offer that was accepted upon the woman's tender of the $299.00.

92. A woman agreed to purchase a used car for her son for $1,499.00, payment within seven days. The used car dealer confirmed the terms of sale by sending a remittance invoice to the woman, which was signed and dated the date the woman visited the dealership. The dealer also placed a "sold" sign on the car. Although the woman received the invoice, she had a fight with her son and decided not to get a car for him, so she discarded the document and called the dealer and told him that she had changed her mind. The dealer sued the woman for breach of contract, and the woman raised the Statute of Frauds as a defense. Will she prevail?

A. No because the remittance invoice signed by the dealer satisfies the Statute of Frauds writing requirement.

B. No because the woman failed to object to the terms of the sale as set forth in the invoice.

C. Yes because the woman is not a merchant and there is no writing signed by her.

D. Yes because the dealer's writing was not contemporaneous with the agreement, thereby permitting fraud or mistake to enter into the writing.

93. A woman and a man made an offer on a home for $200,000. The seller had originally purchased the home five years before for $300,000. The real estate agent presented the offer to the seller, who promptly accepted because of the terrible housing market. Closing was set for the following month. The seller immediately had the real estate agent take the home off the market. Midway through the month, the woman and the man decided that they could not afford the home. They called the real estate agent to withdraw their offer. The real estate agent informed the seller, who sued the woman and the man for breach of contract. The woman and the man asserted the defense that there was no consideration for the offer. Will this defense be successful?

A. No because the seller detrimentally relied when he had the real estate agent take the house off the market, thereby restricting it from further sale.

B. No because the seller's promise to convey the home was sufficient consideration.

C. Yes because the agreement is unenforceable at the price of $200,000 for a home worth more than this amount of money.

D. Yes because the seller did not change his position in reliance on the offer from the woman and the man to pay $200,000.

94. A retailer entered into a contract with a designer from a foreign country. The designer was to supply the retailer with 1,000 fine vases at $500,000 each. Delivery was to occur on October 1. There was a civil war going on in that country at the time. On September 15, the United States Congress passed a law (which the President signed the same day), stating that it was illegal to import goods from that country. What are the rights of the contracting parties on September 15?

    A. The designer is in breach for his inability to tender the vases.

    B. The retailer will be entitled to the benefit of the bargain damages from the designer in the amount of $500,000.

    C. The designer is entitled to the purchase price, but the retailer is not entitled to the vases because of the embargo (it is illegal to import from this particular country).

    D. The designer is excused from tendering the vases, and the retailer is not obligated to pay the purchase price.

95. A woman was severely injured when her vehicle was struck from behind by another vehicle. There were several witnesses to the accident. One witness stated that the woman stopped her vehicle in the middle of the road for no reason at all. Another witness stated that the vehicle that struck the woman's vehicle was speeding. The vehicle that hit the woman's vehicle was driven by a man. The woman sues the man and demands $50,000 in medical bills, lost wages, and pain and suffering. The man believes that the woman's demand is too high in light of the fact that different witnesses believe that either the man or the woman was negligent in the operation of their respective vehicles. However, wanting to avoid litigation, the man offers $20,000 as a settlement offer, which the woman accepts. The man then refuses to pay the $20,000. If the woman institutes an action against the man for $20,000, what result?

    A. The man will prevail because the woman's claim was based on evidence that directly conflicts with the man's evidence, and the woman has the burden of proof on the issue of liability.

B. The man will prevail because an executory contract is not enforceable as an accord and satisfaction.

C. The woman will prevail because the settlement agreement was enforceable as a compromise of a disputed claim.

D. The woman will prevail because tort liability is enforceable without consideration.

96. A piano teacher and her student had a disagreement about how much money was owed to the teacher for piano lessons. The teacher believed that the student owed her $1,000 and filed a lawsuit against the student for $1,000. The student believed that the lessons were useless, but to avoid going to trial, offered to pay the teacher $500. The teacher accepted the settlement offer. The student then refused to pay the $500 because she believed that the lessons were useless and that, as a result, she should not have to pay the teacher anything. The teacher then sued the student for the original $1,000. The student defended on the grounds that her obligation to pay $500 in settlement replaced any liability that may be proven-up at trial. Will the student's defense succeed?

A. No because the student's promise to pay $500 in settlement was void ab initio.

B. No because the teacher had the option of suing on the settlement agreement or amount of the money alleged in her original complaint.

C. No because the settlement agreement was made in compromise of a disputed claim.

D. No because the settlement agreement was enforceable without consideration.

97. A museum administrator sued a woman for allegedly drawing a mustache and beard on a famous painting. The woman states that someone else did this. A witness came forward to support the museum's account of the facts. To avoid litigation, the parties entered into a settlement agreement. After the settlement agreement was entered into, the witness admitted to the woman that he made up his story, but that the museum administrator did not know that he had done so. The museum administrator had already dismissed his complaint because of the settlement agreement. The woman then refused to pay the museum the settlement amount. If the museum administrator sues the woman for the woman's refusal to pay the settlement amount, who will prevail?

A. The museum administrator because the settlement was an accord and satisfaction.

B. The museum administrator because he did not have knowledge of his witness' false statement when he entered the settlement with the woman.

C. The woman because an executory contract is not enforceable as an accord and satisfaction.

D. The woman because the recanted evidence of the museum administrator's witness indicates there is no longer consideration for the settlement agreement.

98. A medical student borrowed $10,000 from a loan shark. When the student was unable to repay the loan, the loan shark threatened to break his knees or worse if the money was not repaid by the following Friday. The loan shark's boss told the loan shark that since this was a medical student, it would be better to simply bring a lawsuit if the student did not pay. The student told his father about his predicament. The father told the loan shark that he would pay the student's $10,000 debt, if the loan shark agreed not to file the lawsuit. The loan shark agreed and refrained from filing the action. The following day, the father informed the loan shark that he had had a complete change of heart because his son was a worthless child who deserved to have his knees broken and that, as a result, the father would not be paying the money. If the loan shark sues the father for $10,000, who will prevail?

A. The loan shark because his agreement to forbear to sue the student is adequate consideration for the father's promise to pay the $10,000.

B. The loan shark because the father's original loyalty to his son was sufficient consideration for the father's promise to pay the $10,000.

C. The father because his promise was not supported by consideration.

D. The father because the rule on contribution requires that the loan shark first sue the student and receive judgment before he can sue on the father's promise to pay.

99. A lumberjack's fingers were cut off by a saw that the lumberjack believed to be defective. He, therefore, sued the saw manufacturer. In order to avoid the high cost of litigation, the saw manufacturer entered into an oral settlement agreement to pay the lumberjack a set amount of money in exchange for the lumberjack's agreement not to pursue the litigation against the manufacturer. Later, the manufacturer changed its mind and refused to pay. The lumberjack then sued the manufacturer. The manufacturer defended on the grounds that the agreement was unenforceable under the Statute of Frauds. Will the manufacturer prevail on this ground?

A. Yes because a promise to forbear to sue for an amount in excess of $500 must be evidenced by a writing.

B. Yes because the promise to pay the debt of another must be evidenced by a writing.

C. Both A and B are correct.

D. No because the lumberjack's promise does not require a writing under the Statute of Frauds to be enforceable.

100. A woman asked a man to loan her $2,000 to purchase some equipment in order to manufacture illegal drugs for sale and to become a 50-50 partner in the enterprise. After the man gave the woman the money, the woman decided to use the $2,000 for a vacation in Hawaii instead. What crime did the woman commit when she failed to repay the money to the man?

A. Larceny.

B. Obtaining money by false pretenses.

C. Embezzlement.

D. Robbery.

END OF QUESTIONS

SIMULATED BAR ANSWERS

1. C is the correct answer. The construction of a home is a service, and service contracts are covered by the common law. In order to modify a contract at common law, there must be new consideration by both contracting parties. Here, the builder was under a pre-existing duty to construct the home with the original roofing tiles. Thus, there was no new consideration for the builder's offer to build the home with new roofing tiles. In addition, the builder offered no new consideration. Also, the contract terms provided that any changes in plans had to be approved in writing. Here, the agreement to accept a different type of tile was by telephone, not in writing and, thus, had no legal effect by the contract's own terms. A is incorrect because there was no waiver by the homeowner. Answer B is incorrect because, although the homeowner and the builder agreed verbally to modify the contract, this modification was not valid for the reasons discussed in Answer C. Answer D is incorrect because the homeowner and the builder verbally expressly agreed to the modification, but the terms of the contract required that modifications be in writing.

2. A is the correct answer. Contracts for tutorial services, like all service contracts, are covered by the common law. (In addition, the fact pattern states that this contract is covered by the common law.) Here, the tutor promised the free tutoring services following the accountant's act of meeting with the IRS and reaching a favorable resolution of the tutor's audit. However, the tutor's promise was not supported by any consideration because the tutor's promise was made after the accountant met with the IRS. Hence, this is a case of past consideration, which is not valid consideration at common law. Answer B is incorrect because the Parol Evidence Rule only applies when a full, completely integrated written contract is entered into between the parties. Here, it appears from the facts that the original contract between the tutor and the accountant was verbal. Thus, the Parol Evidence Rule does not apply. Answer C is incorrect because, although modernly moral consideration might be valid, the fact pattern states that this is a common law contract. Answer D is incorrect because promissory estoppel is triggered when a gratuitous promise is likely to, and does, induce the promisee to rely. Here, the facts state that the tutor's promise followed the accountant's act. Therefore, the accountant was not induced by the promise.

3. D is the correct answer. Where a contract contains gaps in the terms to be performed, the court will ordinarily fill in such gaps by implication, in this case, by requiring a garage door opener of the power rating that is reasonably required for this particular home. Although the installer refused to install the more powerful motor, he is entitled to payment of the contract price for

his substantial performance, less the homeowner's damages for the installer's failure to install the appropriate motor. Answers A, B, and C are incorrect for the same reasons that Answer D is correct.

4. C is the correct answer. When a partially constructed structure is destroyed accidentally through no fault of the parties to the contract, the party constructing the structure cannot recover for the work, including material and labor that was destroyed, because no benefit has been conferred upon the owner. Therefore, the builder may not recover for previously completed work because the warehouse was not destroyed through the fault of either party. Answers A and B are incorrect for the reasons stated in Answer C. Answer D is incorrect because the duty of a contractor to perform on time may be excused by destruction of the structure.

5. A is the correct answer. An express condition that performance must be to the satisfaction of a third person requires that the third person's decision be honest and in good faith. However, where the third person's dissatisfaction is a gross mistake, the condition of personal satisfaction will be excused. Note, Answer A states that IF the agency made a gross mistake, the diamond merchant will prevail. There is nothing in the facts to indicate whether or not such a mistake occurred in this case. Answers B, C and D are incorrect for the reasons stated in answer A.

6. C is the correct answer. Here, the landscaper is in default because he did not complete the job. Where a plaintiff is in default and sues to recover damages, the plaintiff's recovery is measured by the amount of defendant's enrichment, but not more than the contract price. Because the landscaper assigned his rights to the university, the university will recover exactly what the landscaper would have recovered if there had been no assignment. Answer A is incorrect because there is nothing in the facts to indicate that the contract was not assignable. Furthermore, the landscaper merely assigned the right to collect funds. He did not delegate the duty to perform the service. Answers B and D are incorrect for the reasons discussed in Answer C.

7. D is the correct answer. False imprisonment is the intentional confinement of the plaintiff to a bounded area with no reasonable means of escape. The plaintiff must either be aware of his confinement or be injured thereby. Although the nurse intentionally confined the man to the room and locked the door and the man had no reasonable means of escape, the man was neither conscious of the confinement (because he was asleep), nor was he injured by the confinement. Therefore, the nurse is not liable for false imprisonment because all of the elements were not met. Answers A and B are incorrect for the reasons discussed in Answer D. Answer C is incorrect because the nurse may be found liable absent force or threats by creating a physical barrier of confinement, e.g.,

locking the door. However, the fact that the man was neither aware of nor harmed by this action will relieve her of liability, as discussed in Answer D.

8. A is the correct answer. The man's estate will attempt to prove the liability of the bank by a cause of action under negligence per se for violation of a statute. Here, even though the bank violated the statute, once a violation of statute is shown, the plaintiff is presumed to have proven both a duty and a breach of a duty, but the plaintiff must still prove causation and damages. The man's estate must show that the bank's failure to provide a security guard or post a sign was the actual and proximate cause of the man's death in order to impose liability. When there is no actual causation, there is automatically no proximate causation either. Here, the man's death was caused by a killer. Therefore, the bank's actions in violating the statute were not the actual cause of the man's death. Consequently, there was no proximate causation either. Answer B is incorrect because a lack of prior occurrences is no defense. Answer C is incorrect because there is nothing in the facts to indicate that the man was in any way negligent; tourists can reasonably expect that when they use automatic teller machines, even in unfamiliar cities, they will not be killed. D is incorrect because the law as described did not violate the U.S. Constitutional prohibition against ex post facto laws. An ex post facto law criminalizes and punishes conduct that was not a crime at the time it occurred. Here, the statute was already in place at the time the bank violated it. Thus, it had nothing to do with past actions. Furthermore, this is a tort action, not a criminal action. Thus, the ex post facto doctrine does not apply under these facts.

9. C is the correct answer. A plaintiff may recover damages for severe emotional distress caused by observing the negligently inflicted injury of a third person if, but only if the plaintiff is closely related to the injured victim, present at the scene of the injury-producing event at the time it occurs, and aware that the victim is being injured, which results in plaintiff suffering serious emotional distress. Here, although the wife was of course closely related to her the now-deceased husband, she was not present at the scene when he was killed in the plane crash. Therefore, since not all of the elements of negligent infliction of emotional distress have been met, the wife will not prevail in this cause of action. Answer A is an incorrect statement of law. Answer B is incorrect because all of the elements of the tort of negligent infliction of emotional distress must be met for a plaintiff to recover. Here, the wife suffered emotional distress, but that alone will not allow her to recover, for the reasons discussed in Answer C. Answer D is incorrect because foreseeability is not an element of negligent infliction of emotional distress.

10. C is the correct answer. At common law, a conspiracy was an agreement between two or more persons to do an unlawful

act. Here, the woman did not willingly agree to perform the robbery. She was under the compulsion of duress. Therefore, there was no agreement between the woman and the man, such that it amounted to a conspiracy. Answers A and B are incorrect because one can never withdraw from a conspiracy once the agreement is made. Here, the woman was arrested just before she exited the bank. Since this was after the agreement was made between her and the man, there was no effective withdrawal here. However, as discussed in Answer C, the fact that the woman was not a willing participant relieves her of criminal liability. Answer D is incorrect because co-conspirators do not have to agree to all the details of the plan.

11. B is the correct answer. The defense of duress applies where the conduct of another caused the defendant to reasonably believe that, unless he committed the crime, he or a third person would suffer death or serious bodily harm. Here, the man believed he would be killed by the other gang member if he did not rob the old lady. His reasonable belief that the other gang member had a real gun means that the defense applies, even though the gun was in fact a toy, since the man had no way of knowing this. Answer A is incorrect for the reasons discussed in Answer B. Answer C is incorrect because, although the man threatened the old lady with injury if the money was not given to him, the duress defense discussed in Answer B applies. Answer D is incorrect because it is irrelevant whether or not he intended to give the money to the gang, since he intended to permanently deprive the old lady of the money, which is an element of robbery.

12. D is the correct answer. A person can commit a crime through an innocent agent and be subject to conviction as though he committed the crime himself. Here, the facts indicate that the terrorist used the man (an innocent agent) to commit the crime of terrorism by switching the brief cases, so that the man would unknowingly bring the bomb into the building and blow it up. Answer A is incorrect for the reasons discussed in Answer D. Answer B is incorrect because the crime in question is terrorism, not conspiracy. Thus, it is irrelevant whether or not there was an agreement between the man and the terrorist. Answer C is incorrect because it states the reasons why the man was acquitted. It has nothing to do with why the terrorist would be found guilty, since the terrorist knew that the brief case contained a bomb and the terrorist intended for the bomb to be used to blow up the building.

13. A is the correct answer. Pursuant to U.C.C. 2-206, an offer to buy goods shall be construed as inviting acceptance, either by a prompt promise to ship or act of shipment. However, the act of shipping non-conforming goods is not only acceptance of the offer, but also a breach of the accepted contract. Here, the supplier accepted the store's

offer to buy when the supplier shipped the games. However, since the games were not the ones ordered by the store, they were nonconforming goods. As such, the supplier was in breach. As a result, the store will prevail. Answer B is incorrect because, even though the store returned the goods, it had prepaid and was entitled to either a refund of its money or to shipment of the correct games. Answer C is incorrect because the seller must seasonably notify the buyer that the shipment is offered as an accommodation only. Here, the supplier did not send any indication to the store that this was an accommodation. Answer D is incorrect because a buyer is entitled to a reasonable opportunity to inspect goods.

14. D is the correct answer. Negligence is a breach of a duty of care owed to a foreseeable plaintiff. The breach is a failure to meet the applicable standard of care, and the breach must also be both the actual and the proximate cause of harm to the plaintiff. Here, the man must show that the oil company failed to exercise due care in maintaining the pipeline before liability will be imposed. If he is able to do so, then he will recover in negligence, if the damage to him was caused by the oil company's failure to meet this standard. Answer A is incorrect because the facts state there was no danger to the man presented by the leaking pipeline. Answer B is incorrect because Torts Restatement 402(A) provides that liability is limited to persons who sell, produce, or distribute the product. The facts state that the oil company merely owned and operated the pipeline. C is incorrect because the man must show he suffered an injury peculiar in kind (different from the injury suffered by others for the same pipeline crack) in order to recover for public nuisance. Here, there is no showing in the facts that the man suffered such an injury.

15. D is the correct answer. A property owner may use reasonable (non-deadly) force to protect his property from intruders. Here, the facts state that the man's fence only gave a mild shock that ordinarily would not cause a person to die as a result. Although the boy's death was tragic, the amount of force used by the property owner was reasonable. Therefore, the boy's estate will not prevail. Answer A is incorrect because, while the fence was the cause in fact of the boy's death, in order to prevail, the boy's estate needs to show that it was also the proximate cause. For the reasons discussed in Answer D, this was not the case. Answer B is incorrect because the facts state that the force was not, in fact, deadly. Answer C is an incorrect statement of law. Even if the boy were a trespasser, the man would still owe the boy a duty not to use deadly force against him.

16. D is the correct answer. At common law, a burglary is the nighttime breaking and entering into the dwelling house of another with the intent to commit a felony therein. Here, because the woman

entered the man's home to retrieve her own property, she entered without the requisite intent necessary to have committed a felony therein. Therefore, there was no burglary. Answer A is incorrect because, even though she forced open the door, she did so with the intent of retrieving her own property. She had no intent of committing a felony once inside the man's house. Answers B and C are incorrect for the reason stated in D.

17. D is the correct answer. A private citizen is privileged to use deadly force to avert the perpetration of an inherently dangerous felony that involves a substantial risk of death or serious bodily harm to others and that the person against whom the force was used is guilty of that crime. Here, the thief, carrying an automatic rifle, approached the truck, apparently intending to steal the jewelry. He also aimed his rifle at the detective, which constitutes deadly force. Therefore, the detective was privileged to use deadly force against the thief to prevent the perpetration of the inherently dangerous felony. Consequently, he will be found not guilty. Answers A, B and C are incorrect, since crime prevention, under these facts, is a valid defense. The detective will not be found guilty under any degree of murder or involuntary manslaughter.

18. B is the correct answer. Larceny is defined as the trespassory taking and carrying away of the personal property of another with the intent to permanently deprive. Here, when the woman had decided to keep the horse, before obtaining possession of him, she was in unlawful possession of him in violation of the ownership rights of the man at the time she was given possession of the horse. Therefore, all of the elements of larceny are met, and she will be found guilty. Answer A is incorrect because a larceny was committed at the time the woman received the horse. Answers C and D are incorrect for the reasons discussed in Answer B.

19. D is the correct answer. This contract is for clothes, which are goods. It is, therefore, governed by the U.C.C. Under U.C.C. Section 2-306, a requirements contract measures the quantity of goods by the "requirements" of the buyer. The party that will determine the quantity amount is required to exercise good faith and the contract does not lack mutuality, since the requirement of good faith is imposed upon the party determining quantity. A contract in which the parties make an agreement to buy all that is required and an agreement to supply all that is required is sufficient consideration in a requirements contract. Here, the retailer agreed to buy all of its requirements of clothes from the wholesaler. The wholesaler agreed to supply the required clothes. Therefore, there was consideration for this contract and the wholesaler's defense of lack of consideration will fail. Answer A is incorrect because, although all contracts must be supported by consideration, this contract was supported by

consideration, as discussed in Answer D. Answer B is incorrect because the contract is not illusory, as discussed in Answer D. Answer C is incorrect because consideration is needed for requirements contracts. As discussed in Answer D, there was consideration in this particular fact scenario.

20. A is the correct answer. This contract is for sandwiches, which are goods. It is, therefore, governed by the U.C.C. Pursuant to U.C.C. section 2-306(1), no quantity unreasonably disproportionate to any stated estimate, or in the absence of a stated estimate to any normal or otherwise comparable prior output or requirements contract, may be tendered or demanded. Here, the catering company's demand for twenty dozen sandwiches per week was unreasonably disproportionate to its prior year's requirements of seven dozen sandwiches per week. Answer B is legally incorrect as contemplation by the contracting parties is not the proper test under U.C.C. section 2-306(1). Answers C and D are incorrect for the reasons discussed in Answer A.

21. A is the correct answer. This contract is for roses, which are goods. It is, therefore, governed by the U.C.C. Under U.C.C. section 2-306, a party who will determine the quantity amount is required to exercise good faith. A contract in which a party makes an agreement to buy all that it requires and that party fails to buy all its requirements is not acting in good faith (absent additional facts) and, therefore, is in breach of contract. Here, when the florist stopped purchasing and selling roses because the grower refused to lower the price, the florist was in breach because it was not acting in good faith. Answers B, C, and D are incorrect for the reasons discussed in Answer A.

22. C is the correct answer. Requirements contracts generally are not assignable because the assignee (the new company) may have significantly different requirements from the assignor (the original owner of the office), thereby materially changing the duty of the obligor (the office supplier) under the contract. Answers A, B, and D are incorrect for the reasons discussed in Answer C.

23. D is the correct answer. A novation is a three-party agreement by which the obligee (the man) agrees to accept a new obligor (the dealership under the new ownership) in place of the original obligor (the dealership under the original ownership). The novation results in a discharge of the original obligor from its duties under the original contract. Here, the new dealership was under an obligation to service the man's car. Therefore, the man will prevail. Answers A and B are incorrect for the reasons stated in Answer D. Answer C is incorrect because there is no such thing as an implied warranty of serviceability.

24. B is the correct answer. A manufacturer, retailer, or supplier of a product that places an unreasonably dangerous

product into the stream of commerce will be held strictly liable for injuries to a consumer or user of the product. Here, the sled manufacturer placed a sled into the stream of commerce. This sled was unreasonably dangerous because it was equipped with runners that were made of a metal that was less durable than steel. Furthermore, the facts seem to imply that, had the manufacturer used steel, the accident would not have occurred. Answer A is incorrect because liability for a defective product will not be imposed if the product was not unreasonably dangerous. The mere fact that other manufacturers used a different metal on the sled does not mean that the runners on the sled in question were made of an unreasonably dangerous metal. Answer C is incorrect because the plaintiff does not need to be the purchaser of the product in order to recover. Answer D is incorrect because contributory negligence is generally not a defense to a strict products liability cause of action, unless there are facts to support a finding of unreasonable misuse of the product. Such facts are not present in the situation above.

25. C is the correct answer. A manufacturer, retailer, or supplier of a product that places an unreasonably dangerous (defective) product into the stream of commerce will be strictly liable for injuries to a consumer or user of the product. This doctrine applies to retailers and distributors as well as manufacturers because each party is an integral part of the marketing enterprise, enabling them to share the risk of liability with the manufacturer. Here, the drug store was a retailer that sold the fan, which obviously was in a defective condition because the blade flew off and struck the woman in the eye. Answer A is incorrect for the reasons stated in Answer C. Answer B is incorrect because no privity is required to impose liability under the theory of strict products liability. Answer D is an incorrect statement of law because she is suing in strict liability in tort, not negligence.

26. B is the correct answer. Under a negligence products liability theory, a commercial supplier generally has no duty to inspect, test, or provide warnings in regard to products manufactured by another prior to selling the product, unless the seller has reason to know that the product is dangerously defective. There is nothing in the facts to indicate that the dealer had any reason to know that the car was dangerous. Presumably, the dealer conducted an inspection of the car before it was sold (as car dealers normally do), and the type of defect that occurred could not have been discovered upon reasonable inspection. Answer A is incorrect for the reasons stated in Answer B because this is a products negligence action and the retailer has a duty to inspect. Answer C is incorrect because privity and intended use are no longer required. Answer D is incorrect because the dealer's duty of care would extend to a bystander or to another user of the car.

27. B is the correct answer. In order to recover under a theory of negligent infliction of emotional distress, a plaintiff must have witnessed the distressing event, the plaintiff must be a close relative of the person upon whom the distressing event was inflicted, and the plaintiff must have a physical harm. Here, the father witnessed his toddler falling off of the tricycle and striking her head. The father became physically ill. It should be noted that even a de minimis physical injury (such as getting physically ill) will suffice for recovery under negligent infliction of emotional distress, if the other elements are met, which was the case here, since the father by definition was a close relative of the toddler (the person upon whom the distressing event was inflicted, in this case, falling off the tricycle when the wheel came off). Answer A is incorrect because one must not only witness the act, but also meet the other elements discussed in Answer B. Answer C is incorrect because the father did not have to be the one using the tricycle in order to be able to recover for negligent infliction of emotional distress. Answer D is incorrect for the same reasons that Answer B is correct.

28. A is the correct answer. An individual is criminally liable as an accomplice of a crime performed by another if, with the intent to facilitate the crime, encouragement or assistance was given, or he failed to perform a legal duty to prevent the crime of another. Here, the man assisted the thieves to burglarize the house by leaving the bathroom window open. He is, therefore, guilty as an accomplice to the burglary. Answers B, C, and D are incorrect for the same reasons that Answer A is correct.

29. D is the correct answer. At common law, a burglary is defined as the nighttime breaking and entering into the dwelling house of another with the specific intent to commit a felony therein. Here, the boy is not guilty of common law burglary for several reasons. First of all, a store is not a dwelling. Second, there was no breaking and entering into the store, since it was still open to the public when the boy came in. Although Answers A, B, and C address elements of common law burglary, the boy is not guilty for the same reasons that Answer D is correct.

30. C is the correct answer. At common law, arson was defined as the malicious burning of the dwelling of another. Here, the dwelling belonged to the ex-wife and was, thus, "the dwelling of another." However, because the dwelling did not "burn" (but instead only had smoke damage), no arson occurred at common law. Answer A is incorrect because, although he inserted the broom into the home, there was no actual burning of the structure. Answers B and D are incorrect because specific intent is not a necessary element and are not responsive to the question.

31. D is the correct answer. Conspiracy at common law was an agreement between two or more people to commit an unlaw-

ful act. Here, when the defendant (the store's owner) agreed to refurbish the table, knowing that it was stolen, this constituted an agreement between the store's owner and the man. The unlawful act was the sale of the stolen merchandise. The store's owner is, therefore, liable for conspiracy. Answers A and B are incorrect for the reasons Answer D is correct. C is incorrect because it does not address the issue of the agreement between the store's owner and the man, as discussed in Answer D.

32. C is the correct answer. A defendant is entitled to use reasonable force in self-defense to the extent such force is not likely to cause serious bodily injury or death, unless defendant is being threatened with serious bodily injury or death. Thus, the woman will be liable to the man if the force used by the woman in self-defense was unreasonable. Here, the woman merely struck the man with her diploma, which does not appear to be unreasonable excessive force. Answer A is incorrect because, even though the woman intended to strike the man with her diploma, this answer choice does not address the issue of whether that force was unreasonable. Thus, Answer C is correct and Answer A is incorrect. Answer B is incorrect because there is generally no duty to retreat. Answer D is incorrect because it is irrelevant whether or not most women are strong enough to cause a man to suffer a concussion. Guilt is determined by whether or not the force used was unreasonable, as discussed in Answer C.

33. B is the correct answer. The most likely theory that the woman would allege against the store would be negligence, which has elements of duty, breach, actual and proximate causation, and damages. A breach of duty would occur if the store failed to use reasonable care to supervise its premises. There is nothing in the facts to indicate that the store failed to use reasonable care to supervise its premises. Answer A is incorrect because it is irrelevant, since the store still had a duty to supervise its premises, as discussed in Answer B. Answer C is incorrect because it fails to address whether or not the store used reasonable care in supervising its premises, as discussed in Answer B. Answer D is incorrect because the parking lot is still part of the store's premises. Thus, the store's duties to the woman extended to its parking lot, as well.

34. A is the correct answer. An individual may recover damages for the unauthorized use by a defendant of the individual's name or likeness for a commercial advantage. Here, the nun did not agree to have her picture displayed in the magazine. Since the magazine sold extra copies, it received a commercial advantage by using the nun's likeness. Thus, the nun may be able to recover for invasion of privacy. Answer B is incorrect because the picture was taken without consent. Answer C is incorrect because there is nothing in the facts to indicate that the nun was a public figure. D is incorrect because the magazine is liable for the reporter's actions commit-

ted within the course and scope of his employment with the magazine, under respondeat superior.

35. C is the correct answer. A plaintiff may recover for a defendant's highly offensive intrusion into his private life, whether the intrusion was intentional or negligent in nature. Here, however, the plaintiff (the celebrity) is not entitled to recover for invasion of privacy because the photograph was taken while the celebrity was in a public place (he was in a convertible with the top down, driving on a public street, and was, thus, visible to anyone with a camera). The celebrity, thus, had no reasonable expectation that he would not be intruded upon by the photographer. Answers A and B are incorrect because they address elements of a different prong (category) of invasion of privacy, namely, the use of the plaintiff's name or likeness for commercial advantage without the plaintiff's consent. Here, the plaintiff was suing for the prong of intrusion on solitude. Answer D is incorrect because it is not relevant for intrusion on solitude.

36. C is the correct answer. Where property is lost or mislaid, the property is considered to be in the constructive possession of the true owner. When property is found by a third party and that party has a clue to the identity of the property's owner, but decides to keep the property anyway, that person has committed a larceny (which is defined as the trespassory taking and carrying away of the personal property of another with the intent to permanently deprive the owner of lawful possession of the property). Here, when the woman found the book, she intended to keep it even though she had a clue to ownership when she discovered the bookmark with the owner's name on it. Thus, based on these facts, the woman has committed a larceny. Answer A is incorrect because the woman formed the intent to keep the book upon finding it. Answer B is incorrect because there was no uttering in this fact pattern. Answer D is incorrect because the woman was never entrusted with the property (an element of embezzlement), nor did she ever intend to return it.

37. B is the correct answer. The crime of larceny requires a trespassory taking and carrying away of the personal property of another with the intent to permanently deprive. Here, although the man was voluntarily given possession of the bicycle by his friend, a taking with the victim's permission is larceny where the permission was obtained by fraud or deception, such as the deception used by the man, since the man knew that he could not return the bicycle on Sunday, yet told his friend that he would do so. Answers A and C are incorrect because the man did not obtain lawful possession because he obtained possession of the bicycle through fraud, as discussed in Answer B. Answer D is an incorrect statement of the law. Intent can be formed after the act occurs.

38. B is the correct answer. This contract is for the performance of a comedy act, which is a service. The contract is, thus, covered by the common law. Under the common law's "mailbox rule," where the use of U.S. mail, telegram, or overnight mail services is a reasonable method of communicating an acceptance, such acceptance is generally effective upon dispatch and a revocation is generally effective upon receipt. Thus, even though the second comedian received the club owner's attempted revocation before the club owner received the second comedian's acceptance, a contract was already formed when the second comedian mailed his acceptance by telegram. Note that although an offer may invite acceptance by either a promise or an act, and on its face the club owner's offer arguably contains language that invites acceptance by performance, a reasonable interpretation of the club owner's offer was that he required to be contacted prior to Sunday for acceptance. Answer A is incorrect because the method of revocation is generally not limited to the same method as the communication method of the offer. Answer C is incorrect because the second comedian's normal fee can be objectively determined. Answer D is incorrect because a request using such language as "I wish" or "I hope" is considered to be mere inquiry and not a counteroffer.

39. A is the correct answer. An offer is an outward manifestation of present willingness to enter into a bargain made in such a way that the person to whom it is addressed reasonably believes that he could accept the offer by assenting to the stated terms. Here, because the girlfriend had no knowledge that the man's best friend received an identical offer, she reasonably believed that she could accept the offer by sending a telegram to the man. Answers B, C and D are incorrect for the reasons discussed in Answer A.

40. B is the correct answer. This is a contract to paint a house, which is a service. The contract is, thus, governed by the common law. Under the common law, in order to modify a contract, there must be new consideration. Here, although the woman had to pay more money to the window installer, that is no new consideration to modify her contract with the painter. The woman's modification amount offered to the painter is significantly less than the original offer. Thus, the painter is not obligated to accept the modified amount. Therefore, he may recover the contract price ($15,000), plus any profits he would have made (offset by the money he saved by not having to purchase materials, etc., to complete the work). Answers A, C, and D are incorrect for the reasons discussed in Answer B.

41. B is the correct answer. An offer may invite acceptance by either a promise or an act. On its face, the concert hall owner's offer arguably contained language that invited acceptance by performance. A reasonable interpretation of the concert hall owner's offer was

that he required to be contacted prior to Saturday for acceptance. The opera singer should have known that, if the concert hall owner was not contacted by her, he would continue his efforts to secure an opera singer. Answers A, C and D are incorrect for the reasons discussed in Answer B.

42. C is the correct answer. A battery is the harmful or offensive touching of plaintiff without privilege or consent. Here, the woman only consented to have the original dentist perform the root canal. Thus, the second dentist, by performing the root canal without the woman's consent, is liable for battery. Answers A and B are incorrect for the same reasons that Answer C is correct. Answer D is incorrect because the doctrine of res ipsa loquitur only applies in a negligence action where the harm cannot have occurred in the absence of negligence. Here, there was no injury to the woman and, thus, no negligence. Consequently, the doctrine of res ipsa loquitor is irrelevant to these facts.

43. D is the correct answer. The doctrine of res ipsa loquitur applies in a negligence action where the harm could not have occurred in the absence of negligence. The doctrine has been held to apply to establish "exclusive control" in a group of medical personnel when an unconscious plaintiff suffers harm of a type that might be attributable to someone's negligence. In this case, the mixup in the charts (and the resulting incorrect medical procedure being performed on the man) could not have occurred in the absence of negligence by someone at the clinic. Thus, the clinic may be held liable for the man's injuries, even if he cannot establish precisely who was responsible for his injuries. Answer A is incorrect because, as discussed in Answer D, the clinic can be held directly liable under the doctrine of res ipsa loquitur. Thus, vicarious liability is not needed to impose liability on the clinic. Answer B is incorrect for the reasons discussed in Answer D. Answer C is incorrect because battery is an intentional tort. There is nothing in the facts to suggest that the wrong procedure was performed on the man intentionally.

44. D is the correct answer. Conversion is an intentional act, resulting in the unauthorized assertion of dominion and control over the personal property of another. Here, although the shop's owner was mistaken as to his ownership of the violin at the time of the sale, and the woman in good faith believed the violin was owned by the shop's owner, the intent required for conversion is the tortfeasor's intent to deal with the chattel in a manner that exercises dominion and control over the chattel of another. Thus, it is no defense that defendants are not conscious wrongdoers. Answers A, B and C are incorrect for the reason stated in Answer D.

45. B is the correct answer. The general rule is that a defendant who did not place another individual in a position of peril owes no duty to provide assistance to

that person in an emergency. However, defendant must provide assistance to another individual in an emergency where a special relationship exists, e.g., family members, employer-employee, etc. Here, there are no facts indicating that the man either put the woman in peril or had a special relationship with her. Therefore, he owed her no duty to provide assistance. Answers A, C and D are incorrect for the reason stated in Answer B.

46. A is the correct answer. In a criminal case, the burden of proof is on the prosecution to establish beyond a reasonable doubt the elements of a criminal cause of action, including the specific intent to commit a crime where such intent is a necessary element of the crime. Here, the crime charged is larceny, which is a specific intent crime. While intoxication can be a defense to a specific intent crime, the burden of proof is still upon the prosecution to establish that the woman in this case was not so intoxicated that she was incapable of forming the specific intent necessary for larceny. Answers B, C, and D are incorrect because they describe the wrong burdens of proof of a prosecutor in a criminal case, and it is not necessary to get to the defendant's burden of proof.

47. C is the correct answer. This is a contract for the sale of a home. Land sale contracts, such as the one here, are covered by the common law. Under the common law, when a party to a contract will be unable to perform at the time set for his (the man's) performance, i.e., there is a prospective inability to perform, the other party (the woman) is excused from holding herself ready to perform, rendering performance or tendering performance, as an implied condition to the duty of the party who is unable to perform. Here, this is exactly what happened because the man no longer owns the house (he sold it to his uncle prior to the performance date). Answers A and B are incorrect for the reasons discussed in Answer C. Answer D is incorrect because demands for assurances may be required under the U.C.C, but as discussed above, this is a common law contract.

48. A is the correct answer. This contract is for the sale of a car, which is a good. It is, thus, governed by the U.C.C. Under the U.C.C., where a party repudiates a contract in advance of the date set for performance, the innocent party is excused from holding himself ready to perform, rendering performance, or tendering performance. In addition, the innocent party may generally treat the anticipatory repudiation as a present material breach of the contract and bring an immediate action to recover his damages. Here, the woman repudiated the contract before the performance date (April 1). Thus, the man has an immediate cause of action for breach at the time of the repudiation (March 15). Answers B, C and D are incorrect for the reasons discussed in Answer A.

49. C is the correct answer. When a contract fixes the same time for performance by the parties to the contract, tender of

such performance by each party is an implied condition of the other party's duty to perform (concurrent conditions). Thus, the man must tender (offer to pay) the $4,000 to the woman in order for the woman's duty to perform (sell the television) to arise. Here, it may be assumed that the man came to the woman's home ready to pay. When she refused to give him the television, the man had a cause of action for breach of contract. Answers A, B and D are incorrect for the reasons discussed in Answer C.

50. C is the correct answer. Unlike murder or other completed crimes, attempt is always a specific intent crime. Consequently, attempted murder requires the specific intent to cause the death of a particular individual. Here, since the assassin did not intend to kill the passerby, he is not guilty of attempted murder of the passerby. Answers A, B and D are incorrect for the same reasons that Answer C is correct.

51. C is the correct answer. When a person is threatened with immediate bodily harm, that person is privileged to use self-defense to protect oneself. Self-defense does not require a correct belief that such is necessary to protect oneself, but only a reasonable belief. Here, the woman reasonably believed that the man was going to strike her with what she believed to be a knife. Thus, she believed that she was threatened with immediate bodily harm, and this belief was reasonable under the circumstances. Consequently, she was privileged to strike the man in self-defense and is, thus, not guilty of battery. Answer A is incorrect because it does not address the issue of the woman's reasonable belief that she was about to suffer imminent bodily harm. Answer B is incorrect because one who is defending oneself may attack the assailant intentionally, as discussed in Answer C. Answer D is an incorrect statement of law.

52. C is the correct answer. Embezzlement is the fraudulent conversion of rightfully entrusted personal property. Here, because the president of the collection agency intended to extinguish the joint debt and subsequently did so with the money collected from the man, an embezzlement occurred because the collected funds belonged to the truck's owner and were not to be used to extinguish a joint debt between the collection agency and its president. Thus, although the truck's owner gave the collection agency the right to collect the money (giving the collection agency rightful possession of the money), when it was used to extinguish the joint debt, a conversion occurred. Thus, the crime was embezzlement. Answer A is incorrect because the employee was not being charged and because a crime did occur, as discussed in Answer C. Answer B is incorrect because false pretenses requires the defendant to have obtained title. Here, the president of the collection agency obtained possession of the money received, but not title. Answer D is incorrect. Larceny is the trespas-

sory taking and carrying away of the personal property of another with the intent to permanently deprive the owner of rightful possession. Here, as discussed in Answer C, the money was in the lawful possession of the collection agency. Thus, there was no trespassory taking.

53. D is the correct answer. A corporation may be liable for a criminal act, in all jurisdictions, where the act involves a specific intent crime and is authorized, performed or at least tolerated by the board of directors or a high managerial agent acting on behalf of the corporation within the scope of his employment. Here, the facts indicate that the president's act may have been authorized by the board of directors, since they authorized all officers and employees to do whatever was necessary to "kill the competition." Thus, the company is also liable for the crime. Answer A is incorrect because it presumes a corporation cannot be convicted of crime. Answer B is incorrect because a corporation can be convicted of a specific intent crime. Answer C is incorrect because the conviction of the company and its president need not be contemporaneous.

54. D is the correct answer. Generally, ignorance or a mistaken belief as to the law is no defense to criminal liability. Although such ignorance/mistaken belief is based on the good faith reliance on the advice of a professional (in this case, an accountant), it is no defense.

However, where the defendant's good faith reliance is such that he did not have the necessary mens rea to commit the crime, such reliance will act as a defense. Here, if the man believed in good faith that the accountant's advice was correct, he did not have the necessary "willfulness" to evade payment of taxes required under the statute. Answers A and C are incorrect statements of the law. Answer B is incorrect because the mere signing of the tax form does not give the man a valid defense, unless he meets the parameters discussed in Answer D. Furthermore, when a person signs something, he is generally held responsible for what he has signed. Thus, the signing actually goes further toward the man's guilt rather than acting as a defense.

55. D is the correct answer. In general, where defendant criminally acts under the reasonable belief that his actions will prevent the occurrence of a greater harm, the defense of necessity will keep the defendant from criminal liability. Thus, when the man threatened the hiker in order to call for emergency assistance to save the woman's life, no criminal liability will result to the man for such actions. Answer A is incorrect because there is no requirement that the act be performed for the necessity of an acquaintance. Answer B is incorrect because no special statute is required to permit raising the defense of necessity. Answer C is an incorrect statement of the law because the man only used the THREAT of deadly force against the

hiker. Had the man actually used deadly force under the circumstances, the defense would not have been available.

56. B is the correct answer. A conditional promise means that the promisor only needs to perform if a specified condition occurs and is recognized as sufficient consideration for a contract where the conditional promise is not illusory. Further, every contract imposes upon each party a duty of good faith and fair dealing in its performance and its enforcement. Thus, the couple must use good faith efforts to sell the present home and, although the couple is not obligated to buy the home from the developer unless the present home is sold, the couple's promise to sell the present home is sufficient consideration to form a contract. Answer A is incorrect because it does not address the issue of good faith, as discussed in Answer B. Answer C is incorrect for the reasons discussed in Answer B. Answer D is incorrect because a change in position in reliance on a promise is promissory estoppel, which is a consideration substitute. Here, since there is actual consideration (as discussed in Answer B), it is not necessary to discuss promissory estoppel.

57. A is the correct answer. A condition will be excused where a party that is favored by the condition wrongfully prevents or hinders the completion of the condition. Thus, the woman does not need to provide evidence that it would be possible for the man to obtain a bank loan. The fact that he refused to get the bank loan excuses the condition and puts the man in breach of contract. Answer B is an incorrect statement of law. Answers C and D are incorrect for the reasons discussed in Answer A.

58. D is the correct answer. The Parol Evidence Rule states that when there is a fully integrated contract, evidence of prior or contemporaneous oral or written agreements may not be introduced to contradict the words of a fully integrated contract. A fully integrated contract is a contract that has been adopted as a final and complete expression of an agreement between two parties as an expression of an integrated agreement. Here, the contract between the man and the company did not contain their complete agreement because it did not mention the gym membership. Thus, the man can argue that the contract was not fully integrated, and he will be allowed to bring in evidence of a prior oral agreement to provide him with a gym membership. This is, thus, the man's best argument. Answer A is incorrect because the condition of the gym membership was not a modification, but was discussed during contractual negotiations. Answer B is incorrect because there is no ambiguity in the written contract. The written contract simply fails to mention the gym membership, but this is failure to mention a particular term rather than ambiguity. Answer C is an incorrect statement of law for the reasons discussed in Answer D.

59. B is the correct answer. Under general tort principles, a possessor of a domestic animal that has not previously exhibited dangerous propensities is not held strictly liable for the acts of the animal, so long as the possessor was exercising due care at the time. Here, since it appears that the woman was not negligent in allowing the dog to escape, she is not liable for the woman's injuries. Answer A is incorrect for the reasons discussed above. Answers C and D are incorrect because, unless the woman was negligent, she will not be held liable, as discussed in Answer B.

60. B is the correct answer. Liability under the principles of negligence per se for violation of statute requires violation of a statute passed for the purpose of preventing the injury suffered by plaintiff and that that plaintiff was within the class of persons sought to be protected by the statute. Here, the plaintiff is probably within the class of persons sought to be protected by the statute because a pedestrian could potentially be hurt by a vehicle not equipped with chains during the snow. However, the accident that occurred with the tire blowing out had nothing to do with whether or not the woman had chains on her tires, since there was no snow at the time. Thus, because the accident was not within the statutory purpose, the woman will not be liable. Answer A is incorrect because, even if the tire blowout were an Act of God, if foreseeable, it would not relieve the woman of liability. Tire blowouts can usually be prevented by keeping one's car's tires in working order, unless there are hazards on the road that cause the tire blowout. There is nothing in these facts to indicate that there were any road conditions that brought about the tire blowout or that the woman had failed to keep her tires in working order. Thus, the woman should not be found liable under these facts. Answers C and D are incorrect for the reasons discussed in Answer B.

61. B is the correct answer. Under the traditional (subjective) rule, the defense of entrapment will be available where a law enforcement officer has instigated the defendant's illegal conduct, and the defendant was not predisposed to commit the crime. Under the facts, the criminal was predisposed to commit the crime, as he had stolen cars from his own valet parking service in the past. Even though the police officer deliberately left his vehicle with the criminal (valet) to see if he would steal it, since the criminal was predisposed to steal the car, the defense of entrapment is not available to the criminal. Answers A, C, and D are incorrect for the reasons discussed in Answer B.

62. C is the correct answer. The minority (objective) standard for the defense of entrapment looks to whether the crime was performed in response to law enforcement activity that was reasonably likely to cause a reasonable, but unpredisposed person to commit a crime, which is the rule set forth in this answer. Here, although the police

officer was not in uniform (since he was undercover), the police officer had to be out of uniform in order to encourage the confidence of the drug dealer. Therefore, the defense of entrapment is unavailable, since the drug dealer was predisposed to commit the crime. Answer A is incorrect because it does not discuss the issue of predisposition to commit the crime, as explained in Answer C. Answer B is incorrect because a valid contract cannot be formed for a criminal activity. Answer D is incorrect because there was no violation of the drug dealer's due process rights, for the reasons discussed in Answer C.

63. The correct answer is C. Conversion is the intentional exercise of dominion and control over the chattel of another. When a bailee receives possession of the chattel of another and uses the chattel in such a way as to materially breach the scope of his authority over the chattel, a conversion has occurred. Here, the restaurant was a bailee because it was entrusted with the man's coat while he ate dinner. When the restaurant's coat clerk could not produce the man's coat when presented with the ticket, a material breach of the restaurant's authority and, therefore, a conversion occurred. Answer A is incorrect because a waiver of liability does not apply as a defense under the facts given. Liability for conversion cannot be waived; only liability for loss or damage can be disclaimed. Answer B is incorrect because, where the defendant (here, the restaurant) deals with the chattel (here, the coat) in the manner that resulted in the loss of the chattel, even if the defendant did not consciously commit a wrongdoing (permit theft or gave the chattel to the wrong person), the defendant is liable for conversion. The restaurant is vicariously liable for the coat clerk's conduct. Answer D is incorrect because it merely addresses the amount of recoverable damages.

64. B is the correct answer. An owner or occupier of land has the duty to inspect and discover any dangerous conditions or activities on the land, and to correct or warn of such conditions or activities. However, the question asks about the liability of the host, who is an occupier of the land. He would be liable, if he inspected the cage and found that there was a problem with it and did not warn the movie star. However, it is possible that the product (the cage) was defective, and it was the type of defect that could not be discovered upon a reasonable inspection. Therefore, the host would not be liable, unless he failed to exercise reasonable care in removing the movie star from the cage. Answer A is incorrect because the movie star's mother does not have the same duty as the owner or occupier of land due to her status as parent of a minor child. Answers C and D are incorrect for the reasons discussed in Answer B.

65. D is the correct answer. A manufacturer of a product may be held liable for its negligence that results in its product being unreasonably dangerous. A manu-

facturer of a defective product is also strictly liable to consumers and users for injuries caused by the defect. However, a manufacturer is not liable under a premises liability theory ("abnormally dangerous condition") for defects in a product. Here, since the saw was both defective and unreasonably dangerous (since the volunteer was sawed in half), the estate may recover under both negligence and strict products liability. Answers A, B and C are incorrect for the reasons discussed in Answer D.

66. B is the correct answer. In cases involving a "thin skull" plaintiff, all courts will hold defendants liable for the full extent of plaintiff's damages, under the rationale that a defendant takes the plaintiff as he finds him. Therefore, the defendant in this case (the woman) will be liable for the actual amount of the tennis player's lost income resulting from his inability to compete in the tennis match. Answers A, C, and D are incorrect statements of the law, for the reasons discussed in Answer B.

67. B is the correct answer. Generally, where a plaintiff recovers from one of two equally negligent defendants and one defendant pays the entire judgment, that defendant is entitled to contribution from the other negligent defendant, as determined by the amount of the final judgment. That amount will differ depending on whether this is a contributory negligence or comparative negligence jurisdiction. Here, since both hunters were negligent, the first hunter (who paid the entire judgment) will be entitled to contribution from the second hunter. Answer A is incorrect because the call of the question does not involve the manufacturer of the guns. Answer C is incorrect because there is no such thing as the Hunter's Rule. Answer D is incorrect because it fails to recognize the principle of contribution.

68. C is the correct answer. An accessory after the fact is a person who receives, comforts, or assists another to avoid arrest, prosecution, or conviction, knowing that the other has committed a felony. Here, since the woman knew of the theft (and in fact was paid for her services out of the spoils of the theft), and was acting to help the man avoid arrest, she is guilty of being an accessory after the fact. Answer A is incorrect because a principal in the first degree is someone who actually commits the crime by his acts, or through the acts of an innocent person or inanimate agent. Here, the woman did not commit the actual theft. She merely assisted the man after he did so. Also, the man was not an innocent agent, since he did commit the theft. Answer B is incorrect because a principal in the second degree is someone who incites or abets the commission of the crime, and is actually or constructively present at the scene of the crime. None of these elements are present under these facts, since the woman was only present after the theft was committed. Answer D is incorrect for the reasons stated in Answer C.

69. C is the correct answer. Robbery is the trespassory taking and carrying away of the personal property of another from the person or their presence by force or threat of force with the intent to permanently deprive. All elements must be present. Here, there was no taking (control) of the property (the money from the cash drawer), due to the intervention of the security guard. Thus, there was no robbery. Answer A is incorrect because it addresses only one element of the crime. Answers B and D are incorrect statements of law, since the threat can be to third parties. Furthermore, D is not the best answer because it is better to choose an answer that eliminates an element of the actus reas than an answer that raises a possible defense of duress.

70. A is the correct answer because attempt is a specific intent crime in which the underlying crime (here, robbery) would have been completed, if not for some factor. Here, the man had the specific intent to rob the woman, took substantial steps in furtherance of the robbery by putting a gun to the woman's back, and "but for" the woman's ability to wrestle the gun from the man, the crime could have been completed. Therefore, the man is guilty of attempted robbery. Answer B is incorrect because having a gun to one's back puts a person in danger, regardless of whether or not the person is a black belt in jiu-jitsu. Furthermore, Answer B does not address the issue of the man's specific intent to commit robbery, as discussed in Answer A. Answers C and D are incorrect for the reasons discussed in Answer A.

71. A is the correct answer. Larceny is the trespassory taking and carrying away of the personal property of another with the intent to permanently deprive the owner of lawful possession. In circumstances where the owner has lost or mislaid the property, a larceny has occurred, if there is a clue to ownership of the property and the intent to permanently deprive exists at the time defendant takes possession of the property. Here, since the woman received the money in a bag from the restaurant's cashier and immediately discovered the money as she drove away with it, she is guilty of larceny. Answer B is incorrect because the property was not taken by fraud or deception. Answer C is incorrect because embezzlement requires the defendant to obtain lawful possession. However, lost or mislaid goods remain in the constructive possession of the owner. Answer D is incorrect because Answer A is the correct answer.

72. B is the correct answer. Private nuisance is the nontrespassory invasion of the use and enjoyment of plaintiff's land. In order for an interference to permit recovery for damages, the interference must result in substantial and unreasonable harm in the use and enjoyment of realty. Here, the loud noise from the sushi bar's Karaoke machine constituted a substantial interference with the man's use and enjoyment of his real property (i.e., his land). Thus, he will prevail under a private nuisance theory. Answer A is incorrect because a violation of the ordinance does not necessarily constitute a

nuisance. Answer C is incorrect because the man did not come to the nuisance. The noise and crowds did not occur until after he moved in. Answer D is an incorrect statement of the law in that actual trespass is not required for recovery under a private nuisance theory. As discussed in Answer B, private nuisance is the nontrespassory invasion of the use and enjoyment of land.

73. The correct answer is C. Generally, an assault with a deadly weapon is intentionally placing another person in fear of a battery or an attempted battery through the use of an instrumentality calculated to cause severe harm or death. A battery is the intentional and unlawful application of force to another person. Here, since the woman intentionally shot at her ex-boyfriend using a gun (a deadly weapon), but did not actually strike him, she is guilty of assault with a deadly weapon. Although the bullet did not strike the actual person of the ex-boyfriend, it did knock an object out of his hand, which is sufficient to constitute a battery. Answers A and B are incorrect because attempted murder is the specific intent to kill coupled with an act in perpetration to complete the killing. Here, the facts state that the woman only intended to scare her ex-boyfriend, not kill him. Answer D is incorrect because, as discussed in Answer C, the woman is guilty of more than just battery.

74. C is the correct answer. First-degree murder is the premeditated intentional killing of a human being, or via felony-murder. Here, since the man immediately drove his car at the woman, he did not have time to premeditate or deliberate the killing. In addition, there was no underlying felony that triggered the felony murder rule. Therefore, since all murder that is not first-degree murder is second-degree murder, this is the most serious crime of which the man can be convicted. Answer A is incorrect. Involuntary manslaughter is an unintended killing that occurs during a criminal act or as the result of criminal negligence. Here, the facts do not indicate an unintended killing. The killing was intended. Answer B is incorrect. Voluntary manslaughter is a killing that would be murder except for the fact it was committed with adequate provocation, thereby mitigating the defendant's culpability. Here, there was no reasonable provocation. Not getting a promotion does not constitute reasonable provocation to kill someone. Answer D is incorrect for the reasons discussed in Answer C.

75. D is the correct answer. For purposes of criminal homicide, unless the victim is a living human being, there can be no homicide. However, most courts do not recognize a viable living fetus as a "living human being" such that the killing of the fetus would be homicide. Even though the fetus died as a result of the stabbing, the man will not be found guilty of homicide of the fetus. Answers A, B and C are incorrect for this reason. (Note, he may be guilty of attempted murder of the woman, but the call of the question does not discuss attempted murder.)

76. D is the correct answer. Where one party to a contract has made a material misrepresentation regarding the subject of the contract, the contract is voidable by the innocent party. Here, since the woman's statement regarding the defects in her car were likely to induce the man (or any other reasonable person) to purchase the car, the misrepresentation is material. Answers A and C are incorrect because, while the woman was a minor at the time she purchased the car, she was no longer a minor at the time of the attempted sale to the man. Answer B is incorrect because the man's reliance was reasonable, since no facts suggest that he should have known of the misrepresentation.

77. C is the correct answer. A contract entered into by a minor is voidable at the minor's choice, even though the minor may enforce the contract against an adult. Here, since the boy was a minor and stated that he wanted to avoid the contract, the contract is not enforceable. Answers A and B are incorrect for the reasons discussed in Answer C. Answer D is incorrect because contracts with minors are not automatically null and void; they may be voided by the minor, if the minor so chooses, as discussed in Answer C.

78. A is the correct answer. Parol evidence is admissible to show the existence of a mistake in the transcription of the terms of an oral agreement that was subsequently reduced to writing, where the terms of the agreement were not correctly transcribed to reflect the agreement of the parties. Here, since the baker and the supplier agreed that the baker would purchase 400 cakes, parol evidence that the baker did not agree to purchase only 40 cakes is admissible. Answer B is incorrect because it does not address the Parol Evidence Rule. Answer C is incorrect because the Parol Evidence Rule is not applicable when there was a mistake, as discussed in Answer A. Answer D is incorrect because the reasonableness of the price is not at issue here.

79. C is the correct answer. Parol evidence is admissible to show the existence of a mistake in the transcription of the terms of an oral agreement that was subsequently reduced to writing, where the terms of the agreement were not correctly transcribed to reflect the agreement of the parties. Here, there was a transcription error, and the man should not be allowed to take advantage of that error and take the more expensive laptop computer at the lower price. Therefore, the dealer will prevail and does not have to sell the more expensive laptop computer at the lower price. Answer A is incorrect for the reasons discussed in Answer C. Answer B is incorrect because, where only one party (here, the man) knows that a mistake has been made, that party cannot snap up an offer that was made in mistake. Answer D is incorrect because it misstates the facts. There was no mutual mistake, since only the man was aware of the mistake.

80. A is the correct answer. Since a party to a contract is entitled to receive the benefit of his bargain, where the other party to the contract induces the injured party to enter the contract by making fraudulent representations, the injured party is entitled to recover his damages to the extent there is a difference between what he was offered and what he received. B is incorrect because a person is not held to a reasonable discovery standard where his reliance was obtained by fraud. C and D are incorrect because Buyer has not received the full benefit of his bargain.

81. B is the correct answer. Danger invites rescue. The party creating the danger owes a duty of reasonable care to any rescuer who reasonably attempts a rescue. Here, the dangerous situation was the fire in the neighbor's home, which was a result of the neighbor's negligence in falling asleep with a lit cigarette. The man acted reasonably in attempting to rescue anyone who might be in the home, but the defendant (the neighbor) created a dangerous situation by both failing to remove the tricycle from the yard and by falling asleep with a lit cigarette. Thus, under these facts, the man will prevail in his suit against the neighbor. Answer A is incorrect because the Good Samaritan Rule is not applicable here; it is the rescuer rule that applies under these facts. The Good Samaritan Rule states that if a volunteer comes to the aid of an injured or ill person who is a stranger, the person giving the aid owes the stranger a duty of being reasonably careful. In some circumstances negligence could result in a claim of negligent care if the injuries or illness were made worse by the volunteer's negligence. Here, there is nothing in the facts to show that the man's conduct made the neighbor's condition any worse. Hence, the Good Samaritan Rule does not apply under these facts. Answer C is incorrect because, as discussed in Answer B, the man's injury was foreseeable under the circumstances. Answer D is incorrect because intervening negligence does not necessarily exculpate the neighbor from liability.

82. D is the correct answer. When a plaintiff sues a defendant for negligence and the defendant raises contributory negligence as a defense, contributory negligence will be a complete bar to the plaintiff's recovery. Therefore, whether the woman had maintained her car properly, whether the woman was speeding before her car stalled, and whether the man had a last clear chance of avoiding the accident will all be relevant factors in determining whether or not the man will prevail on a contributory negligence defense. Answers A, B, and C are not complete answers because the call of the question asked for which factors are relevant. Since all of them are relevant, Answer D is the correct answer.

83. B is the correct answer. An owner or operator of premises owes an invitee the duty of care to inspect the premises for dangerous conditions and to correct or

warn of such conditions. Thus, premises owner or occupier must correct or warn of conditions about which he knew or should have known. Here, if a customer spilled the grease moments before the woman slipped on it, the grocery store would not have had a reasonable period of time to discover the dangerous condition and will, therefore, not be held liable under the theory of negligence. Answer A misstates the woman's status and is, therefore, incorrect. Since the woman was a customer at the store, she was an invitee. Answer C is an incomplete statement of the duty for a premises owner or operator. It omits the fact that the owner or operator also has the duty to warn about dangerous defects. Answer D is an incorrect application of the law in the premises liability area.

84. A is the correct answer. Implied assumption of risk will be a defense where the plaintiff was actually aware of the particular risk involved and voluntarily encountered the known risk. Here, if the man had actual knowledge of the particular risk of slipping on crushed ice on the floor (if he saw it), then the defense will not apply. Answer B is incorrect because a minor may assume the risk where he fully appreciates the risks involved. Answer C is incorrect because the test is not an objective, but a subjective, standard; there is no way to determine if the man "should have" seen the crushed ice. Answer D is incorrect because it addresses the reasonableness of the man's conduct, not whether he voluntarily encountered a known risk.

85. A is the correct answer. When a defendant counsels, incites or induces another to commit or join in the commission of a crime, he is guilty of solicitation. However, where the solicitation is directed to a specific person, but defendant did not intend to solicit the person who actually received the communication, there is no crime of solicitation as to the person (the rookie) who received such communication. Here, the defendant (the man) intended to solicit a particular private investigator to do the breaking and entering. Since the rookie and not the intended private investigator found the note and committed the crime, the man is not guilty of solicitation. Answer B is incorrect because the standard is not reasonableness for solicitation. Answer C is incorrect because, although the man did ask that evidence from a murder trial be recovered, the person who found the evidence is not the intended party that was being solicited, as discussed in Answer A. Answer D is incorrect for the reasons discussed in Answer A.

86. D is the correct answer. Solicitation is the intentional enticement, advisement, incitement or other encouragement of another to commit a crime. Here, when the woman left the note for her boyfriend, requesting that he obtain a gun and rob a bank, a solicitation occurred. It does not matter that the boyfriend did not receive the note. The solicitation occurred when the note was left at his office. Answer A is incorrect, for the reasons discussed in Answer D. An-

swer B is incorrect both for the reasons discussed in Answer D and because it appears to misstate the facts; it appears that the boyfriend understood precisely what the woman wanted him to do. Answer C is incorrect because the boyfriend had already been solicited by the woman when left the note at his office, which occurred before the telephone conversation.

87. B is the correct answer. Conspiracy is an agreement between two or more persons to accomplish a lawful act by unlawful means or accomplish an unlawful purpose. Here, when the law student and his girlfriend agreed to break into the professor's office to steal his notes, there was an agreement to commit an unlawful act (breaking into the professor's office). Thus, the law student and the girlfriend are guilty of conspiracy. Since the mother only agreed to drive the law student and the girlfriend to campus, she did not agree to any criminal activity and is not guilty of conspiracy. Consequently, Answers A and C are incorrect for the reasons discussed in Answer B. Answer D is incorrect because, as discussed in Answer B, the law student and his girlfriend are guilty of conspiracy.

88. D is the correct answer. A defendant will be liable under the theory of vicarious liability for the crimes committed by another person when such is within the scope of a solicitation or conspiracy. In such instance, causation is established. Here, the woman requested that the boyfriend break into her mother's home and steal the jewelry. Thus, she was the cause of the boyfriend being in the home, and it was foreseeable that in the middle of a break-in, somebody could be shot and killed. The fact that she thought that nobody would be home does not relieve her of liability. Answers A and B are incorrect for the same reasons that Answer D is correct. Answer C is incorrect "Blackstone's Rule" does not exist.

89. D is the correct answer. Defamation is a defamatory statement of and concerning the plaintiff, published to a third party, causing injury to the plaintiff's reputation. When the plaintiff is a public official or public figure, as the producer is here because he is running for state congressman, statements about them are constitutionally privileged, unless published with knowledge of falsity or reckless disregard of the truth. Here, the facts do not indicate whether or not the critic acted with reckless disregard for the truth. Therefore, the producer will recover, unless the critic published her statements with knowing falsity and reckless disregard for the truth. Answer A is incorrect because the fact that the producer's film was doing well does not mean that the producer did not suffer any damages as a result of the critic's statements. Answer B is incorrect because, although opinions generally have constitutional protection, opinions are actionable when they contain known false statements or the statement was made with reckless disregard for the truth. Also, the statement that the producer

"was using the film as a springboard for his recently-announced candidacy for state congressman" is not an opinion; it is either true or false. Answer C is incorrect for the reasons discussed in Answer D.

90. A is the correct answer. Defamation is a defamatory statement, of and concerning the plaintiff, published to a third party, causing injury to the plaintiff's reputation. Since the former president is a private person (i.e., not a public official or figure), he may sue for defamation and recover if the defendant (here, the reporter) acted negligently and failed to use reasonable care in investigating the facts. Therefore, since it is unknown whether or not the reporter used reasonable care in her investigation of the facts before publishing the article, the former president will not recover if it turns out that the reporter used such reasonable care. Answer B is incorrect because the reporter will be liable, despite her belief in the truth, if she fialed to exercise reasonable care, as discussed in Answer A. Answer C is incorrect because the defamation has already occurred and a retraction is usually only effective in limiting general, but not special, damages. Answer D is incorrect because it sets forth the incorrect standard for liability. Negligence and tortious malice (knowing falsity or reckless disregard for the truth) are the standards for defamation, not ill will.

91. B is the correct answer. The general rule is that an advertisement is not an offer because it is usually too indefinite and is construed as an invitation to deal. A valid offer must contain quantity, time of performance, identity of the parties, price, and subject matter. Here, although there was a time of performance ("this weekend only"), the parties were identified (the man and any potential customers who saw the advertisement), the price was not specific because the man simply said "our couches – $299.00." This did not mean that all of the couches that the man was selling would be sold for $299.00. This could just be construed as the lowest-priced couches that he had available. The offer also lacked a specific quantity, even though the subject matter was couches. The man's advertisement did not specify which couches were offered at the $299.00 price, the ad could not be construed to invite acceptance to purchase the higher quality couch at the sale price. Answer A is incorrect because consideration is not normally reviewed by the courts for adequacy, as long as the contract is not unconscionable. Here, it is unlikely that the court would find it unconscionable to pay $299.00 for a couch listed at $1,499.00, particularly since no value of the higher quality couch is given in the facts. Answers C and D are incorrect because the advertisement is not an offer for the reasons discussed in Answer B; thus, acceptance is impossible here.

92. C is the correct answer. This is a contract for the sale of a car, which is a good. Thus, this contract is governed by the U.C.C. Under the U.C.C. Statute of

Frauds, a contract for the sale of goods for $500.00 or more must be in writing, signed by the party to be charged, to be enforceable. Here, the good (the car) was to be sold for $1,499.00, which is more than $500. Thus, this provision may apply. However, the U.C.C. provides an exception to this rule when both parties are merchants, one party sends the other party a written confirmation, which satisfies the Statute of Frauds as to the sender, and the party receiving the confirmation does not send a written objection within 10 days (U.C.C. 2-201). Here, although the dealer, who was a merchant, sent the woman a written confirmation, the woman was not a merchant. Thus, this exception does not apply. In this case, the woman (the party to be charged) did not sign any writing evidencing the terms of the contract. She will, therefore, prevail on her Statute of Frauds defense, and the contract will be unenforceable. Answers A and B are incorrect for the reasons that Answer C is correct. Answer D is an incorrect statement of law.

93. B is the correct answer. This is a contract for the sale of a home. Land sale contracts, such as the one here, are governed by the common law. A valid contract consists of an offer, acceptance, and consideration. Here, the woman and the man offered to purchase the home for $200,000. The seller immediately accepted when the real estate agent presented the offer to him, even though the offer was for a lower amount of money than he had paid to purchase the home five years earlier. Courts will not look into the adequacy of consideration. Consideration is merely a bargained-for exchange, which is the case here (money for the home). Answer A is incorrect. Although the seller had the real estate agent take the home off the market after the woman and the man made their offer (detrimental reliance), detrimental reliance or promissory estoppel is merely a consideration substitute. Here, since there was actual consideration (as discussed in Answer B), it is not necessary to look to a consideration substitute. Answer C is incorrect because courts do not look to the adequacy of consideration, as discussed in Answer B. Answer D is factually incorrect because the seller did detrimentally rely. However, as discussed in Answer A, detrimental reliance is not at issue here, since there was actual consideration (as discussed in Answer B).

94. D is the correct answer. Where performance of a contract becomes illegal as a result of a supervening change in the law after the contract was entered into, the promisor's performance is excused. Thus, the designer is not obligated to deliver the vases, and the retailer is not obligated to pay for them. Answers A, B and C are incorrect for the same reasons that Answer D is correct.

95. C is the correct answer. Public policy favors compromise settlement of disputed claims, and a settlement agreement is enforceable under contract law. Therefore, the woman may bring an action

to enforce the settlement agreement between her and the man. Answer A is incorrect because it merely states that a disputed claim exists, but reaches the wrong conclusion because the woman will prevail for the reasons discussed in Answer C. Answer B is incorrect because an executory settlement agreement (an agreement that has not been acted upon by either party) is enforceable. Answer D is incorrect because this question is based on contract law (the settlement agreement) and not the underlying tort claim.

96. B is the correct answer. After the student repudiated the settlement agreement, the piano teacher had the option of suing on either her original claim or on the terms of the settlement. Therefore, the student will not prevail on her defense that she only owed $500 because of the settlement agreement. Answer A is incorrect because settlement agreements are preferred in law and are not void ab initio (from the outset). Answer C is incorrect because, although the settlement agreement was made in compromise of a disputed claim, the student repudiated the settlement agreement when she refused to pay. Also, Answer C is incorrect for the reasons discussed in Answer B. Answer D is incorrect because the consideration is found in the disputed claim, namely in the piano teacher's agreement to accept a lesser amount of money than the amount of money alleged in her original complaint and the student's agreement to pay the lesser amount of money (accord and satisfaction).

97. B is the correct answer. The court will uphold the settlement agreement because the agreement was not based on any known misrepresentations made by the witness. Here, although the result may seem harsh, since the woman did not draw the mustache and beard on the painting, she willingly entered into the settlement agreement to avoid litigation. It is, therefore, a valid agreement. Answer A is incorrect because under the facts, there has been no satisfaction, since nothing has been paid yet. Answer C is incorrect because courts will usually enforce executory settlement agreements (agreements that have not been acted upon by either party). Answer D is incorrect because the parties were not aware of the witness' false statements at the time they entered into their agreement. Therefore, at the time of the agreement, there was consideration.

98. A is the correct answer. Consideration is required in all contracts. Consideration is a bargained-for exchange. A bargained-for promise to forbear from bringing a reasonable and good faith claim constitutes consideration. Here, the loan shark had a good faith claim for the $10,000 owed to him. Therefore, the father's promise to pay the $10,000 in exchange for the loan shark's promise to forbear from suing the medical student forms an enforceable contract. Answer B is incorrect because loyalty does not constitute consideration. Answer C is incorrect because Answer A is correct. Answer D is incorrect because the agreement between the loan shark and

the father is a contract that is enforceable in and of itself and, therefore, the loan shark does not have to first seek his remedy from the medical student.

99. D is the correct answer. Certain promises must be in writing to be enforceable under the Statute of Frauds. Those promises include promises in consideration of marriage; promises that cannot be performed within one year's time; promises concerning land sales; an executor's promise to pay the debts of the decedent out of his or her own pocket; promises regarding goods in excess of $500; and promises to pay the debt of another under a surety arrangement. A promise to pay an amount in exchange for a promise to forbear from asserting a legal claim does not fall within the Statute of Frauds and, therefore, is not required to be in writing to be enforceable. This should not be confused with the promise to pay the debt of another under a surety arrangement. Answers A, B and C are incorrect because Answer D is correct.

100. C is the correct answer. Embezzlement is the fraudulent conversion of rightfully entrusted property. Here, since the man voluntarily gave the woman the $2,000 for the woman's intended purchase of equipment to manufacture illegal drugs, the woman was in rightful possession of the money. (Note, even though the money was to be used for an illegal purpose, the woman still had rightful possession of the money.) The woman's subsequent using the money for a vacation, rather than for its intended purpose, is a conversion of the money, but because she had rightful possession of the money, it was an embezzlement. Answer A is incorrect because a larceny requires that the property not be in the rightful possession of defendant. As discussed in Answer C, the property (the money in this case) was in the woman's rightful possession. Thus, no larceny occurred here. Answer B is incorrect because it requires a false statement intended to obtain title and possession. There was no false statement at the time possession was obtained, and legal title was never obtained. Answer D is incorrect because robbery requires force or threat of force. Here, as discussed above, the woman obtained the money as a loan; there was no force or threat of force involved in her obtaining the money. Thus, no robbery occurred here.

END OF ANSWERS

PROFESSIONAL RESPONSIBILITY

PROFESSIONAL RESPONSIBILITY - QUESTION BREAKDOWN

1. Scope of Representation
2. Meritorious Claims and Contentions
3. Trial Publicity
4. Fees
5. Advertisements
6. Bar Admission
7. Reporting Professional Misconduct
8. Attorney Misconduct - Universal Jurisdicition
9. Judicial Conduct - Character Witness
10. Client Trust Accounts
11. Judicial Conduct
12. Judicial Conduct - Investments
13. Fees
14. Judicial Conduct - Campaigning for Office
15. Competence
16. Acceptance of Employment - Conflicts of Interests
17. Scope of Representation - Case Strategy
18. Avoiding Impropriety - Perjured Testimony
19. Availability of Legal Services – Fees
20. Availability of Legal Services – Solicitation
21. Availability of Legal Services – Fees
22. Availability of Legal Services – Fees
23. Candor To The Tribunal
24. Accepting Employment
25. Accepting Employment - Contingency Fee
26. Accepting Employment - Fees
27. Accepting Employment - Fee Splitting
28. Accepting Employment - Fee Splitting
29. Accepting Employment – Fees - Receipt of Client Chattels
30. Conflict - Fee Dispute
31. Disclosure - Future Criminal Conduct

PROFESSIONAL RESPONSIBILITY

32. Disclosure - Confidences
33. Competency - Supervising Attorneys
34. Competency
35. Acceptance of Employment - Conflicts of Interests
36. Fairness To Opposing Party
37. Legal Services - Fees
38. Accepting Employment - Imputation of Conflicts of Interest
39. Accepting Employment - Imputation of Conflicts of Interest
40. Accepting Employment - Imputation of Conflicts of Interest
41. Accepting Employment - Imputation of Conflicts of Interest - Waiver
42. Attorney Misconduct - Universal Jurisdicition
43. Confidentiality/Crime Exception
44. Accepting Employment – Fraudulent Conduct
45. Who Is the Client - Entity Conflict
46. Who Is the Client - Entity Conflict
47. Legal Services - Fees
48. Conflicts of Interest - Waiver
49. Client Confidentiality
50. Legal Services - Commingled Funds
51. Commingled Funds
52. Attorney-Client Relationship - Termination
53. Frivolous Claims
54. Candor To Tribunal - Failure To Disclose Legal Authority
55. Candor To Tribunal - Failure To Disclose Legal Authority
56. Perjury
57. Client Trust Accounts
58. Trial Publicity
59. Testimony of Lawyer
60. Communication With Represented Party
61. Role of Subordinate Lawyer
62. Special Role - Supervising Attorney
63. Practice of Law
64. Contingent Fee

PROFESSIONAL RESPONSIBILITY QUESTIONS

1. Paula and Donald are next-door neighbors and bitter personal enemies. Paula is suing Donald for trespass. Both parties believe in good faith in the correctness of their legal positions. Paula is represented by Lawyer Lucy and Donald is represented by Attorney Alexis. At the beginning of the representation, Paula told Lucy, "I don't want you to grant any delays or courtesies to Donald or his lawyer. This is war, and I want you to insist on every technicality." Lucy has served written interrogatories on Donald. Due to a death in Donald's family, he has requested a one-week extension of the deadline for answering the interrogatories. May Lucy grant the extension?

    A. Yes, unless granting the extension would prejudice Paula's rights.

    B. Yes because Alexis was not at fault in causing the delay.

    C. No because Lucy owes a duty of loyalty to Paula.

    D. No, unless Paula changes her instructions and agrees to the extension.

2. Attorney Alfred is in-house legal counsel for the environmental group Save Our Scenery (SOS). SOS is opposed to a proposed shopping center development that would require the clearing of 500 acres of forest in Omega County. SOS has sponsored proposed legislation that would designate the forest as a State Park and prevent the development. However, the legislation is stuck in a legislative committee. In the meantime, the Omega County Council approved the proposed development by a unanimous voice vote. One of SOS's staff members brings to Alfred's attention a rule that requires a secret ballot vote in all County Council matters. Alfred considers a lawsuit seeking to compel the Council to redo its earlier vote using a secret ballot. Though Alfred is certain that the result of a new vote would be the same, a "do over" would give the State Park legislation a chance to make it out of committee and be enacted. May Alfred file the lawsuit?

    A. No because the difference between a voice vote and a secret ballot vote is frivolous.

    B. No because Alfred's primary purpose in filing the suit would be delay.

    C. Yes because protecting the environment is a proper purpose.

    D. Yes because there is a valid legal basis for the lawsuit.

3. Millionaire actress Lana Larson dies unexpectedly of a drug overdose, leaving her entire fortune to her infant daughter, Beatrice. Lana was married to Defendant Daniel at the time Beatrice was born. Under applicable law, Daniel is presumed to be Beatrice's father, but that presumption can be rebutted by a DNA test ordered pursuant to a parentage case. Plaintiff Patrick has come forward and claimed a long-time affair with Larson, and that he is Beatrice's father. Beatrice's father will exercise control over the child's now substantial fortune. Plaintiff Patrick has hired Attorney Alice to file a paternity action on his behalf. The matter has attracted substantial media attention, and as soon as Alice files the action, Attorney Alice is surrounded by reporters seeking a comment. Which of the following statements, if believed by Alice to be true, would be proper for her to make?

I. "As stated in our pleadings, we believe that a DNA test will prove conclusively that Patrick is the father of Beatrice."

II. "Lana was no longer in love with Daniel by the time Beatrice was conceived."

III. "We have been unable to locate several people whose testimony will be helpful to us, and we implore them to contact us immediately."

A. II only.

B. III only.

C. I and III, but not II.

D. I, II, and III.

4. Calico Corporation hires Attorney Albert to defend it in a products liability lawsuit. Calico's General Counsel, Gary, becomes dissatisfied with Albert's handling of the case, so he fires Albert and hires Lawyer Lois to continue the representation. While reviewing the file, Lois notices billing statements from Albert to Calico, which reflect outrageously excessive charges for things like photocopying, travel expenses, and meals. When Lois asks Gary about the charges, Gary makes the following statement: "Look, I realize we made a mistake in hiring Albert, but we didn't pay those charges, and we're done with Albert, so I'd appreciate it if you would not pursue those charges any further." Is Lois subject to discipline if she fails to report her knowledge of Albert's overcharges to bar authorities?

A. No, unless Gary changes his mind and allows Lois to report the wrongdoing.

B. No, if Gary is convinced Calico was not harmed by the overcharges.

C. Yes, unless Lois believes the overcharges were a mistake.

D. Yes, if Lois believes Albert was guilty of professional misconduct.

5. A lawyer places an advertisement in a raunchy magazine. In the ad, he states that he has never lost a drunken driving case. The lawyer is subject to discipline because:

   A. Advertising is per se unlawful.

   B. Advertising is per se in violation of the rules.

   C. The ad must be in a dignified forum.

   D. The ad is misleading.

6. Many years ago, in college, a woman was suspended for being caught with a small amount of marijuana on her person. She was suspended for one semester, then later returned to graduate with honors. On her bar application, she is asked if she was ever suspended from any school. She writes "no." Five years after being admitted, a former boyfriend of hers informs the bar. The bar investigates and finds that she knowingly lied. The lawyer is suspended from practice for 6 months. Is the suspension lawful?

   A. No because of the statute of limitations.

   B. No because it is unrelated to present moral turpitude.

   C. Yes because it is a very clear violation of the rules.

   D. None of the above.

7. A lawyer learns that his boss, who is also an attorney, is embezzling funds. Because the lawyer fears for his job, he does nothing. The lawyer's silence is:

   A. Proper.

   B. Proper, if he asks the boss to do the right thing and turn himself in.

   C. In violation of the rules of professional responsibility.

   D. In good faith, thus, excusable.

8. A lawyer goes on a hunting trip to Canada. One evening, he gets in a bar room brawl and kills two men. He is convicted of two counts of involuntary manslaughter. The lawyer's home state decides to discipline him. Is this permissible?

   A. No because it was outside the state.

   B. No because it was outside the country.

   C. No because the actions were unrelated to the practice of law.

   D. Yes.

9. A man is on trial for willful tax fraud. His old friend, who is a municipal judge, knows that the man is of the highest moral character. The man could really use the judge's testimony, but only as it relates to the man's good character. Should the judge so testify?

A. No because it appears improper.

B. No because judges can never be witnesses.

C. No because the man may be of bad character.

D. Yes.

10. Attorney represented Plaintiff, who agreed to a settlement of $25,000. Attorney received a check in that amount from Defendant, payable to Attorney's order. Attorney endorsed and deposited the check in Attorney's Clients' Trust Account. Attorney promptly notified Plaintiff and billed Plaintiff $5,000 for legal fees. Plaintiff disputed the amount of the fee and wrote Attorney stating, "I will agree to pay $3,000 as a reasonable fee for the work you did, but I will not pay anything more than that." It is proper for Attorney to:

I. Send $20,000 to Plaintiff and retain $5,000 in Attorney's Clients' Trust Account until the fee dispute is settled.

II. Send Plaintiff $20,000, transfer $3,000 to Attorney's office account, and retain $2,000 in Attorney's Clients' Trust Account until the dispute is settled.

III. Send Plaintiff $20,000 and transfer $5,000 to Attorney's office account.

A. I only.

B. II only.

C. I and II, but not III.

D. I, II, and III.

11. A state appellate judge teaches law for a local law school and is paid for her teaching. Which of the following are true?

A. She should not be paid, but since she is paid, she should report her income.

B. She should not be paid at all.

C. She should report her income.

D. She should not be teaching law.

12. A judge invests in the stock market for herself and her immediate family. She does quite well. Is this permissible?

A. Yes because she does well.

B. Yes because judges can do anything they want.

C. Yes because a judge can manage her own finances.

D. Yes because this business is unrelated to the practice of law.

13. Defendant Danny hires Lawyer Lucy to represent him in a driving under the influence (DUI) of alcohol case. They agree in a written retainer agreement

that Lucy will be paid $200 per hour for her work. Unbeknownst to Danny, Lucy begins work on researching, writing, and filing an innovative motion to keep the results of the breathalyzer test Danny took out of evidence. The motion is ultimately successful, and the charges against Danny are dropped. However, as a result of the motion, Lucy bills Danny for approximately 100 more hours, or $20,000 more than an attorney would typically charge for a DUI defense.

Is Lucy subject to discipline?

A. No because Danny was ultimately exonerated.

B. No because $200 is a reasonable hourly fee.

C. Yes, unless Lucy really worked for all of the extra 100 hours for which she billed Danny.

D. Yes because the fee charged was significantly more than other lawyers in the jurisdiction would have charged and Danny did not approve the additional fees in advance.

14. A lawyer is campaigning for judicial office. It is a tough race. The lawyer, thus, pledges that, "If there is any doubt, I will order the maximum sentence." Is this proper?

A. Yes.

B. No.

C. More facts are needed.

D. It depends on the jurisdiction.

15. A lawyer has just passed and been admitted to the bar, after having failed it three times prior. He decides to set up his own criminal law practice, even though he has virtually no experience in this area. When he opens up a law office immediately after being admitted to the bar, he is:

A. Subject to discipline because he is per se incompetent in this legal area.

B. Subject to discipline because he is actually incompetent in this area.

C. Not subject to discipline because he is presumed competent.

D. Not subject to discipline because he is actually competent.

16. Lawyer Louis is one of the top communications lawyers in the country. The federal government announces that a limited number of new broadcast licenses will be made available next year. Two major broadcasting companies, CNNC and KBCJ, separately contact Louis and ask him to represent them in their applications for one of the new licenses. Though in some sense, the two companies will be competing for one of

the limited number of licenses, Louis is confident that he can adequately represent each in their applications. May Louis represent both companies?

A. Yes, as long as each gives informed written consent and agrees to waive any actual and potential conflicts that may arise from the representation.

B. Yes, provided that each agrees to waive their right of confidentiality owed to them by Louis.

C. No because the companies' interests are directly adverse in relation to obtaining a license.

D. No because a lawyer owes each of his clients a duty of loyalty.

17. A lawyer represents a client who is charged with the statutory offense of "Driving an Automobile while under the Influence of Alcohol." The client talks with a slight lisp and tends to be snide when he is questioned. The lawyer, therefore, decides that the client must not take the stand in his own defense. The client insists that he be so allowed. The trial ends with the client fully acquitted, even though he does not take the stand. Should the lawyer have let the client take the stand?

A. Yes because this is an area of client decision.

B. Yes because a client's funda-

mental desires should always be followed.

C. Yes because the jury may have drawn an adverse conclusion from the client's silence.

D. No, because this was an area of attorney strategy.

18. A client is on trial for murder. He has pled not guilty. However, before trial, the client admits to the lawyer that he actually did commit the crime of which he was accused. If the lawyer coaches the client as to how to best lie on the stand, the lawyer is:

A. Behaving within the norms of the profession.

B. In technical violation of the norms, but is not subject to discipline.

C. Subject to discipline.

D. Not subject to discipline.

19. A lawyer charges only $25 to prepare simple bankruptcy papers, intentionally undercutting the price of his peer lawyers. The lawyer's undercutting the price of his peer lawyers is:

A. In technical violation of the disciplinary norms.

B. In substantial violation of the norms.

C. Proper.

D. Improper.

20. A probate attorney prepares several wills for a client. Two weeks after preparing the last of such wills for that client, the client's sole beneficiary dies. The attorney finds out about the death of the sole beneficiary. However, the attorney has not made subsequent contact with the client.

    Which of the following is true?

    A. It is improper for the attorney to contact the client; the attorney must wait for the client to contact him first.

    B. It is proper for the attorney to contact the client regarding changing the will, and the attorney should, in fact, make such contact.

    C. The attorney will be disciplined for his failure to contact the client.

    D. None of the above.

21. A client comes to see a lawyer about a drunk driving case. The lawyer determines that this is a routine case and charges $10,000 to represent this client. This fee:

    A. May be excessive and, thus, subjects her to possible discipline.

    B. Is probably not excessive and, thus, is proper.

    C. Is totally within her own discretion.

    D. Is improper.

22. An attorney is contacted by the State Bar for potential discipline for charging "excessive fees." In order to discipline the attorney for charging an excessive fee, which of the following are relevant:

    A. Her expertise, her reputation, and the difficulty of the case.

    B. The difficulty of the case and the fees charged by similarly situated attorneys.

    C. The attorney's expertise, her reputation, the difficulty of the case, and the fees charged by similarly situated attorneys.

    D. The attorney's expertise, her reputation, the difficulty of the case, the fees charged by similarly situated attorneys, and the fees charged by one of the attorney's direct competitors.

23. Plaintiff Patty is suing her former employer Evenco for wrongful termination. On cross-examination, Evenco's lawyer asks Patty if she ever came to work under the influence of alcohol after March 31, 2009, a date upon which the parties agree Patty came to work

drunk. Patty answers "no." While the answer is literally true, Patty's lawyer Lucas knows that Patty in fact went to work under the influence of a number of other narcotics besides alcohol on dates after March 31, 2009. Must Lucas disclose to the tribunal the fact that Patty appeared for work under the influence of narcotics after March 31, 2009?

A. No because an attorney owes a paramount duty of confidentiality to his client.

B. No because Patty's testimony was literally true.

C. Yes because an attorney owes a duty of candor to the tribunal.

D. Yes because an attorney must take remedial measures if the attorney reasonably believes the tribunal will draw a false inference from the evidence presented.

24. An attorney in a large law firm is contacted by a woman who wants that attorney to represent her in her divorce case. The attorney's firm charges a minimum of $20,000 to handle divorce cases. The woman cannot afford to pay more than $5,000. The attorney already does a great deal of pro bono work and, therefore, decides to refuse to represent the woman for less than $20,000. The attorney's refusal to represent the woman:

A. Is proper because rarely are attorneys required to accept clients.

B. Is improper because attorneys are not permitted to turn away clients in need.

C. Is improper because $20,000 is an excessive fee.

D. Is proper because the woman should not have contacted a large law firm to handle her case for only $5,000.

25. On one occasion, a client sought the services of an attorney for a criminal matter. The attorney refused to represent the client because the client could not afford the attorney's retainer. Finally, the attorney agreed to lower the retainer to just $2,000. However, the client told the attorney that he could not afford even a $2,000 retainer. The attorney felt sorry for the client and agreed to represent him "for $500 now, and you can pay me $1,500 if you are acquitted." The client lost the case and was sent to prison. The attorney did not bill him for the $1,500.

The attorney's fee agreement with the client:

A. Was in good faith. Thus, the attorney is not subject to discipline.

B. Is a violation of the ethical norms, only if the attorney acted in good faith.

    C. Is a violation of the rules, under the <u>Leon</u> case.

    D. Subjects the attorney to discipline.

26. A transactional attorney charges different fees for clients, depending on the difficulty of the transaction. He also charges some clients with virtually identical cases different fees. Is this proper?

    A. Yes because attorneys do not need to bill the same amounts.

    B. No because, although different attorneys can bill different amounts to different clients, each individual attorney must bill the same amount to every client who has similar legal work. It is also a violation of the Equal Protection Clause.

    C. No because, although different attorneys can bill different amounts to different clients, each individual attorney must bill the same amount to every client who has similar legal work.

    D. No because it is a violation of the Equal Protection Clause.

27. A client seeks the advice of an attorney regarding highly complex litigation. The attorney calls a lawyer friend to see if he is willing to help out. The lawyer agrees, as does the client. The fee is not raised and the client agrees to this arrangement in writing. The attorney and the lawyer spend equal time on the client's case and split the fee equally.

Based on the above facts, is the attorney subject to discipline for utilizing the lawyer friend's services on this case?

    A. Yes because fee splits, with attorneys outside the firm, are per se violations of the norms of the profession.

    B. Yes because the fee split was not in proportion to the actual work performed.

    C. Yes because the client did not consent to the fee split.

    D. No.

28. One attorney decides to associate with an attorney from another firm to assist him with a client's case. He obtains the client's consent, but fails to tell the client that he has the option to contact another attorney before consenting. The attorney and the associated-in attorney do equal work and split the fee equally. With regard to the fee split, it would have been preferable for the first attorney:

    A. To have asked the client's permission prior to even calling the second attorney.

    B. To have asked the client's permission prior to calling the second attorney or to have withdrawn completely.

C. To have either asked the client's permission prior to calling the second attorney or to have given the associated-in attorney the greater portion of the fee.

D. To have either asked the client's permission prior to calling the second attorney, to have withdrawn entirely, or to have given the associated-in attorney the greater portion of the fee.

29. A lawyer accepts an engagement ring from her client in lieu of a $1,000 payment. The ring was worth approximately $1,100. Such a fee arrangement is:

    A. Improper.

    B. Proper.

    C. A violation of the Model Rules.

    D. None of the above.

30. A client contacts a lawyer to represent him in a criminal case. The client pays the lawyer's fee of $20,000 up front. Despite the lawyer's best efforts in court, the client is convicted. The client then demands the return of his $20,000. What should the lawyer do?

    A. Nothing.

    B. Return the fee.

    C. Tell the prosecutor.

    D. Recommend arbitration of the dispute.

31. A lawyer represents a client in a case involving an alleged contractual misrepresentation the client made to his roommate. At one point, the client says, "If this [expletive] continues, I'm going to have to get someone to kill my roommate."

    The lawyer tells the client, "Do not do that. It will only make your problems worse."

    The client responds, "Perhaps so, but I'm getting very close to having him taken out, and I mean it."

    The lawyer does nothing, and, unfortunately, the roommate is murdered, apparently by the client.

    Which of the following is most correct?

    A. The lawyer is subject to discipline because he was required to reveal the danger to the roommate.

    B. The lawyer is subject to discipline because he was required to withdraw from the case.

    C. The lawyer behaved properly because the crime was not reasonably apparent.

D. The lawyer behaved properly because the case involved his client.

32. An attorney is called before the State Bar's disciplinary board regarding the fact that the attorney was told by her client that the client intended to commit tax fraud and the attorney failed to notify the Internal Revenue Service. Which of the following is correct?

    A. The attorney is permitted to reveal the conversation between herself and the client to the disciplinary board because the client had no reasonable expectation that the attorney would keep such information confidential.

    B. The attorney is not subject to discipline for failing to notify the Internal Revenue Service. However, the attorney is permitted to reveal the conversation between herself and the client to the disciplinary board, if it is relevant to the attorney's defense.

    C. The attorney is subject to discipline.

    D. The attorney is subject to discipline only if the Internal Revenue Service has subpoenaed the information from the attorney because the Internal Revenue Service has the right to know about potential frauds.

33. Questions 33 and 34 relate to the following facts:

    Lawyer Lucy is an expert in securities regulation law. Corp, a corporation, retains Lucy's law firm to qualify Corp's stock for public issuance. After accepting the representation, Lucy assigns the matter to Associate Abe, a newly hired associate with Lucy's firm who is just out of law school, so Lucy can pursue other matters. Abe does not want to take the case, telling Lucy that he knows nothing about securities law and doesn't have time to get up to speed on the matter. Lucy tells Abe, "Tough luck. I learned how to sink or swim on my own with these cases and you will, too. I've got no time to hold your hand while you learn how to be a lawyer." Was Lucy's conduct proper in this matter?

    A. No, unless Corp had given Lucy express permission to assign an associate to work on the matter.

    B. No because Lucy knew Abe was not competent to handle the matter, and she failed to provide supervision adequate to protect the client's interest.

    C. Yes because as a member of the bar, Abe is licensed to handle any legal matter.

    D. Yes because Lucy could have turned the case down in the first place.

34. Despite his misgivings, Abe agrees to work on the matter. However, as he feared, Abe makes a variety of mistakes that result in the public offering being invalidated, and Corp being subjected to a variety of lawsuits. A more experienced securities lawyer would not have made such mistakes. Is Abe subject to discipline?

A. Yes because Abe had a duty to refuse to work on the matter.

B. Yes because Abe failed to provide competent legal representation.

C. No, as long as he worked diligently on the matter.

D. No because Abe was entitled to defer to Lucy's judgment that he was competent to handle the matter.

35. Brothers Bobby and Benji are charged with robbery of a gas station and felony murder, as the cashier was shot and killed during the robbery. It is alleged that Bobby committed the robbery and the killing while Benji waited outside in the car. In fact, the evidence showing that Benji was a knowing participant in the crime is extremely weak. The brothers want Attorney Alpha to represent them jointly, and are willing to waive any conflicts of interest. Alpha expects the D.A. to offer leniency to Benji in exchange for his testimony against Bobby. May Alpha represent both Bobby and Benji concurrently?

A. No because Alpha cannot reasonably believe that he can represent adequately the interests of both brothers in these circumstances.

B. No because Federal Rule of Criminal Procedure 44 prohibits joint representation in such circumstances.

C. Yes, unless the brothers' testimony will be directly conflicting.

D. Yes because the brothers are willing to waive any conflicts of interest.

36. Catina is a long time client of Tax Attorney Alberto. After filing her most recent tax return, Catina meets with Alberto. She tells Alberto that she took some pretty aggressive positions in preparing the return, and fully expects to get audited by the IRS. She then hands Alberto some paperwork that contains receipts and calculations relating to the tax return. Catina asks Alberto to hold onto the documents in anticipation of an IRS audit. Alberto agrees and places the paperwork in one of his file cabinets. Is Alberto subject to discipline?

A. Yes because it is improper for a lawyer to tamper with or conceal evidence.

B. Yes because a lawyer must turn over the fruits or instrumentalities of a crime that come into the lawyer's possession.

    C. No because what Catina told him about the documents is confidential.

    D. No because there is no duty to turn over evidence of potential wrongdoing before any audit by the IRS.

37. A lawyer agrees to represent a client on a murder case. The client is indigent, so the lawyer agrees to do the case for 50% royalties on a book about the case that the lawyer "may write after the trial is complete." Before the trial, the client pleads guilty to negligent homicide. The lawyer never writes the book and, thus, receives no fee. The lawyer's fee agreement is:

    A. Proper because the client consented.

    B. Proper because there was no actual prejudice.

    C. Proper, but only because the book was never written and the case did not go to trial.

    D. None of the above.

38. A lawyer worked for one law firm for many years. She then switched to another firm. While at the previous firm, the lawyer had a minor role in a suit against a woman by a client. In the course of that suit, the lawyer learned some confidential information about her then client. Presently, a third party approaches the lawyer regarding representing her in a suit against that former client. The suit is somewhat related to the earlier case. If the attorney accepts the case, she is:

    A. Subject to discipline.

    B. Subject to discipline, only if she compromises anything she learned about that former client.

    C. Subject to discipline, unless she is screened from any participation in the case.

    D. Not subject to discipline.

39. A law firm enters into an agreement to represent a new client. Shortly thereafter, the senior partners learn that one of their new attorneys had represented another individual who was suing that client. Which of the following actions will prevent the partners from being subject to discipline?

    A. Immediately terminating the new attorney and then taking the case.

    B. Taking the case but screening the new attorney from any participation in the case.

    C. Immediately terminating the new attorney, or screening the new attorney from any participation in the case, or obtaining written consent from all involved.

D. Immediately terminating the new attorney or screening the new attorney from any participation in the case.

40. An associate in a small firm once represented a man in a lawsuit against a woman. Some time later, the associate left and joined a big firm. The woman then contacted the big firm about possible representation. After interviewing her, the firm decided to not take his case. Shortly afterward, one of the big firm's partners left and started his own solo practice. The solo practitioner was then contacted by an individual looking for representation in a lawsuit against the woman. May the solo practitioner take the case?

   A. Yes because there is no longer the imputation of conflicts of interest.

   B. Yes because the solo practitioner was never disqualified from this representation.

   C. No because once there has been a conflict of interest, the taint of that conflict can never be vitiated.

   D. No.

41. A firm is about to represent a plaintiff who is suing a defendant. However, in the course of their due diligence, they discover that, prior to being hired by the firm, one of their associates once represented someone who had sued the plaintiff. Both opposing counsel and the defendant are made aware of the potential conflict and consent in writing to the firm's representation of the plaintiff, so long as the associate is screened off. Under these facts, are the firm's partners subject to discipline if they take the case?

   A. Yes.

   B. No.

   C. No. However, the associate is subject to discipline if the firm takes the case.

   D. No. However, the associate is subject to discipline because she will probably assist opposing counsel in the case.

42. Lawyer Linda is admitted to practice in State A, but not in State B. Her cousin asks her to write a letter recommending him for admission to practice law in State B. Linda knows that her cousin is educationally well-qualified to be a lawyer, but she regards him as thoroughly dishonest. May Linda write a letter, stating that her cousin is fit to practice law?

   A. No because Linda is not a member of the bar of State B.

   B. No because Linda would be making a false statement of a material fact.

C. Yes because her belief about her cousin's lack of honesty is merely her own opinion.

D. Yes because the bar of State B will decide for itself whether her cousin is a person of good moral character.

43. A lawyer is representing a client accused of theft from a store. The client then asks his lawyer for advice on the best time and way to violently rob a bank, since the lawyer had spent many years working for banks and would be likely to know the answer. What should the lawyer do?

A. Withdraw from further representation of the client.

B. Inform the managers of the bank that the client intends to rob that bank.

C. Inform the court of the client's intentions to violently rob the bank or keep silent; it is up to the lawyer's discretion.

D. Assist the client in the bank robbery so as to minimize injuries to bystanders.

44. A lawyer works for a corporation. The corporation's president is contemplating a complex business transaction that the lawyer believes to be fraudulent. The lawyer informs the president of his belief that the contemplated transaction is fraudulent, but the president says, "I think we'll go ahead anyway." If the lawyer goes directly to the Board of Directors, requesting that they override the president's decision, the lawyer is:

A. Behaving properly.

B. Subject to discipline.

C. Behaving improperly.

D. None of the above.

45. An attorney works as in-house counsel for a corporation. One day, an employee of the corporation approaches the attorney about illegal acts that the employee's direct supervisor has requested the employee to perform, some of which the employee has already performed. What should the attorney do?

A. Tell the corporation that he is no longer the corporation's attorney but will, instead, be the employee's attorney from here on out.

B. Counsel against the fraud.

C. Tell the employee that the attorney is not the employee's lawyer.

D. Tell the employee not to be concerned about his past fraudulent actions.

46. Plaintiff Polly slips, falls, and injures herself while shopping in a Whole Grains supermarket. Polly sues Whole

Grains in Federal Court and alleges that the store negligently caused her injury by placing too much wax on its floor, making it unreasonably slippery. In response to the lawsuit, Whole Grains' CEO hires Lawyer Lucas to conduct an investigation to determine the merits of Polly's claim. During the course of his investigation, Lucas interviews Janitor Jones, who is responsible for waxing the floors in the supermarket. During discovery, Polly's Attorney Abe makes a discovery request for "the results of any internal investigation relating to the claim." Is Abe entitled to the results from Lucas' interview with Jones?

A. No, pursuant to the corporate attorney-client privilege from Upjohn v. United States.

B. No because each side must do its own work in preparing a lawsuit for trial.

C. Yes because Jones is not part of Whole Grains' control group and is not of manager status.

D. Yes, as long as Jones consents.

47. A lawyer agrees to represent a criminal defendant. Since the defendant is hard pressed for cash, the lawyer agrees to accept an expensive watch as an advance of the first $10,000 owed. Since the lawyer has not earned the $10,000 yet, he is in a quandary as to what to do with the watch. What is the lawyer's best course of conduct?

A. Wear the watch.

B. Sell the watch and put the $10,000 in his client trust account.

C. Place the watch in a client-only safety deposit box.

D. Give the watch to his girlfriend.

48. Attorney Alex represented Husband Hugh and Wife Winona in setting up their family business, a restaurant. During the course of the representation, Alex became highly familiar with the personal financial circumstances of both Hugh and Winona. Running the business puts a strain on the couple's marriage, and Hugh and Winona decide to divorce. Winona is served with a divorce petition from Hugh. After reading the petition, Winona notices that Alex is representing Hugh in the divorce case. Angry, Winona calls Hugh to complain. A short time later, Winona receives a letter from Alex asking her to consent in writing to his representation of Hugh in the divorce. Winona reluctantly agrees. Has Alex acted properly?

A. Yes because there is no substantial relationship between the divorce case and the business representation.

B. Yes because he obtained a conflict waiver from Winona.

C. No because the conflict in the divorce case was not waivable.

D. No because Winona's conflict waiver came after the representation had already begun.

49. Insured Ivan is involved in a car accident. Pursuant to the terms of his contract with Insco, his insurance company, Insco, provides Ivan with Attorney Alison to represent him in the ensuing litigation. There is no separate retainer agreement governing the representation. During the course of the representation, Ivan admits to Alison that he had been drinking prior to the accident. Alison includes this information in the monthly summary she prepares for Insco regarding each of the cases she handles on behalf of the company. As a result, Insco writes a letter to Ivan informing him that his policy does not cover accidents involving the use of alcohol. Has Alison acted properly?

   A. No because Ivan's confession was confidential.

   B. No because Ivan was the primary client and Insco the secondary client.

   C. Yes because she could not assist Ivan in defrauding Insco.

   D. Yes because Ivan committed a crime by drinking and driving.

50. A lawyer settles a case for a significant amount of money, on behalf of a client. The lawyer, unknown to the client, then invests the entire settlement in a business gamble and wins big. He then confesses this to the client and offers the client half of his profits, in addition to the amount of money that the client owed as part of the settlement. Is the lawyer subject to discipline?

   A. Yes because he has commingled funds.

   B. Yes because lawyers must not gamble.

   C. No because there was no harm to the client.

   D. No because the client profited substantially.

51. A lawyer wins a lot of money on behalf of a client. The lawyer promptly distributes the client's money to the client. However, the lawyer keeps his own fees in the client trust account for two more months, so as to avoid paying taxes. If the lawyer is called before the State Bar for discipline, the State Bar's best argument in favor of disciplining the lawyer is:

   A. There was harm to the client.

   B. There was commingling.

   C. Lawyers are never allowed to try to minimize their taxes.

   D. The lawyer should have closed the client trust account immediately upon the conclusion of this case.

52. A lawyer is representing a client on a "slip and fall" case. The lawyer is performing excellent work and is nearing settlement of the case. For no good reason, the client terminates the lawyer's employment. Under these circumstances, the lawyer:

   A. Should withdraw.

   B. Shall withdraw.

   C. May withdraw.

   D. Should seek arbitration.

53. An attorney is an excellent and tough lawyer. She is representing a client in a civil rights action. In order to motivate the opposing party to settle, she attempts to "wear down" his desire to sue. She does this by opposing every discovery request and by making several discovery requests that are not necessary. Is the attorney subject to discipline?

   A. No because this is an acceptable tactic.

   B. No because ours is an adversary system.

   C. No because discovery is, per se, acceptable.

   D. Yes.

54. State X and State Y each have state trademark registration statutes that are substantially similar in purpose and wording to the Lanham Act (the federal trademark registration statute). For many years, Daisy Dairy has used the mark "Daisy" on dairy projects it sells in State X, and it has registered the mark under the State X statute. Recently Noxatox Chemical began using the "Daisy" mark on cockroach poison it sells in State X. Daisy Dairy sued Noxatox under State X law in a State X court for intentional infringement of the "Daisy" mark. The complaint asks for an injunction, for an award of the profits made by Noxatox, and for money damages. Noxatox moved for summary judgment on the grounds that dairy products and cockroach poison do not compete with each other, that no sensible consumer could be deceived by the use of the same mark on such widely different goods, and that Daisy Dairy could not possibly have suffered monetary injury. The trial judge who will hear the motion is not well versed in trademark law, and the lawyer for Daisy Dairy failed to discover several pertinent court decisions. Which of the following decisions MUST the lawyer for Noxatox call to the judge's attention?

I. A United States Supreme Court decision, which holds that the Lanham Act authorizes an injunction to stop intentional infringement, even where the defendant's goods do not compete with the plaintiff's goods.

II. A decision of the United States Court of Appeals for the circuit that includes State X and State Y, holding that an injunction can be issued under the Lanham Act where the nature of the defendant's goods could cast a distasteful or odious image on the plaintiff's goods.

III. A decision of the Supreme Court of State Y which holds that the State Y registration statute authorizes an accounting of the defendant's profits in a case of intentional infringement, even where the plaintiff cannot prove monetary injury.

IV. A decision of the Supreme Court of State X which holds that in actions for intentional trespass to real property, State X trial judges have the power of courts of equity to fashion equitable remedies, even where the plaintiff cannot prove monetary injury.

A. All of the above.

B. None of the above.

C. I, II, and IV only.

D. I and IV only.

55. A lawyer is representing a client in a complex securities case. The opposing counsel has failed to cite two cases on two different points. Both are directly on point. One case is in State P (where this case is being litigated.) The other case is in sister State Q (State P usually follows the lead of State Q.) The lawyer reveals neither case to the court. Moreover, in closing argument, the lawyer alludes to facts that she did not offer in the case-in-chief (she believes she can "get this by" the inattentive and ill-informed jury.) The opposing party prevails in the verdict. Which of the following will subject the lawyer to discipline?

A. Losing the case.

B. Not revealing the State P case, as well as the lawyer's closing argument.

C. Not revealing the State Q case.

D. The lawyer's failure to inform opposing counsel about the opposing cases outside of court.

56. A client tells his attorney that he must perjure himself regarding the use of self-defense. The attorney tries to convince the client not to proceed, but the client is adamant. The attorney makes a decision that it is better that she help. She coaches the client on the best method to utilize this defense. Utilizing the perjury, the client is acquitted.

A. The attorney is subject to discipline, but is not subject to malpractice liability.

B. The attorney is not subject to discipline, but is subject to malpractice liability.

C. The attorney is subject to discipline and is also subject to malpractice liability.

D. The attorney is neither subject to discipline nor to malpractice liability.

57. Client Fujitomi entrusted Lawyer Lee with $10,000, to be used six weeks later to close a business transaction. Lee immediately deposited it in her client trust account; at the time, it was the only money in that account. Later that same day, the local bar association called Lee and asked her to rush out to the Municipal Court to take over the defense of an indigent drunkard, Watkins, who was being tried for violating an obscure municipal statute. Because of chaos in the Public Defender's Office, Watkins was being tried without benefit of counsel. By the time Lee arrived, the judge had already found Watkins guilty and sentenced him to pay a fine of $350 or spend 30 days in jail. Under a peculiar local rule of court, the only way to keep Watkins from going to jail was to pay the fine immediately and to request a trial de novo in the Superior Court. Therefore, Lee paid the fine with a check drawn on her client trust account, and Watkins promised to repay her within one week. Which one of the following statements is correct?

A. Lee's handling of the Watkins matter was proper.

B. Lee would have been subject to litigation sanction if she had allowed Watkins to go to jail.

C. If Lee had paid Watkins' fine out of her personal bank account, that would have been proper.

D. Lee would be subject to discipline for handling the matter in any manner other than she did.

58. An attorney holds a pretrial news conference regarding his client's case. The client was allegedly beaten up by the police without provocation. The attorney's motivation for holding the news conference is to motivate the other side to settle. On these facts alone, the attorney's conduct is:

A. Proper.

B. Not proper.

C. In violation of the disciplinary rules.

D. Not proper because the attorney's motivation is in violation of the disciplinary rules.

59. At the close of a lawyer's case, after a verdict has been obtained in favor of the lawyer's client, the lawyer takes the stand to state her fees (which the losing party must pay). Such is:

A. Proper.

B. Not proper.

C. In violation of the disciplinary rules.

D. Not proper because disclosure of the lawyer's fee is in violation of the attorney-client privilege.

60. A lawyer is representing a man in a case against a woman. The woman is being represented by an attorney from a nearby city. The man's lawyer calls the woman's attorney repeatedly to make an objectively fair offer of settlement. The attorney does not return the lawyer's calls. The man's lawyer then makes a written settlement offer with the request that, even if the offer is rejected, the woman's attorney must make phone or written contact. Still, the woman's attorney makes no contact. Finally, the man's lawyer contacts the woman directly. The woman is shocked that such generous offers were made and that the woman had never heard about them. The woman's attorney files a complaint with the State Bar against the man's lawyer for "interfering in the sacrosanct attorney-client relationship." This complaint will:

   A. Fail because of the bad faith of the woman's attorney.

   B. Fail because the man's lawyer had no reasonable alternative.

   C. Fail because no settlement was actually made.

   D. None of the above.

61. An associate works for a partner. The partner tells the associate to mislead the opposing party. The associate believes that doing so is against the rules of the State Bar. However, the partner insists. If the associate acquiesces, he is:

   A. Subject to discipline.

   B. Not subject to discipline.

   C. Civilly liable.

   D. Not civilly liable.

62. The senior partner at a law firm instructs a newly-hired attorney to mislead the court in a particular manner. Is the senior partner subject to discipline for giving the new attorney these instructions?

   A. No because the partner's advice does not violate the norms.

   B. No because it is not a violation of the rules if the senior partner himself does not engage in misleading the court but, rather, has another attorney do so.

   C. Yes because the senior partner's advice is both a vicarious violation of the norms and constitutes failure to adequately supervise junior attorneys.

   D. Yes because senior partners are supposed to set an example of ethical behavior.

63. A lawyer is licensed in State P. He decides to relocate to State Q where he is

not yet licensed. State Q will waive the lawyer in, for a nominal fee, without the need for the lawyer to sit for the bar examination. The lawyer relocates to State Q. While waiting to be sworn in, the lawyer does a few simple wills in State Q without being paid, primarily as favors. Is the lawyer subject to discipline?

A. Yes because he was practicing law without a license.

B. No because in effect he had a license.

C. No because he had no pecuniary motive.

D. No because he did not appear before a court.

64. Criminal Defense Lawyer Loman agreed to represent Defendant Demon at Demon's trial for burglary. Loman and Demon orally agreed on the following attorney fee arrangement. If Demon was acquitted, the fee would be $25,000. If Demon was convicted of any lesser included offense, the fee would be $5,000. If Demon was convicted of burglary, the fee would be $500. Loman further agreed to advance all litigation expenses, subject to Demon's promise to repay Loman whatever the outcome of the case. Which of the following statements are correct?

I. Loman is subject to discipline for not putting the fee agreement in writing.

II. It was proper for Loman to agree to advance the litigation expenses.

III. Loman is subject to discipline for charging a contingent fee in a criminal case.

IV. It was proper for Loman to require Demon to repay the advanced litigation expenses whatever the outcome of the case.

A. Only I, II, and IV are correct.

B. Only I and III are correct.

C. Only II and IV are correct.

D. All of the statements are correct.

END OF QUESTIONS

PROFESSIONAL RESPONSIBILITY ANSWERS

1. A is the correct answer. Lucy may properly grant the delay of one week. The issue in this question concerns ABA Model Rules of Professional Conduct Model Rule [MR] 1.2, Scope of Representation. Under Model Rule 1.2, the client directs the objectives of the representation but the lawyer is permitted to direct the means or strategies to achieve those objectives. Here, Paula wanted Lucy to "observe every technicality." Technically, Lucy could have objected to the delay. However, the details of the representation are properly left to the lawyer and a court would have likely granted Donald an extension under these circumstances. Lucy, as the lawyer, is permitted to make this call. B is incorrect because "fault" as to why the delay occurred does not come into play in this analysis. C is incorrect because, although Lucy certainly owes her client a duty of loyalty, the duty of loyalty is not breached here by permitting the short delay. D is incorrect because Lucy does not need Paula to agree to the extension.

2. D is the correct answer. Here, Alfred has a valid legal basis for requesting that the Council redo the vote. Under ABA Model Rules of Professional Conduct, Model Rule [MR] 3.1, Meritorious Claims and Contentions, Alfred would only be violating this rule if the lawsuit is frivolous. However, nothing prevents Alfred from bringing a technically valid lawsuit requesting the Council to comply with the law. The fact that it is the delay caused by the lawsuit that is more beneficial to Alfred's client than the actual result of the lawsuit does not change the analysis. A is incorrect because nothing in the facts suggests that the difference between a voice ballot and a secret ballot is frivolous. B is incorrect because "delay" can be a wise strategy for Alfred's client and this alone is not problematic, unless there is no basis in law or fact for the lawsuit. C is incorrect because we are not required to assess under the rules whether there is a proper purpose or not. The standard is whether the lawsuit is frivolous.

3. C is the correct answer. This type of question is called an Option Type of Question. You can handle these best through a process of eliminating a wrong answer option, and then eliminating answer choices with that option. Here, Option I is correct. Under ABA Model Rules of Professional Conduct, Model Rule [MR] 3.6, Trial Publicity, an attorney can provide limited information to the public in terms of trial publicity as long as it does not prejudice the case. Option I is permissible because it states what is in the public record, i.e., the pleadings. Option II is not permissible nor is it relevant. It would be considered an extrajudicial statement that could prejudice the proceedings, and therefore, this would be disallowed under Model Rule 3.6. Option III is

correct because a lawyer is allowed to request the public's help in identifying key witnesses or individuals with needed information. Therefore, answer choice C is correct because it properly states the right options of I and III, but not II. A and B are incorrect because they allow only one answer option, i.e., either II only or III only. And D is incorrect because it contains Option II, which is not permissible.

4. D is the correct answer. Under ABA Model Rules of Professional Conduct, Model Rule [MR] 1.5, Fees, it is improper to charge an excessive or unreasonable fee. Under Model Rule 8.3, Reporting Professional Misconduct, an attorney who "knows that another lawyer has committed a violation of the Rules of Professional Conduct that raises a substantial question as to that lawyer's honesty, trustworthiness or fitness as a lawyer in other respects, shall inform the appropriate professional authority." Here, Lois knows Albert violated the rules, i.e., violated Model Rule 1.5, and this was clearly dishonest as Albert himself admits that that he lied in his statement. Therefore, under Model Rule 8.3, Lois is required to report Albert. A is incorrect because the client's opinion does nothing to change the duty Lois has under Model Rule 8.3. B is incorrect because under the rules, there is no assessment of "damage" to a client; in other words, a client does not have to be damaged in order for there to be a violation of the rules (a damage assessment *is required* for malpractice). Here, Albert clearly violated Rule 1.5 and that is sufficient. C is incorrect because whether Lois believes it was a mistake or not is irrelevant.

5. D is the correct answer. Advertisements must not be misleading. ABA Model Rules of Professional Conduct Model Rule [MR] 7.1. A statement that a lawyer has never lost a case, even if true, is misleading because it sets up an unreasonable expectation regarding cases that no lawyer could claim; Quinn's ad is in violation of the rules. A and B are incorrect because lawyer advertising is given limited First Amendment protection. C is incorrect because there is no requirement that lawyer ads appear in a dignified forum.

6. C is the correct answer. Lawyers must not lie on their bar applications. To knowingly make a false statement of material fact shows a lack of good character, which subjects an attorney to discipline. ABA Model Rules of Professional Conduct Model Rule [MR] 8.1. Here, the woman lied on her bar application by concealing her suspension for marijuana use while she was in college. Thus, she is subject to discipline. A and D are incorrect because discipline is not for the purpose of punishment. Rather, it is to protect the public from dangerously inept or corrupt attorneys. Moreover, there are no statutes of limitations regarding disciplining attorneys. B is incorrect because it is permissible to discipline an attorney for past acts unrelated to her present psychological state.

7. C is the correct answer. A lawyer must turn in his delinquent peers provided that what they know is unprivileged. ABA Model Rules of Professional Conduct Model Rule [MR] 8.3(a). Here, the boss is not the lawyer's client. Thus, the lawyer's knowledge of the boss' embezzling funds is not privileged information. Consequently, A and B are incorrect, since the silence is not proper for the reasons discussed in C, and even the attorney's request for the boss to turn himself in (Answer B) does not relieve the attorney of the duty to turn in a delinquent peer (the boss). D is incorrect for two reasons. First, the lawyer's silence is not in good faith (since the attorney knows that the boss' activities are improper). Second, good faith is not an excuse for this kind of violation. (Note: California has no such requirement. However, the California rules are not tested on the MPRE, but they are tested in the essay portion of the California Bar Examination.)

8. D is the correct answer. A state can discipline a lawyer for actions performed anywhere, if such actions involve moral turpitude. Since manslaughter is morally wrong, discipline is acceptable, even if it occurred in another state. ABA Model Rules of Professional Conduct Model Rule [MR] 8.4; MR 8.5. Therefore, A and B are incorrect for the reasons discussed in Answer D. C is incorrect because the actions of moral turpitude need not be directly related to the practice of law.

9. A is the correct answer. Judges should not be character witnesses because it appears improper. ABA Model Code of Judicial Conduct Rule 3.3. Here, the man has asked his friend who is a municipal judge to be a character witness. It would be improper for the judge to do so. Therefore, D is incorrect. B is incorrect because judges may on occasion be required to testify, e.g., if they are a party to their own litigation. C is incorrect because the man's good or bad character is not the issue. The issue is whether the judge is permitted to testify.

10. C is the correct answer choice. Again, this is an Options Question so the best course of action is to go through each option to determine which ones are correct and incorrect. Option I is a correct option. Under ABA Model Rules of Professional Conduct, Model Rule [MR] 1.15, Client Trust Accounts, the rule states that an attorney cannot commingle client funds with attorney funds. Further, any amount in dispute needs to be kept in the Client Trust Account. Here, Lawyer billed client for $5,000. Client agreed that Lawyer earned $3,000, but there was $2,000 in dispute. Lawyer has a couple of different options as to how to handle this, but the main concern is not to commingle funds. Option I is correct because Lawyer should send the client the $20,000 that is client's award. Lawyer can keep the $5,000 in the Client Trust Account because that amount of Lawyer's fee is in dispute. Option II is also correct. Here, Lawyer can send the $20,000 to client. Lawyer is required to keep any disputed amount in the Cli-

ent Trust Account. Here, $2,000 is in dispute; $3,000 is not in dispute. Lawyer can properly transfer the amount "earned" and not in dispute to lawyer's office account. (As in Option I, Lawyer could have left the whole $5,000 in the Client Trust Account as well). Option II, however, is not correct. Because there is $2,000 in dispute, Lawyer cannot put the full amount into his office account.

11. C is the correct answer. Under ABA Model Code of Judicial Conduct Rule 3.15(A)(1), a judge is permitted to teach law and be paid. Judges should also make a public report of their extra judicial income. Thus, Answers A, B, and D are incorrect.

12. C is the correct answer. Judges are permitted to manage and participate in the investment of their financial resources. A judge must avoid financial and business dealings that would reasonably appear to exploit the judge's judicial position. ABA Model Code of Judicial Conduct Rule 3.11(A). A is incorrect because a judge may manage or participate in investments whether or not the judge does well. B is incorrect because judges cannot do anything they want. Their conduct is controlled by the Code of Judicial Conduct. D is incorrect because the business can be related to law, e.g., law teaching. ABA Model Code of Judicial Conduct Rule 3.1, Comment [1].

13. D is the correct answer. Under ABA Model Rules of Professional Conduct, Model Rule [MR] 1.5, a lawyer's fee must be reasonable. Here, Lucy's fees were significantly more than other lawyers in the jurisdiction and were unreasonable. A is wrong because whether the client wins or not is irrelevant to a discipline issue. B is incorrect because although $200 per hour is reasonable for an hourly fee, Lucy's overall fees were unreasonable. C is incorrect because, even if Lucy did work all of the hours, the fee would still be unreasonable.

14. A is the correct answer. Judges, when campaigning for office, generally should not make pledges regarding the way they would sentence. ABA Model Code of Judicial Conduct Rule 4.3 [Comment 1]. However, in this case, the lawyer/candidate is simply stating that the candidate will order the maximum sentence. This is not a specific comment about any particular case or particular area of law, and therefore, this is permissible. The First Amendment does allow candidates/judges to make general statements about what he/she intends to do if elected. B is incorrect because the First Amendment is applicable to judges, so judges can take a "law and order" stance. C is incorrect because ample facts were given. D is incorrect because the First Amendment controls in all United States jurisdictions.

15. C is the correct answer. Passing the bar exam, on its face, is proof of reasonable competence. Perhaps where the law is complex, a new lawyer should not begin practice in that area, but in any general

area of law, new lawyers are permitted to start right out. ABA Model Rules of Professional Conduct Model Rule [MR] 1.1. Here, criminal law is a general area of law in which anyone who has passed the bar exam is presumably competent. A and B are incorrect for the same reason that C is correct. Furthermore, B is incorrect because no facts indicate that the lawyer is actually incompetent. D is incorrect because no facts indicate that the lawyer is actually competent.

16. A is the correct answer. Under ABA Model Rules of Professional Conduct, Model Rule [MR] 1.7, a lawyer cannot represent concurrent clients with interests adverse to each other, unless the attorney believes she can do so and the client gives informed, written consent. Here, although it may initially seem like the clients would be adverse to each other, even a conflict with a current client can be overcome with client's written, informed consent. (Note that it would be rare for a client to actually do this, but the rules do permit it and that is what the MPRE tests). A correctly states the requirement that to get around a concurrent conflict of interest, you can obtain a client's written, informed consent. B is incorrect because there is nothing in the conflicts rules that require a waiver of confidentiality. C is incorrect because under Model Rule 1.7, a lawyer can get around a conflict through informed, written consent. D is incorrect because, although a lawyer does owe the client's a duty of loyalty, this does not trump the ability for a client to waive a conflict under Model Rule 1.7.

17. A is the correct answer. As a general rule, strategy is entirely within a lawyer's discretion. There are, however, certain fundamental choices that are entirely to be made by the client. Whether or not to take the stand is one of those areas. ABA Model Rules of Professional Conduct Model Rule [MR] 1.2(a). Thus, the lawyer should have let the client testify. B is incorrect because. if a client disagrees as to strategy, the lawyer may follow his own decisions and desires. C is incorrect because the real issue is not what the jury might think but, rather, the client's right to take the stand. D is incorrect for the same reasons that A is correct.

18. C is the correct answer. A lawyer must not make use of perjured testimony. ABA Model Rules of Professional Conduct Model Rule [MR] 3.3(a)(3), 3.3(b). The lawyer not only plans to make use of the client's perjured testimony, he also aids in the fraud on the court by coaching the client as to how to lie on the stand. A and D are incorrect for the same reason that C is correct. B is incorrect because a technical violation of the mandatory rules subjects an attorney to discipline. Of course, if it is merely a technical violation, the discipline will probably be light, e.g., private reprimand only.

19. C is the correct answer. There is nothing in the code that prohibits a lawyer from

charging low fees. On the contrary, lawyers are encouraged to compete and also to do some pro bono work (work for free). ABA Model Rules of Professional Conduct Model Rule [MR] 6.1. Thus, the lawyer's undercutting of fees is within his own discretion and is, thus, "proper." Choices A, B and D are incorrect for the same reasons that C is correct.

20. B is the correct answer because there is an exception to the rule barring solicitation of clients when the solicitation concerns a former client. ABA Model Rules of Professional Conduct Model Rule [MR] 7.3(a)(2). When a client is to be prejudiced, as is the case here (because the will needs to be changed, since the sole beneficiary is now deceased), the best course of conduct is for the attorney to initiate contact with that former client (on the related matter). Model Rule 1.3. A and D are incorrect for the reasons discussed in B. C is incorrect because, although lawyers "should" contact clients in like situations, such contact is within their discretion, unless of course, they tell the client that they will periodically inspect the legal document. Because this is a matter for attorney discretion, not doing so will not subject the attorney to discipline.

21. B is the correct answer. For the most part, attorneys can set their own fees, which are permitted to be substantial within the broad parameters of reasonableness. ABA Model Rules of Professional Conduct Model Rule [MR] 1.5. A and D are incorrect because, although excessive fees will subject an attorney to discipline, this fee was likely not excessive, for the reasons discussed in B. C is incorrect because attorney fees must be reasonable.

22. C is the correct answer. Expertise is a factor in whether the attorney fee is excessive or reasonable. The attorney's fame (reputation) is another legitimate factor. The more difficult the case, the higher the fee can be. Although not completely controlling, the fees of similarly situated attorneys are relevant in determining whether a particular attorney's fee is excessive. See generally ABA Model Rules of Professional Conduct Model Rule [MR] 1.5. Therefore, A and B are incorrect because they do not include all of these factors. D is incorrect because the fees charged by one particular competitor are not taken into account in determining the reasonableness of the attorney's fees.

23. B is the correct answer. ABA Model Rules of Professional Conduct, Model Rule [MR] 3.3, Candor to the Tribunal, requires a lawyer to correct any false testimony made by a client. Here, however, Patty answered the question truthfully. B is correct in that Patty's testimony was "literally" true. The attorney for the employer did not ask about other narcotics, and Lucas is under no obligation to offer additional information (which would actually breach Lucas' duty of confidentiality

to Patty). A is incorrect because, although an attorney does owe a duty of confidentiality to all clients, this is not the rule applicable to this question. C is incorrect because Lucas can comply with the duty of candor to the court, since Patty was technically truthful. D is incorrect because this misstates the rule; an attorney has no duty under Model Rule 3.3 to correct "inferences."

24. A is the correct answer. Nothing in the ABA code requires an attorney to accept all walk-in clients. The fees need only be reasonable. ABA Model Rules of Professional Conduct Model Rule [MR] 1.5. Attorneys are encouraged to perform some legal work for the poor for no charge, but are not required to do so. Model Rule 6.1. Thus, B and C are incorrect. D is incorrect because a client is free to contact law firms of any size and attempt to negotiate a fee.

25. D is the correct answer. Allowing the client to pay an additional $1,500 only if he is acquitted is essentially a contingency fee contract. Contingency fee contracts in criminal cases are per se prohibited. ABA Model Rules of Professional Conduct Model Rule [MR] 1.5(d)(2). A and B are incorrect because the attorney's good faith is no defense. C is incorrect because the Leon case is not relevant here. In the Leon case, the Connecticut attorney charged a fee that he did not earn, and he failed to properly communicate with the client or even prosecute the client's case. Here, the client lost his case, but there is nothing in the facts to indicate that this was due to the attorney's failure to communicate with the client or adequately prosecute the case. Thus, the Leon case is irrelevant here. (Note: California law does not, per se, prohibit such an arrangement. However, the MPRE does not test the California rules.)

26. A is the correct answer because attorney fees need only be reasonable, not equal. ABA Model Rules of Professional Conduct Model Rule [MR] 1.5. B and C are incorrect for the same reasons that A is correct. Furthermore, there is no State action; thus, the Equal Protection Clause is not relevant. Thus, D is also incorrect.

27. D is the correct answer. Fee splits with attorneys outside the firm are acceptable, if the client consents and the fee is not raised. ABA Model Rules of Professional Conduct Model Rule [MR] 1.5(e); MR 1.5 Comment [7]. Here, the client agreed and the fee was not raised. Thus, the attorney is not subject to discipline under these facts. A is incorrect for the same reasons that D is correct. B is incorrect because it misreads the facts. This fee split was in proportion to actual attorney work performed. C is incorrect because the client did consent to this fee split.

28. A is the correct answer because the original attorney must have asked his client's permission prior to even contacting the second attorney. ABA Model Rules of Professional Conduct

Model Rule [MR] 1.5(e). Both B and D are incorrect because withdrawal is not necessary. Both C and D are incorrect because the code does not suggest that disproportionate attorney fee splits are always preferable.

29. B is the correct answer. Although the receipt of client chattels as payment of the fee is not preferable, it is not prohibited. See ABA Model Rules of Professional Conduct Model Rule [MR] 1.5, Comment [4]. Here, the engagement ring is a client chattel. Thus, the attorney does not violate any of the Model Rules in accepting it. A, C and D are incorrect for the same reason that B is correct.

30. D is the correct answer. When there is a fee dispute between the lawyer and client, the lawyer should recommend arbitration. However, it is not required. See ABA Model Rules of Professional Conduct Model Rule [MR] 1.5, Comment [9]. (Note: it would be a different fact pattern entirely if the funds were in the attorney's trust account. This is not the case when the fee is paid up front, as here.) A is incorrect for the same reason that D is correct. B is incorrect because lawyers are not required to return fees that they reasonably believe they have earned. C is incorrect because lawyers must not threaten or harm clients so as to keep their fees, which are in dispute. Telling the prosecutor might appear to be a threat.

31. D is the correct answer. Somewhat surprisingly, there is no requirement that an attorney reveal an intended future crime of her client. The option is given, if the crime involves physical danger or corporate fraud under ABA Model Rules of Professional Conduct Model Rule [MR] 1.6 and [MR] 1.13. Here, although the crime involved physical danger, the lawyer had the option, but not the requirement, to warn the victim. The lawyer in this case chose to honor the attorney-client privilege instead. A is incorrect for the same reason that D is correct. B is incorrect because an attorney need only withdraw when the crime (or fraud) is on the court itself. C is incorrect because it misreads the facts – the crime was reasonably apparent.

32. B is the correct answer. An attorney is permitted to keep to herself her client's spoken intent to commit a future fraud. ABA Model Rules of Professional Conduct Model Rule [MR] 1.6(b)(2). Furthermore, an attorney is permitted to reveal a confidence, if it is reasonably related to and reasonably necessary to the defense of herself. Model Rule 1.6(b)(5). A is incorrect because it is irrelevant whether the client had a reasonable expectation that the information would be kept in confidence. Except where permitted by the rules, attorneys must keep all client conversations confidential regardless of the client's apparent reasonable expectations. C and D are incorrect for the same reasons that B is correct.

33. B is the correct answer. Under ABA Model Rules of Professional Conduct,

Model Rule [MR] 5.1, an attorney is required to supervise other attorneys when the more experienced attorney gives work. Here, Lucy knew that Abe was a new lawyer who was inexperienced in securities work. Her statement that she had to learn by "sinking" or "swimming" is irrelevant; she had a duty under Model Rule 5.1 to supervise Abe and she will be responsible for Abe's negligence. A is incorrect because the law firm did not have to approve Abe working on the case. C is incorrect because, although Abe is presumed to be competent as a licensed attorney, this does not mean that Abe can handle "any legal matter." Clearly the rule of competence contemplates that lawyers need to study and associate with more experienced attorneys when they are taking on a new matter.

34. B is the correct answer. Under ABA Model Rules of Professional Conduct, Model Rule [MR] 1.1, a lawyer must provide competent service. Here, if Abe was unsure of how to handle the securities issue, he was obligated to "gain competence" by either studying the area and/or associating with another lawyer with experience in that area. Just because Lucy was not willing to help him did not take away Abe's obligation to render competent legal work. Abe was required under Model Rule 1.1 to gain competence, i.e., ask another lawyer. A is incorrect because there is no duty to refuse work; in fact, the rules allow new lawyers to take on work, but to do so in a competent manner. C is incorrect because Abe is required to be competent as well as diligent. D is incorrect because Abe had his own ethical obligations; these are not negated simply because Lucy was his supervisory attorney.

35. A is correct. Under ABA Model Rules of Professional Conduct, Model Rule [MR] 1.7, a lawyer cannot undertake representation of clients that have interests adverse to each other. However, this conflict can be waived in some circumstances if the lawyer reasonably believes he can represent both parties, and the clients give informed, written consent. However, there are certain non-waivable (sometimes called non-consentable) conflicts. Two examples are joint clients in a criminal cases and parties in a domestic relations (divorce) case. Here, there is clearly a conflict; further, the conflict is not waivable by the clients. B is incorrect because Model Rule 1.7 disallows the representation; not Rule 44 of the Rules of Criminal Procedure. C is incorrect because, although true, i.e., the brothers will have conflicting testimony, this is not the reason why the representation is inappropriate. D is incorrect because the conflict cannot be waived.

36. D is the correct answer. Under ABA Model Rule 3.4, Fairness to the Parties, a party is not allowed to obstruct another party's access to evidence. Here, Alberto is not obstructing access to evidence; there is no case against the client yet and he is under no obligation

to turn over evidence for a potential case. A is incorrect because, although a lawyer cannot tamper with evidence, the facts do not suggest that Alberto was tampering with evidence. B is incorrect because there is no crime yet, if at all. C is incorrect because, although confidentiality always applies, that is not the issue here, and the duty of confidentiality would not allow Alberto to conceal or obstruct evidence if there were a case by the IRS.

37. D is the correct answer. An attorney is not permitted to receive as his fee rights to a book about the subject matter of the litigation. ABA Model Rules of Professional Conduct Model Rule [MR] 1.8(d). Thus, A, B and C are incorrect and D is the correct answer. (Note: California law may permit such an arrangement. See California Business and Professions Code §§6146-6149.5 and California Rules of Professional Conduct, Rule 4-200. However, the California rules, while tested on the California Bar Examination, are not tested on the MPRE.)

38. A is the correct answer. When a lawyer has learned something confidential and relevant about a client, she is not permitted to oppose that client in a later case. ABA Model Rules of Professional Conduct Model Rule [MR] 1.9(a). B is incorrect because it misreads the facts. The facts indicate that the prior confidence is "somewhat related." Thus, the lawyer cannot take the case. C is incorrect because screening the lawyer from participation in the case is not an option under the facts, which indicate that she accepts the case. D is incorrect for the same reason that A is correct.

39. C is the correct answer. When a lawyer in a firm is disqualified, generally all lawyers in the firm are disqualified. ABA Model Rules of Professional Conduct Model Rule [MR] 1.10. Here, the firm would be disqualified because of the direct conflict of interest caused by the fact that the new attorney had previously represented a party adverse to the new client. Although terminating the new attorney is harsh and may open the firm to civil liability for wrongful termination, the termination will remove the conflict of interest. Screening the attorney from participation in the case is acceptable, provided there is written consent from all involved. A, B, and D are incorrect for the same reasons that C is correct.

40. A is the correct answer. A vicariously disqualified attorney (here the solo practitioner) is no longer disqualified if he discontinues an association with the disqualified attorney (the associate). See generally ABA Model Rules of Professional Conduct Model Rule [MR] 1.10. In this case, the big firm was disqualified from representing the woman because the associate had once represented a party adverse to the woman. This disqualification was imputed to everyone else at the firm. However, once the solo practitioner left and started his own solo practice, he was

no longer vicariously disqualified. B is incorrect because, as discussed above, the solo practitioner was vicariously disqualified while working at the big firm. However, once he left and started his own solo practice, he was no longer disqualified. C and D are incorrect for the reasons discussed in A.

41. B is the correct answer. Disqualification can be waived by the opposing party. Thus, since this is what occurred here, B is the correct answer. ABA Model Rules of Professional Conduct Model Rule [MR] 1.10(c). A is incorrect because in no way does it appear that the firm's lawyers compromised his case. The associate had to be screened from participation in the case. C is incorrect because, as discussed above, disqualification can be waived by the opposing party, as it has been here. Thus, neither the firm nor the associate will be subject to discipline under these facts. D is incorrect since no facts whatsoever suggest that the associate will assist opposing counsel.

42. B is the correct answer. If Linda tells the bar of State B that her cousin is fit to practice law, when in fact she believes him to be thoroughly dishonest, she would knowingly be making a false statement of material fact in violation of ABA Model Rules of Professional Conduct, Model Rule [MR] 8.1(a). A is incorrect because State A can discipline Linda for actions that she took in State B if they involved moral turpitude. ABA Model Rule 8.5 allows a lawyer to be disciplined even when the activity occurs in a different state. Answers C and D are incorrect because the issue is whether Linda lied. If she did, she can be disciplined, regardless of where the conduct occurred.

43. C is the correct answer. A lawyer may reveal to a court a client's intentions to commit a crime involving potential serious bodily harm or death. ABA Model Rules of Professional Conduct Model Rule [MR] 1.6(b)(1). Here, violently robbing a bank is an action that involves potential serious bodily harm. Thus, the lawyer may reveal to the court the client's intention to commit this action. Note, the rule says that the lawyer may reveal this. It does not say that the lawyer must reveal it. Hence, it is up to the lawyer's discretion whether or not to reveal the actions here. (Note, under California Business and Professions Code § 6068(e)(2), California lawyers are given similar discretion. However, the California rules are not tested on the MPRE, but they are tested in the essay portion of the California Bar Examination.) A is incorrect because the lawyer is not required to withdraw; he is merely given the discretion to inform the court if he so chooses, as discussed in C. B is incorrect because informing the bank managers would be a violation of the attorney-client privilege; the rules allow the lawyer to inform the court, not the managers of a private business (such as a bank). D is incorrect because there is no rule that permits lawyers to commit crimes; in fact, they are subject to

discipline, as well as criminal liability for doing so.

44. A is the correct answer. Going over the head of the individual in the business entity who intends to do the fraud is the correct course of conduct. Thus, A is correct. ABA Model Rules of Professional Conduct Model Rule [MR] 1.13(b). Here, the lawyer intends to tell the Board of Directors about the president's proposed fraudulent transaction. He is, thus, complying with the rule. B, C and D are incorrect for the same reason that A is correct.

45. C is the correct answer. The attorney is in a difficult position. Not only should he counsel the direct supervisor and the corporation, but he also may have some duties to the employee who apparently is seeking the attorney's legal advice. Because what the employee says may hurt the employee if revealed, but may possibly aid the corporation, the attorney should as soon as possible tell the employee that he represents the corporation, not the employee. Otherwise, there might arise an impermissible conflict of interest between the duties owed to the corporation and those owed to the employee. Without this kind of warning, the employee's interests might be severely compromised. See ABA Model Rules of Professional Conduct Model Rule [MR] 1.13, Comment [10]. A is incorrect because the attorney, over the course of his employment with the corporation, has already learned many corporate secrets. Even if the attorney withdraws from representing the corporation, the attorney's duties to safeguard these secrets will remain. However, in representing the employee, the attorney may have to reveal these secrets. Thus, because there is a potential conflict, the attorney should not represent the employee, even if he withdraws from representation of the corporation. B and D are incorrect because counseling against the fraud constitutes legal advice, as does telling the employee not to worry about his past fraudulent conduct. As discussed in C, the attorney is not the employee's lawyer. Thus, he should not be giving legal advice to the employee.

46. A is the correct answer. This question illustrates that occasionally the MPRE will test case law that interprets the Model Rules. This question tests your understanding of ABA Model Rules of Professional Conduct, Model Rule [MR] 1.13, Corporation as a client. Under Model Rule 1.13, a lawyer for the corporation has a duty to represent the corporation as a client. The other rule implicated by this question is ABA Model Rule 1.6—in which Upjohn v. United States interpreted the attorney-client privilege to cover the corporation as the client. A is correct because the interview was conducted as a confidential communication between Lucas, the corporation's lawyer, and Janitor Jones—an employee of the corporation. B is incorrect because the reasoning is not correct and does not refer to a rule. C is incorrect because the U.S. Supreme Court in Upjohn did not narrow its deci-

sion to include a corporate privilege that only applied to higher-level corporate employees; the privilege covers even the janitor. D is incorrect because Jones does not have to consent.

47. C is the correct answer. Although receiving property as advance payment of fees from a client is not preferred, it is acceptable if it is kept separate from the property of the attorney. Putting the property in a client-only safe deposit box is the ideal method. See ABA Model Rules of Professional Conduct Model Rule [MR] 1.15, Comment [1]. Here, the lawyer received a $10,000 watch as a fee advance. The lawyer must, thus, put the watch in a client-only safe deposit box. A and D are incorrect for the same reason that C is correct. The lawyer may neither wear the watch nor give it to his girlfriend (or anyone else); he must keep it in a client-only safe deposit box. B is incorrect because a problem will arise if less money is earned than the value of the watch.

48. D is the correct answer. ABA Model Rules of Professional Conduct, Model Rule [MR] 1.7, a conflict of interest between two concurrent clients can only occur if both clients waive the conflict, in writing, before the representation begins. (Note that in many states, representing two adverse parties in a divorce would be un-waivable). Here, the best answer is D because Alex must obtain a waiver before the representation. He waited too long. A is incorrect because there is a substantial relationship between the divorce case and business representation. B is incorrect because Alex still violated the rules, even if Winona did consent. C is incorrect because it is possible to waive a divorce conflict in some situations.

49. A is the correct answer. Under ABA Model Rules of Professional Conduct, Model Rule [MR] 1.6, a lawyer has a duty of confidentiality to a client with regard to all information concerning the representation. Here, the question tests the unique situation of insurance counsel for the client—also called the insured—and the duty of the lawyer to represent the client. Even when the lawyer is being paid by the insurance company, the lawyer owes a duty of confidentiality to the insured, the client. B is incorrect because there is no designation between primary and secondary client. The only client is Ivan, the insured. C is incorrect because keeping the information confidential is not defrauding the insurance company. The insurance company has an independent obligation and opportunity to investigate its own facts concerning any coverage issues. D is incorrect because Ivan was not charged with a crime.

50. A is the correct answer. That the client is not injured is irrelevant to the rule prohibiting commingling. ABA Model Rules of Professional Conduct Model Rule [MR] 1.15. Since taking the client's funds was without consent, it is commingling. (Note, this would be dif-

ferent if the question dealt, instead, with a malpractice suit by the client against the lawyer. In that case, the client would not prevail because he was not harmed. However, the Model Rules, which deal only with discipline of lawyers, do not care about harm or lack of harm to the client.) B is incorrect because lawyers are permitted to gamble with their own money outside of their practice of law. C and D are incorrect for the same reasons that A is correct.

51. B is the correct answer. When the attorney left his fee in the client trust account, this constituted comingling, which is prohibited under ABA Model Rules of Professional Conduct Model Rule [MR] 1.15. A is incorrect because harm to the client is irrelevant when there is commingling. (Note, this would be different if the question dealt, instead, with a malpractice suit by the client against the lawyer. In that case, the client would not prevail because he was not harmed. However, the Model Rules, which deal only with discipline of lawyers, do not care about harm or lack of harm to the client.) C is incorrect because lawyers are permitted to try to minimize their tax liability, so long as they do it legally. D is incorrect because lawyers are not required to close their trust accounts when they conclude cases; they should keep the trust account open for use in the next case(s).

52. B is the correct answer. Because the attorney-client relationship is fiduciary in nature and because it is the client who is in the position of trust, clients are generally permitted to terminate the services of their attorneys "at will" with little or no penalty. ABA Model Rules of Professional Conduct Model Rule [MR] 1.16(a)(3). Attorneys, when terminated, as a general rule, must withdraw; thus, when the client terminates the lawyer, the lawyer must withdraw, regardless of the reason for the termination. A and C are incorrect for the same reasons that B is correct; the attorney must withdraw (it is not optional). D is incorrect because there is no need for arbitration as to whether the attorney must withdraw after being fired by the client. The lawyer shall withdraw, as discussed in B.

53. D is the correct answer. Attorneys must not either harass an opposing party or pursue a frivolous argument. ABA Model Rules of Professional Conduct Model Rule [MR] 3.1. Since it is stipulated that the attorney merely desired to "wear down" the opposing party, such action is definitely prohibited. A, B and C are incorrect for the same reason that D is correct.

54. B is the correct answer. The lawyer is not required to alert the judge to any of these authorities because none are binding on the jurisdiction in which the court sits. ABA Model Rules of Professional Conduct, Model Rule [MR] 3.3(a)(2) concerns a lawyer's duty to alert the court to adverse legal authorities. In Option I, the U.S. Supreme Court case is adverse

only by analogy between the State X statute and the federal Lanham Act. Further, the U.S. Supreme Court's interpretation of federal law is not controlling on a State X judge who is applying State X law. For the same reasons, the U.S. Court of Appeals case in Option II need not be disclosed. Further, the State Y case in Option III need not be disclosed because it is adverse only by analogy between trespass to real property and infringement of a trademark. There may be sound tactical reasons for counsel for Noxatox to use these cases, but the rules do not compel it.

55. B is the correct answer. Attorneys must reveal cases within the jurisdiction that are directly on point. ABA Model Rules of Professional Conduct Model Rule [MR] 3.3(a)(2). (Note, there is no such requirement to reveal contra cases in California.) Furthermore, attorneys must not purposely mislead the jury in closing argument. MR 3.3(a)(1). Here, the attorney both failed to reveal a case in the jurisdiction that was directly on point and, in closing argument, alluded to facts that were not offered in the case in chief, which seems to have been done in an attempt to mislead the jury. ("She believes she can 'get this by' the inattentive and ill-informed jury.") A is incorrect because attorneys are generally not disciplined for simply losing cases. There must be another factor, such as neglect. C is incorrect because attorneys need not reveal cases on point that are outside the jurisdiction, such as the State Q case. (The lawyer's case takes place in State P.) D is incorrect because, while attorneys must reveal cases within the jurisdiction that are directly on point, this is only required to be done on the record in court. There is no rule that requires lawyers to inform opposing counsel off the record prior to court.

56. A is the correct answer. An attorney must not help a client commit perjury. ABA Model Rules of Professional Conduct Model Rule [MR] 3.3(a)(3). Because the attorney did this, she is subject to discipline. For an attorney to be civilly liable for malpractice, two elements must occur: 1) an attorney error (usually shown by referring to the state's code of ethics) and 2) harm/damages to the client. Because the client was acquitted, the second element is missing, and there is no malpractice liability. B, C and D are incorrect for the reasons discussed in A.

57. C is the correct answer. ABA Model Rules of Professional Conduct, Model Rule [MR] 1.15 governs the issue that a lawyer must keep all client money in the Client Trust Account. An attorney cannot remove client money for any reason. C is correct because Lee could have paid the amount out of her personal account so that no client money was used. Further, under ABA Model Rules of Professional Conduct, Model Rule [MR] 1.8(e), a lawyer is permitted to advance litigation costs. A is incorrect because Lee's handling of the matter was improper. B is incorrect because

Lee would not have been subject to sanctions for allowing Watkins to go to jail. She could choose to pay the fine; but she was not obligated to do so. D is not correct because Lee misappropriated funds.

58. A is the correct answer. Attorneys enjoy First Amendment free-speech protection. Thus, they are permitted to speak to the press pre-trial. Attorneys can be disciplined only if they know or reasonably should know that there is a substantial likelihood that their comments will prejudice the trial. See generally ABA Model Rules of Professional Conduct Model Rule [MR] 3.6. Here, since the attorney's conduct fell short of that standard (since he was merely trying to motivate the other side to settle), the conduct was proper. B, C and D are incorrect for the same reasons that A is correct.

59. A is the correct answer. A lawyer is permitted to testify as to the value of her legal services. ABA Model Rules of Professional Conduct Model Rule [MR] 3.7(a)(2). B, C and D are incorrect for the same reason that A is correct.

60. D is the correct answer. A lawyer must not communicate with a represented party, unless the lawyer has the consent of the other lawyer or is authorized to do so by law or a court order. ABA Model Rules of Professional Conduct Model Rule [MR] 4.2. Here, there was no consent by the woman's attorney for the man's lawyer to contact the woman directly, nor was there a court order. Thus, A, B and C are incorrect.

61. A is the correct answer. It is no defense to a charge of discipline that the charged lawyer was simply obeying the orders of his superior. ABA Model Rules of Professional Conduct Model Rule [MR] 5.2(a). It is a disciplinary violation to intentionally mislead the opposing party. Model Rule 4.1(a). Thus, B is incorrect. C and D are incorrect because they deal with civil liability, and more facts are needed to determine if there is tort liability, e.g., were there damages?

62. C is the correct answer. A lawyer is responsible when he directs another lawyer to violate the rules of ethics. Similarly, senior a lawyer must supervise junior attorneys in his employ. See generally ABA Model Rules of Professional Conduct Model Rule [MR] 5.1. A and B are incorrect for the same reasons that C is correct. D is incorrect because failure to set a good example is not in and of itself a violation of the rules.

63. A is the correct answer. Until a lawyer has been sworn in, he is not licensed to practice law. Because the lawyer was not sworn in, did not receive a waiver from the court, was not practicing with a licensed attorney of record (or practicing within some other exception), he was practicing law without a license. Here, the lawyer's drafting of wills in State Q prior to being waived in constituted the practice of law without a license. B is incorrect because he did

not have a law license – he was waiting to be sworn in. C is incorrect because profit-motive is not the test for the unauthorized practice of law. D is incorrect because a lawyer need not be in court to be practicing without a license. ABA Model Rules of Professional Conduct Model Rule [MR] 5.5.

64. D is the correct answer because all of the Option statements are correct. Item I is correct because ABA Model Rules of Professional Conduct, Model Rule [MR] 1.5(c) disallows a contingent fee agreement in a criminal case; further, all contingency fee agreements should be in writing. Loman should not have taken this case on contingent fee, but since he did, he should at least have put the contingent fee agreement in writing. Items II and IV are also both correct. ABA Model Rules of Professional Conduct, Model Rule [MR] 1.8(e) permits Loman to advance the litigation expenses, and Demon's promise to pay back the advance is proper under Model Rule 1.8(e).

END OF ANSWERS

A

PROFESSIONAL RESPONSIBILITY